To order or to receive additional information on these or any other McGraw-Hill titles, please call 1-800-822-8158 in the United States. In other countries, contact your local McGraw-Hill representative.   **WM16XXA**

SO-BDP-458

The McGraw-Hill
High-Speed LANs
Handbook

The McGraw-Hill High-Speed LANs Handbook

Stephen Saunders
News Editor, Data Communications
New York, New York

McGraw-Hill

New York   San Francisco   Washington, D.C.   Auckland   Bogotá
Caracas   Lisbon   London   Madrid   Mexico City   Milan
Montreal   New Delhi   San Juan   Singapore
Sydney   Tokyo   Toronto

Library of Congress Cataloging-in-Publication Data

Saunders, Stephen.
    The McGraw-Hill high-speed LANs handbook / Stephen Saunders.
       p.   cm. — (McGraw-Hill series on computer communications)
    Includes index.
    ISBN 0-07-057199-6 (hc)
    1. Local area networks (Computer networks) I. Title. II. Series.
TK5105.7.S277 1996
004.6'8—dc20   95-45981
                                                      CIP

McGraw-Hill

A Division of The McGraw·Hill Companies

1 2 3 4 5 6 7 8 9 0 DOC/DOC 9 0 1 0 9 8 7 6

ISBN 0-07-057199-6

The sponsoring editor for this book was Jerry Papke, the editing supervisor was Bernard Onken, and the production supervisor was Donald Schmidt. It was set in Century Schoolbook by Dina John of McGraw-Hill's Professional Book Group composition unit.

Printed and bound by R. R. Donnelley & Sons Company.

McGraw-Hill books are available at special quantity discounts to use as premiums and sales promotions, or for use in corporate training programs. For more information, please write to the Director of Special Sales, McGraw-Hill, 11 West 19th Street, New York, NY 10011. Or contact your local bookstore.

 This book is printed on recycled, acid-free paper containing a minimum of 50% recycled de-inked fiber.

For Mum and Dad

Contents

Part 4   Cross-Comparison Tables

Part 5   High-Speed LAN Design Issues

Preface

Ignore a problem long enough, and it becomes a crisis. Let a crisis linger, and it turns into a potential catastrophe.

Organizations that continue to rely on aging Ethernet and token ring local-area networks to meet their data communications needs are now flirting with disaster. Those networks, first devised when the Intel 8088 chip was state of the art, simply don't have the speed to keep up with the growing legions of users, faster workstations, killer applications, and huge files that make up today's LAN environments.

The truth is, conventional Ethernet LANs (which operate at 10 Mbit/s) and token ring networks (which run at 4 or 16 Mbit/s) have been straining under the growing data burden for some time. Back in 1990, about 26 percent of all PCs in the world were connected to LANs; that proportion has grown steadily, to 85 percent by 1996, according to Electronic Trend Publications (San Jose, CA), a market researcher. PC processing power—from the 8088 to the Intel 80286, 386, 486, and Pentium chips—has grown exponentially since the mid-1980s, and they're driving applications that dwarf the simple file and print services that characterized early LANs.

The first line of defense used by network managers to ward off LAN performance problems was to break Ethernets and token rings into smaller segments by installing bridges or routers. This approach does boost the amount of network bandwidth available to each workstation within segments. But segmented networks are a headache to manage, they can be fantastically expensive, and they can be even slower than larger LANs when traffic is sent between segments.

This patchwork approach to solving chronic LAN bandwidth shortages is now giving way to a different strategy, one that calls for deploying high-speed LAN technologies. Network managers have an array of high-speed LAN options to choose from, each of which promises to deliver a long-term solution to the bandwidth squeeze.

In fact, there may be an overabundance of high-speed LAN technologies as far as network managers are concerned. Standards organizations like the American National Standards Institute, the Institute of Electrical and Electronics Engineers, and the ATM Forum have ratified no fewer than eight competing specifications for high-speed LANs. These include ATM (asynchronous transfer mode), FDDI (fiber distributed data interface), FDDI II, Fibre Channel, HIPPI (high-performance parallel interface), IsoEnet (isochronous Ethernet), 100Base-T (a.k.a. fast Ethernet), and 100VG-AnyLAN. That's not all—well over 100 equipment vendors now sell proprietary LAN switches based on Ethernet, token ring, FDDI, or 100Base-T network designs. These devices, which replace conventional hubs and concentrators, dramatically increase the performance of shared-media networks by converting them to switched networks made up of dedicated LAN segments.

With at least a dozen high-speed LAN options staring them in the eye, network managers can't help but flinch at the prospect of making a wrong choice. Depending on which way the market winds blow, chances are that some high-speed options will float away into oblivion or be relegated to niche roles attracting minimal interest from technology developers. When that happens, investments in those failed technologies—which can reach into the millions of dollars for large organizations—are put at risk.

For net managers, the real challenge of high-speed networking lies in choosing the right combination of technologies, working out when to implement them, and matching them to the right applications. Some high-speed LANs are suited to delay-sensitive multimedia traffic; others only come into their own when pushing asynchronous data packets. Some can serve in the backbone; others are intended primarily for desktop connections. Some can run over the cables now in place in walls and risers; others are only going to get the green light once fiber optic cabling has been pulled.

And that's just for starters. Performance issues need to be analyzed very closely: Even something as straightforward as line speed can be complicated by architectural considerations. Network overhead also must be evaluated carefully. Compatibility with existing networking gear and cabling requires very close attention, and cost—the net manager's perennial worry—must be factored into any decision.

This book is aimed at helping network managers sort through the high-speed LAN alternatives to minimize the risks and ease the worries. The book is organized into six parts. The first three sections discuss each of the different high-speed LAN options: the ANSI and IEEE standards, ATM networking, and proprietary switching technologies. Part 4 comprises a series of matrix-like tables that compare the different high-speed LAN options, complete with "at a glance" summaries of each alternative's strengths and weaknesses. Part 5 offers design guidelines for implementing these networks in the real world. Finally, Part 6 covers issues regarding network cabling and high-speed LANs.

The information in this book is drawn from a wide variety of sources, including interviews with equipment vendors and the standards organizations, as well as feedback from pioneer users of high-speed LAN technologies. Results of high-speed LAN evaluations from independent test organizations like the National Software Testing Laboratories (NSTL, Plymouth Meeting, PA) and the Tolly Group (Manasquan, NJ) are included as well.

In a perfect world, the migration from yesterday's LAN standards to high-speed networks would be a straightforward move. Unfortunately, reality for network managers is anything but perfect.

The real reason net managers have so many high-speed LAN standards to choose from has little to do with their best interests and a lot to do with the self-interests of the vendors that manufacture and market network gear. Equipment makers are under the gun to deliver products that conform to industry standards—any standards. Standards-based products sell better than proprietary offerings; in fact, some venture capitalists are making standardization a condition of further investment in networking companies. Most companies in the networking business are tiny by today's global business standards, which means they can't afford to ignore demands by potential investors.

Rather than pool their efforts into creating a single set of standards, vendors have pushed hard to get their various technologies stamped with an ANSI or IEEE seal of approval—a procedure that has proved ludicrously easy since standards committees are made up almost exclusively of vendor representatives. This approach may legitimize competing technologies, but it can only spell trouble for network managers, who lack an official ombudsman to voice their opinions and concerns.

The IEEE's search for a 100-Mbit/s shared-media successor to Ethernet stands as a prime example of the standards approval process gone awry. The IEEE's original request for proposals yielded two alternatives; 100VG-AnyLAN (nee 100Base-VG) and 100Base-T. Rather than choose one of these options as a standard, the IEEE bowed to vendor pressure and ended up ratifying both specifications. As a result, net managers must now choose between two standards that ostensibly deliver the same goods: high-speed, low-cost, shared-media network connectivity.

Along with the obvious confusion, the IEEE's dual specifications are causing interoperability problems in corporate networks. Companies that are deploying products that conform to the two IEEE standards are finding that different equipment suppliers support incompatible interfaces. This can lead to situations where, for example, a router from one vendor cannot be connected to a hub from another.

Some industry experts contend that all this confusion about high-speed networking will fade away once ATM technology reaches full maturity. ATM has several big factors in its favor: It's a high-speed, scalable technology that can handle asynchronous data and time-sensitive multimedia traffic equally well, it's the only standard capable of straddling both local- and wide-area networks, and it has garnered almost universal support among equipment makers.

But ATM has several major hurdles to clear before it becomes the LAN technology of choice. Equipment prices still have a long way to fall. Standards must be fully defined (and successfully implemented). Interoperability problems must be ironed out. And applications must be written to take advantage of ATM's best features. For these reasons, ATM is unlikely to become the predominant LAN technology for desktop connections until the end of the decade.

Even then, ATM isn't going to eliminate other high-speed alternatives overnight. Two things stand between ATM and world domination. First, there's networking's installed base—including some 100 million (and growing) Ethernet and token ring nodes, along with all the network operating systems and applications built expressly for that installed base. Most organizations are going to want to preserve their investment in this infrastructure for as long as possible. One big reason that LAN switches are so popular is that they work with LAN adapters and cabling already in place—a huge consideration for companies with networks that can span tens of thousands of nodes.

Second, although ATM is very good at carrying all applications, it is not the best choice for each of those applications. For instance, both Fibre Channel and HIPPI provide a much more efficient and much faster path for applications that send very large asynchronous data files.

What all this means is that corporate networks for the forseeable future will comprise a hodgepodge of high-speed technologies (see Fig. 1). A manufacturer of household appliances, for instance, might upgrade the 10-Mbit/s Ethernet in its accounting department using LAN switches, add a 100-Mbit/s 100VG-AnyLAN network to service the graphics workstations in marketing, tack on a switched 400-Mbit/s Fibre Channel LAN to tie together the Sun workstations in its R&D lab, then connect the whole site to the enterprise backbone via a router with ATM interfaces.

Clearly, this kind of mix-and-match approach is going to put an even greater burden on network managers as they scramble to keep pace with soaring demand for LAN bandwidth. In the long run, however, it's easier to solve a problem today than to face a catastrophe tomorrow.

Stephen Saunders
ssaunder@mcgraw-hill.com

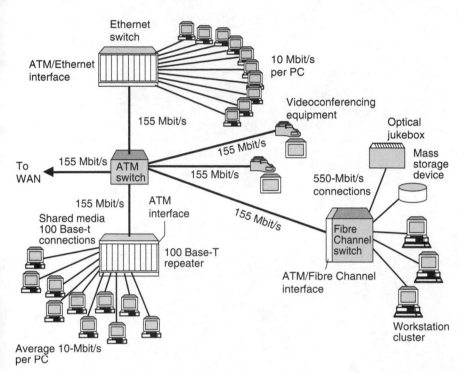

Fig. 1 The high-speed LAN cocktail. For the forseeable future net managers will mix and match high-speed LAN technologies, putting standards-based schemes to work alongside proprietary LAN switches.

Acknowledgments

So many people to thank, so little space to do it in.

Writing this book would have been impossible without the help I received from my friends at *Data Communications* magazine. My thanks go to Joe Braue for allowing me to re-use many pertinent *Data Comm* articles in this book. Also, to Don Marks, David Newman and Johna Till Johnson, all of whom gave me permission to reprint their work without hesitation (or, more significantly, compensation).

Likewise, this seems a good opportunity to thank Aaron Fischer and Dennis Mendyk, whose peerless and anonymous editing skills at *Data Comm* have, over the years, succeeded in exaggerating my own writing ability in a most satisfactory fashion. I'm also grateful to my current boss, Lee Keough, who was a constant source of encouragement during the preparation of this manuscript, as she has been throughout my career at *Data Comm*.

Further, I would like to thank Peter Heywood, the editor of *Data Communications'* international edition, for giving me my first break in journalism when he hired me out of the McGraw-Hill postroom back in 1989. Since then my work for *Data Comm* has taken me from London, to California (via an unfortunate hiatus in Wimbledon) and now, finally, to New York. I think, all in all, I can say that things have worked out rather well. Thanks, mate.

Many equipment vendors also contributed information for this book; the contributions from Amberwave, Bay, DEC, Centillion (now part of Bay), Madge, Network Peripherals, Stratacom and 3Com were particularly useful. I'd also like to thank Bob Mandeville of the European Network Laboratories (ENL) and Kevin Tolly of the Tolly Group for supplying me with several papers that proved invaluable to the preparation of this work.

Finally, I'd like to say thanks to Jay Ranade, Jerry Papke, Bernie Onken and Donna Namorato at the McGraw-Hill, Inc. Professional Book Group for their kind help and advice in preparing this book.

Stephen Saunders

The McGraw-Hill
High-Speed LANs
Handbook

Tutorials on Seven High-Speed LAN Standards

Part 1 of this book provides tutorials on seven high-speed LAN standards. Four of them are on the books at the American National Standards Association (ANSI): FDDI, FDDI II, Fibre Channel, and HIPPI. Three have been defined by the IEEE (Institute of Electrical and Electronics Engineers): 100Base-T, 100VG-AnyLAN, and IsoEnet. ATM, which falls in the bailiwick of both the Internet Engineering Task Force (IETF) and the ITU-TSS, is dealt with in Part 2.

Net managers wondering why they have a total of eight high-speed LAN standards to choose from in the first place will find the answer familiar: big business. Equipment vendors have been quick to catch onto the fact that standards-based networks sell better than proprietary ones. The fact that the membership of standards bodies like ANSI and the IEEE is made up almost exclusively from the ranks of vendors themselves has made it childishly simple for them to gain the necessary stamp of approval.

The following chapters analyze and explain the different standards, and to make for easier comparisons, each of the tutorials uses a similar structure: starting with an overview of the technology (including its benefits and disadvantages) and then going into detail on how it works, how easy (or hard) it is to migrate to, how well it handles time-sensitive multimedia, cost, and so on. A list of the most significant points to note about each standard is provided in a panel at the opening of each chapter.

Chapter 1 describes FDDI, a shared-media 100-Mbit/s LAN.

Chapter 2 describes FDDI II, a follow-on to the original FDDI standard, which endows it with multimedia capabilities.

Chapter 3 describes Fibre Channel, which uses a low-latency, switched architecture to carry data at speeds up to 800 Mbit/s.

Chapter 4 describes HIPPI, which is primarily designed as a high-capacity data transport for specialized asynchronous data applications.

Chapter 5 describes IsoEnet, which uses a combination of shared-media and circuit switching technology to add voice and video capabilities to conventional Ethernet LANs.

Chapter 6 describes 100Base-T, a shared-media 100-Mbit/s LAN that retains much of the technology found in 10-Mbit/s Ethernet.

Chapter 7 describes 100VG-AnyLAN, a 100-Mbit/s LAn with some prioritization features for time-sensitive traffic.

One more thing. Some ratified standards have been intentionally omitted from this book. Two examples are ANSI's FDDI Follow On LAN (FFOL), and the IEEE's P1394. Neither has attracted enough industry support to make it a viable high-speed LAN option.

1

An FDDI Tutorial

Focusing on FDDI

Speed: 100 Mbit/s

Architecture: shared media with token-passing access methodology

Cabling: single-mode and multimode fiber; an addendum to the standard defines transmission over Category 5 UTP, STP

Distance: 2 kilometers over multimode fiber; 100 meters over copper

Latency: variable; synchronous facilities can be enabled

Products: network interface cards, routers, concentrators, switches, analyzers

Cost per shared-media node: $2000 (fiber), $1500 (copper)

Number of vendors: more than 100

Snapshot: a stable, dependable high-speed LAN standard that is already losing ground to switch-based technologies

---

Some information in this chapter is taken from research by John Curtis and Randy Bao of The Tolly Group (Manasquan, NJ), an independent testing facility.

Section 1.   Overview

Fiber distributed data interface (FDDI) was ratified in 1988. Compared with the youth of the other networking technologies vying for net managers' attention, that makes it the grand old man of the high-speed networking world. But FDDI's age is also its biggest asset, making FDDI the most stable, standardized, and interoperable of today's high-speed LANs. It is also the most available. FDDI products are now on sale for many classes of servers and workstations, and it is supported in hubs, routers, switches, analyzers, and concentrators. More than 100 vendors manufacture FDDI equipment.

The FDDI standard was developed by ANSI, and defines a shared-media LAN (local-area network). Its ring topology and the token-passing mechanism it uses to allocate access to network nodes are similar to those deployed in token ring LANs. The big difference between the two is that FDDI runs at 100 Mbit/s (token ring tops out at 16 Mbit/s). Also, FDDI implements its token-passing scheme with dual fiber-optic rings, so it's highly fault-tolerant. FDDI's token-passing access methodology provides highly efficient utilization of network bandwidth; it has been shown to deliver 97.5 Mbit/s at user sites.

FDDI development began back in the early 1980s; initially, it was envisioned as a high-speed link for supercomputers (one of the applications now targeted by Fibre Channel networks). As FDDI began to take shape, some proponents expected the technology to replace Ethernet as an enterprise LAN protocol. That never happened. Today's network professionals largely implement FDDI for two applications: to accommodate scientific and technical applications in high-performance work groups and to expand backbone capacity (see Fig. 1.1). Despite recent enhancements to FDDI—including an addendum to the standard which enables it to run over low-cost unshielded twisted-pair (UTP) cable as well or fiber-optic cable—its long-term future remains in doubt.

For one thing, FDDI is among the most expensive of the high-speed LAN alternatives. Also, FDDI's shared-media design imposes some disadvantages. Because all the nodes on a network must contend for a portion of the common 100-Mbit/s pool, the capacity available to each user decreases in proportion to the size of the LAN. Simply put, FDDI networks do not scale as well as switched networks. Further, the fact that nodes have to wait their turn before transmitting means FDDI is poorly suited to voice-sensitive and other time-sensitive applications.

There are also some interoperability issues that must be ironed out. Right now, the FDDI standards from ANSI (American National Standards Institute) and ISO (International Organization for Standardization) do not address source route bridging, which opens

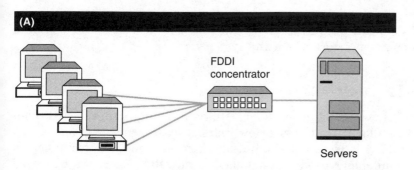

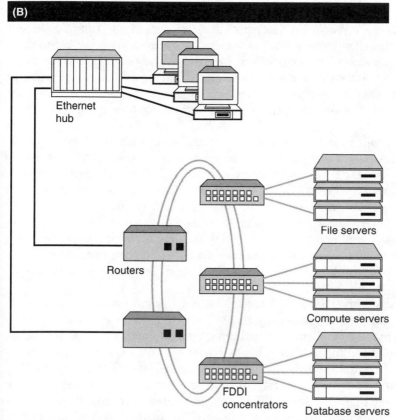

Figure 1.1 Typical uses of FDDI. In a work group setting (a) FDDI can be used to supply high-speed links to high-performance desktop machines. FDDI also can be deployed as a backbone technology (b) to link routers and concentrators.

the way for proprietary (hence incompatible) schemes. What's more, FDDI network adapters don't always work as well as they should with popular network operating systems.

Section 2.   The FDDI Fight-Back

It's not all doom and gloom for FDDI, however. For one thing, its continued popularity for the next few years at least is virtually assured by the fact that it is one of the only high-speed backbone technologies widely available. A good part of today's bandwidth crunch can be traced to conventional wisdom, which typically assumes that backbones needn't be much faster than the feeder LANs they join. After all (so the reasoning goes), a single LAN is generally running only at 10 to 20 percent of full capacity. Ironically, advancements in bridge/router technology have exacerbated the situation. Formerly, bridge/routers slowed the flow of data between LANs (unintentionally, of course) because of inherent frame-handling limitations or excessive latency. Now that some vendors offer wire speed boxes, bridge/routers no longer act as throttles.

New applications on the way are only going to make things worse. Character-based applications used for word processing and inventory control are fast becoming more powerful. LU6.2 applications, increasingly common in many corporations, can easily transfer data across a 16-Mbit/s token ring at close to wire speed. Further, it's already obvious that Netware 4.x can easily saturate Ethernet or token ring. And when multimedia gets here, it's going to hurt. A single, uncompressed, black-and-white document scanned at 300 dots per square inch will yield a 1-Mbyte binary file. Scanning in a color image could create 10 times as much data.

Installed correctly, FDDI can provide an answer to these problems. FDDI vendors are also taking steps to make the technology more desirable to managers. Some are bringing out products which make FDDI better at handling multimedia by using a little-known feature in the original FDDI standard—called *synchronous FDDI*. Synchronous FDDI products give special priority to time-sensitive traffic. A second group are selling FDDI switches. These products deliver many of the advantages of asynchronous transfer mode (ATM) switches—dedicating up to the full bandwidth of the network to each network node, and providing automatic call setup and closed virtual work groups. Still another group of vendors are making products which support an altogether new version of the standard, called FDDI II. The new standard also is optimized for carrying both asynchronous and time-sensitive traffic (see Chap. 2, "An FDDI II Tutorial").

Section 3. How FDDI Works

Like the other high-speed LAN standards, the original FDDI is a
link-layer protocol. This means that higher-layer protocols operate
independently of the FDDI protocol. Applications pass packet-level
data using higher-layer protocols down to lower-layer FDDI, in the
same way that they would do over an Ethernet or token ring LAN.
The FDDI standard defines four layers: media access control (MAC),
physical media dependent (PMD), physical layer protocol (PHY), and
station management (SMT). Here's a breakdown of their responsibilities:

- The MAC layer defines addressing, scheduling, and routing of
  data. It also communicates with higher-layer protocols, such as
  TCP/IP, SNA, IPX, DECnet, DEC LAT, and AppleTalk. Upper-layer
  protocols pass protocol data units (PDUs) to the MAC layer, which
  adds a MAC header and then passes the packets (or frames) up
  4500 bytes long to the PHY layer.

- The PHY layer handles the encoding and decoding of packet data
  onto the wire, using a scheme called 4B5B encoding. It also handles clock synchronization on the FDDI ring.

- The PMD layer handles the analog baseband transmission between
  nodes on the physical media (or cabling).

- The SMT layer is an overlay function that handles the management of the FDDI ring. Functions handled by SMT include neighbor identification, fault detection and reconfiguration, insertion
  and deinsertion from the ring, and traffic statistics monitoring.

Section 4. Twin Topologies

A LAN is only as good as it is robust. Ethernet and token ring—if
implemented correctly—are very reliable. Still, only a single cable
connects even the most important station or server to the LAN. If
that cable goes, the node is down. FDDI, in contrast, is designed to be
far more fault-tolerant. As mentioned, a network actually consists of
two rings. If a fault occurs on the primary ring, the technology automatically "wraps" the primary ring onto the secondary ring, bypassing the fault. In essence, wrapping detours the traffic around the
problem. Wrapping is available only with a dual-attached station
(DAS) or a dual-attached concentrator (DAC), each of which is physically linked to both rings. The drawback to this approach is that if
more than one dual-attached node is turned off, entire sections of the

FDDI ring are isolated and cannot communicate. Thus, dual attachment should be used only when nodes are rarely going to be powered off. Routers and servers, for instance, are good candidates for dual attachment; client PCs are not. (It's possible to install optical bypass switches in dual-attached nodes that shunt the signal past the station when the power is off. These switches tend to be expensive, however, and may reduce network performance.) The other way to link to FDDI is via a single-attached station (SAS) or single-attached concentrator (SAC). These are physically connected to only one of the rings, through a user port on a concentrator. When a single-attached node is turned off, the concentrator merely bypasses that port. Single attachment isn't fault tolerant, but it's the way to go with stations that are frequently turned on and off (see Fig. 1.2).

FDDI's fault tolerance doesn't stop there. Network managers also can take advantage of the fact that an individual FDDI network interface card in a bridge, router, or server can be simultaneously linked to two FDDI concentrators. This feature, which is not very well known, is called *dual homing* (see Fig. 1.3). It establishes an active connection as well as a hot standby that's automatically activated in the event of a failure. Dual homing can be implemented using any dual-attached FDDI adapter. The beauty of the scheme is that it's implemented at layer 1 (the physical layer). Thus, both physical connections share the same address at the MAC (media access control) layer, and the switch from the hot link to the standby is accomplished transparent to higher-layer applications or bridge/routers.

Dual homing is often confused with seemingly similar capabilities that can be implemented on token ring or Ethernet. It is possible to

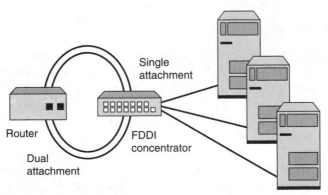

Figure 1.2   Dual or single attached stations. FDDI concentrators function like token ring MAUs or Ethernet hubs. Concentrators make FDDI networks more reliable by isolating failures that occur at end stations and by providing SNMP management functions.

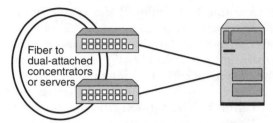

Figure 1.3 Dual homing. In dual-homed applications, mission-critical servers are connected to redundant concentrators, which in turn are connected to a dual-attached ring for maximum redundancy.

connect a token ring or Ethernet bridge/router to the LAN using multiple interfaces, which establish a redundant link. But in this case, each connection has its own MAC address, so routing software must be used to activate the standby link in the event of a failure. If the routing protocol can make the switch quickly enough—a process known as *reconvergence*—sessions may not be lost. But there's considerable industrywide controversy over whether even the newest routers are fast enough.

Section 5.   FDDI Network Utilization

That FDDI has reliability features means that it can be safely deployed in the backbone—but how much of its 100-Mbit/s bandwidth can actually be used? All too often, potential bandwidth proves impossible to attain because of real-world problems. This is particularly true of Ethernet and 100Base-T LANs, where collisions limit throughput to only a percentage of the "available" 10 Mbit/s or 100 Mbit/s. The same, to a lesser extent, holds true for token ring; when small frames are used, today's software drivers cannot achieve the technology's 16-Mbit/s maximum. To determine how much bandwidth FDDI really makes available, The Tolly Group, a private testing firm, ran a high-speed LU 6.2 application between stations on two different token ring LANs bridged across FDDI. Throughput between the LU 6.2 stations was first measured without any competing traffic on the backbone. Frame generators were then used to simulate other traffic on the network—using 4-kbyte frames loads ranging from 10 to 87 Mbit/s—and the LU6.2 throughput was measured again. If the FDDI backbone were passing any less than 100 Mbit/s (our initial expectation) the throughput for the LU6.2 application would naturally trail off—at some point, drastically. After all, any application is sensitive to frame loss. Degradation was surprisingly low, even insignificant, which indicated that FDDI was able to handle all the traffic being sent. With no competing frames on the backbone, the LU 6.2 application clocked in at 10.13 Mbit/s. When the backbone was loaded with 10, 30, and even 60 Mbit/s, throughput fell only slightly. And when the FDDI backbone was loaded with 87 Mbit/s of competing traffic (the most the generator could get onto it), application throughput dropped only slightly, to 9.79 Mbit/s. The total traffic on the LAN amounted to over 96 Mbit/s. Certainly, the results of this test show that FDDI's useful capacity verges on 100 percent. FDDI's token-passing technology obviously works as intended.

Section 6.   FDDI Cabling

The original FDDI standard called for the use of pricey monomode or multimode fiber cable. One recent change that has boosted FDDI's stock among corporate networkers is a new ANSI wiring specification that allows for 100 Mbit/s transmission over Category 5 unshielded twisted-pair (UTP) copper wiring.

The new document, called TP-PMD, replaces the proprietary (or prestandard) approaches previously used for running FDDI traffic over copper wires. The TP-PMD standard is based on an MLT-3 encoding scheme; prestandard implementations used a less reliable NRZ encoding scheme. TP-PMD interfaces are compliant with U.S. and international emission standards and provide reliable transmission over distances up to 100 m. With TP-PMD in place, network managers now have a standard means to implement FDDI over inexpensive Category 5 UTP cable.

Network diameter is a point in FDDI's favor. When run over fiber cabling, FDDI networks can function as either a local area network or, even, a metropolitan area network (MAN). A dual-attached multimode fiber FDDI ring can run for up to 200 km in length, without requiring additional repeaters, bridges, or routers to boost the data signal. Each desktop workstation node can be up to 2,000 meters away from the next station—and a single FDDI ring can accommodate up to 500 nodes. Of course, when Category 5 UTP cabling is used, the distances covered shrink considerably. The TP-PMD standard specifies that Category 5 UTP copper wiring can handle links of up to 100 meters from a concentrator (attached to the fiber ring) to the desktop node (see Fig. 1.4).

Section 7.   The Upgrade Path

In the past, a key reason for limited FDDI uptake has been outrageously high equipment costs. FDDI vendors apparently felt that being first on the block with a high-speed LAN technology gave them a right to charge astronomical prices for their products. Even today,

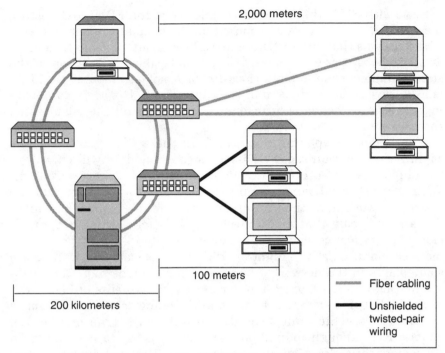

Figure 1.4 FDDI cabling options. The TP-PMD standard for FDDI cabling specifies a maximum distance between end-stations and concentrators of 100 meters when Category 5 unshielded twisted-pair wiring is used and 2 km when fiber is used. Dual-attached fiber rings can span up to 200 kilometers in total circumference, connecting as many as 500 dual attached nodes.

after drastic price cutting in the face of competition from the new wave of LAN standards, FDDI still costs upwards of $2,000 per connection (that price includes the cost of a port on a concentrator and an adapter in the workstation).

That's better than the $5,000 per connection prices vendors were charging until about 1993, but it's still an awfully long way from being a bargain. FDDI remains one of the most expensive high-speed standards covered in this book.

The price problem is unlikely to go away, despite a recent enhancement of FDDI which is designed to bring prices down. Version 7.3 of SMT (the part of the FDDI standard that handles ring management) includes specifications for bringing unmanaged, single-attached (known as null-attached) concentrators into FDDI networks. Null-attached concentrators don't need the management processing hardware associated with dual attachment, and their cost is about two-thirds that of their dual-attached counterparts. They are best suited to small work group installations, which generally don't require dual-attached connections.

Even with SMT, the inherent complexity of the FDDI architecture means FDDI will always cost more than its simpler competitors. One of the reasons that the FDDI standard took about 10 years to develop was that it is over-engineered. For example, the SMT section of the standard alone runs to more than 400 pages of documentation. FDDI is expensive to implement in other ways as well. Upgrading an existing Ethernet or token ring means swapping out all the adapters on the network.

What's more, depending on what's in the walls, changes to the cabling may be required. FDDI-over-copper adapters will only work with high-quality Category 5 UTP; lower quality Category 3 won't do. With the cost of labor now running at about $45 per hour (and the cost of network downtime an order of magnitude higher), net managers may decide that an Ethernet LAN switch—which can supercharge performance using the adapter already in place—provides a more economical path to higher performance. Nevertheless, there are some places in the network where managers may be more than willing to cough up the money in order to reap the benefits of FDDI. For example, FDDI is particularly adept at providing access to high-speed superservers, which must (by definition) serve large numbers of clients. Even though individual users aren't going to need much in the way of throughput, multiple users will quickly eat up bandwidth. On Ethernets or token rings, the accepted way of increasing throughput is by installing additional network interface cards in the server. This approach is not without problems, however. High-performance network adapters aren't cheap, and additional cards take up server slots that could be used for other resources. And once more adapters are added, network managers have to start worrying about load balancing, something that most network operating systems are notoriously poor at. Worse, once additional adapters are added, separate LAN segments must be created. After all, if one adapter is overutilized, so is the LAN that's tied into it. The added adapters can only be utilized fully if new segments are created (by running cable), and that also means deploying more bridge/routers. FDDI offers a far cleaner solution. A single FDDI card theoretically raises the I/O capacity of an interface to 100 Mbit/s. Thus, users on a number of Ethernet or token ring LANs can reach the server simultaneously. In addition, dual homing is available for many of the FDDI cards now on the market.

Section 8.   Source Route Bridging Over FDDI

Interoperability is a critical concern for any network manager who's considering FDDI as a backbone technology—especially since there is no standard for token ring source route bridging over FDDI. Ethernet bridges aren't a problem, since the FDDI spec addresses transparent/translation bridging between Ethernet and FDDI. Thus, all vendors have implemented it the same way. Without a source routing standard, though, FDDI bridge vendors have pretty much gone their own ways. Some are using true source routing, as defined by the IEEE 802.5 token ring spec. The problem with this approach is that source routing uses framing and control bits that FDDI declares as "unused," which can lead to conflicts under certain conditions. But true source routing is the highest-performance scheme and the only way to guarantee interoperability. Some bridges encapsulate the entire token ring packet inside FDDI frames (a second bridge strips off the encapsulation on the other side of the ring). The trouble with this approach is that it adds significant overhead and makes it impossible for the encapsulated frames to be delivered directly to stations on the FDDI ring. On the other hand, it's generally the least expensive approach. Some bridges employ source route conversion. With this approach, the source routing information on the token ring is termi-nated at the bridge (which appears to the sending station as the desti-nation) and converted into either routed or transparent bridged traffic on FDDI. Unfortunately, this routing scheme can't handle Netbios and SNA (which must be bridged). What's more, translation bridges exhib-it high latency and poor performance. But network managers needn't despair: A new FDDI standard, known as FDDI MAC-2, is likely to be adopted soon by ANSI. It will specify true 802.5 token ring source routing on FDDI. Vendors that already have implemented this tech-nique are exhibiting products with both high performance and interop-erability. Network managers may run into other FDDI compatibility problems when it comes to network adapters. Although most adapters will work with any client or server NOS, some combinations of prod-ucts will prove problematic. One no-go situation occurs when bridging Novell Netware traffic between token ring and FDDI (bridging Netware traffic from Ethernet to FDDI is not a problem). Simply put, incompatible addresses make it impossible to bridge IPX clients on token ring to Netware servers on FDDI. Routing must be used instead.

Section 9. Multimedia Shortcomings

Ultimately, it is not price, complexity, or standards issues which could spell the end of FDDI, but its inability to provide guaranteed delivery for time-sensitive multimedia traffic like voice and video—the kind of traffic that will be a big part of the interactive multimedia applica-tions expected to sweep through corporate networks in the coming years. In this regard, FDDI's main competition in corporate networks will come from ATM, which is designed from the ground up to carry both multimedia and asynchronous data.

Bear in mind that not all multimedia applications are interactive. Such multimedia features as voice annotation of text files or access to stored motion video or still images can be handled asynchronously, like any other data file. In such cases, receiving stations wait until the whole file has been received before displaying it. Network delays don't affect the quality of these applications, which means asynchronous FDDI can handle them. In fact, FDDI makes a strong medium for noninteractive applications.

FDDI vendors have been known to boast—somewhat desperately— that FDDI's 100 Mbit/s of bandwidth is enough to make sure that time-sensitive, real-time applications arrive on time. But anyone who uses asynchronous FDDI for interactive multimedia applications has to keep in mind one major caveat: If the network gets congested, the quality of delay-sensitive voice and video traffic will fall through the floor. Asynchronous FDDI uses a token-passing scheme to send traffic along the network. A token travels around the FDDI ring, stopping at each station to give it the chance to transmit frames. If enough stations use the token, all traffic is subject to delay. The delay doesn't have much of an effect on asynchronous traffic, but it can wreak havoc with isochronous traffic like video and voice.

To alleviate this problem, video cards installed in desktop PCs to support multimedia applications can capture video and voice frames as they come off the network, buffer them in memory, and then reassemble them and pass them to the PC in a continuous stream. This approach can salvage the quality of interactive video and voice transmissions, but it detracts from the real-time nature of applications like desktop videoconferencing by introducing delays between sending and receiving stations. One way to get around this drawback is to limit the number of devices transmitting asynchronous data on the network to ensure that multimedia traffic doesn't get squeezed out. But that's not always practical, and it certainly isn't ideal.

Section 10.   Synchronous FDDI

Vendor claims aside, network managers probably will feel more comfortable implementing a version of FDDI that supports prioritized traffic. Some FDDI vendors are working on a way to implement a feature included in the original version of the FDDI standard to do just that. The feature allows some traffic to be given preferential treatment, by dedicating bandwidth to isochronous voice and video data. This approach, known as synchronous FDDI, uses a variation of the token-passing access mechanism. In essence, stations handling delay-sensitive traffic are segregated from those handling asynchronous data. This is done by configuring the network to apportion a given amount of bandwidth for synchronous communications only. The token timers in the asynchronous stations are configured to assume that bandwidth dedicated to synchronous stations has already been used up. Thus, synchronous stations are always able to transmit data up to their specified bandwidth limit.

For instance, in a network with 40 stations running time-sensitive applications and 80 stations running asynchronous data applications like file transfer and database access, the network administrator could dedicate 2 Mbit/s of bandwidth to each synchronous station, leaving the asynchronous stations to share the remaining 20 Mbit/s. If a synchronous station does not need all of its reserved bandwidth, it just returns the token to the network early, making the remainder of its dedicated bandwidth available to asynchronous stations for the rest of that token circuit.

Because synchronous FDDI adapters obtain bandwidth using a modified version of FDDI's token-passing facilities, they should interoperate with installed asynchronous products. It's worth noting, however, that no independent interoperability testing has taken place between synchronous and asynchronous products. To eliminate potential problems that are inherent to synchronous FDDI, such as the risk of overallocating synchronous bandwidth to the exclusion of asynchronous stations on the network, an ad hoc group of vendors has defined a document called the Synchronous Bandwidth Implementors Agreement, which defines a procedure for allocating synchronous bandwidth to network stations.

Because synchronous FDDI is part of the original FDDI standard, some users will be able to field-upgrade their asynchronous FDDI adapters via software. Others won't be so lucky, and will have to resort either to sending their cards back to the manufacturer or buying new ones altogether. The issue here is that if the adapter vendor hasn't built enough memory into its board to service both the synchronous and asynchronous traffic queues, the adapter can't be upgraded in software.

Despite the alleged advantages that accrue from synchronous FDDI, vendors have been slow to bring out products which implement it. One reason is that synchronous FDDI only provides a minimum sustained data rate—it cannot deliver fixed, dedicated bandwidth—or constant delays. The bottom line is this means there is no way to guarantee the quality of multimedia applications over synchronous FDDI networks. In other words, while synchronous FDDI provides a better transport for multimedia than asynchronous FDDI, it is still by no means perfect.

Section 11.   FDDI Switches

Rather than implement standards-based variations on FDDI's original shared-media architecture, a growing number of equipment vendors are now starting to offer FDDI switches. Their pitch is that FDDI switches combine the advantages of a switched, dedicated architecture with those of FDDI itself—that is, 100-Mbit/s raw throughput and internodal drive distances up to 2 kilometers. The Gigaswitch from Digital Equipment Corp. (Maynard, Mass.) was the first example of an FDDI switch. It handles up to 22 switched FDDI connections to devices attached via fiber cabling.

FDDI switches are expensive—usually costing an average of $10,600 per port. In terms of both price and application, the main competitor for FDDI switches are ATM switches. Like ATM switches, FDDI switches can dedicate up to the full bandwidth of the network to each node. Although at 100 Mbit/s FDDI doesn't match ATM's 155-Mbit/s throughput, it's fast enough to handle many applications envisioned for ATM products, such as high-speed work group computing and backbone interconnection of Ethernet and token ring LANs. And because FDDI switches are based on the established FDDI standard, they are guaranteed to work with FDDI products (including adapters) from third parties.

The one area in which FDDI switches can't match ATM technology is in the handling of time-sensitive traffic like voice and interactive video. FDDI's large frame sizes (up to 4,478 bytes) are optimized for carrying asynchronous data. ATM switches, in contrast, use much smaller (53-byte) cells, which help minimize delivery delay when different traffic streams are sent through a switch.

Although their vendors bill their products as switches, they typically function more like very large multiport bridges. Here's how they work. As an FDDI frame comes into the switch, the bridging engine looks up the frame's destination address in a table to see which of the other ports to send it to. It then adds a proprietary header to route the frame across an internal matrix. At the destination port, the header is stripped off and the frame is sent out over the second FDDI connection. All this takes place automatically. To reduce switching delay (or latency), some FDDI switches can be set to operate in so-called cut-through mode. In this mode, the port receiving a frame starts to transmit it to the destination port as soon as the front of the frame is received, instead of waiting for the entire frame to arrive.

Digital's Gigaswitch supports this feature. With cut-through enabled, latency within a switch is kept to less than 20 microseconds, according to Digital. Without it, latency for a full-size (4,478-byte) FDDI frame is 300 microseconds.

Switches with bridge-based architectures typically allow managers to set up closed virtual work groups. Traffic filters designating address domains can be set up at the port bridges, allowing only those ports in a closed group to communicate with one another.

A recent technology development from Digital promises to boost switched FDDI's prospects even further. Digital recently patented and is licensing to other FDDI manufacturers a technology called FFDT (for FDDI Full-Duplex Technology), which allows the transmit and receive channels of an FDDI connection to function simultaneously, effectively doubling throughput to 200 Mbit/s. Full-duplex operation requires changes to SMT software in the adapters and the switch. One restriction with full duplex operation is that it only operates on point-to-point connections—for example, between two switches, or between a switch and a single end node. Digital's Gigaswitch is FFDT capable. All of Digital's FDDI adapters also support FDDT.

2

An FDDI II Tutorial

FDDI II—The Sequel

Speed: 100 Mbit/s

Architecture: a hybrid of shared-media and circuit switching

Cabling: Category 5 UTP, multimode fiber, monomode fiber

Distance: 100 meters over copper, 2 kilometers over multimode fiber

Latency: variable for packets, fixed for circuits

Products: adapters, concentrators

Cost per node: $2600

Vendors implementing: one

Snapshot: a good example of why sequels rarely live up to the original.

Section 1.   Overview

FDDI's 100-Mbit/s bandwidth can go a long way to alleviating today's bandwidth crunch on corporate LANs. That advantage sounds great to net managers until they start to think a year or two down the road, when multimedia applications are likely to begin appearing in force.

The original FDDI standard was primarily designed for carrying asynchronous applications. Multimedia applications, involving interactive voice and video communications, will require networks that can guarantee timely delivery of that traffic. Quite simply, asynchronous FDDI can't meet that guarantee. That's where FDDI II comes in. The FDDI II standard was ratified by the ANSI X3T9.5 committee in 1994. It defines a hybrid network that allows simultaneous packet transfer of traditional asynchronous data, as well as circuit-switched transfer of time-sensitive multimedia data. By using circuit-switching (also called isochronous) services, FDDI II can deliver low and constant delays for time-sensitive signals.

Circuit switching aside, FDDI II otherwise is similar to the original FDDI standard. PMD, PHY, and SMT functions are identical to those in the original document. This means that the dual ring topology is retained, no modifications are required to existing applications, and installed FDDI wiring can be used unaltered. Despite its multimedia capabilities, the future of FDDI II looks bleak. Like asynchronous FDDI, FDDI II adapters are expensive. And like FDDI, FDDI II is at heart a shared-media technology—which means it doesn't scale well.

Ultimately, the majority of net managers will feel more comfortable opting for a mainstream alternative—such as ATM, Ethernet switching, or token ring switching—rather than stick their neck out by staking their network's future on a technology that has so far failed to foster even a small level of support among network vendors. Currently, only one vendor offers a network adapter implementing FDDI II: Loral Federal Systems (Manassas, VA). The fiber version of its IsoFDDI adapter costs around $2600. In comparison, the latest 25-Mbit/s ATM products can be had for less than $1000 per node.

Section 2.   How It Works

FDDI II provides circuit-switched service in addition to the packet service offered on conventional FDDI LANs. The new standard uses a multiplexing technique to divide FDDI's 100-Mbit/s bandwidth into sixteen 6.144-Mbit/s circuits. Each of the sixteen circuits is in turn subdivided into ninety-six 64-kbit/s channels, each of which can be allocated to carrying asynchronous data or isochronous traffic.

To facilitate this hybrid operation, the FDDI II standard adds two new components to the MAC layer defined in the original FDDI standard: (1) An isochronous MAC (IMAC), which processes time-sensitive traffic, and (2) a hybrid multiplexer (HMUX), which is used to transfer both circuit-switched and packet traffic onto the FDDI II ring (see Fig. 2.1).

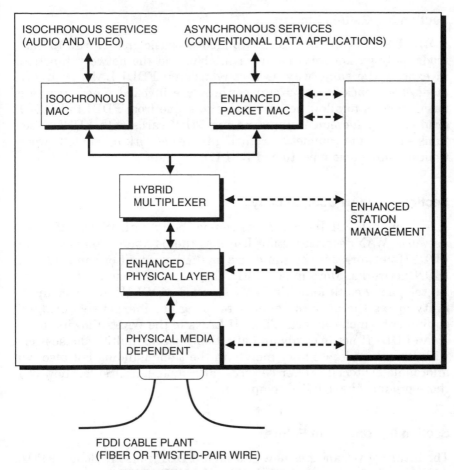

Figure 2.1 The FDDI II MAC. Network adapters conforming to the forthcoming FDDI II spec feature separate media access control (MAC) circuitry to handle isochronous traffic and conventional asynchronous traffic, shrinking isochronous circuit delay to 125 microseconds.

FDDI II's circuits allow a constant, fixed-rate connection to be set up between stations that need to exchange time-sensitive traffic. This trims node-to-node network delay to 125 microseconds (an amount which stays the same regardless of how much other traffic activity is taking place on the network at the same time). In contrast, the delays on asynchronous and synchronous FDDI fluctuate depending on the amount of traffic on the network, and can easily stretch to milliseconds. Even though video card buffering can alleviate some of this problem with FDDI, applications benefit from the predictability of FDDI II.

Section 3.   Getting Started

FDDI II LANs can operate in two modes—basic and hybrid. In basic mode, only packet services are available, and the network functions in exactly the same way as a conventional FDDI LAN. In hybrid mode, both packet and circuit services are invoked. The purpose of basic mode is to allow net managers to segue from FDDI to FDDI II gradually, by incrementally replacing FDDI cards with FDDI II editions—instead of completely refitting their network in one fell swoop. Concentrators also have to be FDDI II compliant.

Section 4.   WAN Compatibility

A feather in FDDI II's cap is its compatibility with ISDN wide-area network (WAN) services. Like IsoEnet, the 64-kbit/s channels on an FDDI II network are the same size as the basic unit of bandwidth on ISDN networks. More importantly, they use the same 8-KHz universal telephony clock found in WAN services. FDDI II's ISDN compatibility opens the door to vendors to bring out inexpensive bridging equipment which connects FDDI II LANs to the WAN, allowing users on an FDDI II net to easily and affordably set up multimedia sessions with coworkers located not merely in the same building but also (via affordable switched-carrier services) at remote sites. So far, however, those products have failed to appear.

Section 5.   Uncertain Future

The future of yet another new edition of FDDI is also in doubt. FFOL, which comes under the jurisdiction of ANSI's X3T9.5 committee, is supposed to define an ultra-high-speed fiber network capable of handling both isochronous and asynchronous traffic simultaneously. No firm decision has been made on exactly how fast FFOL will run, although speeds in excess of 2 Gbit/s are being considered. To date, the total output of the ANSI X3T9.5 committee that is preparing FFOL has been limited to one working paper, a slim tome about 20 pages long. Work on FFOL is mired down because it lacks a technology champion to push its development. FFOL products are years away, at best. If ATM proves to be as much of a hit with corporate managers as predicted, FFOL will never get off the ground.

3

A Fibre Channel
Tutorial

Fibre Channel at a Glance

Speeds: 100 Mbit/s, 200 Mbit/s, 400 Mbit/s, 800 Mbit/s supported today; 1 Gbit/s and 2 Gbit/s planned—all versions can operate full duplex

Cabling types: single-mode and multimode optical fiber, coaxial, shielded twisted pair

Distance limits: up to 10 kilometers using single-mode fiber; up to 50 meters using shielded twisted pair

Latency: 10 to 30 microseconds

Products available: switches, arbitrated-loop hubs, adapter cards for PCs, workstations, storage servers, supercomputers

Cost per switched port: $1500

Cost per adapter card: $1200 to $3000

Cost per node: $2700 to $4500

Snapshot: its low-latency, high bandwidth, switched architecture will win it significant market share in high-end computer networks

---

This chapter contains some information from an article originally published in *Data Communications* magazine and written by Edward M. Frymoyer, a consultant at EMF Associates (Mountain View, CA).

Section 1.   Overview

It hasn't received half the publicity of some of the new wave of high-speed LANs, but Fibre Channel is fast becoming a mainstream option for multivendor, multiprotocol high-speed networking. Fibre Channel was originally developed in concert by Hewlett-Packard, IBM, and Sun Microsystems. It is now a ratified ANSI standard, and after a slow start net managers are finally catching onto the potential of Fibre Channel. That's reflected in market researchers' predictions. Dataquest (San Jose) forecasts that the Fibre Channel market will be worth $850 million by 1997. Ryan-Hankin-Kent Inc. (San Francisco) is even more bullish, predicting a $1.4 billion market (see Fig. 3.1).

Designed to meet the data rate demands of high-end systems, Fibre Channel enables multiple workstation, server, and host platforms to access a high-speed, low-latency, switched communications infrastructure. Ironically, Fibre Channel is actually based on a channel design usually associated with "old" applications like host-peripheral connections, and uses the channel-based architecture found in network adapters used for host-peripheral connections or point-to-point data storage. Generally speaking, channel-based adapters are designed to carry data packets at the highest speed, and with the least network delay (latency) possible.

Fibre Channel development started in 1988 when the ANSI X3T9.3 (now X3T1.1) committee began reviewing the requirements for high-

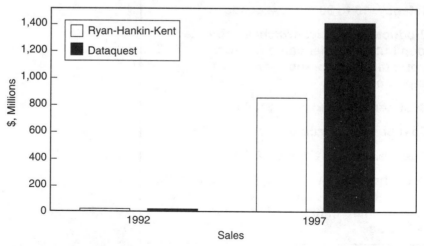

Figure 3.1   Fibre Channel markets. $850 million to $1.4 billion market by 1997. *Source: ANCOR Communications, Inc.*

speed channel attachments and LAN connections. The committee concluded that a new technology was needed to meet the rising input/output (I/O) demands of distributed networks, and that this technology, which later came to be known as Fibre Channel, would need to be:

- Interoperable—meeting diverse application and protocol needs: small computer systems interface (SCSI), intelligent peripheral interface (IPI), high-performance parallel interface (HIPPI), and others

- Scalable—both speed and application support would need to extend beyond current requirements to provide room for future growth (Fibre Channel presently supports throughput of up to 800 Mbit/s)

- Inexpensive—able to support computer systems at costs comparable to existing LAN technologies

Fibre Channel's proponents can today certainly claim to have met the first and second of these aims, but as far as price goes, the technology is still prohibitively expensive. Current Fibre Channel switches average about $1500 per connection, while Fibre Channel adapter cards range from $1500 to $3000 each. In its defense, Fibre Channel vendors say that prices are falling fast.

Nevertheless, Fibre Channel still faces significant competition from both HIPPI, the standard supercomputing protocol, and—of course—ATM. Also, it's worth noting that not all the vendors pushing the Fibre Channel standard are touting it as appropriate for switched-LAN service. Sun is interested in Fibre Channel as an I/O technology, not as a local area network technology.

ANSI approved the first Fibre Channel spec in 1990, and the first Fibre Channel products reached the market in 1991. The current version of the specification (Version 4.3) received approval from ANSI in October 1994. Version 4.3 also has been accepted by the International Standards Organization (ISO) as a standard-in-process, ISO 14165-1.

If Fibre Channel is to find favor as a network solution, it will need to ensure interoperability among different vendors' gear. Oddly, the standard itself stops short of providing some specific technical details about how its features should be implemented. To address the interoperability issue, Fibre Channel's three most influential supporters—Hewlett-Packard, IBM, and Sun—formed the Fibre Channel Systems Initiative (FCSI). The triumvirate has developed a set of documents, called *profiles,* that give vendors implementation information to develop interoperable products.

Applications Envisioned for Fibre Channel

In a medical imaging facility, a local work group harnesses high-speed file transfers and the horsepower of a supercomputer to perform enhanced visual analysis of a scanned X-ray image. Upon discovering previously unseen patterns and correlations in the image data, a member of the group sets up a data pipe connection (via a high-speed enterprise or campus switch) to a workstation in the office of the patient's primary physician.

After viewing the data and consulting with other on-line physicians in real time, the primary care physician directs further inquiries on the basis of the analysts' findings. But before the physician takes action, these inquiries are logged in a database on the hospital mainframe, where an expert system evaluates them against operating procedures followed for similar cases in the past. Within minutes, the expert system reports back its findings, complete with documentation, X-ray and scanned-image data, case histories, research references, and success rates.

This state-of-the-art high-speed LAN application offers a hospital more efficient utilization of its medical imaging facilities. And the rapid transfer of image data enables implementation of higher-resolution equipment, permitting finer sectioning of tissue, more detailed analysis, and more exact diagnosis. Patients receive more extensive lower-cost care that limits the need for invasive medical procedures. Hospitals get higher productivity, better consultation, high-integrity data retention for future reference, greater protection against malpractice—and, possibly, happier patients.

Section 2.   End-to-End Standard

Fibre Channel permits a plug-and-play channel extension interface to mainframes and supercomputers, as well as to many peripherals, including mass storage, media storage, medical devices, process equipment, data acquisition equipment—such as real-time sensors—and other hardware (see Fig. 3.2). At the same time, it offers a high-speed LAN interconnect technology that accommodates today's distributed, multivendor, multiprotocol networks. To existing network applications, Fibre Channel can look the same as Ethernet, token ring, FDDI, or even ATM, but it delivers significantly higher throughput.

In some ways, Fibre Channel is one of the most comprehensive of the high-speed networking standards to reach market. It delivers a

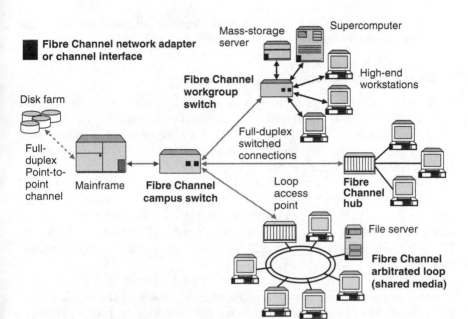

Figure 3.2 The Fibre Channel network. Fibre Channel supports point-to-point, shared-media and switched topologies. It also delivers the throughput needed for mainframe channel extensions, mass storage, and supercomputer and workstation clusters.

wide range of data rates, from 100 Mbit/s to 800 Mbit/s, running on fiber-optic (hence the "Fibre" moniker) media at distances up to 10 kilometers, and copper media at distances of up to 50 meters. And, in an unusual twist, it can function both as a switched (dedicated) network or in a shared-media, ring-based environment. It also provides multiple classes of service to accommodate different types of network applications and data, including mainframe channel attachments (thus the "Channel" portion of the name) and isochronous multimedia traffic. And it transparently supports several LAN protocols, both old and new, including ATM protocol data units (PDUs), HIPPI, SCSI, and TCP/IP.

Also important, Fibre Channel does all these things across a network infrastructure that can incorporate multiple topologies, including point-to-point direct channel connections, ring topologies (known as arbitrated loops), and either work group or campuswide switching fabrics. Proponents of Fibre Channel envision hundreds of small high-speed work groups populating commercial enterprise nets. These local work groups would access distributed system resources and peripherals via shared-media Fibre Channel loops or hubs, then connect to a Fibre Channel campus backbone switch. High-performance workstation clusters could also access their own local switches that front-end the larger network switch.

Section 3. Fibre Channel, Layer by Layer

Fibre Channel employs a five-layer network stack. These five layers define the physical media and transmission rates (FC-0), the data encoding and decoding scheme (FC-1), framing protocol and flow control (FC-2), common services and feature selection (FC-3), and upper-layer protocol and application interfaces (FC-4).

The lower three layers of the Fibre Channel stack (layers FC-0 through FC-2) form what is known as the Fibre Channel physical standard (FC-PH). These layers define all the physical transmission characteristics for Fibre Channel, while the upper layers (FC-3 and FC-4) handle interfaces with other network protocols and applications (see Fig. 3.3).

Unlike other LAN technologies, such as Ethernet and token ring, Fibre Channel keeps the various functional layers of the stack physically separate. This separation enables vendors to build products from separate functional pieces, such as media connect modules, processing chip sets, or bus interfaces, that handle specific portions of the protocol stack. It also allows vendors to easily implement some stack functions in hardware, while putting others in software or firmware.

Section 4. Speeds Supported

The lowest layer in the Fibre Channel stack, FC-0, defines the basic physical link. Fibre Channel, unlike other high-speed LAN technologies such as 100Base-T (fast Ethernet), 100VG-AnyLAN, and FDDI, supports a selection of signaling rates—not just one. Even ATM, the high-speed technology most noted for throughput scalability, does not deliver the range of data rates that Fibre Channel can provide. These include 133 Mbaud, 266 Mbaud, 531 Mbaud, and 1.062 Gbaud. Note that these signaling rates include the overhead involved in establishing and maintaining connections. The true data throughput rates are somewhat lower: 100 Mbit/s for 133 Mbaud; 200 Mbit/s for 266 Mbaud; 400 Mbit/s for 531 Mbaud; and 800 Mbit/s for 1.062 Gbaud. The difference between signaling and data throughput rates is attributable to overhead generated by Fibre Channel's encode/decode mechanism.

Today, 200 Mbit/s is the most widely used Fibre Channel data rate for high-speed work group environments. In most cases, including switched environments, users will be able to upgrade to higher rates

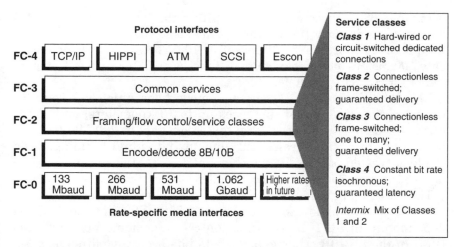

ATM = Asynchronous transfer mode   HIPPI = High performance parallel interface
Escon = Enterprise Systems Connection   SCSI = Small computer systems interface

Figure 3.3   Fibre Channel's five layers. Fibre Channel employs a five-layer stack. The layers define transmission rates (FC-0); data encoding and decoding (FC-1); framing, flow control, and service classes (FC-2); common services (FC-3); and protocol and application interfaces (FC-4). Service classes characterize distinct types of Fibre Channel transmissions.

by means of an adapter card swap. Future data rates for Fibre Channel will go well beyond today's 1.062 Gbaud ceiling. Specifications for 2.134 and 4.268 Gbaud are in place, and vendors are planning to launch products supporting these signaling rates soon. However, users buying into the faster products will pay a penalty both in cost (especially because optical fiber cabling is required) and in additional overhead as Fibre Channel scales up to higher throughput rates.

Section 5.   Cabling Concerns

Fibre Channel supports a wide range of physical cabling media, including single-mode fiber-optic cable, 50- and 62.5-micrometer multimode fiber, video, and coaxial cable, and shielded twisted pair. At this point, Fibre Channel does not support unshielded twisted-pair wiring—a major drawback. For optical fiber connections, Fibre Channel uses what is known as a duplex SC connector. For coaxial interfaces, it uses a TNC receiver connector and a BNC transmitter. And for STP, it uses a standard 9-pin D-type connector.

Each of these different cabling media supports a range of data rates and entails specific distance limitations, and Fibre Channel can support a mix of all these wiring types within the same network. All this makes designing a Fibre Channel LAN somewhat more complicated than other networks like 100Base-T or 100VG-AnyLAN—which mandate 100 meters as the maximum distance over Category 5 or Category 3 UTP, or STP copper cable.

In a Fibre Channel LAN, a single-mode fiber-optic cable could be used across a campus for distances up to 10 kilometers; multimode fiber, which spans distances of up to 2 kilometers at 200 Mbit/s, could be used to distribute traffic throughout individual buildings; and shielded twisted pair (STP), which supports 100 Mbit/s at distances of up to 50 meters, could provide connections to individual workstations.

The encoding scheme used in Fibre Channel is defined in layer FC-1 of the five-layer stack. Like some ATM implementations, FC-1 depends on an 8B/10B transmission coding scheme licensed from IBM. In the 8B/10B scheme, eight data bits are transmitted as a 10-bit group with the two extra bits used for error detection and correction, known as *disparity control*. The 8B/10B scheme supplies sufficient error correction to permit use of low-cost transceivers as well as timing recovery methods to ensure balanced, synchronized transmissions and reduce the potential for radio frequency interference.

Section 6.   Working Classes

FC-2 is the workhorse of the Fibre Channel protocol stack. It performs the basic signaling and framing functions and defines the transport mechanism for data from the upper layers of the stack.

FC-2 frames and sequences data from the upper layers to transmit via the FC-0 layer, then receives transmissions from the FC-0 layer and reframes and resequences it for use by upper layers. Fibre Channel frame sizes can vary and must be negotiated by the transmitter/receiver pair for each connection. Frame sizes typically range from 36 bytes to 2 kbytes, but can be larger in some cases. The amount of overhead required to transmit a frame remains constant regardless of the frame's size. This makes Fibre Channel very efficient for high-volume data transfers, such as storage reads and writes or a TCP/IP file interchange in which large message sizes are the norm.

FC-2 signaling defines the connection between at least two Fibre Channel node ports (also known as N ports), one of which must act as an originator sending outbound traffic and at least one of which must act as a responder, receiving inbound traffic and sending traffic back. Connections between N ports are full duplex—each connection can accommodate simultaneous, bidirectional traffic flow. This means, for example, that the 200-Mbit/s data rate of Fibre Channel's 266-Mbaud signaling option actually delivers 400 Mbit/s of aggregate through-put—200 Mbit/s in each direction (provided, of course, that an operating system capable of transmitting data in both directions is running on the Fibre Channel workstations).

The FC-2 layer also provides essential traffic management functions, including flow control mechanisms, link management functions, buffer memory management, and error detection and correction.

Section 7.   Different Service Levels

Most importantly, FC-2 defines four classes of service which allow it to meet a variety of communications needs (see Fig. 3.4). Message classes provide a structure for dynamic resource management as well as for prioritization, data and application integrity, and flow control.

Class 1.   Hard-wired or circuit-switched connections. Class 1 connections are dedicated, uninterruptible links, like telephone connections. This service provides exclusive use of the connection for the period of time of the connect. In this respect, it is sometimes called a selfish connection. When two Fibre Channel N ports are connected via a Class 1 link, these ports—and the path followed to establish the connection—are not available to other N ports. Class 1 service is designed for time-critical, nonbursty, dedicated links, such as those between two supercomputers.

Class 2.   Connectionless, frame-switched transmission, which guarantees delivery and confirms receipt of traffic. As in conventional packet-switching technologies such as frame relay, Class 2 switching is performed on the data frame rather than on a connection. No dedicated connection is established between N ports. In other words, each frame is sent to its destination over an available route.

In Class 2 service, delivery is guaranteed; when congestion occurs, the frame is retransmitted until it successfully reaches its destination. Class 2 signaling blocks a frame; the transmitting N port receives a busy signal. It works this way so that retransmissions can be performed immediately during periods of network congestion, rather than having to wait for a time-out, as is the case with TCP/IP and other protocols.

Class 3.   One-to-many connectionless frame-switched services, similar to Class 2, but with no delivery guarantee or confirmation mechanism. Class 3 transmissions are faster than Class 2 because they don't wait for confirmation. However, if a transmission does not arrive at its destination, Class 3 service does not retransmit. Class 3 is most

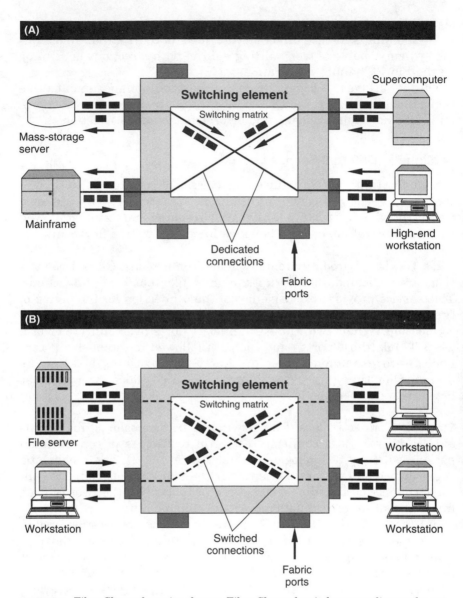

Figure 3.4 Fibre Channel service classes. Fibre Channel switches according to the service class of the traffic. Class 1 requires dedicated point-to-point connections, so the switch establishes direct paths from one port to another (a). For Class 2 service, individual frames are switched (b). Each frame takes the most economical path to its destination.

often used for real-time broadcasts of scientific visualizations, process control data, and other applications which cannot wait for acknowledgments, but are not sufficiently time-critical to warrant Class 1 service, and can tolerate some lost data.

Class 4. Connection-based service offering guaranteed fractional bandwidth and guaranteed latency levels. In this service class, which is still under development, users will be able to lock down specific paths through a Fibre Channel switch fabric. These paths will guarantee constant latency as well as a constant fraction of the switch's aggregate bandwidth.

Constant latency requires a defined physical path through the switch fabric, as opposed to a virtual path, where the actual physical connection can vary. Overall Fibre Channel offers very low latency levels for all its service classes—lower than those of ATM. Even when only moderately congested, latency in an ATM network can typically rise to several hundred microseconds. Fibre Channel's proponents claim it can provide connection-based service with 10- to 30-microsecond latency and can deliver similar performance for Class 2 frame-based service, unless the network is severely congested. These claims have yet to be put to the test, however.

Class 4 also will support an isochronous service, which will carry real-time voice and video traffic. Isochronous means time-consistent, so data, voice, and video transmitted isochronously all arrive at the same time and at the same rate. Fibre Channel can carry packetized video in any class of service, but applications such as high-definition video require consistent latency and minimum jitter connections without buffering, which only isochronous service can provide.

Class 4 was designed with multimedia and ATM in mind and should provide a better interface to ATM networks, which also guarantees specific traffic parameters, including latency levels and isochronous service. Like ATM constant bit rate (CBR) service, Class 4 provides a dedicated number of bits in a specified unit of time.

Intermix. Combines features of Class 1 circuit-switched connections and Class 2 frame-switching service. Essentially Intermix service reserves Fibre Channel bandwidth for Class 1 service, but transmits Class 2 traffic when the Class 1 connection is idle. In this way, Intermix provides inherent prioritization, Class 1 traffic always goes through at the committed data rate, while Class 2 traffic is automatically retransmitted until the link is idle and the frames reach their destination.

Section 8.   Flow Control

FC-2 also supplies additional flow control and error correction mechanisms. For flow control, FC-2 employs a sliding-window flow control scheme similar to that of TCP/IP, although flow control functionality varies somewhat according to the class of service defined. Error detection is performed using a 32-bit cyclic redundancy check (CRC) mechanism. Also, a link control facility manages operation of the Fibre Channel connection and maintains information necessary to recover links in the event of failure.

The crowning layer of the Fibre Channel stack is FC-4, also known as the multiple service interconnect. At this layer, Fibre Channel provides interfaces to several legacy upper-layer protocols (ULPs). In other words, FC-4 allows Fibre Channel to carry data from other networking protocols and applications. So far specifications have been defined for many of the most widely used networking protocols, including TCP/IP, HIPPI, and ATM Adaptation Layer 5 (AAL-5) protocol data units (PDUs), and channel connection protocols including SCSI, IPI, and ESCON.

Section 9.   Loops and Switches

To meet the diverse needs of work group and campuswide applications, Fibre Channel supports three topologies: point-to-point, arbitrated loop, and crosspoint or fabric switching. The topology of a Fibre Channel network is transparent to the attached devices. That is, whether the Fibre Channel link is hard-wired, established over a shared media, or set up via a switch is irrelevant to the end station or its application. The Fibre Channel ports involved in a given link negotiate the means and nature of the connection or transmission.

All three topologies are fully interoperable. Fibre Channel switch ports (also known as fabric ports, or F ports) can provide individual end stations (N ports) or loops with access to the overall Fibre Channel network. All point-to-point and loop topologies require that all nodes use the same data rate at all times. In a Fibre Channel switch topology, however, dynamic rate conversion is possible. For example, in the switched topology, a 266-Mbaud unit could connect to a 1.062-Gbaud unit. The two ports involved in the connection simply negotiate to the lowest available signaling rate—in this case, 266 Mbaud.

The arbitrated-loop topology provides a low-cost solution for attaching multiple devices, without requiring hubs or switches. The loop provides shared bandwidth for up to 127 Fibre Channel ports (which in the loop topology are also known as loop ports, or L ports). Each L port requests use of the loop when it needs to communicate with another port; if the loop is free, the requesting port sets up a bidirectional connection to the destination port. This connection can then deliver any class of service appropriate to the traffic between the two L ports.

Only one pair of loop ports may communicate at one time. When these two L ports relinquish control of the loop, another point-to-point connection between two L ports may be established. The entire loop may be attached to a Fibre Channel switch fabric port known as an FL port or directly to a single host system via an NL port. Autosensing capabilities enable L ports to identify the other ports in their environment and to negotiate connections with switch ports.

Arbitration occurs according to the address of the L port for the sending end station. Like ATM, Fibre Channel uses a 24-bit addressing scheme. This address is used to identify a destination end station. The L port with the lowest address is given highest priority for access to the arbitrated loop. The loop is self-configuring, so that host connections, NL ports, are always given the lowest addresses and therefore the highest priority. Switch fabric connections, FL addresses, are given the second priority (next to the lowest addresses), and N ports are given highest addresses and the lowest priority.

Section 10.   Switched Service

Crosspoint switching is the highest-performing and most versatile of the three Fibre Channel topologies. It provides a fabric of possible connections between multiple switched ports (F ports). The way switching works depends on the service class of the traffic being transmitted.

Class 1 service, which calls for dedicated point-to-point connections, requires the switch to establish a fixed path from one F port to another. The transmitting end station (N port) sends information to the F port to which it is attached, then that F port passes the traffic directly to its destination F port via the dedicated switched connection. The destination F port then forwards the traffic to the destination N port. This transmission continues—in one or both directions—until one of the N ports drops the connection.

In the case of Class 2 service, in which individual frames are switched rather than dedicated point-to-point connections, the process works differently. In this case, when one end station (N port) attached to the switch fabric sends frames destined for another N port, the traffic can follow several different paths through the switch fabric.

Because the data is transmitted and processed one frame at a time rather than via a dedicated point-to-point link, the switch can send each frame through the most economical available route. If a Class 1 dedicated connection makes use of one path through the switch fabric, a Class 2 frame may take another path. When the Class 1 connection relinquishes its path, the next Class 2 frame may use it.

Section 11.   The Future of Fibre Channel

Fibre Channel offers a natural follow-on to the SCSI peripheral interface, which supplies lower data rates with significantly higher latency. Fibre Channel also offers up to 127 connections on the same arbitrated loop or hub and unlimited switched connections, whereas SCSI is limited to a maximum of 15. And Fibre Channel extends to distances of up to 10 kilometers, while SCSI is restricted to 20 meters. Best of all, Fibre Channel allows reuse of existing SCSI drivers with little modification.

Yet it is as a high-speed switched networking technology for campus and local area networks that Fibre Channel has its greatest promise. Faster than most of the other high-speed LAN alternatives, and equipped with a full complement of flow control and class of service features, Fibre Channel is poised to leave the supercomputer laboratory and enter mainstream commercial environments. As prices fall, performance increases, and the installed base expands, Fibre Channel could penetrate the conventional LAN market now dominated by Ethernet and token ring.

Fibre Channel could play an especially useful role in organizations downsizing from mainframes to distributed networks. With the aid of Fibre Channel, centralized mainframe computing resources can evolve toward distributed file servers, workstations, and server and disk farms. Old and new architectures can be interconnected in a structured, prioritized fashion at high speeds using Fibre Channel's support for multiple servers, service classes, and topologies. Workstation and supercomputer clustering applications for Fibre Channel are also growing, although further development of the appropriate clustering software is still required.

Additionally, Fibre Channel's support for multiple protocols and data types allows users to integrate special-purpose data sources such as imaging equipment and real-time sensors into their information networks. Its higher throughput permits greater distribution of processing resources, which in turn makes possible the wider use of visualization and analysis tools, particularly in campus environments. Essentially, any applications producing megabits to gigabits of data per second, from on-line transaction processing services to satellite imaging systems, are ripe for Fibre Channel.

Section 12.   User Perspective

Fibre Channel has already made quite a hit with users. For instance, a 6-month comparison of ATM with Fibre Channel by the University of Minnesota (Minneapolis) recently concluded that Fibre Channel offers lower overall latency and higher overall throughput than ATM—at a lower cost, and with higher overall reliability.

Others report that Fibre Channel is so fast that actual data throughput is currently limited by the internal system bus of the workstations it is used to connect, and not by the network itself. According to SSESCO Inc. (Minneapolis), a value added reseller (VAR) that has installed equipment from Ancor at sites in Japan and the United States, the lowest actual throughput it has measured is around 100 Mbit/s, between each pair of sixteen RS-6000 Model 520/530 workstations connected by a single Ancor switch at Florida State University (Tallahassee). The highest is roughly 230 Mbit/s, between each pair of (faster) RS-6000 Model 590/990 workstations connected by a switch at the Research Information Processing Systems (RIPS) division of the Ministry of International Trade and Industry (MITI) in Tsukuba, Japan.

SSESCO notes that performance does not degrade at either site, even when all eight pairs of workstations simultaneously communicate via the switches. Both sites are installed over multimode fiber cable. They run IBM's AIX operating system, plus additional parallel processing software, and are used to perform high-end scientific applications.

A HIPPI Tutorial

HIPPI at a Glance

Speeds: 800 Mbit/s and 1.6 Gbit/s

Architecture: switched

Cabling: 50-pair STP, single-mode and multimode fiber

Distance: 25 meters over copper (cascaded switches can be extended 200 meters); 300 meters over multimode fiber; 10 kilometers over single-mode fiber

Connection time: less than 1 microsecond for a dedicated connection

Latency: 2 microseconds

Products: switches, routers, mainframe and supercomputer channels, interfaces for mass-storage devices, frame buffers, adapters for PCI workstations and PCs

Cost per switched port: $2000

Cost per adapter card: $2000 to $3500

Cost per node: $4000 to $5500

Snapshot: the ultrahigh throughput it delivers for asynchronous applications will win HIPPI a small but fervent fan club in high-end data networks

This chapter contains extracts from an article originally published in *Data Communications* magazine and written by Don Tolmie of Los Alamos National Laboratory and Don Flanagan of the HIPPI Networking Forum.

Section 1.   Overview

Network managers on the hunt for high throughput don't have time
to play games. Still, they may want to spare a moment to consider
this brief riddle: "What do supercomputers, workstations, and other
high-end devices have in common?"

"Bandwidth—and lots of it" is the obvious answer. But it's not the
only one. How about HIPPI? That's right, HIPPI (high-performance
parallel interface). True, the gigabit-per-second ANSI standard was
originally developed to allow mainframes and their supercomputing
kin to communicate with one another, and with directly attached storage devices, at supersonic speeds. But HIPPI is no longer just for
supercomputers.

In the past, HIPPI networking solutions have been far too expensive for most net managers' pockets—costing up to $30,000 per node.
The high cost has confined HIPPI to use primarily with supercomputers, supporting applications such as special-effects creation for
movies, medical imaging, seismic analysis, molecular modeling, and
component design for electronic firms. However, recent product intro-
ductions have dramatically lowered the cost per HIPPI seat to as little as $4000. HIPPI's followers reckon this factor makes possible
much broader use of HIPPI technology—unleashing its power for
more mainstream applications like connecting data center networks,
accessing mass storage devices, supporting client/server applications,
and clustering high-end workstations.

Proponents of the nascent network technology posit its use either
as a very high-speed autonomous network or as an adjunct technology
that can be connected to another network—such as Ethernet, FDDI,
or ATM—via routers. The original series of ANSI (American National
Standards Institute) standards that define HIPPI have been extended
on several fronts. HIPPI over copper now allows several switches to
be cascaded via local connections that can reach to 200 meters all
told, though switch to end-node drive distance is still limited to a pal-
try 25 meters. Multimode connections can run to 300 meters. And the
HIPPI-Serial extension allows fiber runs of up to 10 kilometers over
monomode fiber, 2 kilometers over multimode.

Since HIPPI is a standard, it gives users a clearly defined way to
connect a range of devices at very high speeds—without having to
worry about interoperability and workarounds. What's more, both the
HIPPI Networking Forum and the ANSI X3T11 Technical Committee
are looking to make HIPPI easier to deploy and manage. A HIPPI
MIB (management information base) proposal is in process, and several developers are working on capacity planning applications and
looking to integrate HIPPI with management platforms like

Openview from Hewlett-Packard Co. (Palo Alto, CA) and Netview from IBM. Finally, there have been several developments aimed at linking HIPPI to other LAN and WAN technologies, including ATM, Fibre Channel, and Sonet (synchronous optical network).

HIPPI's most noticeable attribute is speed. The committee charged with developing the HIPPI standard set itself a straightforward goal: to develop a simple "fire hose" for moving data at the highest speeds possible. The group succeeded. HIPPI provides full duplex data throughput at speeds up to 3.2 Gbit/s, making it far and away the fastest of the high-speed LAN technologies covered in this book.

Despite its gargantuan data rates, HIPPI faces serious competition from two other networking technologies—ATM, and Fibre Channel (which similarly has its origins in channel-attached architectures). Both have received far more publicity than the HIPPI standard to date, and have some advantages over HIPPI when it comes to utilizing bandwidth efficiently between multiple nodes. Further, the genuinely astonishing data rates supported by HIPPI may actually dissuade some managers from experimenting with the technology as a run-of-the-mill LAN, since the rates are so much higher than anything that their desktop equipment could conceivably utilize.

Section 2.   HIPPI Hardware

Enough vendors are now selling HIPPI products to allow net managers to create an end-to-end HIPPI network and integrate it into their existing LAN environment.

Four vendors—including Network Systems Corp. (Minneapolis)— are now shipping HIPPI switches; these come with up to 32 ports, and can be cascaded to support a network comprising hundreds of nodes. Copper network interface cards (NICs) are available for all supercomputers, as well as workstations from Sun, SGI, Hewlett-Packard, and IBM. Recently, Essential Communications became the first adapter vendor to ship a fiber interface card, which fits inside PCI bus machines. Front-end processors (FEPs) are shipping for some mainframes. Most importantly, perhaps, Essential Communications (Albuquerque, NM) and Netstar Inc. (Minneapolis) have routers with HIPPI interfaces—enabling them to link HIPPI networks with other LANs and WANs. Essential also has a Sonet-HIPPI gateway. Another gateway is being developed by Los Alamos National Laboratory (Los Alamos, NM). And the GTE Government Systems Corp. (Needham Heights, MA) has an ATM (asynchronous transfer mode) switch with a HIPPI interface.

One thing all these products have in common is that they can now be had for far less than ever before. In the early days of HIPPI, manufacturers spared no expense in engineering their products with a wide variety of high-end features—such as hot swappability, high-end management, and redundancy. The result was very high prices: switches cost around $10,000 per port; adapters went for an astonishing $10,000 to $20,000. Those prices were almost insignificant compared with the cost of the supercomputers which the HIPPI kit was hooking up (often $20 million).

All that has changed now. HIPPI switches and adapters are being used to connect far less expensive desktop devices. To meet that application, vendors have brought out slimmed-down versions of their earlier products. Switches can now be had for as little as $2000 per port; adapters, for between $2000 and $3500.

Section 3.   The Basics

The best way to get a sense of what HIPPI has to offer is take a look at some of its more important characteristics:

- *Very high-speed data transfers*—HIPPI can be configured for either of two speeds—800 Mbit/s or 1.6 Gbit/s, both either simplex or full duplex.

- *Very simple signaling sequences*—Basically, HIPPI connections can be set up with just three messages: Request (which the source uses to ask for a connection); Connect (which the destination uses to indicate that the connection has been established); Ready (which the destination uses to indicate that it's ready to accept a stream of packets).

- *Protocol independence*—HIPPI channels can handle so-called raw HIPPI (data formatted with the technology's framing protocol, without any upper-layer protocols), TCP-IP datagrams, and IPI-3 (intelligent peripheral interface) framed data. (IPI-3 is the protocol used to connect peripherals like RAID [redundant array of inexpensive disks] devices to computers). Thus, HIPPI is equally adept at internetworking (with Ethernet and FDDI) and high-speed data storage and retrieval.

- *Physical layer flow control*—HIPPI also offers a credit-based system for reliable and efficient communications between devices operating at different speeds. In effect, the source keeps track of the Ready signals and sends data only when the destination can handle it.

- *Connection-oriented circuit switching*—Nonblocking circuit switches allow multiple conversations to take place concurrently. Thus, the aggregate bandwidth of these switches can be very high—equal to 800 Mbit/s or 1.6 Gbit/s times the number of ports.

- *Compatibility with copper and fiber*—HIPPI uses 50-pair STP (shielded twisted pair) cable for short distances. It works with single-mode and multimode cable across the campus or metropolitan area. Sonet is used for long-distance communication.

The bulk of the HIPPI standard is defined in four documents:

1. X3.183 (HIPPI-PH1) defines the physical layer, detailing mechanical and electrical specifications.

2. X3.210 (HIPPI-FP2) defines the HIPPI packet format and header. Information is carried in packets measuring either 1 Kbyte or 2 Kbytes in length. These can be combined into a single "burst" measuring in excess of a gigabyte.

3. X3.218 (HIPPI-LE3) defines an encapsulation scheme enabling IEEE 802.2-compliant protocols—such as TCP/IP—to be carried over HIPPI networks.

4. X3.222 (HIPPI-SC4) defines the operation of HIPPI switches.

A fifth advisory document (not a standard) has subsequently been defined. Called HIPPI-5, it details how HIPPI can run over fiber cabling.

Section 4.   Network Topology

At its very simplest, a HIPPI network consists of two computers with HIPPI channels linked by two 50-pair copper cables (HIPPI adapters and the ports on HIPPI switches come with two sets of connectors to accommodate the dual cables). This configuration furnishes a full-duplex (or dual-simplex) 800-Mbit/s channel that can extend up to 25 meters. One cable is used to send data, the other to receive. A full duplex HIPPI connection running at 800 Mbit/s thus provides aggregate throughput of 1.6 Gbit/s.

As if that wasn't fast enough, HIPPI defines a second speed—1.6 Gbit/s—which is implemented by running a pair of cables in each direction. By running a total of four cables between two computers, full duplex performance of 3.2 Gbit/s is achievable. In reality, almost all the roughly 2500 HIPPI nodes now installed run at 800 Mbit/s, for the very simple reason that practically no device can either send or receive a 1.6-Gbit/s stream of data.

HIPPI switches can be cascaded locally over 200-meter cabling runs. The number of switches that can be cascaded depends upon the size of the switches themselves. HIPPI addresses are 24 bits long. Some switches work with 3-bit addresses; others, with 4 bits. If eight-by-eight switches are deployed (which use 3-bit addresses on their eight inbound and eight outbound ports), a maximum of eight boxes can be cascaded (for a total of 24 bits). Connections on a HIPPI network are made in a similar way to telephone calls. Once a connection has been set up, a stream of packets can be sent from the source to the destination. HIPPI connections between two nodes are nailed up—that is, other traffic cannot use the link until the transmission is over.

Section 5.   Gigantic Cable

The HIPPI physical layer specifies use of a 50-pair, shielded copper cable for distances up to 25 meters. While useful in small networks within computer centers, this type of cable is way too cumbersome, and provides insufficient drive distances, to be viable in mainstream LANs. When greater distances are required, fiber can be deployed to extend the node-to-node range of the HIPPI network; to either 10 kilometers over monomode fiber cable or 2 kilometers over multimode fiber cable (see Fig. 4.1). Fiber can be implemented in one of two ways: (1) by using adapters and switches that support fiber cable natively or (2) by converting copper cable connections to fiber using conversion "modems."

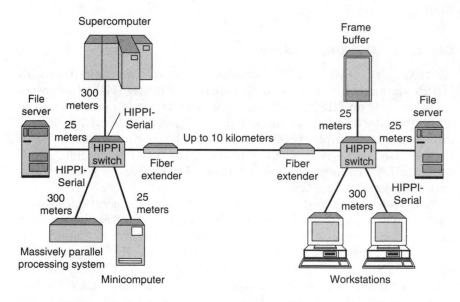

HIPPI = High performance parallel interface

Figure 4.1 The HIPPI backbone. HIPPI makes it possible to link a variety of high-speed devices. Copper connections can extend 25 meters; HIPPI-Serial interfaces allow runs of 300 meters over multimode fiber. With fiber extenders, devices can be separated by 10 kilometers.

HIPPI's power as a backbone technology was demonstrated at the Supercomputing '94 conference held in Washington, D.C. An all-fiber HIPPI backbone, consisting of some 18 miles of multimode cable, connected 16 exhibitors and delivered over 90 Gbit/s of aggregate capacity. The backbone was used for numerous tests and demonstrations. For example, three HIPPI switch makers—Avaika Networks Corp. (Mountain View, CA), Essential, and Netstar—conducted the first public interoperability demo of HIPPI-Serial. The switches were linked directly via their serial ports—without fiber extenders—and ran at the full HIPPI speed of 800 Mbit/s. Direct switch-to-switch fiber connections will go a long way toward simplifying HIPPI networking.

Section 6.   The Internetworking Angle

HIPPI switches are an accepted technology for LAN interconnect. RFC (request for comment) 1347 from the IETF (Internet Engineering Task Force) specifies how these boxes are to be used on IP networks. Most vendors of computers with HIPPI channels also have software drivers for TCP/IP.

HIPPI is architected toward servicing applications that require very large data transfers, and some observers have questioned the efficiency of using a HIPPI switch to carry small LAN packets, such as TCP/IP datagrams. The standard's backers defend it by saying that the connection times offered with HIPPI switches are so fast (as little as 740 nanoseconds) and the delay caused by HIPPI switches is so low (typically under 2 microseconds) that an individual HIPPI port can easily outperform conventional bridges and routers, even when tiny packet sizes are invoked. Of course, HIPPI's connection-oriented design really comes into its own when delivering huge data sets. HIPPI's architects have not yet come up with a way to support broadcast transmissions—an integral part of most mainstream network operating systems. One way around the problem would be to attach an address server to the switch. On receiving a multicast message, it would store it temporarily, then forward it to a list of destinations one by one. Other parties are positing support internal to the switch. Both solutions are under consideration.

HIPPI also is suited to hierarchical internetworking. In a three-tier arrangement, for example, Ethernet segments are connected via FDDI rings, which in turn are connected by one or more HIPPI switches (see Fig. 4.2). And HIPPI works equally well with fast Ethernet, full-duplex Ethernet, and straight Ethernet—anything, in fact, that speaks TCP/IP.

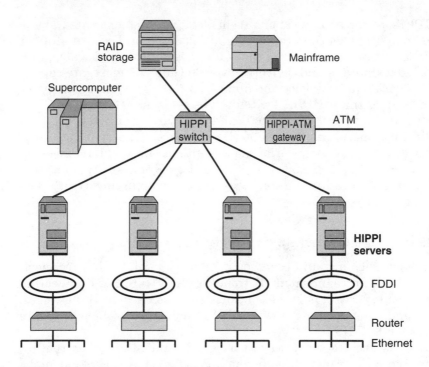

HIPPI = High performance parallel interface
RAID = Redundant array of inexpensive disks

Figure 4.2 The HIPPI hierarchy. HIPPI can be used to impose a hierarchical structure on a corporate internetwork, thus ensuring more efficient use of resources.

Section 7.   The HIPPI Channel

HIPPI has long been employed as a high-speed channel to peripherals like disk and tape controllers. HIPPI switches also can be used to link diverse storage devices, thus allowing for shared access across a network. Further, IPI-3 is employed for host-peripheral communications. This protocol is specifically designed to deliver high I/O with minimal CPU overhead.

But HIPPI can serve for more than data access. In another demonstration at Supercomputing '94, Triplex Systems Corp. (Columbia, MD) transmitted full-motion video through a HIPPI switch to a high-resolution monitor—with no loss of quality. Scenes from the Clint Eastwood thriller *In the Line of Fire* were shipped from a tape unit through a HIPPI switch to a frame buffer from Psitech Inc. (Fountain Valley, CA); they were displayed on the high-resolution monitor at a rate of five frames per second. Given that each frame contained more than 6 Mbytes of data, the sustained throughput was over 30 Mbyte/s. By comparison, ATM running at OC-3 (155 Mbit/s) can deliver a maximum of 55 percent of that throughput.

Section 8. Cluster Controller

So-called workstation clusters could well become the high-performance computing paradigm of the future, capturing a good portion of the supercomputing market thanks to their dramatically improved price/performance ratios. But realizing this promise means that networking technologies must deliver the exponential increase in bandwidth required in such environments. HIPPI makes it simple and relatively inexpensive to build gigabit-speed, switched networks running TCP/IP.

HIPPI has four major roles to play in such networked systems. First, it can link workstations and other hosts. Second, it can connect workstations with storage systems at higher speeds than any other currently available technology. Third, it can attach display peripherals for real-time visualization. Fourth, it can connect the entire system to another network.

There are several potential wide-scale applications for HIPPI in workstation clusters—especially animation, scientific visualization, and high-fidelity imaging. All of these require very high data transmission rates to display large-size, high-quality color video. HIPPI-Serial connections, in combination with desktop HIPPI, make it possible to transfer images to their point of use at the requisite speed. HIPPI also makes it easy to set up affordable parallel-processing workstation clusters that can be used to divide and conquer complex problems.

Section 9. Standards Progress

The HIPPI standard isn't standing still. Work is under way to improve the technology and integrate it with other networking schemes. For instance, a HIPPI MIB proposal is being prepared for SNMP. It features self-discovery of switch addresses and address resolution between MAC (media access control) addresses and HIPPI addresses. Developers also are working on performance and capacity planning applications and exploring ways to integrate HIPPI network management with Openview, Netview, and other platforms. HIPPI interoperability with ATM, Fibre Channel, and Sonet also is garnering some interest.

Section 10.   HIPPI and ATM, Fibre Channel, and Sonet

Like HIPPI, both ATM and Fibre Channel combine very high data rates with a switched architecture that delivers deterministic, scalable performance. Both share a critical advantage over HIPPI: the ability to multiplex traffic from different nodes onto a single connection. With HIPPI, in contrast, if node A is sending several megabytes of information to node B, node C must wait until the transfer is complete before it can transmit its message. There is no way for C to inject its data onto the connection, even if it is only waiting to send a control message a few bytes in length.

Even so, HIPPI does have at least one thing over both ATM and Fibre Channel: it has been around for much longer. HIPPI was first proposed to a working group of the ANSI X3T9.5 Task Group in January 1987, and the first HIPPI implementations were available in late 1988. HIPPI's creators have had enough time to develop fully fledged solutions to problems which have only recently been addressed by the committees working on ATM and Fibre Channel. An example is flow control, or congestion control. The HIPPI standard fully defines a credit-based scheme, whereby nodes at each end of a connection exchange "ready"" messages which notify each other that they have sufficient buffer capacity to handle incoming data. Flow control in ATM has only recently been resolved. This issue has not yet been formally addressed by the Fibre Channel committee within ANSI.

Because of ATM's strong momentum, and its technological advantages, some in the industry assume that it will displace HIPPI. But such a scenario isn't likely—if for no other reason than simple arithmetic. Any of today's ATM switches can deliver an aggregate bandwidth of 3.2 Gbit/s. That's fast, but it pales in comparison with the 12.8 to 25.6 Gbit/s offered by HIPPI switches. In addition, the ATM market is primarily focused on services at 155 Mbit/s and below, with some interest in 25 Mbit/s. There's a good reason for that: it's what the majority of users need. However, it cannot satisfy the small minority of power users who need gigabit throughput right now.

Finally, HIPPI—unlike ATM—allows storage devices to be directly connected to a network at high speeds. That's a critical concern, since end users on high-speed networks must be able to access computer and storage servers. Actually, it's not a question of HIPPI or ATM. A gateway from a HIPPI workstation cluster to ATM would give end users the best of both worlds—the unsurpassed throughput of HIPPI on the local area and the ATM's wide area connectivity. With such a gateway, even multimedia data could fan out from HIPPI-attached servers to multiple ATM desktops.

Creating such a gateway is hardly a trivial undertaking. HIPPI is a connection-oriented, circuit-switched transport. ATM is a connection-less, cell-switched scheme. HIPPI can handle raw HIPPI, as well as IP and IPI-3 datagrams. ATM slices and dices everything into 53-byte cells. For all the complexity, though, the ANSI Technical Committee and the HIPPI Networking Forum are hammering out HIPPI-ATM interfaces. HIPPI-ATM connections work by encapsulating HIPPI data, shipping it over the ATM network, and then reconstituting the HIPPI data and format at the other end. In other words, HIPPI is tunneled through the ATM network. This is done at AAL 5 (ATM adaptation layer 5). Netstar is beta-testing a version of its Gigarouter with a HIPPI-ATM interface based on this draft standard. GTE's HIPPI-ATM switch uses an interface based on an earlier version of some of this work.

Ironically enough, HIPPI and Fibre Channel are both the work of the same ANSI committee. Fibre Channel is more complex. It specifies four data rates, three kinds of media, four transmitter types, three distance categories, three classes of service, and three possible fabrics. Despite their differences, HIPPI and Fibre Channel can be complementary technologies. An ANSI standard has already been defined that specifies how to send upper-layer Fibre Channel protocol over the lower-layer HIPPI media. The complementary ANSI standard (defining how to ship HIPPI upper-layer protocol over Fibre Channel lower-layer media) is in process. IP-level routing offers another way to map HIPPI to Fibre Channel, and vice versa.

As discussed, HIPPI takes advantage of Sonet to extend over long distances. Of course, that means that until a national Sonet infrastructure is in place, most HIPPI applications will span metropolitan areas. When HIPPI and Sonet are used in conjunction, the HIPPI network is effectively terminated at a HIPPI-Sonet gateway, which frames HIPPI data for transport over Sonet. This can be done fairly easily, since HIPPI maps well both to a single Sonet OC-12c (622-Mbit/s) circuit or multiple Sonet OC-3 circuits. In the latter scenario, the gateway stripes data onto the 155-Mbit/s circuits. This scheme has been demonstrated successfully for a sustained throughput of 783 Mbit/s over 2000 kilometers. A HIPPI-Sonet gateway has even run successfully over a satellite link.

5

An IsoEnet Tutorial

Inside IsoEnet

Speed: 16.144 Mbit/s divided into one single-segment 10-Mbit/s channel for Ethernet packet data, and ninety-six 64-kbit/s ISDN B channels for time-sensitive voice and video traffic; also contains one 64-kbit/s D channel for signaling

Architecture: a hybrid of shared-media and circuit switching

Cabling: Category 3 UTP, Category 5 UTP, STP

Distance: 100 meters

Latency: variable for packets, fixed for circuits

Products: adapters, concentrators

Cost per network interface card: $500

Cost per hub port: $900

Cost per node: $1400

Vendors implementing: ten

Snapshot: IsoEnet's main usefulness is as a jump-off to wide-area networks; that isn't enough to garner it more than a wafer-thin slice of the LAN market

Section 1. Overview

Of all the LAN standards currently vying for network managers' attention, IsoEnet is one which has remained steadfastly out of the spotlight. IsoEnet (short for isochronous Ethernet) is the handiwork of the IEEE's 802.9a committee. Simply put, the IsoEnet standard defines a 16-Mbit/s network incorporating facilities for carrying multimedia traffic. It is intended as a successor to existing 10-Mbit/s Ethernet networks.

While it hasn't received much publicity to date, IsoEnet contains a feature which could guarantee it a loyal if limited following among net managers in the long term: it uses wide-area Integrated Services Digital Network (ISDN) services to carry multimedia data over the LAN.

IsoEnet's use of ISDN is significant for two reasons. First, ISDN is an inexpensive, proven way to carry multimedia. Second, it has the potential to allow users on an IsoEnet LAN to set up multimedia sessions with coworkers located not merely in the same building but also (via affordable switched carrier services) on the other side of the country—or even the world.

Section 2. How It Works

IEEE 802.9a IsoEnet is based on a modified version of the existing shared-media Ethernet specification defined in the IEEE 802.3 standard. It comprises a new physical layer standard, and adds data link layer and network layer signaling and call setup to the original Ethernet specification. The charter of IsoEnet is to provide real-time interactive communication—combining video, voice, and data—for peer devices. It supports a so-called superior class of service (COS) to achieve this—one which includes guaranteed bandwidth, latency, and latency variation.

The 16 Mbit/s of total network bandwidth on an IsoEnet LAN is divided into two logical parts. First, 6.144-Mbit/s of the network bandwidth is parceled off into ninety-six 64-kbit/s circuits. These are used for carrying time-sensitive multimedia traffic such as voice and video. The other 10 Mbit/s of bandwidth is used as a conventional contention-based shared-media Ethernet network by asynchronous data traffic. IsoEnet also features one 64-kbit/s channel which is used to carry call setup and signaling information for the ninety-six 64-kbit/s circuits (see Fig. 5.1).

Traffic is passed to and from the LAN using IsoEnet adapters installed in each user's workstation. These come equipped with two MACs. One multiplexes the time-sensitive traffic (like videoconferencing sessions) from the workstation onto the LAN in 64-kbit/s circuits.

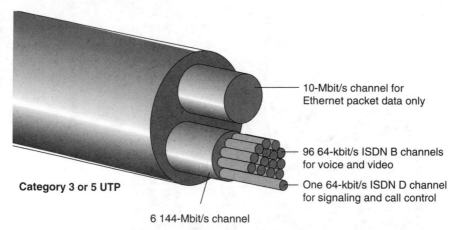

Category 3 or 5 UTP

10-Mbit/s channel for
Ethernet packet data only

96 64-kbit/s ISDN B channels
for voice and video

One 64-kbit/s ISDN D channel
for signaling and call control

6 144-Mbit/s channel

Figure 5.1 The IsoEnet channels. The 16.144 Mbit/s of available bandwidth on an IsoEnet network is divided into one single-segment 10-Mbit/s channel for Ethernet packet data, and 96 64-kbit/s ISDN B channels for time-sensitive voice and video traffic. There is also one 64-kbit/s D channel for signaling.

The other transmits asynchronous packets onto the shared-media portion of the LAN bandwidth (see Fig. 5.2).

Section 3.   The Upgrade Path

The good news for network managers thinking about upgrading their current 10-Mbit/s Ethernet LANs to IsoEnet is that the new standard will run quite happily over the same cabling they already have in place. Because IsoEnet summons up just 16-Mbit/s of bandwidth, it has no difficulty in running over Category 3, 4, or 5 unshielded twisted-pair (UTP) or shielded twisted-pair (STP) cabling.

On the other hand, the fact that IsoEnet runs over copper cabling means that it is suitable only for providing desktop connectivity. The 100-meter maximum drive distance supported by IsoEnet over copper cables precludes it from serving as a backbone technology—for example, as a link between hubs in a campus network. While IsoEnet is compatible with existing cabling, net managers will have to change out their existing IEEE 802.3-compliant Ethernet modular hubs and their old Ethernet adapter cards for new IsoEnet models. (If a network manager inadvertently plugs a IsoEnet adapter into an Ethernet hub, the card is supposed to automatically fall back to functioning as an IEEE 802.3-compliant adapter, without crashing the network.)

IsoEnet cards and hubs now go for more than six times as much as their Ethernet equivalents, but supporters of the new standard say that premium will drop fast. However, more significant than the cost of

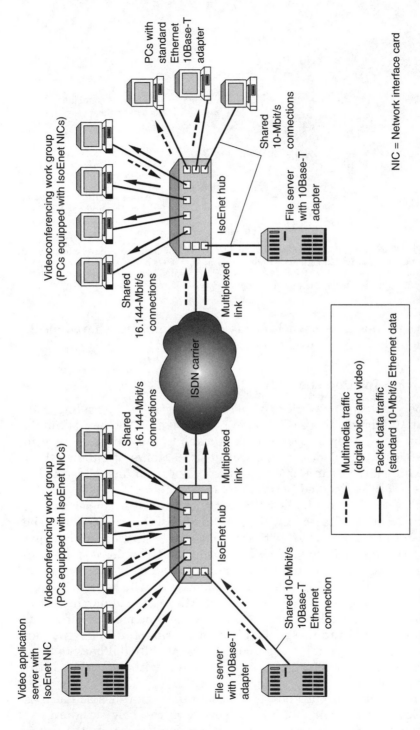

Figure 5.2 The IsoEnet network. Workstations and servers equipped with IsoEnet adapters can transmit multimedia and asynchronous data within the same building or over wide-area ISDN connections. An IsoEnet concentrator takes the place of the conventional Ethernet repeater in the wiring closet.

the hardware itself is the cost of the labor required to change out the equipment (currently about $45 per hour in the United States), and the cost of network downtime while the cards and hubs are replaced.

Section 4.   An Application Tradeoff

By carrying video and voice in 64-kbit/s circuits (or streams), IsoEnet LANs ensure that delays not only are kept low, they are also kept constant—at 10 milliseconds over the LAN. Low, predictable node-to-node latencies are a prerequisite of high-quality videoconferencing. As a rule of thumb, the higher and more varied the delay, the lower the quality of the interactive application. But while the hybrid architecture invoked by IsoEnet certainly improves on the ability of conventional Ethernet to carry multimedia, it does precisely zero to increase Ethernet's capacity for carrying asynchronous data. As with ordinary Ethernet, when network nodes are using applications like file transfer, they contend with each other for the same 10 Mbit/s of bandwidth.

In fact, the collision detection phase of the CSMA/CD (carrier-sense multiple access with collision detection) protocol, which IsoEnet uses to allocate network access to asynchronous data, actually reduces the bandwidth available even further—typically to around 6.5 Mbit/s. (What happens is that when several stations try to send data over the network simultaneously, collision detection interrupts and cancels the transmissions from all but one station, slowing network throughput down.) IsoEnet's limited capacity for asynchronous data will limit its appeal to those network managers who are not currently experiencing congestion on their Ethernet LANs, and do not expect to do so for the foreseeable future—and that's an increasingly tiny number of people.

It is in recognition of this fact that some vendors are lobbying to have IsoEnet capabilities added to the 100Base-T standard—which defines 100-Mbit/s data throughput. This hybird spec is not expected to see ratification until 1977.

Section 5.   PBX Proponents

The bandwidth shortfall is one reason the vast majority of vendors of modular LAN hubs and concentrators are refusing to commit to manufacturing IsoEnet products. In fact, it is vendors of PBXs (voice switches) that are turning out to be IsoEnet's biggest fans. They see their products as the logical point of convergence between IsoEnet LANs and ISDN WANs, and are counting on IsoEnet to provide them with a standards-based path to reinvent their switches as a vehicle for carrying both voice and data on the customer premises. PBX vendors are adamant that a significant number of companies will want to take advantage of the synergy between IsoEnet and ISDN.

Three factors make IsoEnet a good fit with ISDN. First, the call setup procedures which are used to initiate a multimedia session over an IsoEnet LAN are compatible with those used on ISDN networks. Second, the 64-kbit/s circuits used on IsoEnet are the same size as the basic unit of bandwidth on ISDN networks. Third (and most importantly), IsoEnet uses the same 8-kHz universal telephony clock as found in wide-area network services. In fact, IsoEnet's designers have actually gone beyond current ISDN signaling specifications by adding a so-called C channel signaling band to IsoEnet. The C channel allows multiple 64-kbit/s ISDN B channels to be combined end to end for carrying high-speed video services. Manufacturers of equipment for ISDN networks currently support the same amalgamation facilities using proprietary techniques.

One of the first companies to ship an IsoEnet-compliant product is Incite Inc. (Dallas). Incite's Multimedia Hub uses IsoEnet to transport isochronous and asynchronous traffic to every desktop. Incite also offers a WAN hub that connects the LAN to switched WAN services via a PBX or public network. Incite's product line also features a server control software package, called the Multimedia Manager, which is used to set up and route voice and video calls between users and the switched network.

Section 6.   ATM Antagonism

The aim of IsoEnet's PBX supporters is to deliver low-cost products which allow net managers to build multimedia networks that extend through both the local and wide-area network domains. Clearly, those products will come in for competition from ATM technology—which also is being touted as a network that can span the enterprise. In the short term, IsoEnet actually has one significant advantage over ATM: it utilizes low-speed, economic ISDN links. For voice and low-quality videoconferencing, ISDN is now a much better price fit than ATM. Much faster wide-area ATM connections are likely to remain way beyond most managers' budgets for the foreseeable future. For instance, to connect offices in Chicago, New York, and San Francisco over 128-kbit/s ISDN lines costs a few hundred dollars per month. To link the same sites using 45-Mbit/s ATM services from AT&T costs $94,500 per month.

6

A 100Base-T Tutorial

100Base-T at a Glance

Speed: 100 Mbit/s

Architecture: shared media with CSMA/CD
Ethernet collision detection access
mechanism

Cabling: Category 3 UTP, Category 5 UTP,
STP, fiber

Distance: 100 meters over copper, 2
kilometers over fiber

Latency: variable

Products: network interface cards,
concentrators, routers

Cost per shared-media node: $450

Number of vendors: 20

Snapshot: affordable and easy to work
with, but appeal is limited by its has-been
shared-media design

Section 1.   Overview

It's no secret that after 10 years of service on corporate networks,
Ethernet is starting to show its age. Bigger networks, larger files, and

more powerful applications all are conspiring to choke up installed Ethernet LANs (and frustrate their 40 million or so users).

The IEEE 802.3 committee's solution to the problem is a new edition of the 10-year-old 10-Mbit/s standard, which runs ten times as fast, called 100Base-T (a.k.a. fast Ethernet). Finalized in the fourth quarter of 1994, 100Base-T defines a 100-Mbit/s shared-media LAN, and retains much of the original Ethernet standard (see Table 6.1). Proponents of 100Base-T claim that it is the natural choice for net managers with installed Ethernets looking for an easy upgrade to higher-speed performance.

100Base-T provides a smooth migration path because it uses the same packet format as the original standard. This confers two benefits. First, users can run their existing applications over 100Base-T unaltered. Second, hybrid networks consisting of both 10-Mbit/s Ethernet and 100-Mbit/s fast Ethernet connections can be interconnected by low-cost bridging hardware—instead of expensive routers.

Other plus points: The new standard is designed to run over the cabling that managers already have installed, and 100Base-T adapters and hubs are available for only two or three times the cost of their 10-Mbit/s antecedents. On the down side, the fact that 100Base-T is based on the same principles as Ethernet means—inevitably— that it is subject to the same failings. Network managers trying to make up their minds about whether to buy into a shared-media 100Base-T LAN should imagine a tenfold increase in the performance of their existing LAN. If that doesn't seem fast enough, neither will 100Base-T.

Broadly speaking, 100Base-T's shared-media architecture has several effects: the amount of bandwidth available to each user decreases in proportion to the total number of network nodes, network delay is variable (making 100Base-T inherently unsuitable for carrying time-

TABLE 6.1   Ethernet vs. 100Base-T (Fast Ethernet)

	Ethernet	Fast Ethernet
Speed Cost	10 Mbps	100 Mbps
IEEE Standard	802.3	802.3
Media Access Protocol	CSMA/CD	CSMA/CD
Topology	Bus or Star	Star
Cable support	Coax, UTP, Fiber	UTP, Fiber
UTP cable support	Category 3, 4, or 5	Category 3, 4, or 5
UTP link distance (max)	100 meters	100 meters
Network diameter (UTP max)	500 meters	210 meters
Broad multivendor support	Yes	Yes
Availability	Now	Now

sensitive applications like videoconferencing), and effective through-put can be severely impaired by the standard's CSMA/CD network access control method. Another drawback is that the diameter of an unbridged 100Base-T network is limited to 210 meters. That's less than half the maximum diameter of old Ethernet LANs, and amounts to a rather small network.

Vendors are taking two approaches to solving the distance problem. Some are building a low-cost repeater port into their products to regenerate the signal. Other vendors, like Bay Networks Inc. (Santa Clara, CA), are now touting 100Base-T LAN switches which have the same effect. By switching traffic between nodes using dedicated 100-Mbit/s connections, 100Base-T switches also increase the amount of bandwidth available to each user, and minimize network delay and overhead by eliminating contention.

There are two moves afoot to improve 100Base-T's capabilities. First, the IEEE is now considering developing an even faster version of the standard, which would run at one gigabit. The new spec is not expected to be ratified until 1977. Second, some vendors are pushing the idea of merging 100Base-T with parts of the IsoEnet standard—thus improving its multi-media capabilities. This idea is still on the whiteboard.

Section 2.   How It Works

100Base-T adapters, hubs/repeaters, and switches all use the same CSMA/CD (carrier-sense multiple access with collision detection) MAC protocol that is at the core of 10-Mbit/s Ethernet. The 100Base-T specification simply reduces the bit time (the time taken to transmit each data bit) by a factor of 10—enabling a tenfold increase in band-width. 100Base-T repeaters serve exactly the same function as they do on 10-Mbit/s Ethernet: broadcasting incoming packets out over all outgoing ports; making the networks star topology act as a logical bus; and resolving collision conflicts.

100Base-T's supercharged MAC leaves the rest of the 10-Mbit/s MAC unchanged. Packet format, packet length, error detection, and management information are identical to those in the earlier standard.

Section 3.   The Upgrade Path

To upgrade an existing Ethernet LAN to 100Base-T, net managers must swap out their old workstation adapter cards and repeater hubs (see Fig. 6.1). That's a major inconvenience, involving substantial downtime and labor costs (it's accepted wisdom that the capital cost of the new equipment is nothing compared with the cost of installing the

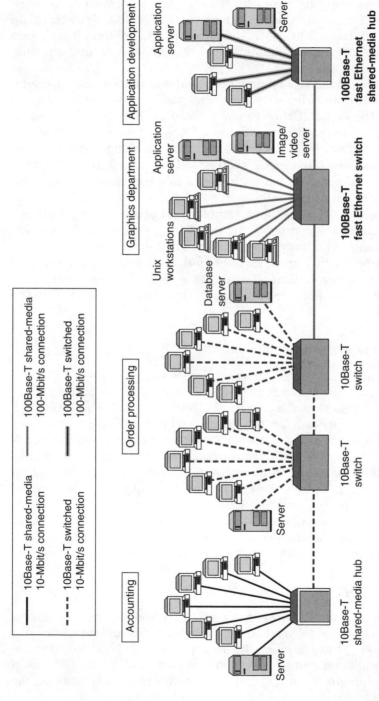

Figure 6.1 Mixed networks. 100Base-T (fast Ethernet) technology can be installed alongside existing 10Base-T (Ethernet) equipment to provide additional bandwidth where needed. In this example, a company has enhanced the performance of its application development team using shared-media 100Base-T, and given its power-hungry graphics team an even bigger boost by hooking them up to a 100Base-T switch.

new gear and downloading new drivers). To soften the blow, the 100Base-T standard comes with an optional feature, called Nway, which allows managers to move their Ethernet networks to 100Base-T gradually. Here's how it works. 100Base-T adapters, hubs, and switches that support Nway are able to sense whether they are communicating with equipment that can transmit at 10 Mbit/s or 100 Mbit/s. At power-up, Nway devices exchange status packets—called *fast link pulses*—that indicate basic status information, including what cabling media they are attached to and what transmission speeds are supported.

Nway devices automatically adjust themselves to the lowest speed supported by the other devices on their segment. Thus, if a 100Base-T Nway adapter is installed on the same segment as 10-Mbit/s adapters, it will default to operating in accordance with the 10-Mbit/s standard until all the other devices with which it communicates are 100-Mbit/s-capable (see Fig. 6.2). This is important because it means that instead of making wholesale changes to their networks, net managers can

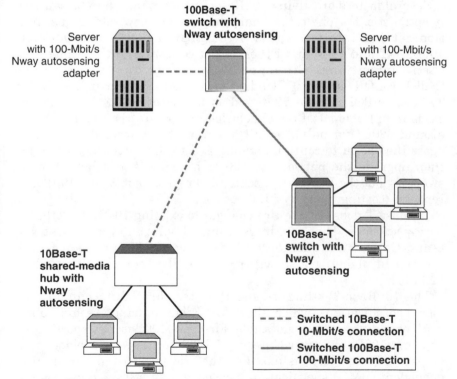

Figure 6.2 Nway detection. Nway autosensing logic enables fast Ethernet adapters, hubs, and switches to tell whether attached equipment can transmit at 10 or 100 Mbit/s. What's more, Nway-capable devices automatically adjust to the speed supported by other gear on the same segment.

swap out old Ethernet adapters for new 100Base-T adapters individually, as they find the time. When the changeover is complete, the segment will automatically start running at 100 Mbit/s.

Net managers shopping for 100Base-T hardware should check that it supports Nway before reaching for their checkbooks. The spec is optional. While most vendors are moving to support Nway, some do not. Even with Nway autosensing, the aggravation and expense of swapping out old equipment means that few, if any, network managers will choose to upgrade their existing Ethernets via 100Base-T. A far easier and cost-effective approach for these networks is to buy and install a low-cost Ethernet LAN switch. In fact, many of 100Base-T's proponents admit that the standard has little chance of taking off in existing Ethernet LANs. They believe that 100Base-T will become the network of choice as new nodes are installed. That's a huge market; some analysts estimate that the world's PC population is increasing by as much as 30 million devices a year. Of that number, about 30 percent (or 10 million) of those PCs are being hooked up to local area networks.

Several factors are giving 100Base-T vendors reason to be cautiously optimistic. For one thing, many vendors are now selling dual-function network interface cards (NICs) that support both 100-Mbit/s 100Base-T and 10-Mbit/s Ethernet but cost only 1.5 to 2 times more than conventional Ethernet NICs. For instance, Intel Corp. (Hillsboro, OR) sells a PCI adapter for $249. Networth Inc. (Irving, TX) sells a PCI card for $220 and an ISA card for $130. The low-end cards from Cogent Data Technologies Inc. (Friday Harbour, WA) cost around $200. For only a small premium, these products give managers the option to continue adding PCs to their Ethernet LAN, and then upgrade the network to 100-Mbit/s speeds at a later time by swapping out the Ethernet repeater and replacing it with a 100Base-T repeater (costing typically $190 per port).

100Base-T does not require changes to existing 10-Mbit/s Ethernet wiring schemes. The 100-Mbit/s standard will run over the Category 3 and Category 5 unshielded twisted-pair (UTP) copper cabling already in place. It also will run over fiber-optic cabling, where installed.

The 100Base-T standard incorporates three different physical media specifications, which allow Fast Ethernet adapters and hubs to work over different types of cable. First, the 100Base-TX specification supports 100Base-T over Category 5 UTP and Type 1 shielded twisted-pair (STP) cable. It is based on the proven MLT-3 physical media dependent (PMD) specification developed by ANSI's X3T9.5 committee for use in the FDDI-over-copper products. 100Base-TX transmits data using two copper pairs. Practically all the LANs in the United

States are cabled using cabling containing four pairs, but this doesn't mean that net managers can use the two remaining pairs for other traffic, such as voice. In order to meet FCC emissions regulations, the other two pairs must be left idle.

Second, the 100Base-T4 specification allows users to run 100Base-T over Category 3 UTP, using four copper pairs. Data is transmitted using 8B/6T encoding, which allows a lower signal frequency and decreases electromagnetic emissions. Companies implementing 100Base-T4 claim that its encoding scheme provides a much more reliable path for data than 100Base-TX, and can easily support drive distances up to 150 meters over Category 4 and Category 5 UTP (though the standard specifies distances only up to 100 meters). To prove this point, Broadcom Corp. (Los Angeles), a silicon developer, has demonstrated 100Base-T running over barbed wire at trade shows. Third, 100Base-FX defines transmission over fiber-optic cable.

Section 4. Poor Coverage

Net managers expecting the forthcoming 100Base-T fast Ethernet standard to provide the same coverage as its 10-Mbit/s 10Base-T cousin will be sadly disappointed. The maximum diameter of a 100Base-T network running over Category 5 unshielded twisted-pair (UTP) cable is 210 meters. That compares with the 500-meter maximum size permitted with 10-Mbit/s Ethernets. The diameter dilemma comes courtesy of a simple fact: network diameter is inversely proportional to bit rate. This distance constraint will have two effects. First, it will prevent users from cascading repeaters (a common topology in 10-Mbit/s LANs). Second, in order to extend the coverage of their 100Base-T networks, users will have to install LAN switches (or bridges and routers) between repeaters—at a cost premium that may well discourage many users from implementing fast Ethernet. To get around this problem, vendors such as Networth build a low-cost repeater into their 100Base-T hubs. This allows the signal to be regenerated, and increases interrepeater distance to 100 meters.

Network diameter is not so much of a problem with 100Base-T's main competitor, the 100-Mbit/s 100VG-AnyLAN standard, which supports a network diameter of 600 meters over Category 3 UTP, and 1200 meters over Category 5 UTP.

Section 5. Multimedia Shortfalls

At first sight, 100Base-T's 100-Mbit/s bandwidth appears to be more than enough to handle time-sensitive multimedia applications. A VCR-quality video stream compressed using the MPEG standard takes up about 1.5 Mbit/s of bandwidth. Videoconferencing can be done with as little as 56 kbit/s of bandwidth. But bear in mind that 100Base-T is based on a shared-media architecture, which means that the available bandwidth is divided among all the nodes on the network.

Further, the CSMA/CD network access mechanism used by 100Base-T was originally designed exclusively for carrying character-based text files. It contains no provisions for prioritizing multimedia packets; thus, there is nothing in the specification to prevent a multimedia transmission from hogging the network and leaving other user applications hanging in the breeze. What makes life worse for users running multimedia applications is that delays on a 100Base-T network are not simply long, they are variable as well. The way 100Base-T is designed, only one node can transmit data over the network at any time—the rest of the devices have to wait their turn. Waiting time fluctuates depending on the number of devices trying to access the network at the same time. This fluctuation causes video images to appear jerky and distorts the quality of audio signals.

One solution is to equip desktop multimedia gear with memory buffers that collect video and voice frames as they arrive and deliver them in a smooth stream. But even then, some loss of quality will be apparent to users. And this approach increases the cost of running multimedia applications. Supporters of 100Base-T says that the secret to keeping latency down to a tolerable level is careful network design, which limits the number of devices on the network. A well-built network should exhibit variable latency of no more than 30 milliseconds, they say.

But working out exactly how many devices to put on the network is much easier said than done. There are no hard-and-fast rules for network design; that is a job which must be undertaken on a site-by-site basis. A number of factors have to be taken into account—in particular, what sorts of applications are being run, on what types of workstations, and (most importantly) how often. Similarly, critics point out that regardless of how carefully a 100Base-T network is put together, there is simply no way to anticipate when multiple users will attempt to access the network simultaneously, and thus ultimately there is no way to guarantee multimedia quality.

Section 6.   Deceptive Appearances

When is 100 Mbit/s not 100 Mbit/s? A closer look at the 100Base-T specification reveals that it is not only managers who put multimedia over this network who may get less than they bargained for. 100Base-T may define a 100 Mbit/s network, but the fact is that the new standard suffers from a form of network overhead that will typically keep it from ever attaining that level of throughput—when carrying even asynchronous data.

The problem can again be traced to the carrier sense multiple access with collision detection (CSMA/CD), which is used to resolve contention problems. When more than one station tries to send data over the network simultaneously, the collision detection scheme tells each node to stop transmitting. It then runs an algorithm that allows one station to access the network ahead of the others. Tests by LANquest Labs (San Jose, CA) show that collision detection reduces available bandwidth on a 10-Mbit/s Ethernet (with 4 servers and 12 PCs) to 6.8 Mbit/s (by 32 percent). On really busy networks, it is not unusual for collision detection to reduce available bandwidth even further—to as little as 3 Mbit/s (a 70 percent reduction).

Again, because the amount of overhead increases in proportion to the number of nodes attempting to access the network, the simplest solution to the problem is to limit the number of devices on any given Ethernet segment. In contrast, high-speed LANs that employ a token-passing scheme to assign access are far more efficient. In tests conducted by The Tolly Group (Manasquan, NJ), a private testing facility, FDDI delivered 96 Mbit/s, or 96 percent of available bandwidth.

Net managers with 10-Mbit/s networks have learned the hard way that careful network design can do only so much to prevent slow-motion performance in their networks (it is not unusual for users on some of today's Ethernets to be kept waiting for minutes before they can send data). 100Base-T's speed increase should reduce those problems by a factor of 10, but that may not be enough to convince users that a shared-media design that originated more than a decade ago is a suitable platform on which to build next-generation networks.

Section 7.   The Switching Panacea

An increasing number of equipment vendors see switching as the only solution to 100Base-T's shortcomings. 100Base-T switches are installed in the wiring closet, with networking gear connected in a star topology. Essentially they act like very fast multiport bridges, allowing 100Base-T LANs to be segmented in order to increase performance.

Each port on a 100Base-T switch can be used in two ways. First, the port can support multiple 100Base-T workstations (connected via a shared-media 100Base-T hub). Second—for maximum performance—each port can be allocated to a single network device, establishing a dedicated segment to the individual node. On switched LANs in which each node gets its own pipe, line speed ceases to decrease in proportion to the number of nodes. Instead, each link runs at full line speed, as does every link that is added. What's more, putting each node on its own switch port provides a better vehicle for time-sensitive multimedia traffic, since it eliminates contention entirely and establishes multiple paths between workstations. Better, but not perfect. The vast majority of switches available today contain no facilities to ensure that bandwidth is allocated equally among switch ports.

Similarly, when networks change from a shared to a switched environment, network managers lose the ability to connect a LAN analyzer to a backbone and thus trace all network traffic. Most switches fall short when it comes to providing analysis facilities, forcing network managers either to manually shift a single analyzer [or remote monitoring (RMON) agent] between ports or to fork out exorbitant sums to equip each port with its own test agent. A better alternative are the switches from vendors like Fore Systems Inc. (Warrendale, PA) and Madye Networks Inc. (San Jose, CA), which feature components that can copy packets from any port and forward them to an analyzer.

To further boost bandwidth, the 100Base-T standard incorporates a technology called full-duplex fast Ethernet. This specification allows data to be passed in two directions simultaneously on switch-to-PC connections, effectively doubling network throughput to 200 Mbit/s on each link. On conventional 100Base-T LANs, data cannot be transmitted in both directions at the same time because the collision detection part of the CSMA/CD protocol forces one end of the connection to stop transmitting. (Full-duplex fast Ethernet requires a full-duplex-capable adapter to be installed in the workstation, and doesn't work if more than one workstation is attached to a switch port.)

7

A 100VG-AnyLAN
Tutorial

100VG-AnyLAN at a Glance

Speed: 100 Mbit/s

Cabling requirements: four-pair voice-grade Category 3, 4, and 5 unshielded twisted pair (UTP), with two-pair Category 5 UTP planned; two-pair shielded twisted pair (STP); single-mode and multimode fiber-optic cable

Distance limitations: 100 meters over four-pair Category 3, 4, 5 UTP; 150 meters over two-pair Category 5 STP; 2000 meters over single-mode or multimode fiber-optic cable

Legacy packet formats supported: Ethernet and token ring

Costs: adapter cards, $225 to $350; shared-media hubs, $300 per port

Snapshot: technologically superior to 100Base-T, though with less industry support; 100VG AnyLAN is destined to play a modest role in future high-speed networks

---

This chapter contains some information from an article originally published in *Data Communications* magazine and written by Peter Rauch and Scott Lawrence, both of Thomas-Conrad Corp. (Austin, TX).

Section 1. Overview

The 100VG-AnyLAN standard didn't get off to the most auspicious start. Faced with intense competition from all the other high-speed LAN technologies vying for a slice of the next-generation LAN market, 100VG-AnyLAN initially lacked sufficient vendor backing and risked slipping into oblivion. Lack of publicity, combined with lack of products—including switches, network analyzers, and hubs or adapters that fully implement the technology's ability to support both Ethernet and token ring—slowed AnyLAN's initial rollout.

But marketing and product development problems like these belied the value of 100VG's underlying technology. To paraphrase Mark Twain's famous quip, reports of 100VG-AnyLAN's demise were greatly exaggerated. In addition to 100-Mbit/s throughput, 100VG-AnyLAN offers off-the-bat support for both Ethernet and token ring applications, simple network design and configuration, and an aptitude for multimedia. Pricing for 100VG-AnyLAN is another strong advantage. 100VG-AnyLAN adapters run about $225 to $350, and hub prices average $3700 for a 12-port hub (approximately $300 per port). After a rocky start, vendors gradually picked up on 100VG-AnyLAN's potential, and the technology has since made headway in the LAN marketplace.

Moves are now afoot to enhance 100VG-AnyLAN to run at faster speeds—possibly up to one gigabit. However, products implementing such high data rates are not expected until 1997 at the earliest.

Section 2. 100VG-AnyLAN History

Developed by the IEEE 802.12 committee, the 100VG-AnyLAN standard, like its closest 100-Mbit/s rival, the IEEE 802.3 100Base-T (fast Ethernet) standard, is designed as a shared-media network. Also like 100Base-T, 100VG-AnyLAN supports existing network topologies without significant reconfiguration. Unlike 100Base-T, however, the enhanced throughput that 100VG-AnyLAN affords does not necessitate more restrictive distance limits than does conventional Ethernet 10Base-T.

In addition, 100VG-AnyLAN promises to deliver three primary advantages over 100Base-T (see Fig. 7.1):

- As the "AnyLAN" tag indicates, 100VG-AnyLAN is designed to support both Ethernet and token ring legacy applications, albeit not on the same network. (A 100VG-AnyLAN bridge or router is required to move traffic between 100VG-AnyLAN Ethernet and 100VG-AnyLAN token ring networks.)

- 100VG-AnyLAN's demand priority access scheme, which replaces the CSMA/CD (carrier sense multiple access with collision detec-

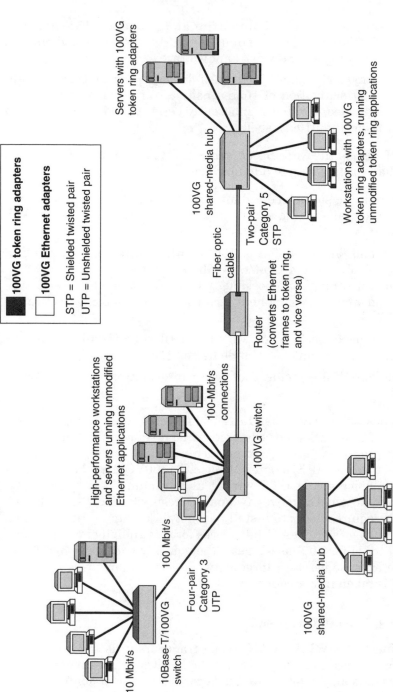

Figure 7.1 A heterogeneous 100VG-AnyLAN network. 100VG supports current Ethernet and token ring applications, as well as a range of cabling options, but requires new adapter cards, hubs, and switches. A router is used to communicate between Ethernet and token ring segments.

tion) scheme used in conventional 10Base-T Ethernet and 100Base-T (fast Ethernet), eliminates packet collisions and enables more efficient use of network bandwidth.

- 100VG-AnyLAN, again by virtue of demand priority, permits rudimentary prioritization of time-sensitive traffic, such as real-time voice and video, making it inherently better suited for multimedia applications than 100Base-T.

The IEEE is still working on some new features for 100VG. Task groups have been set up to add four new specifications:

1. The ability to set up redundant links between hubs, so that if one connection fails traffic can be automatically routed to the backup connection.

2. A new and faster version of 100VG, which will run at a speed of from 400 Mbit/s to 4 Gbit/s. (4 Gbit/s is the predicted theoretical maximum throughput possible with 100VG technology, and supposes advances in component technology which have not yet taken place.)

3. A full-duplex specification which will allow traffic to flow in two directions on a point-to-point dedicated 100VG link.

4. A line encoding scheme that will run over two-pair Category 5 UTP.

Like most of its rival fast LAN technologies, 100VG-AnyLAN has its share of drawbacks. For example, while it supports a wide range of cabling options, its wiring requirements are not quite as flexible as those of traditional Ethernet 10Base-T. (100VG-AnyLAN requires four-pair voice-grade UTP wiring at minimum—hence the "VG" label—and does not run over two-pair Category 3 UTP.) Also, 100VG-AnyLAN requires users to install new network adapter cards, as well as new hubs or switches. While prices for this equipment are comparable to those for 100Base-T gear, they quickly add up to significant upgrade expense across a large network—particularly when the cost of labor is taken into account.

Section 3.   The Physical Fit

Migrating to 100VG-AnyLAN, while transparent as far as network software is concerned, requires a basic hardware investment in new adapter cards and hubs, as well as a certain degree of administrative effort. Also, unless network designers have had the forethought to pull more expensive voice-grade cable, some new wiring may be required as well.

Fortunately, replacing Ethernet 10Base-T or token ring adapters with 100VG-AnyLAN adapters is relatively easy. Some 100VG-AnyLAN vendors even offer side-by-side 10/100 implementations that enable one card to serve either as a 10Base-T or a 100VG-AnyLAN adapter. To change from one technology to the other, the user simply moves the network cable to the desired connector and reboots the PC. This flexibility permits PCs to remain on 10Base-T Ethernet segments until the entire work group is ready to upgrade to 100 Mbit/s via 100VG-AnyLAN. Replacing old hubs, bridges, and routers with 100VG-AnyLAN-capable gear is equally straightforward.

Section 4. Cabling Considerations

One of 100VG-AnyLAN's shortcomings right now is that it does not support as wide a variety of cable types as do existing 10Base-T or token ring networks. (These same limitations, incidentally, apply to 100Base-T fast Ethernet as well.) At present, 100VG-AnyLAN requires four-pair, voice-grade Category 3, 4, or 5 unshielded twisted-pair (UTP) wiring, whereas 10Base-T can get by with two-pair Category 3, 4, or 5 UTP. Like 100Base-T, 100VG-AnyLAN can operate over two-pair Category 5 shielded twisted-pair (STP) cable. Other (future) implementations of the 100VG-AnyLAN spec will provide support for two-pair Category 3, 4, and 5 UTP, as well as single-mode and multimode fiber-optic cable. But the IEEE 802.12 committee is still working on these options.

In 100VG-AnyLAN's defense, the 100Base-T camp is still developing support for these cable types as well. Unlike 100Base-T, however, 100VG-AnyLAN provides for full interoperability among its implementations for different cabling media. At present, because different encoding schemes are used, the 100Base-TX fast Ethernet specification, which operates over two-pair Category 5 UTP, cannot be implemented on the same shared-media hub as the 100Base-T4 Fast Ethernet specification, which operates over four-pair Category 3, 4, or 5 UTP wiring. By contrast, all current and future 100VG-AnyLAN implementations for various cable types use the same encoding scheme and can be implemented in a single shared-media hub.

Section 5. Distances Covered

Node-to-node cabling distance limits for 100VG-AnyLAN are 100 meters for four-pair Category 3, 4, or 5 UTP wiring, 150 meters for two-pair Category 5 STP wiring, and 2000 meters for multimode fiber. This means that multimode fiber can support a network diameter of up to 4000 meters—2000 meters in any direction radiating in a star topology from a central hub.

As with Ethernet 10Base-T, 100VG-AnyLAN permits network designers to place up to four hubs between any two nodes on the network, with up to 100 meters of Category 3 UTP cabling between nodes. This is a distinct advantage over 100Base-T fast Ethernet, which allows only two hubs between any two nodes with 10 meters of Category 3 UTP cable between the two.

In an ideal scenario, little in the user's cable plant or wiring closet would need to change to support 100VG-AnyLAN. Unfortunately, the real world is not always going to conform to this ideal—particularly in the United States, where there is a considerable amount of two-pair Category 3 wiring. Also, many network designers have terminated their networks using two-pair cabling. Although they wouldn't have to repull cable to install 100VG-AnyLAN, these net managers would have to reterminate their networks.

All 100VG-AnyLAN networks make use of a scalable star topology (see Fig. 7.2). The network design rules followed by 100VG-AnyLAN allow it to support all topologies used by either Ethernet 10Base-T or IEEE 802.5 token ring LANs. This means that any existing 10Base-T or token ring network could be upgraded to 100VG-AnyLAN without changing the network's topology or design. 100VG-AnyLAN hubs, like 10Base-T hubs, can be deployed in a cascading hierarchical fashion as in an Ethernet network (see Fig. 7.3). So long as all hubs on the network use the same frame format (Ethernet or token ring), a single 100VG-AnyLAN network can contain several tiers without requiring a bridge.

Each hub in a 100VG-AnyLAN network may be configured to support either IEEE 802.3 10Base-T Ethernet frames or IEEE 802.5 token ring frames. A single hub cannot support both frame formats at the same time, and all hubs on the network must be configured to use the same frame format. However, because 100VG-AnyLAN supports both Ethernet and token ring frames, a 100VG-AnyLAN bridge can move traffic between a 100VG-AnyLAN network using Ethernet frames and a 100VG-AnyLAN network using token ring frames. To move between either type of 100VG-AnyLAN network and an ATM, FDDI, or other network, a router or translating bridge is required.

Section 6.   MAC Layer Modifications

The hottest point of contention for opponents of 100VG-AnyLAN is, without question, its unique media access control (MAC) layer, the

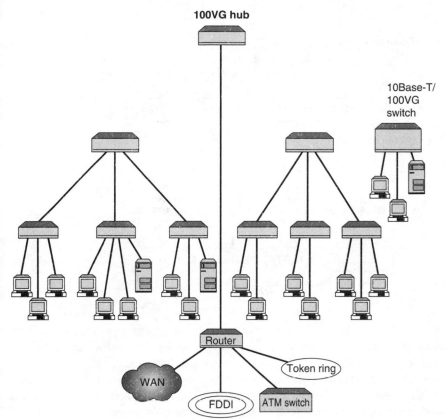

Figure 7.2 Scalable Star topology. Because it can be configured as a scalable star, 100VG supports all the topologies used by 10Base-T Ethernet or 802.5 token ring LANs. 100VG hubs can be cascaded hierarchically; a 100VG network can contain several tiers without requiring a bridge.

demand priority access scheme. Defined in the IEEE 802.12 standard, demand priority replaces the CSMA/CD algorithm used in the 10Base-T and 100Base-T Ethernet standards. Instead of the collision detection scheme of traditional Ethernet—and the circulating token in token ring environments—demand priority uses a round-robin polling scheme, implemented via a hub or switch (see Fig. 7.4).

Unlike traditional Ethernet, 100VG-AnyLAN is a "collisionless" technology. Using the demand priority scheme, the 100VG-AnyLAN hub or switch permits only one node to access the network segment at a time, so there is no possibility of packet collisions. The hub or switch acts as a network traffic cop. When a node needs to send something over the network, it places a request with the hub or switch. The hub

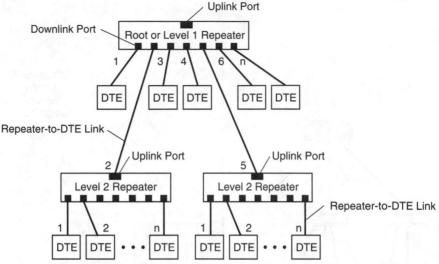

Figure 7.3   A Cascaded Hierarchical network.

or switch then services each node on the segment in sequence. If the node has something to send, the hub or switch permits access to the segment. If it does not, the hub moves on to the next node.

Each round-robin polling sequence provides every single-port node on the network with the opportunity to send one packet. Because all nodes requesting access are served during each polling round, all nodes are assured fair access to the network. If a multiport hub or switch serves as a node in a larger 100VG-AnyLAN network, it too must request network access from the next level up the network's cascading hierarchy. This device is known as the *root hub* for the attached nodes, hubs, or switches it supports. When granted access to the larger network by the root hub, the multiport node is permitted to transmit one packet from each port it supports.

Demand priority follows the same procedure in 100VG-AnyLAN networks using token ring frames. In the token ring scenario, the 100VG-AnyLAN hub or switch essentially performs the role of the circulating token. Instead of waiting to catch the token before transmitting, a token ring node waits to receive permission from the hub or switch. As in a traditional token ring environment, only one node has permission to transmit across a network segment at one time. Multiport 100VG-AnyLAN nodes adhere to the same procedures when using token ring packets as they do in the Ethernet environment. When granted access to the root hub in a 100VG-AnyLAN

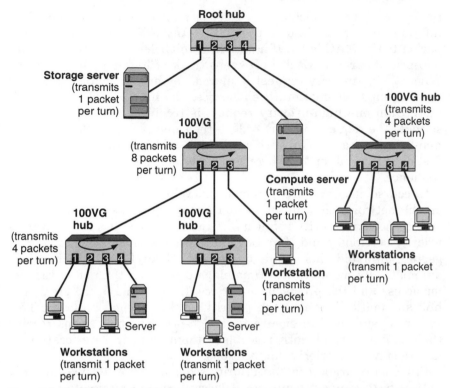

Figure 7.4 100VG's round-robin access. Round-robin polling makes it possible for every single-port node on a 100VG network to send one packet. If a multiport hub or switch serves as a node on the network, it must request access from the "root hub" at the next higher level. Multiport nodes can transmit one packet for each of their ports.

token ring environment, the multiport 100VG-AnyLAN hub or switch may transmit one packet per port.

In addition to its democratic polling of network nodes, the demand priority scheme permits rudimentary prioritization of LAN traffic. Time-critical network applications, such as voice and video, can be designated as high priority. When the 100VG-AnyLAN hub or switch polls the network segment, it will pick up high-priority traffic first, then go back to less time-sensitive normal traffic. In effect, 100VG-AnyLAN allows applications to separate traffic into two classes—high priority and normal—according to their throughput requirements.

As applications require, the transmitting 100VG-AnyLAN node labels each packet it wishes to send as either normal or high priority. The actual prioritization of data is performed by upper-layer applications at each node, such as the video or multimedia application. This information is passed down the 100VG-AnyLAN stack as part of the packet to the MAC layer. If a packet is unlabeled, it is treated as normal-priority traffic. Each hub keeps track of high-priority requests. When a high-priority request is placed, the hub or switch completes the current transmission, then services the high-priority request. If more than one high-priority request is received, the hub or switch services the requests in port order—the same order it follows for normal-priority traffic. Only when all high-priority requests are satisfied does the hub or switch return to its normal round-robin polling sequence.

Of course, if there were a tremendous volume of high-priority traffic on the network, the hub or switch might take considerable time to service normal-priority requests. If the wait were too long, normal-priority sessions could time out and the network could become congested. To avoid this problem, the 100VG-AnyLAN hub or switch automatically monitors the time elapsed between the node's request for access and the provision of service. If that time is too great, the hub automatically raises the priority level of normal requests. This system is supposed to ensure that high-priority applications receive the maximum bandwidth possible without causing deterioration or failure of normal-priority applications.

Proponents argue that its priority scheme equips 100VG-AnyLAN networks to support time-sensitive multimedia applications quite capably, enabling the network to distinguish between high-priority and normal-priority traffic to ensure that bursty data applications in high-volume networks won't overwhelm time-sensitive multimedia traffic. The reality is that 100VG-AnyLAN as defined by the IEEE 802.12 committee is still—at heart—a shared-media LAN. By definition, this means that it is incapable of providing the same fixed, low latency as switched technologies—two qualities that are prerequisite for high-quality multimedia support.

Section 7.   When Worlds Collide

Ironically, the demand priority scheme, which was originally designed to enhance Ethernet for use with voice and video applications, is under attack from many in the Ethernet community. CSMA/CD purists in the 100Base-T fast Ethernet camp argue that if the technology doesn't use CSMA/CD it's not truly Ethernet. Introducing a new MAC layer technology, critics claim, runs counter to the goal of making incremental improvements to Ethernet and opens the door to consideration of non-Ethernet technologies.

Still other critics in both the Ethernet and token ring user communities suggest that the introduction of demand priority requires network managers to abandon the MAC layer technologies that they understand well and undergo significant additional training to learn a new scheme. This requirement, they claim, raises the cost of implementing 100VG-AnyLAN and creates organizational roadblocks to acceptance of the new technology.

In truth, these concerns are actually religious arguments on behalf of those committed to 100Base-T (fast Ethernet), as opposed to valid technical critiques. Some vendors and net managers who cut their teeth on Ethernet may strongly associate the technology with CSMA/CD. However, from the application standpoint, the frame is what matters, not the underlying network access scheme. If the way that the MAC layer functions is critical to the deployment of a technology, then switched Ethernet or 100Base-T (fast Ethernet) should be equally burdensome in the eyes of these critics. Introducing switching significantly changes the function of the CSMA/CD access scheme because, as with 100VG-AnyLAN, intelligence in the switch—not the collision detection algorithm alone—determines which traffic is transmitted.

Actually, demand priority can overcome some limitations of CSMA/CD access. With CSMA/CD, users must limit the size of their networks; the more devices the network supports, the more collisions and contention for bandwidth. Granted, even with 100VG-AnyLAN and demand priority, adding users adversely affects network performance, but access to the network is always fair. In theory, at least, the orderly operating procedure of demand priority should make it easier to add more users to the network.

Another criticism leveled against the demand priority scheme is that it requires too much sophistication at the hub or switch. Demand priority does place more responsibility on the hub than 10-Mbit/s Ethernet using the CSMA/CD access scheme. But in 100-Mbit/s networks, this sophistication is a necessary evil. In a 100VG-AnyLAN demand priority environment, the hub determines what happens and in what order. In a 100Base-T shared-media network, by contrast, the hub can quickly be overwhelmed with collisions. The answer to this problem, of course, is to segment the network, and this is done by adding intelligence—in the form of switches or routers.

Finally, some critics of 100VG-AnyLAN suggest that demand priority networks will become gridlocked with high-priority packets. Of all the arguments against demand priority, this is perhaps the weakest. The ability to assign high- and low-priority packets is a tool for network managers and application developers to allow an application to operate at a higher level or a lower level. And when implemented properly, 100VG-AnyLAN will raise the priority level of normal traffic, so that sessions will not time out.

In reality, unless the application developer or the network manager is completely irresponsible, they will use that feature to their benefit rather than to their detriment. Any network technology can be abused and still follow the technical standard, but make performance miserable for everybody. If gridlock occurs on a 100VG-AnyLAN-AnyLAN network, it's more likely to be the fault of the application developer or network designer than of the demand priority access scheme.

Section 8. Token Ring Capabilities

When arguing with 100Base-T fast Ethernet supporters, 100VG-AnyLAN's proponents like to emphasize the technology's ability to provide an upgrade path for token ring networks. 100Base-T (fast Ethernet) can't offer this functionality because of its reliance on CSMA/CD. But despite 100VG-AnyLAN's importance as a differentiator, its token ring promise has received relatively little industry attention.

To date, no 100VG-AnyLAN vendors have introduced products that support token ring frames, although several vendors are promising to deliver these devices. And some early token-ring-compatible products may not offer the full complement of 100VG-AnyLAN's token ring capabilities. For instance, when they are introduced, 100VG-AnyLAN hubs may not perform token ring source route bridging—a necessity for any large token ring network.

What's more, 100VG-AnyLAN soon may face stiff competition in the next-generation token ring market. IBM has positioned 25-Mbit/s ATM as its follow-on technology for token ring networks, and many token ring vendors have followed suit. Promising low-priced ATM adapter cards ($300 to $600 each, as opposed to $300 to $700 for current token ring adapters) and a rapid decrease in price per port of work group ATM switches, these vendors envision a smooth growth path from token ring to ATM.

But 25-Mbit/s ATM to the desktop has several limitations. Most significantly, an ATM network requires considerable modification to work with legacy environments. Although the ATM Forum has finalized its LAN emulation user-to-network interface (L-UNI), standard ATM LAN emulation that supports existing Ethernet and token ring applications is not widely available as yet. 100VG-AnyLAN offers this capability today.

Despite its critics, 100VG-AnyLAN is winning its share of adherents. Although its initial introduction met with little fanfare, 100VG-AnyLAN now has the backing of several high-profile networking and system vendors, including IBM, Cisco Systems Inc. (Santa Clara, CA), Proteon Inc. (Westborough, MA), Compaq Computer Corp. (Houston), Texas Instruments Inc. (Dallas), and Thomas-Conrad Corp. (Austin). Some industry heavyweights, such as 3Com Corp. (Santa Clara) and Standard Microsystems Corp. (Hauppauge, NY), still haven't boarded the 100VG-AnyLAN bus—and may never feel the need to do so—but enough vendors have enlisted now to give the technology a fighting chance.

ATM

Of all the technologies covered in this book, ATM (asynchronous transfer mode) clearly holds the most promise for corporations looking for a future-proof LAN. What is strange is that ATM actually has its roots planted firmly in the world of wide-area networking, or telecommunications. In fact, it's possible to trace the initial development of ATM as far back as the late 1960s, when scientists at Bell Laboratories began experimenting with cell switching.

ATM may have had to wait a quarter of a century before reaching LAN prime time, but it is now receiving an unprecedented level of support—from equipment vendors, software developers, and network managers. Predicted revenues from ATM products are expected to reach nearly $2.5 billion by 1998 (see Fig. 1). The ATM Forum—the primary organization

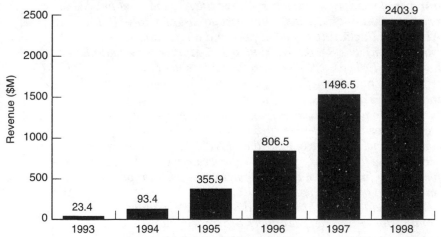

Fig. 1 Total U.S. ATM market revenue. Source: *Electronic Trend Publications* (San Jose, CA).

developing and defining ATM standards—now boasts over 700 members. All are adamant that networks for the foreseeable future will be based on ATM technology.

A quick glance at the ATM feature set lends credence to that belief. ATM is a high-speed, connection-oriented switching and multiplexing technology that uses 53-byte cells (5-byte header, 48 byte payload) to carry different types of traffic simultaneously— including data, time-sensitive multimedia (such as videoconferencing), and voice. The technology is known as asynchronous because it allows information streams to be sent independently without a common clock, not because it is designed to carry asynchronous data. ATM connections can be automatically set up and torn down. Quality-of-service parameters—such as guaranteed data rate and maximum delay—can be set on a link-by-link basis, allowing users to run diverse applications without incurring a tradeoff with performance or quality. When used in the LAN, ATM supports a variety of speeds—currently 25 Mbit/s, 51 Mbit/s, 155 Mbit/s, and 622 Mbit/s. Different speeds can be mixed within the same network. In large part, ATM also owes its popularity to the fact that it is the only networking technology with the potential to span both the local and wide-area domains. In other words, it is a single, homogeneous technology that can span the enterprise.

Two factors have conspired to bring ATM into play on LANs earlier than had first been anticipated. First, standards for ATM have been defined at a blistering pace, enabling vendors to bring interoperable equipment to market fast (it took ANSI over 10 years to define the FDDI standard; the ATM Forum completed the vast majority of ATM in fewer than 3). Second, the high number of vendors vying for a slice of the ATM market has led to price cutting. Back in 1993, the average cost of a 155-Mbit/s ATM node (including a switch port and an adapter in the workstation) was $4500. By 1995 a 155-Mbit/s node could be had for as little as $2250, and a 25-Mbit/s node cost only $700.

Its undisputed benefits have some net managers convinced that ATM is about to execute a networking shutout, taking over the LAN domain to the exclusion of all other networking technologies. The reality is rather different. For most corporations, the days of end-to-end ATM networking lie many years in the future—if, indeed, they ever arrive at all. For the foreseeable future most corporate networks will comprise a mish-mash of technologies.

In particular, two things stand between ATM and world domination. First, net managers are under financial and practical pressure to preserve at least some of the existing infrastructure—the installed base of some 50 million Ethernet *and token ring nodes, and the applications and network operating systems (NOSs) designed to run over them—for as long as possible. Second, while ATM is very good at carrying all applications, it is not the best at carrying all of them. For certain applications, some of the other high-speed LANs are superior to ATM. For instance, both Fibre Channel and HIPPI provide a much more efficient, and much faster, path for applications that send very large asynchronous data files. Similarly a network such as IsoEnet can provide better quality when carrying voice.*

These shortfalls are not surprising given that ATM is actually a compromise technology—one that is designed to meet the needs of both telco carriers and LAN equipment manufacturers. During the early days of ATM, phone companies argued in favor of using a 32-byte cell, which would provide better quality for voice calls. LAN purists wanted a 64-byte data unit, which would mean less overhead when carrying asynchronous applications. Today's cell size—48 bytes plus header—is a tradeoff between the needs of the two groups.

Nevertheless, ATM is such a significant technology that it is impossible to cover it in a single chapter. Consequently, Part 2 of this book is dedicated in its entirety to a discussion of ATM. The following eight chapters look at ATM from every angle:

- Chap. 8, "The History of ATM," provides a history of ATM; understanding ATM's development puts its advantages and drawbacks in perspective.

- Chap. 9, "ATM LAN Emulation," discusses the technology that provides a way for the MAC-layer protocols and applications running on legacy networks like Ethernet and token ring to work transparently across an ATM network.

- Chap. 10, "The ATM MPOA Specification," describes a standard still under development which aims to define how to implement routing on ATM networks.

- Chap. 11, "The ATM PNNI Specification," describes the ATM specification that enables switches from disparate vendors to interoperate.

- Chap. 12, "ATM Service Classes," deals with the four classes defined by the ATM Forum in its user network interface (UNI) 3.0 specification. These specs are designed to allow switch designers, and the companies that buy those switches, to make optimum use of the bandwidth available on ATM networks.

- Chap. 13, "25-Mbit/s ATM," describes the low-speed (and lower-cost) 25-Mbit/s ATM switches and adapters which are responsible for jump-starting the uptake of ATM in local area networks.

- Chap. 14, "Assessing the ATM State of the Art," describes a hands-on test of ATM switches. It gives a picture of what today's ATM switches are currently capable of, debunking vendor hyperbole about their products.

- Chap. 15, "An ATM Glossary," translates the esoteric language of ATM into plain English.

The History of ATM

Section 1. Overview

ATM has a reputation in the networking industry as an overnight sensation. With wide-area networks facing chronic and ever-growing bandwidth shortages, ATM came seemingly from nowhere in 1986 to serve as the core foundation for tomorrow's high-speed networks. The sudden arrival of ATM not only dispelled worries about WAN capacity but also helped spur the development of high-powered applications that previously had little hope of extending beyond the LAN.

Appearances aside, ATM obviously didn't simply materialize. Its underlying technology evolved over a period of time in research labs around the world. Yet even the most seasoned network professionals may be surprised at just how long it took for ATM to achieve its instant stardom. ATM's roots extend all the way back to the late 1960s, when researchers at Bell Laboratories began tinkering with cell switching (See Fig. 8.1). That places ATM technology in roughly the same generation as packet switching, which has served as the basis for data networking for about the past quarter century.

Why did it take so long for cell switching to catch on as a real-world technology? Part of the reason is expediency. Packet switching was developed to accommodate bursty data transmissions over the low-speed links that characterize the circuit-switched public network. With cell switching, developers had a nobler purpose in mind: They

---

This chapter first appeared as an article in *Data Communications* magazine and was written by Jeff Gould, a consultant based in Paris.

1960s

mid-60s
The Bell System begins deploying digital TDM in the public network.

1967
T1 transmission debuts in the U.S. network.

late 1960s
Bell Labs engineers start to tinker with blending label-based switching (later to be known as packet switching) with TDM.

1968
A Bell Labs researcher coins the term *asynchronous time-division multiplexing*—cell relay is born.

Figure 8.1

wanted to build a technology that would overcome some of the public networks' more intractable engineering limits. When it came to deploying technologies, the world's telecom monopolies opted for packet switching's quick fix.

But the ATM saga involves a lot more than that. To understand where ATM is and where it may be heading, it's important to know how and why it was created in the first place.

Section 2.   In the Beginning...

Ever since the first phone wires were strung together to form a network, telecommunications has involved an unending struggle to dole out a limited resource—bandwidth—to accommodate the demands of an ever-growing pool of users. Early phone networks relied on analog transmissions over copper wire pairs, with one physical link devoted to each voice conversation. This approach proved to be a logistical nightmare, especially in the United States. In the 1930s, a single voice call from New York to Los Angeles required its own contiguous physical circuit (comprising several tons of what after all is a semi-precious metal) spanning an entire continent.

In a first step to alleviate such massive inefficiencies, communications researchers came up with a form of frequency division multiplexing that allowed several voice calls to run over a single trunk line. The relief afforded by frequency division multiplexing was temporary; the post-World War II years brought a huge expansion of the U.S. phone network, with demand for circuits threatening to overwhelm a somewhat fragile infrastructure. The first really adequate solution for handling the public network bandwidth problem was digital time division multiplexing (TDM), pioneered by Bell Labs in the early 1960s. (Actually, computer pioneer Alan Turing used a form of digital TDM during World War II to encrypt transatlantic radio conversations between Winston Churchill and Franklin D. Roosevelt.)

The first TDM systems deployed by Bell Labs digitized 24 voice conversations and piped them into separate, sequential 64-kbit/s channels, which were then multiplexed onto a single four-wire copper trunk running at 1.544 Mbit/s (T1). Each channel was represented by an 8-bit voice sample, placed in a frame along with samples from the other 23 channels. The entire 24-byte frame (plus one framing bit) was then repeated 8000 times a second. Channel banks at either end of the line used a byte's position—also known as *temporal alignment*—within the frames to determine which call or circuit it belonged to.

Early T1 channel banks were decidedly feeble minded, with an IQ somewhere between that of a pocket calculator and a footstool. The primitive microelectronics of that era required fewer than 8000 framing bits per second to discern the boundaries between channels on a T1 line. In fact, the single most important driver of networking technology since those early days has involved efforts to cram as much computing power as possible into a small space. TDM is an efficient way to carry predictable, delay-sensitive voice traffic, because it uses an implicit method—time synchronization—to identify individual traffic sources. But it also wastes bandwidth, because individual time slots in each synchronous frame are dedicated to specific calls in progress. If a given call goes silent—for instance, if there's a lull in the voice conversation—there's no easy way to reallocate that call's time slot to another call, such as a bursty data transmission that could use the bandwidth.

This basic inefficiency drove data networking pioneers to invent packet switching, an overlay technique that masks the time-synchronous nature of the public voice network by using labels (packet headers) instead of time slots to identify separate connections. Packets are variable-length bundles of data that are generated out by a process running on a host computer, wrapped in a frame with an address or a virtual circuit identifier (together with some housekeeping functions such as error correction and perhaps flow control), and then dropped into a TDM circuit. Once the basic packet-switching mechanism was in place, data networkers began working on incompatible variants of the new technology. The most noteworthy of these range from X.25 for public networks and SNA for IBM mainframe networks, to such diverse venues as corporate networks (SNA), public packet networks (X.25), and the Internet.

Meanwhile, the world's telephone companies decided to pursue an entirely different technology: ISDN, or integrated services digital network. Essentially a switched form of TDM tailored for the local loop, basic-rate ISDN multiplexes two 64-kbit/s transparent bearer channels and a packet-based 16-kbit/s signaling channel onto a single twisted pair. In other words, it's an economy version of T1 transmission decorated with basic call setup and handling facilities.

For network managers who still have trouble getting ISDN from their local phone companies in the mid-1990s, it may seem hard to believe that the technology was developed and almost completely specified by the CCITT in the 1970s, about the same time that a college dropout named Bill Gates was writing a Basic interpreter for a now-forgotten microcomputer. Today, Gates's software runs on nearly 100 million computers around the planet, but ISDN is still a niche product with only a few hundred thousand users worldwide.

When the telecom monopolies dreamed up ISDN two decades ago, they knew that data traffic was going to be important, and they thoughtfully provided end-to-end digital channels to accommodate it. At the time, they considered 64-kbit/s channels more than generous—after all, modems at the time were the size of refrigerators and ran at 300 bit/s. Although the phone companies anticipated the arrival of large-scale data networking, they couldn't bring themselves to tamper with the inherently synchronous, circuit-based infrastructure at the core of their networks. With first-generation ISDN, they left untouched the problem of TDM's bandwidth inefficiency. The inefficiency issue wasn't addressed until the mid-1980s, when the CCITT began its work on the second generation of ISDN, known as broadband ISDN (BISDN).

Section 3.   The Plot Thickens

The CCITT's initial plan for BISDN involved simply extending the TDM used in the first-generation ISDN (now known as narrowband ISDN) to higher speeds. But the experts on the CCITT's broadband committee recognized that user needs in the 1990s were likely to extend beyond data. In particular, committee members expected video—both for entertainment and for business applications like videoconferencing—to become a major traffic source. Acting on the then-received wisdom that compression techniques would at best reduce a full-motion, broadcast-quality digital video signal to 140

Mbit/s, the CCITT decided that BISDN would require a user-to-network interface running at more than 150 Mbit/s to accommodate video, data, and voice traffic on a single line. Each physical interface would provide multiple switched TDM channels running at various speeds depending on the traffic type, from 64 kbit/s to "$n \times 64$," or multiple 64-kbit/s channels, right up to 140 Mbit/s.

It didn't take the CCITT long to realize that the synchronous transfer mode (STM) approach to broadband networking would make switch design a nightmare. The widely variable speeds called for in STM would make the inherent inefficiency of TDM grow exponentially. A working STM switch would have to reserve enormous pools of bandwidth in its switching fabric to accommodate calls requiring 140 Mbit/s, without being able to reallocate this bandwidth during periods of silence in the high-speed calls. There had to be a better way.

Section 4. Cell Theory

And there was. Back at the lab, a handful of telephone company engineers had been experimenting since the late 1960s with the idea of blending label-based switching (the basis of packet networks) with TDM. Unlike designers of packet protocols, the phone company researchers didn't want to hide the underlying network's division into fixed time slots; instead, they wanted to change the way the network identified which bits or bytes belonged to which circuits.

Their idea was to put a short indicator, basically no more than a virtual channel identifier, at the start of each time slot. This method allowed a given traffic source to put its bit stream onto the line asynchronously, using up labeled slots as needed rather than being compelled to march in synchronous lockstep with the network clock. In other words, the idea of building a network around short, fixed-length units (now known as *cells*) had its origins in TDM. Cell relay required more overhead bits than conventional TDM, but it did a much better job of accommodating unpredictable traffic from many sources. It also held the promise of making broadband switches much easier—and therefore much less expensive—to develop.

Work on cell relay continued throughout the 1970s, but it never reached the commercial stage (see Fig. 8.2). The key missing ingredient was cheap, application-specific silicon that could crunch through the millions of repetitive operations per second required to make cell relay feasible on a large scale. Once low-cost chips became available, cell switching took a big step closer to reality.

W. W. Chu, a researcher at Bell Labs, had coined the term ATDM (asynchronous time division multiplexing) back in 1968 to describe cell relay. But when the CCITT decided to make cell relay the core of

1970s

1971
The CCITT begins exploring technologies that later form the basis of ISDN.

1972
Ethernet formulated by Xerox; IBM introduces synchronous data link control (SDLC).

1974
IBM unveils SNA.

1976
The CCITT adopts the X.25 recommendations for public packet-switched networks.

Figure 8.2

BISDN in 1986, it decided to come up with a new label for the technology. Thus was born asynchronous transfer mode, or ATM. The CCITT ratified the foundation documents for BISDN in 1988. The broadband network of the future was to be based on an alliance of ATM and synchronous digital hierarchy (SDH), providing a cell-based user interface over a synchronously framed transmission media at 155 Mbit/s—the speed of SDH STM-1 or Sonet (synchronous optical network) OC-3c lines (SDH is the European equivalent of Sonet).

The 1988 CCITT documents defined the ATM cell format, which includes a 48-byte payload and a 5-byte header. They also defined the following layers of the ATM model:

- The physical layer, which is concerned with putting bits on the wire and taking them off again

- The ATM layer, which handles cell multiplexing and assorted housekeeping functions (such as header error correction)

- The ATM adaptation layers (AALs)—complex sublayered protocols that package various kinds of higher-level user traffic into 48-byte cells, together with the overhead needed to meet specific quality-of-service requirements, such as constant or variable bit rate and constant or variable delay (see Fig. 8.3).

Services type   **ATM adaptation layers**

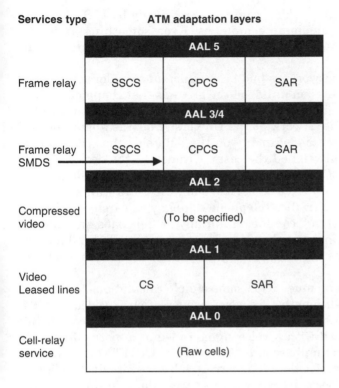

CPCS = Common-part convergence sublayer
CS = Convergence sublayer
SAR = Segmentation and reassembly
SMDS = Switched Multimegabit Data Service
SSCS = Service-specific convergence sublayer

Figure 8.3 ATM's different layers. ATM adaptation layers (AALs) are responsible for segmenting and reassembling data to be sent over the network. Different layers are intended to handle different traffic types.

Section 5. Turf Wars

At the time, the CCITT's work on BISDN looked like so much pie in the sky. After all, T1 was still a big-ticket item in the United States, and most European postal, telegraph, and telephone agencies (PTTs), or public carriers, weren't even offering 64-kbit/s digital leased lines. And the phone companies undoubtedly were motivated in part by a need to protect their fiefdoms from up-and-coming delivery systems like coaxial-based cable TV and VSAT (very small aperture terminal) satellite networks. In fact, turf protection played a large part in those early ATM standards efforts, with the main battle lines drawn between the data networking camp—led primarily by U.S. computer makers—and the telephone companies. Even something as fundamental as the length of the ATM cell was the subject of a bitter struggle.

For years, data networkers had been reluctant to endorse the use of fixed-length transmission units, on the grounds that chopping up long data packets into short cells made for inefficient use of bandwidth. But Jonathan Turner's work at the University of Washington on fast packet switching persuaded many on the data side that the benefits of cell switching outweighed the costs. Ultimately, the data networking lobby within CCITT agreed to endorse the use of 128-byte cells. Europe's PTTs quickly cried foul. Above all, the PTTs wanted to keep BISDN safe for voice traffic. Telephone company research on cell multiplexing and switching, conducted initially at Bell Labs and later at France Telecom's Cnet, was based on the assumption that cell lengths would be short—as short as 16 bytes, twice the size of a standard TDM time slot.

The telephone companies used some simple calculations to come up with their ideal cell length. If a voice conversation is coded in a 64-kbit/s circuit, a 16-byte cell can be filled in only 2 milliseconds. But filling a 128-byte cell with a voice signal coded at a more efficient 16 kbit/s would take 64 milliseconds. According to CCITT standards, the maximum tolerance for delay on terrestrial voice circuits is slightly more than 20 milliseconds. Beyond this threshold, operators are supposed to install expensive echo cancellation equipment. For U.S. carriers, echo cancellation wasn't much of an issue. Since it takes a signal at least 30 milliseconds to go coast to coast on fiber, long-distance operators have long since learned to live with this constraint. But in Europe, long-distance calls that stay within national boundaries cover much shorter distances. That meant PTTs didn't need to bother with echo cancellation—unless large cell sizes forced the issue.

After much bickering, each side made a concession: The phone companies offered to go up to 32 bytes, while the data networking camp agreed to drop down to 64 bytes. At this point the CCITT split the difference and set the ATM cell length at 48 bytes, plus header. This momentous decision, whose consequences the world's networking and telecom communities will be living with for decades to come, had the virtue of leaving all parties unhappy—the ultimate kind of compromise.

Section 6.   LAN Assault

After this auspicious start, a funny thing happened to ATM on the road to BISDN: it got hijacked. A handful of savvy researchers familiar with both Turner's work on fast packet switching and the CCITT's grand scheme for global cell switching put 48 and 5 together and decided that ATM would be just the ticket for corporate LANs in the 1990s (see Fig. 8.4).

The first two companies to announce ATM LANs were Adaptive Corp. (Redwood City, CA) and Fore Systems Inc. (Warrendale, PA). Adaptive was started by a group spun off from multiplexer maker Network Equipment Technologies Inc. (NET, Redwood City); Fore was led by a band of refugees from the computer science department of Carnegie-Mellon University. (Adaptive has since been folded back into NET.) Adaptive and Fore weren't the first vendors to sell commercial ATM products. That honor belongs to Stratacom Inc. (San Jose, CA), which in the late 1980s developed the IPX, a landmark multiplexing and switching product. IPX uses a proprietary 24-byte cell format (exactly half the official ATM payload size, and just enough to fill a T1 frame) to multiplex voice and data in private corporate networks.

Of course, Stratacom was and is a WAN company, as are ATM WAN pioneers Newbridge Networks Inc. (Kanata, Ontario) and Netcom Systems (Chatsworth, CA), which recently was acquired by General Datacomm Inc. (Middlebury, CT). For telephone operators, these companies didn't represent nearly as big a threat as the LAN upstarts. The reason: LAN vendors were almost certain to force a much faster

1980s

1984
The CCITT issues its first formal standards for ISDN.

1986
The CCITT decides to make ATM the core technology for broadband ISDN (BISDN).

1987
ANSI adopts the first standards governing Synchronous Optical Network (Sonet).

1988
The CCITT ratifies the foundation documents for BISDN.

Figure 8.4

migration to ATM. In essence, that's exactly what's been happening. In utter contrast to the CCITT's study-it-for-10-years-before-you-do-anything approach, the ATM LAN companies raced to market with hastily designed but innovative products that took both American corporate customers and European switch makers by surprise. With their early switches, Adaptive and Fore deployed easy-to-design, cheap-to-build bus architectures, leaving the more ambitious space division switching fabrics for the second generation. Fore's original adapter cards for Unix workstations didn't even handle the cell segmentation and reassembly (SAR) function of the AALs (ATM adaptation layer), leaving that task for the workstation's interrupt-harassed CPU.

Although first-generation ATM LAN products sold only a few hundred units worldwide in 1993, their first full year on the market, they succeeded in grabbing the imagination of just about anyone who had anything to do with data networks. What was ATM doing in a LAN product? Would it work? Did anybody need it? Would anybody buy it? Since 1992, when the first products rolled off the assembly line, ATM LAN switching has had a profound effect on both broadband wide-area networking and conventional shared-media LANs (see Fig. 8.5).

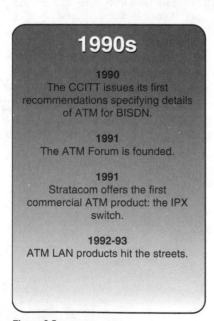

1990s

1990
The CCITT issues its first recommendations specifying details of ATM for BISDN.

1991
The ATM Forum is founded.

1991
Stratacom offers the first commercial ATM product: the IPX switch.

1992-93
ATM LAN products hit the streets.

Figure 8.5

Section 7.   Ethernet Has Left the Building

The fundamental argument of the ATM LAN vendors is that the shared-media model, introduced in the 1970s in the form of coaxial bus Ethernet, is dead. The reasons backing this contention are well known:

- High-powered PC clients and servers continue to double in processing power every 18 months, putting ever-greater strains on shared-media networks.

- LANs are breaking out of their isolated clusters of small work groups to offer enterprisewide connectivity spanning hundreds or even thousands of intelligent nodes, with aggregate traffic flows far exceeding anything Ethernet and token ring were designed to handle.

- With multitask operating systems, PCs can handle several network tasks at once, resulting in a corresponding need for more bandwidth.

- New, high-bandwidth buses like Intel Corp.'s PCI, which can reach peak block transfer rates on the order of 1 Gbit/s, are rapidly finding their way into desktop PCs.

- Client-server application components behave as if they are running on a single machine, with no network between them.

- Process-to-process protocols such as remote procedure calls (RPCs) are extremely sensitive to network delays.

- The expected rise of distributed computing and networked multimedia applications, including real-time video, will require more bandwidth than conventional LANs can deliver.

Whether individual desktop PCs really need ATM over a 155-Mbit/s Sonet/SDH connection or could settle for 25 Mbit/s or even less is beside the point. The key idea that ATM vendors are selling is that tomorrow's LANs should become a kind of cell-based PBX, where end-to-end virtual circuits are set up and torn down on demand between individual user processes.

And one factor that ultimately may ensure ATM's long-term success is its ability to bridge the LAN and WAN worlds, a talent that sets ATM apart from its LAN-based rivals. Once data starts flying through the network at ultrahigh speeds, the fewer boxes and algorithms needed to sort that information out, the better.

ATM LAN Emulation

Section 1. Overview

No matter how fast or versatile ATM (asynchronous transfer mode) ultimately proves to be, most corporate networkers simply can't afford forklift upgrades to cell-switching technology. And that basic fact of life means that ATM LAN emulation is going to be a critical issue for the foreseeable future. The ATM Forum has addressed this issue via the L-UNI (LAN emulation user-to-network interface), its LAN emulation standard.

L-UNI (pronounced "loony") defines how Ethernet- or token ring-attached PCs and workstations connect to their counterparts over an ATM network. It also specifies how ATM-attached servers communicate with devices on legacy LANs. L-UNI was approved by the ATM Forum in the summer of 1995. In essence, LAN emulation is a way to render the ATM switching fabric invisible to legacy LANs. Thus, it makes it possible to reap all the benefits associated with ATM without requiring extensive or expensive changes to end-station hardware and software. What's more, it allows legacy LAN adapters, NDIS (network device interface specification) and ODI (open data link interface) drivers, and all protocols at layer 2 and above to continue to be used.

There's more: LAN emulation enables applications on legacy LANs to access ATM-attached servers, workstations, routers, and other network equipment. What this means is that LAN emulation forwards

---

This chapter first appeared as an article in *Data Communications* magazine and was written by Ron Jeffries, principal at Jeffries Research (Santa Maria, CA).

upper-layer protocols across ATM connections without requiring any modifications to legacy software. At the same time, it makes it possible to convert LAN packets into ATM cells (and vice versa) without generating too much overhead at the ATM-attached devices. L-UNI also spells out how legacy LAN applications and protocols can run over an all-ATM network. Thus, even when ATM adapters have replaced all the legacy LAN adapters on a network, legacy protocols and applications can continue to run unchanged. Here again, the goal is to help companies protect the huge investment they've made (see Fig. 9.1).

For all its obvious benefits, the future of LAN emulation has been put in doubt by another ATM specification, called MPOA (multiprotocol over ATM). Unlike LAN emulation, which bridges traffic at the MAC layer, MPOA will define how traffic can be routed across a switched ATM network (see Chap. 10). Defining MPOA is the biggest

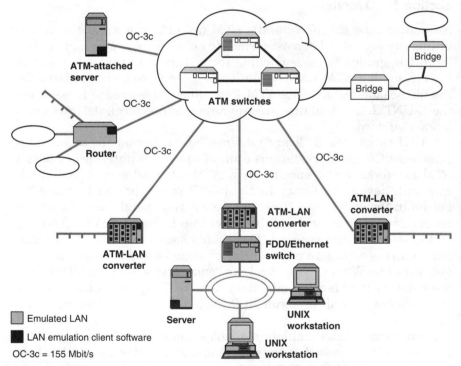

Figure 9.1 ATM LAN emulation in action. An emulated LAN allows legacy LANs to communicate across a high-speed ATM backbone without having to modify existing applications or infrastructure. It also enables legacy end stations to access ATM-attached servers, routers, and other devices. Emulated LANs also allow end-to-end ATM applications to run legacy LAN protocols and applications. LEC (LAN emulation client) software is used to establish connections to the backbone; LAN-to-ATM converters accept native LAN packets and modify them for transport over ATM.

challenge that the ATM Forum has faced to date—partly because of MPOA's technical complexity, and partly because vendors already are competing to twist the spec toward their own particular product strategies. Consequently, work on MPOA is not due to be complete until late 1996, and possibly not until 1997. In the meantime, it is unclear how networks using LAN emulation will communicate with those using MPOA, though one likely scenario is that routers supporting both specifications will be used to hand off data between the two. Given that MPOA will actually perform a superset of LAN emulation's duties (i.e., allowing traffic to be routed *and* bridged), it is not impossible that it eventually will take over from the simpler specification as the de facto way to transfer legacy traffic over ATM.

MPOA and LAN emulation are not the only games in town. The IETF (Internet Engineering Task Force) has defined "Classical IP over ATM," described in RFC (request for comment) 1577. This mechanism specifies a new IP-specific MAC layer for ATM.

Section 2.   LAN Emulation Service

The goal of LAN emulation is to use ATM's connection-oriented fabric to mimic (emulate) the connectionless nature of a LAN. ATM LAN emulation is actually a service on the ATM network that allows end stations on legacy LANs to connect both to other legacy end stations and to high-performance ATM-attached servers, routers, bridges, and similar devices. As indicated, all the devices on the Ethernets and token rings require no modification; they simply plug into a legacy LAN-to-ATM converter. This is a layer 2 device that accepts native LAN packets and slightly modifies them by adding an ID header, stripping off the frame check sequence (FCS), and sending them out onto the backbone as AAL 5 PDUs (protocol data units). Segmentation and reassembly (SAR) take place once the LAN packet has dropped into the PDU. Switches which can convert from LAN to ATM are now available from a variety of vendors—including Agile Networks (Concord, MA), Bay Networks Inc. (Santa Clara, CA), and Netedge Systems Inc. (Research Triangle Park, NC).

L-UNI also addresses FDDI. In this case, however, it requires FDDI frames to be translated into either Ethernet or token ring frames. Once that's done, the converter takes care of them. There are a couple of other basic issues to understand at the start. Emulated LANs can't mix and match legacy media: They have to be strictly Ethernet, strictly token ring, or strictly FDDI. Routers must be used to connect an emulated token ring, say, with an emulated Ethernet. Similarly, a bridge must be used to link like emulated LANs—two or more

Ethernet emulations, for instance. L-UNI does allow for multiple emulated LANs—each completely independent of the other—on the same physical LAN.

Classic Concerns for Legacy Nets

The ATM Forum's LAN emulation specification is not the only way to transport legacy traffic over an ATM backbone. The IETF (Internet Engineering Task Force) has defined a new IP-specific MAC (media access control) layer for ATM, "Classical IP over ATM," described in RFC (request for comment) 1577. Despite superficial similarities, the goals of LAN emulation and Classical IP are completely different. LAN emulation works with all protocols, both routable and unroutable, and completely hides ATM from the upper layers. It succeeds by simulating the legacy LAN—delivering a completely transparent, higher-bandwidth replacement for Ethernet or token ring.

Classical IP over ATM, by contrast, supports one protocol and does not attempt to emulate the existing MAC layer. This makes it much simpler than the ATM Forum's take on LAN emulation. Since Classical IP has to handle only one ATM-aware protocol, it generates much less overhead. But there's a price to be paid for simplicity. Any device with a legacy LAN adapter must go through a router or bridge to reach a workstation or server using Classical IP over ATM. With the ATM Forum's LAN emulation, in contrast, legacy LAN devices can directly connect to servers that have ATM adapters, without the extra overhead (and substantial extra delay) associated with routers.

There are some significant advantages to IETF's protocol-specific approach, however. Because they did not have to maintain compatibility with the existing MAC layer, the Classical IP designers elected to have a maximum frame size of more than 9000 bytes. This large frame size reduces packet overhead, which is particularly advantageous in performing bulk data transfers. With LAN emulation, if either end of a connection is on a legacy LAN, the maximum frame size can't exceed the limit for the LAN. If both end stations are using ATM, however, they are free to negotiate an AAL 5 PDU that could easily accommodate over 9000 bytes. This ability is inherent in ATM, however, and is not a feature of LAN emulation.

Finally, unlike the ATM Forum's LAN emulation interface, the Classical IP over ATM protocol stack knows it is running over ATM. Because it was designed to take advantage of ATM, Classical IP over ATM allows users to invoke ATM's quality-of-service features, such as specifying the maximum cell delay or acceptable cell loss for a connection.

Section 3.   Two Components

An emulated LAN has two main components: LAN emulation clients (LECs) and a single LAN emulation service (thus, it follows a client-server model). LEC software can be deployed in the converter or as part of the driver in an ATM-attached network server or other device. The client software has several jobs; one of the most important is to map MAC (media access control) addresses to ATM addresses. This function also is known as *address resolution*.

The software that delivers the LAN emulation service is implemented on three logical servers—the configuration server, the LAN emulation server (LES), and the broadcast and unknown server (BUS). The ATM Forum has left a lot of leeway for implementers as far as the physical location of these servers is concerned. For example, all three could be implemented in an ATM switch as a single application. They also could be distributed across the network, with the LES, say, running in an ATM backbone switch, while the configuration server sits on an ATM-attached server and the BUS runs in a LAN-to-ATM converter.

LAN emulation is a layer 2 service; it is completely independent of upper-layer protocols (see Fig. 9.2). Thus, it handles not only common routable protocols like IPX, APPN (advanced peer-to-peer networking), DECnet, and TCP/IP but also end-to-end communication using unroutable protocols like NetBIOS, LAT (local area transport), and SNA. It's important to understand that an ATM switch does not directly participate in LAN emulation. Rather, it simply sets up a virtual connection and switches 53-byte cells as it would with any other protocol that uses AAL 5. Likewise, a host computer attached to an ATM converter acts just as it would in a pure Ethernet or token ring environment. All the work of converting packets from the legacy LAN into ATM cells is handled by the LEC software and the LAN emulation service itself.

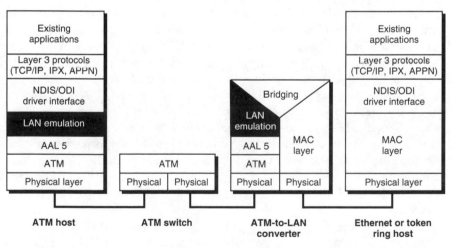

ATM host   ATM switch   ATM-to-LAN   Ethernet or token
                                      converter   ring host

AAL = ATM adaption layer   NDIS = Network Device Interface Specification
MAC = Media access control   ODI = Open Data-link Interface

Figure 9.2 LAN emulations' logical structure. LAN emulation is a layer 2 service. As such, it bridges LAN and ATM addresses at the MAC (media access control) layer. It is completely independent of all services, protocols, and applications running at the higher layers.

Section 4.   Server Scenario

Working together, the servers on an emulated LAN perform three functions: transfer data point to point between one end station and another (unicast); transfer data point to multipoint from one end station to many (broadcast or multicast); and resolve MAC addresses to ATM addresses.

The LES is the command and control center for an emulated LAN. It's responsible for registering and resolving MAC addresses or route descriptors to ATM addresses. The BUS takes care of all the broadcasting and multicasting done over the ATM network. As its name suggests, the server furnishes configuration information about the ATM network; it also supplies the address of the LES to the client. LECs communicate with these servers via two types of ATM connections (see Fig. 9.3). Control connections are used for housekeeping tasks such as finding the address of another client; data connections are used for everything else. The key control connection runs between the client and the LES and is set up by a client when it joins an emulated LAN. This is a bidirectional point-to-point link. The spec also allows for an optional unidirectional link to be set up by the LES to the client. This can be either a point-to-point or a point-to-multipoint connection.

The data connections do the heavy lifting on the emulated LAN. These are used to connect one client to another as well as to link clients to the BUS. The client-to-client link is bidirectional and is known as a *data-direct virtual connection*. This is the path that all unicast traffic travels over. The client-to-BUS data connection is actually a pair of unidirectional links, one carrying data from the client to the bus, the other transmitting data from the BUS to the client.

All these connections, coordinated according to L-UNI, are what allow applications on legacy LANs to run over an ATM network. On a shared-media LAN, a packet travels to every node on a network; the target picks it up and reads it. On an emulated LAN, a packet is converted into cells and sent to the target—either directly, via the data connection, or indirectly, via the BUS. LAN emulation also takes care of correlating ATM addresses with the MAC addresses used by legacy LANs.

The link to the BUS has two purposes. It's used for multicast/broadcasts and it's employed to send unicast traffic to the BUS while the LES and the client are involved with address resolution. This is done for two reasons. First, it takes time to set up a data-direct connection. Rather than have the data sit idle while all the necessary handshaking takes place, the client forwards it to the BUS, which shoots it out to every station on the emulated LAN. Second, the LES can't know

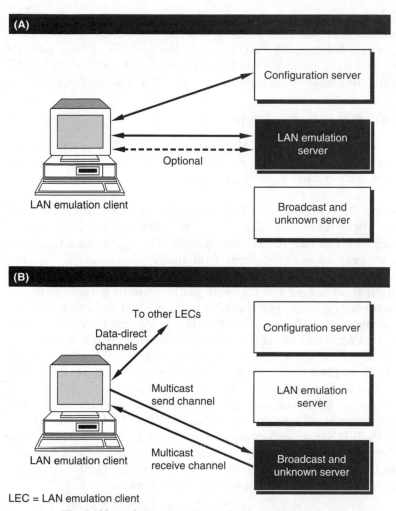

LEC = LAN emulation client

Figure 9.3 The LAN emulation connection. LAN emulation clients use two types of ATM connections to communicate with the configuration server, LE server, and broadcast and unknown server. Control connections are employed for administrative tasks (a). Data connections are used to link clients and to allow the client to broadcast cells over the ATM network (b).

the MAC address of every device on the network. The problem lies not with LAN emulation but with the way a bridged network is built. Once LANs are tied together by bridges, it's impossible for the LAN-to-ATM converter to keep tabs on the addresses of every end station on the far side of a bridge. So when the LES is asked for a MAC address that it doesn't have, it sends out an LE-ARP (LAN emulation address resolution protocol) asking the target to identify itself. While the LES is waiting for an answer, the LEC sends the data to the BUS, which broadcasts it onto the emulated LAN.

Connections between the BUS and individual clients are usually implemented as a single point-to-multipoint link (although L-UNI allows point-to-point connections configured in a star topology).

Section 5.   Five-Step Procedure

Given the complexity of the ATM Forum's LAN emulation scheme, the best way to understand it is to see it in action. Basically, all the activity on an emulated LAN follows five steps.

Initialization.   To establish an ATM connection, the first thing the LAN emulation client must do is find the ATM address of the LAN emulation server so it can join the emulated LAN. The spec allows this to be done in several ways. The client first must use the ATM Forum's ILMI (interim local management interface) to try to get the address of the configuration server from a table in the switch. It then attempts to set up a connection to get the LES address. If it fails to locate the configuration server, it can go back to the ILMI and look for another configuration server or see if the address of the LES itself is listed.

If it is once again unsuccessful, the LEC uses what is called a "well-known ATM address," an agreed-upon address for the configuration server that will be specified by L-UNI and used on every ATM network. If this too fails, another option is to use a "well-known virtual path identifier/virtual channel identifier" (VPI/VCI). This also will be specified in L-UNI; it corresponds to an already established virtual connection to the BUS. Finally, the LEC can try to find a previously configured LES address or a predefined PVC (permanent virtual circuit) between the client and the configuration server.

Configuration.   Once the LEC has the address of the LES, it needs to determine what type of emulated LAN it is about to join and the maximum frame size allowed on the LAN. It typically gets this information from the configuration server; it also can get what it needs using one of the methods described above. The LEC tells the configuration server its ATM address, its MAC address, the type of LAN it supports, and the maximum frame size it accepts. Optionally, it also tells the name of the emulated LAN it wants to join, such as "finance" or "engineering."

Joining.   Once the LEC has all the foregoing information, it joins the emulated LAN. To do so, it first creates a bidirectional control connection to the LAN emulation server. Then it sends a Join request to the

LES, containing its ATM address, LAN type, maximum frame size, and proxy indication (if the client is acting on behalf of other end stations, as would be the case with a LAN-to-ATM converter). The LEC provides all this information to the LES in case it has not successfully reached a configuration server.

The LES can either set up its own control connection or use the LEC's. In either case, it sends back a LAN emulation Join response, either registering the client with the emulated LAN or refusing to allow it to join. If the client is refused, it must terminate its Join request and tear down the bidirectional connection. It may then start the initialization process from scratch. If the communication times out before the LEC receives the response, it may terminate the request or opt to try again.

Registration and BUS initialization.   Once the client registers with the LES, it asks it to supply the ATM address that corresponds to the broadcast MAC address, which is used to indicate that a message goes to all stations on a network. This is actually the ATM address of the BUS. The client then sets up the data connection with the BUS, and the broadcast and unknown server either adds the client to its point-to-multipoint virtual connection or adds another point-to-point connection to its star topology.

Transfer data.   At this point, the LAN emulation client is ready to do useful work: sending data to another station on the emulated LAN. Here's how it's done. When the LEC receives an Ethernet or token ring packet from the driver interface at layer 2, it checks to see if it knows the ATM address of the target. The leading bit of the destination MAC address indicates whether the packet is to be unicast or multicast/broadcast.

If the bit is set, indicating that it is a multicast/broadcast packet, the packet is then passed to the BUS to be sent out over the network. If the bit is not set—indicating a unicast packet—the LEC checks to see if it knows the ATM address that corresponds to the MAC address. If it has the address, it looks to see if it has a virtual connection already established. If it does, it sends the packet. If it has the ATM address but doesn't have a connection, it uses UNI 3.0 signaling to set one up.

If the LEC doesn't know the corresponding ATM address, it issues an LE-ARP to the LES asking for it. While it's waiting for a response, it sends the packet to the BUS, which broadcasts it over the emulated LAN. After the LES responds with the ATM address, the client sets up a data-direct connection. If the LES can't find the address, the LEC continues to broadcast packets using the BUS.

Section 6.   LAN Emulation Benefits

Although the goal of LAN emulation is to allow an ATM network to look like a conventional legacy LAN, it offers a number of other advantages. For one thing, today's Ethernets and token rings suffer from distance limits. In contrast, a LEC can be located anywhere on the ATM switching fabric; it need not reside at the same geographic location as the other members of its emulated LAN. In fact, the physical connection it uses can be shared by several emulated LANs. What's more, congestion is far less of a problem on an emulated LAN. In order to keep conventional shared-media LANs from bogging down, they must be segmented when traffic reaches a certain level. Since most traffic on an emulated LAN is carried on independent point-to-point connections (only multicast/broadcasts are point-to-multipoint), there's far more capacity available. This is not to suggest that an emulated LAN can support an unlimited number of end stations. Theoretically, only one factor limits the size and scope of an emulated LAN: total broadcast and unknown traffic cannot exceed the bandwidth of the slowest participating legacy client. In other words, multicast/broadcast traffic on an emulated LAN could not exceed 10 Mbit/s when emulating an Ethernet LAN or 16 Mbit/s when emulating a token ring LAN. It would take many more end stations than could be accommodated on a legacy LAN to generate this much broadcast traffic on an emulated LAN.

10

The ATM MPOA Specification

Section 1. Overview

Now that the ATM Forum has finished up its LAN emulation specification—which defines a way to bridge traffic from legacy LANs like Ethernet and token ring over ATM—it's turning its attention to a new challenge: defining how traffic can be *routed* over ATM. Developing the standard, called multiprotocol over ATM (MPOA), is by far the most ambitious project the forum has taken on to date. LAN emulation servers require about 25,000 lines of code. MPOA servers will require at least a quarter of a million.

But not all the hurdles that the forum must overcome are technical. Already, the work undertaken in the MPOA committee is being overtaken by a business dynamic, as Cisco Systems Inc. (Menlo Park, CA) seeks to use the MPOA spec to reinforce its dominance in the router industry, and its internetworking competitors take any action necessary to stymie its efforts—even if that means prolonging the amount of time it takes to bring MPOA solutions to market. Cisco itself estimates that it will be 1997 before an implementable version of MPOA gets here. Others say it could be longer.

Section 2. A Network Layer Spec

MPOA is a follow-on to the forum's LAN emulation standard, which was finalized in 1995. Both enable legacy LANs like Ethernet and token ring to work transparently across an ATM network. However, unlike LAN emulation, which bridges traffic at the MAC layer, MPOA will allow traffic to be routed at the network layer. Internetworking equipment supporting MPOA will be able to divide enterprise-size LAN and ATM networks into virtual LANs (vLANs), and route data between them, on the basis of network layer information such as IP subnet addresses. (The only way to do this with LAN-emulation-based networks is by handing off all inter-vLAN traffic to a separate router—a highly inefficient workaround.)

That's the plan, anyhow. To date, the working group charged with developing the spec has got only as far as developing a statement of intent describing what MPOA should ultimately achieve. According to the document, MPOA will define a route server architecture in which switches consult a centralized routing entity when they need to know where to send data. To achieve that, the MPOA spec will have to define several different protocols, including a switch-to-server protocol (which will allow the route server and switches to communicate) and an interserver protocol (which will keep the information in different route servers in the same network in sync).

Section 3.   Divided They Stand

The MPOA committee is split into two camps on the question of what form these protocols should take. In one, Cisco. In the other, everyone else. Originally, Cisco tabled a motion suggesting that MPOA should be largely based on a combination of two standards: LAN emulation and the IETF's next-hop routing protocol (NHRP), which is still in development. (Principally, NHRP defines a way for routers to use a separate server to perform multiprotocol LAN-to-WAN address mapping.) Cisco also argued in favor of developing the standard in stages. Specifically, it wanted to leave defining the server-to-server protocol until later, arguing that existing router protocols like its own IGRP or the standards-based OSPF could suffice in the meantime.

The Cisco proposal was voted down by 21 to 1 in favor of a motion to take a top-down approach, in which MPOA will be mainly developed from scratch. The committee's decision to throw out Cisco's proposal has as much to do with business wheeling and dealing as it does with technology. Other companies believe that Cisco wanted to base MPOA on LAN emulation and NHRP for no other reason than that it has already implemented the LAN emulation spec, and is a leading player in the NHRP committee. Consequently, supporting the motion would have meant giving Cisco a head start in developing MPOA implementations. Likewise, the MPOA committee's decision to go ahead and define a new server-to-server protocol comes as no surprise, since it has the potential to diminish Cisco's dominance in the routing market by reducing companies' reliance on IGRP.

These arguments are far from over. In particular, Cisco still maintains that developing a new server-to-server protocol is a waste of time. The result of this particular debate is almost certain to be a compromise—with the server-to-server protocol defined, but made optional, observers say.

The MPOA committee has three other problems to resolve. First, it must determine how MPOA should handle unroutable protocols like LAT, NetBIOS, and SNA, if at all. Second, it needs to resolve the problem of route servers accidentally instructing switches to send data over paths that are not actually available, or over looped paths. Conventional routers exchange routing information over the same lines that they use to carry applications data. If a connection fails, they know the line isn't there because they stop receiving their router updates. Not so in a route server network, where the routing information is sent over a *different* path (between switch and route server) to the applications data (which travels switch to switch). Today's routing protocols (like IGRP, OSPF, and RIP) don't have to deal with this eventuality, so they don't address it. NHRP does, but the IETF committee responsible for it is still working on a solution.

Third, the MPOA group has to decide how nodes attached to dissimilar LANs can exchange traffic (from Ethernet, over ATM, and onto token ring again, for example). Some companies, including Newbridge, want to include a translational bridging capability in MPOA itself. Others, including Cisco, say that bridging will make MPOA too complicated, and too slow. They recommend omitting translational bridging from the spec, making vendors responsible for supporting it in their switches.

11

The ATM PNNI Specification

Section 1. Overview

Few network managers haven't heard about the benefits of ATM. From local-area work group to campus backbone to wide-area infrastructure, ATM promises a homogeneous enterprisewide technology delivering speeds above and beyond those offered by today's LAN architectures. With ATM, a PC in Paris could connect to a workstation in Washington, D.C. with greater speed and efficiency than two machines communicating on the same shared-media 10Base-T Ethernet. A video server in Vienna could connect to a teleconferencing station in Tokyo over an ATM link that provides better reliability and fidelity than if client and server shared a local 100-Mbit/s FDDI ring.

The power of ATM switching derives from its ability to set up and tear down these far-flung communications links as needed and to guarantee the data rate that a given application requires. ATM links, whether wide-area or local, are switched virtual circuits (SVCs) rather than physical communications links, such as those provided by conventional time division multiplexers. ATM SVCs offer users the ability to define the class of service that they need. ATM applications can specify quality-of-service parameters that determine the characteristics of a connection; these characteristics include features such as allowable delays and committed information rates. Because ATM's speed and quality-of-service features enable users to run diverse, sophisticated applications across wide areas, most if not all ATM net-

---

This chapter first appeared as an article in *Data Communications* magazine and was written by George Swallow at Lightstream Corp. (Billerica, MA).

works are likely to employ switches from several different vendors. Rarely could a large global network rely on one vendor's products for all work group, campus, and backbone nodes. At present, however, there is no standard method governing how one vendor's ATM switch can establish a connection with a switch from another vendor.

The ATM Forum is now working on the standard that will enable switches from disparate vendors to interoperate. This standard, known as the private network-to-network interface (PNNI), defines a protocol that enables users to establish SVCs between any two PNNI-compliant ATM devices. When complete, the PNNI specification will offer users the ability to build elaborate switched networks using products from several vendors. PNNI-compliant devices will interoperate efficiently, and virtual connections between them will support the ATM quality-of-service parameters needed for multimedia and other applications. Most ATM switch vendors have already deployed mechanisms for handling interswitch routing and managing SVCs. However, they have implemented proprietary solutions that define connections between their own switches only. The PNNI specification enables switches from different vendors to establish SVCs between each other. PNNI also will define ways of routing SVCs across heterogeneous backbone, campus, and local networks. In other words, if an organization uses one vendor's ATM switch in a local-area work group, another vendor's product for a campus backbone, and a third vendor's switch as part of a carrier-supplied ATM WAN service, the PNNI standard ensures that each of these switches can connect to the others.

PNNI solves the problem of routing SVCs across a network of multivendor switches, while meeting required quality-of-service objectives. It offers a scalable solution to navigating a complex network topology without requiring each switch to maintain detailed maps of the overall network. PNNI also accommodates existing proprietary interswitch communications protocols. Users who already have configured proprietary networks of switches from a single vendor don't have to sacrifice the value-added features within those groups to take advantage of PNNI elsewhere in their networks.

Although it does support all the value-added automatic configuration and routing features that many vendors' proprietary protocols provide, PNNI requires a minimum of manual configuration. To permit construction of an ATM network using switches from more than one vendor, PNNI must be flexible enough to support many diverse switching architectures—from the most sophisticated to the most rudimentary. It cannot rely on the availability of enormous amounts of buffer memory in every switch, and it cannot assume that the existing proprietary protocol of one switch can interoperate with that of another. PNNI must be sufficiently simple and elegant to allow the most rudimentary switches with the least amount of buffer memory to fulfill all these functions.

And although it cannot make use of them, PNNI must be able to accommodate existing proprietary interswitch protocols that offer value-added features. Finally, PNNI must do all this without requiring network managers to perform elaborate, complex configuration procedures. ATM switches must be able to "learn" the topology of the network they participate in, or at least learn enough of that network to establish efficient paths from one end station to another. Also, switches must know enough about the capabilities of the other switches in the network to choose a route that has a high probability of establishing the needed connection, while at the same time meeting the bandwidth requirements and quality-of-service parameters for a given application.

All this is a tall order, and the ATM Forum's work on PNNI has taken some time. At this point, however, most of the high-level design work on PNNI is complete, and the forum's PNNI committee is working out the details of switch-to-switch communications, including SVC processing, hierarchical source routing, and the exact packet formats and field lengths in which switches will share PNNI data. Although the PNNI specification is well on its way to completion, there are some network managers who would like to build multivendor ATM networks today. For these users, the ATM Forum has agreed on a temporary protocol, known as the interim interswitch signaling protocol (IISP), which vendors could implement prior to the completion of PNNI.

Stopgap PNNI

The ATM Forum was due to finish up PNNI by the end of 1995. Prior to that time, it ratified an interim solution, called the interim interswitch signaling protocol (IISP), which was initially known as PNNI Phase 0. Because IISP is significantly less sophisticated than PNNI, the ATM Forum decided to indicate in the specification's name that it is an interim solution—in order to reduce confusion between IISP and make clear that there will be no migration path from IISP to PNNI. IISP is purely a stopgap solution, to be replaced by PNNI when that specification is complete.

Like PNNI, IISP uses user network interface (UNI) 3.1 signaling procedures. Unlike PNNI, however, the switches using IISP are not peers. Rather, one switch functions as the network node and the other as an end station. There is no support for dynamic distribution of routing information. This is an important difference between IISP and PNNI. IISP uses preconfigured routing tables, which it consults hop by hop. PNNI dynamically distributes topology information throughout the network and employs sophisticated hierarchical source routing, using summarized information about various levels of the network.

The efficiency of PNNI results from its ability to distribute routing information throughout the network. IISP has no such ability. In IISP, routing decisions are made on a hop-by-hop basis rather than according to a hierarchy. That is, one switch sends a request for an SVC to another, and the receiving switch then looks for the destination address in its address table. If the receiving switch does not have the destination address, it passes the request on to another switch in the network. At subsequent switches, the process repeats until the call reaches its destination. The network manager must specify the routing procedure in advance so that each switch knows where to pass the requests it can't fulfill.

Section 2.   The Topology

The first problem faced by designers of PNNI was how to represent the topology of the ATM network. How would a switch "see" the overall network? Essentially, this problem requires striking a balance between the value of topology information for making routing decisions and the cost of distributing, storing, and processing that information. In an ideal scenario, every ATM switch in a network would know not only the address of every ATM-attached end station but also the current available capacity for new SVCs through every switch. The more information a switch has about the network, the easier it is to build optimal routes to the destination. Of course, as ATM networks scale to include hundreds or even thousands of switches supporting tens of thousands of users and devices, this information would require more and more memory to store and more and more processing power to compute. If each switch maintained a detailed map of the network, it would need to know of every change in available carrying capacity throughout the network, requiring ever more administrative messaging to update and maintain the map. In short, it quickly becomes uneconomical to replicate a detailed map of the entire ATM topology in every switch.

Yet finding the shortest or best available path from one point to another across the network does require that a given switch know something about what the network looks like. It must know its own whereabouts in the network and be able to locate other switches or ATM end stations so that it can establish virtual circuits offering the appropriate speed and quality-of-service parameters. The solution is a scheme that distributes and summarizes network topology so that switches have detailed information about their local topology and summarized information about more distant regions of the network. The PNNI specification manages this through the use of a hierarchical topology, along with an addressing scheme akin to that used in telephony networks.

Section 3.   The PNNI Maps

Just as road maps provide varying levels of detail depending on the scale and area covered, the various levels of the switching hierarchy established by PNNI map different segments of the overall network in different degrees of detail. By breaking a large network of ATM switches into smaller domains called peer groups, PNNI allows switches to navigate paths through the network without requiring them to store an entire map of the network in memory. PNNI organizes similar switches into peer groups and the leaders of like peer groups into higher-level peer groups, each of which contains one switch that is designated as a leader. The leader switch also becomes the peer of other peer group leaders at its level in the network. It summarizes information about the devices that can be reached in its peer group and acts as the peer group's conduit for information about the peer groups above it.

Using PNNI, switches in an ATM network automatically form a hierarchy of peer groups according to addresses assigned by the network manager. The switches' ATM addresses provide the key to the structure of this hierarchy. Each peer group has its own address identifier, similar to a telephone exchange or area code. For a lower-level peer group, this address would be similar to an area code and exchange. For a higher-level peer group, it would be analogous to just the area code. Finally, each switch within a peer group has a unique address, similar to the way each line in a telephone exchange has a unique number.

To create a PNNI hierarchy, the network manager needs only to configure the switches' ATM addresses. By default, the switch with the lowest address within a given peer group is automatically "elected" leader of that peer group. The leader learns the necessary topology information regarding the next-highest level of the switching hierarchy and feeds this information to the other switches in its peer group. This process can be repeated several times to create multiple levels of hierarchy. In this way, every switch has all the information it needs to communicate with switches outside its peer group and to create a hierarchical source route to a destination end station.

When switches power up, they automatically initialize links to any other ATM devices they are connected to. When they initialize these links, they exchange the node IDs that the network manager has assigned to them. By comparing IDs, the nodes determine if the neighbor node is in the same peer group or in a different peer group. If they're in the same peer group, they begin exchanging topology and routing information. For example, a hypothetical enterprise ATM network could contain four wide-area domains—in New York, Atlanta, London, and Paris (see Fig. 11.1). Each domain could consist of two or more campus switches, each of which in turn support several local-area work group switches, which in turn support multiple end stations. Campus and work group switches throughout these locations could be from different vendors.

PNNI can automatically define a hierarchy for routing through this switching network. Nodes in the local-area peer groups communicate with their neighboring switches. Each group selects the switch with the lowest ATM address as the peer group leader, and leaders of the local-area peer groups participate in a campus-level peer group. The leaders of the campus-level peer groups then participate in the peer group that includes the leaders from each of the campus locations in

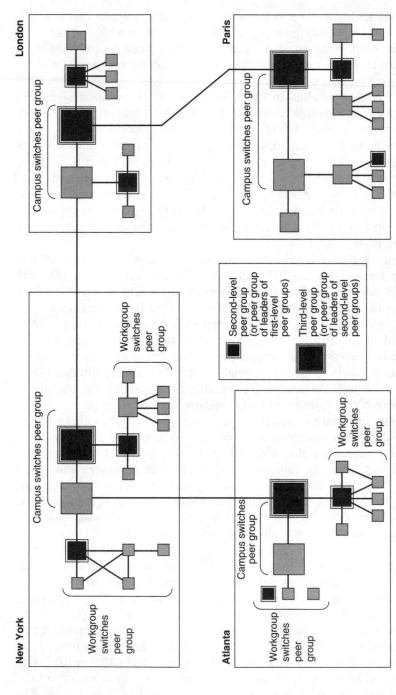

Figure 11.1 PNNI peer groups and physical topology. A hypothetical enterprise ATM network using campus and workgroup switches from different vendors could contain four wide-area domains, in New York, Atlanta, London, and Paris. PNNI automatically defines a hierarchy of peer groups and leaders of peer groups for distributing routing information through the network.

New York, Atlanta, Paris, and London. Each peer group leader summarizes the topology information relevant to its peer group and distributes information regarding the campus switches and higher levels of the hierarchy to the members of that local-area peer group. The leaders of campus peer groups in turn summarize topology information about their peer groups and distribute routing information regarding the switches above them to the other members of the campus group. In this way, the logical nodes discover which nodes are their neighbors and establish routing maps for navigating through the network hierarchy.

Section 4. Consistent Implementation

The same PNNI protocol and procedures apply at the level of the leaders in New York and Paris as at the work group switch peer group leaders in Atlanta and London. Unlike the IP protocol suite, which uses interior and exterior routing protocols depending upon whether a destination address resides on the same subnet as the source, the PNNI protocol remains consistent throughout the hierarchy. The protocol used between the members of the lowest-level peer group also is used between the leader of a peer group and the leaders of higher-level peer groups. It is important to note that this process occurs from the bottom up. When the work group switch leaders are selected, they then discover that they have peers in the next level up the hierarchy. In the case of the work group and campus switches, for example, the leader of each of the New York work group switch peer groups recognizes that it is a member of the peer group of leaders of peer groups. It then exchanges routing information with this second-level peer group, which then elects its own leader, and the process continues up the hierarchy.

Once the hierarchy is established, topology information is passed back down through the various peer group leaders to the members of their respective peer groups. In the PNNI protocol exchange, all routing information is shared among peers and then fed down via the peer group leader to the lower layers in the hierarchy. Using PNNI, a given switch never maintains more routing information than it needs. A source switch knows its local topology, which includes the other members of its peer group, and the topology of the levels above it. It uses this information to create a hierarchical source route. That is, it creates a route to the next-highest or -lowest level of detail. At the lowest level of the topology hierarchy, where nodes correspond to individual switches, routing information consists simply of the list of end-station devices physically attached to a switch. At the highest level of the hierarchy, however, nodes represent summarized regions of the topology. Routing information associated with a node at this level consists of a single summary address, which represents all the devices within the lower-level peer groups.

Section 5.   Exceptions to the Rules

It is important to note that addresses need not necessarily be configured in hierarchical order for the switches to perform their hierarchical functions. The network manager can override the default hierarchy by specifying that a particular switch always be considered the leader of its peer group. The network manager also can specify a given switch as the leader's designated backup in event of failure. This allows the network manager to prevent a change in the leader when new switches with lower addresses are added to the network.

For example, in a three-level hierarchy, nodes addressed A.1., A.1.1, A.2.1, and A.3.1 would all belong to the second-level peer group of leaders of peer groups. When they are powered up, these switches exchange routing updates with their peers and, because they have the lowest addresses in their peer groups, they are elected leaders. Following the PNNI protocol, these four leader switches form a peer group, which by default would choose A.1. as their peer group leader because it has the lowest address in the group. However, the network manager could customize the PNNI hierarchy and specify that A.2.1 always be selected the leader of the peer group (see Fig. 11.2). This capability is particularly useful if the network manager prefers to use a particular switch with a more powerful processor or an uninterruptible power supply as a peer group leader.

Also, it is important to note that not all lowest-level peer groups within the PNNI hierarchy must use the PNNI protocol for intra-peer group communications. A network that already has deployed proprietary routing and connection management protocols, for example, can continue to use those protocols. This proprietary network becomes a separate peer group within the PNNI hierarchy, and only one switch within that group needs to communicate with the surrounding PNNI hierarchy. The proprietary network simply appears to the rest of the network as a single node, as would any other lowest-level peer groups (see Fig. 11.3). Information destined for switches and end stations within the proprietary segment is routed to the leader of this peer group using PNNI. At that point, the proprietary interswitch protocol can take over and route the connection to its destination. The fact that a different set of protocols is run internal to that network is completely transparent to all other PNNI nodes in the network.

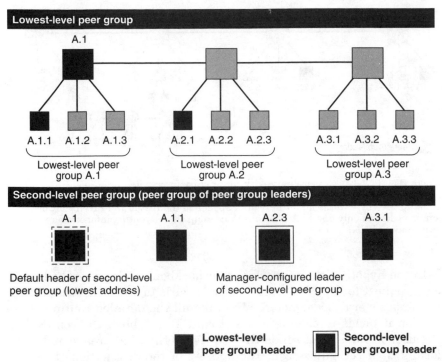

Figure 11.2 The PNNI hierarchy. In a three-level PNNI hierarchy, nodes addressed A.1, A.1.1, A.2.1, and A.3.1 belong to a peer group of leaders of lower-level peer groups. By default, these switches would choose A.1 as leader because it has the lowest address. However, a network manager could customize the hierarchy and specify A.2.1 as leader.

Section 6.   Making Connections

Once the PNNI hierarchy is created, peer group leaders are elected, and routing information is exchanged, the ATM switches can begin to establish SVCs between various end stations on the network. Using the PNNI protocol, end stations on remote networks can easily establish SVCs across the hierarchy with other end stations in different peer groups.

With the PNNI protocol, signaling—the physical establishment of SVCs between two switches—is fully symmetrical, which means both parties involved in the communication perform the same functions. Although PNNI signaling is based on standard user network interface (UNI) 3.1 signaling, the PNNI protocol carries additional information needed to perform hierarchical source routing. Also, unlike standard UNI signaling, which defines distinct roles for the switch and the end station, the PNNI protocol is the same for each node, avoiding the need to configure one node in a connection as master and the other as slave.

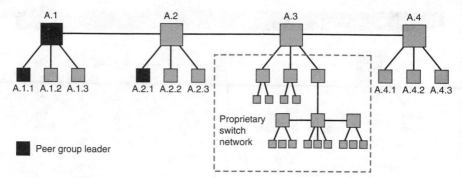

Figure 11.3 PNNI interoperability with proprietary interswitch protocols. PNNI allows a network that has already deployed proprietary interswitch routing protocols to continue to use them. Proprietary networks appear to the rest of the PNNI network as a single node and only one switch within that group shares routing information with the surrounding PNNI hierarchy.

In the hypothetical network of four backbone nodes described earlier, a request for an SVC from a user in Paris to a user in Atlanta will traverse several nodes before obtaining all the detailed routing information it needs to complete the circuit. To establish the connection, the user in Paris first sends the request to the local-area switch. The local switch recognizes that the address of the destination station is contained in the highest-level peer group associated with the node that represents the entire Atlanta campus. It then constructs a detailed path across its work group to the Paris campus backbone and a more general path that specifies that the request cross the campus backbone, access the international links, and cross to Atlanta.

As the SVC request progresses through the network, detail is supplied about the network topology, which was previously known only in summary form by the source. The campus switch in Paris knows from its peer group leader that, in this network, there is no direct connection between Paris and Atlanta. Any SVC request between Paris and Atlanta must first go through New York. But in New York, there are two campus switches, only one of which has connections to Atlanta. Because the Paris campus switch sees only a summarized version of the New York network, it does not distinguish between the two switches. If the request goes to the New York campus switch that is not connected to Atlanta, the switch uses the PNNI routing information, which it has received from its peer group leader, to forward the request to the switch that does have the connection to Atlanta.

At the Atlanta campus, the SVC request journeys down the PNNI hierarchy. The Atlanta campus switch, which receives the request, recognizes that the destination address belongs to one of its local work groups and routes the request to the appropriate work group switch, which can then complete the SVC request and establish a connection with the desired end station. Once the SVC between Paris and Atlanta is established, no additional route computation is required. The connection remains in place until it is no longer needed.

Although this routing process sounds complex, it occurs only when an SVC is set up—unlike IP traffic, which routes each individual packet. Once the connection is established, ATM cells are forwarded by simple table lookups. PNNI serves to set up the tables in each switch along the path so this can happen.

Section 7.   Quality and Quantity

Because PNNI defines the way in which SVCs between ATM switches are established, it also must provide a way to maintain quality-of-service guarantees. To guarantee quality of service, the network must allocate resources to SVCs as they are established. This leads to the possibility that unallocated capacity on some links will be insufficient to meet the quality-of-service requirements of a new SVC. Routing needs to deal with this situation. Paths must be selected that can deliver the specified quality of service for a particular SVC. PNNI distributes a rich set of metrics describing the abilities and capacities for various links in the network. These metrics can be used to establish quality-of-service objectives for the various traffic classes offered on an ATM network (such as constant bit rate, variable bit rate, and available bit rate). When an SVC is set up, nodes employ these metrics to eliminate links that are unable to meet the requested bandwidth and quality of service from the routing calculation. Routing then chooses the best path from this pruned topology.

An added challenge is created by the need to summarize routing information. Any description of the capacity of some summarized region has to strike a balance between being too optimistic and too pessimistic. Pessimistic metrics may cause a call to be blocked—equivalent to getting a busy signal in the phone network—when it could have been completed. Optimistic metrics may result in call setup attempts that cannot be completed, wasting network resources in processing and rerouting these false attempts. The balance between optimism and pessimism is made simpler by distributing more detailed information. This, however, must be traded off against the cost of distributing and processing the added detail. The way in which these tradeoffs are made depends upon the size of the network, the capacities of the links, and the SVC usage patterns. By default, each logical node in the PNNI hierarchy produces a summary representation of its capacity; however, a network manager can require a node to provide more complete information about available capacity, such as the quality-of-service parameters it can support to particular locations.

An additional mechanism called crank-back helps deal with the problems created by overly optimistic quality-of-service metrics. Each SVC setup message contains some basic routing information—at least enough to get from one point in the PNNI hierarchy to the next. At some node along that route, it may be discovered that resources are not available to complete the SVC. This can occur because summarized topology information gave the wrong indication for a particular path or because the resources required were allocated to another SVC while this SVC was in process. Crank-back allows a blocked SVC to be partially torn down and retried without intervention from the originating station.

12

ATM Service Classes

Section 1. Overview

Waste not, want not. ATM developers have taken that old saw to heart and come up with a new class of service that makes more efficient use of ATM network resources. The new service class, called available bit rate (ABR) service, lets users and carriers tap into idle bandwidth to transport data traffic across asynchronous transfer mode networks.

ABR relies on one key traffic management technique to balance the needs of its applications against those that use other ATM service classes: closed-loop rate-based flow control. Rate-based flow control allows switches to inform end stations of congestion in the network. Without it, transmitting end stations run a much higher risk of having cells dropped because of network congestion. This is a key issue for high-speed ATM networks, particularly given that they can provide service in wide-area as well as local-area environments, where huge amounts of data can be in transit at any one time (see Fig. 12.1).

Although requirements for ABR service have been agreed upon for more than a year, it has taken the ATM Forum some time to develop the standard flow control mechanisms required by ABR. Now that those mechanisms are in place, ABR can join the three other service classes already defined by the ATM Forum in accordance with its user

---

This chapter first appeared as an article in *Data Communications* magazine and was written by David Hughes and Kambiz Hooshmand at Stratacom Inc. (San Jose, CA).

Speed of link	No. of bytes in transit
9.6 Kbps	24
256 Kbps	640
155 Mbit/s	387,500
622 Mbit/s	1,555,000

Figure 12.1 Much at stake. It takes around 20 Ms for an ATM cell to travel via a transatlantic connection. ATM's very high bandwidth means that, at any instant, hundreds of thousands, or even millions, of bytes of data will be in transit. This makes efficient flow control a prerequisite for ATM. Source: IBM.

network interface (UNI) 3.0 specification. Those classes are constant bit rate (CBR), variable bit rate (VBR), and unspecified bit rate (UBR) service.

Services at a Glance

The ATM Forum has defined four distinct service classes for ATM networks:
- CBR (constant bit rate) service provides a virtual fixed-bandwidth transmission circuit. CBR is aimed primarily at applications that need a steady bandwidth supply, such as real-time video and voice traffic.
- VBR (variable bit rate) service is intended for bursty traffic, such as transaction processing applications and LAN interconnect. Applications can send data at higher burst rates, as long as overall data rates don't exceed a specified average. VBR includes real-time and non-real-time service classes (VBR-RT and VBR-NRT).
- UBR (unspecified bit rate) is the ATM Forum's equivalent of flying standby. Applications send data across the network with no guarantee when or if that data will arrive at its destination.
- ABR (available bit rate), like UBR, makes use of any available bandwidth, but intelligence built into the network helps guard against data loss by instructing sending stations to throttle back when the network is congested. Also, ABR service does provide minimum bandwidth guarantees to keep applications running.

Section 2. Class Distinctions

Although there is likely to be a great deal of excess bandwidth on ATM networks, it is almost impossible to predict exactly how much will be available at any given time. To make use of idle bandwidth, ABR traffic must be able to pick its spots and fill bandwidth that other applications don't need (see Fig. 12.2). In an ATM network, every time an application needs to set up a connection between two

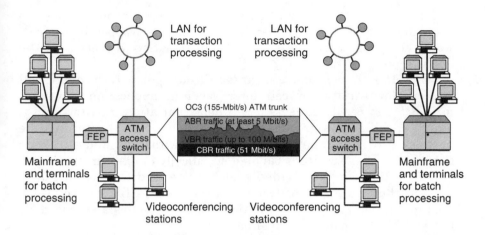

ABR = Available bit rate   FEP = Front-end processor
CBR = Constant bit rate   VBR = Variable bit rate

Figure 12.2 Filling the pipe with ATM traffic. The available bit rate (ABR) service class lets ATM users access idle bandwidth to transmit delay-tolerant traffic like data from batch-processing applications. Part of the ATM trunk can be dedicated to constant bit rate (CBR) traffic like real-time voice and video, with most of the balance allotted to variable bit rate (VBR) traffic like LAN data. Even when VBR traffic is heavy, ABR is assigned a minimal amount of bandwidth to keep applications running.

users, it must negotiate a traffic contract that specifies the connection's class of service. The ATM service classes cover a range of service parameters and quality-of-service guarantees. Service guarantees can define minimum levels of available bandwidth and ceilings on cell delay and cell loss (see Fig. 12.3).

CBR is the most straightforward type of ATM service class. When a network application sets up a CBR connection, it negotiates a peak cell rate (PCR), which is the maximum data rate the connection can support without risking cell loss. Data is then transmitted over that

Class of service	Bandwidth guarantee	Delay variation guarantee	Throughput guarantee	Congestion feedback
CBR	●	●	●	○
VBR	●	●	●	○
UBR	○	○	○	○
ABR	●	○	●	●

● YES   ○ NO

Figure 12.3 Classes of service.

connection at the requested rate—no more and, in most cases, no less. Any traffic above the specified rate may be dropped by the network; anything below the PCR will fail to satisfy the needs of the application.

CBR connections must guarantee throughput with minimal cell loss and low variation in cell delay. When an application negotiates for CBR service, it requests a cell delay variation tolerance limit, which specifies the greatest amount of jitter (variation in time between cells) that the transmission can withstand and still keep data intact. CBR service is tailored specifically to real-time voice and video traffic. Voice and video are characterized by constant data streams that are very sensitive to network delay. CBR service also is appropriate for T1 circuit emulation, which simulates a standard T1 (1.544-Mbit/s) line over an ATM network.

There are no defined data rate limits for CBR connections, and every virtual circuit on the ATM network can request a different constant data rate. The network must reserve the full bandwidth requested by the particular connection.

Section 3.   Variable Variations

VBR traffic includes two subclasses: VBR real-time (VBR-RT) and VBR non-real-time (VBR-NRT). VBR-RT imposes fairly tight bounds on cell delay and can be used to transmit information in real-time applications able to tolerate small amounts of cell delay variation, such as video generated by a variable-rate codec or aggregated voice traffic with silence removal. VBR-NRT, on the other hand, imposes less stringent limits on cell delay. It is designed specifically for transmission of short, bursty data messages, such as those encountered in transaction processing.

Compared with CBR service, VBR requires more complex negotiations between the application and the network. In addition to peak rates, VBR connections are subject to another negotiated cap: the sustained cell rate (SCR), or the average throughput rate the application is permitted. The user can burst above the SCR (up to the PCR) for short periods, but the VBR connection will maintain the SCR as the average by adjusting subsequent traffic flow at a lower rate for a corresponding period of time.

As with a CBR connection, the application and network must agree on the PCR and the cell delay variation tolerance. But unlike CBR, VBR connections must set a limit on how long they can transmit at the PCR. If this limit, known as the *burst tolerance,* is exceeded, a period of lower activity must follow to meet the SCR. These periods of lower activity, during which vast amounts of network bandwidth may be idle, offer an opportunity for other types of traffic, such as ABR, to access the network.

As with CBR, VBR users receive guaranteed quality of service with respect to cell loss, cell delay variation, and bandwidth availability so long as traffic meets the specified criteria. However, for many data applications, which can be particularly bursty and hard to characterize, it is impossible to accurately predict traffic contract parameters. Transaction processing and LAN-to-LAN traffic, for example, are intrinsically unpredictable, with variations too large for a meaningful traffic contract to be negotiated.

As a result, network managers responsible for these applications have three options. They can pay for additional bandwidth that may remain unused. They can try to manage transmission bursts carefully (a difficult task in most applications). Or they can exceed the traffic contract and sacrifice quality-of-service guarantees. For those who choose the third course, the most likely consequence is also the most costly: cell loss. Dropped cells must be retransmitted by the sending device. This can be a severe problem in mission-critical applications. In lower-priority applications, such as electronic mail, cell retransmissions are a resource- and time-consuming nuisance.

Section 4.   The UBR Spec

Unlike CBR and VBR service, UBR provides no specified bit rate, no traffic parameters, and no quality-of-service guarantees. It offers only "best effort" delivery with no guarantees regarding cell loss, cell delay, or cell delay variation. Devised originally to make use of excess bandwidth, UBR offers a partial, but inadequate, solution for those unpredictable bursty applications that don't readily conform to traffic contract parameters.

UBR's biggest deficiencies are its lack of flow control and inability to take other traffic types into account. When the network becomes overloaded, UBR connections go right on transmitting. Network switches can buffer some of this incoming traffic, but once the buffers are full, cells are dropped. And because UBR connections have no traffic management contract with the network, theirs are the first cells to go. UBR cell loss can be so great that "goodput" (successful throughput) can easily fall to below 50 percent—an unacceptable level.

Section 5.   Bursty Data Transport

Like UBR, ABR exploits excess network bandwidth, but it uses traffic management techniques to gauge network congestion and avoid cell loss. ABR is the first ATM class of service to provide reliable transport for bursty data applications.

As with CBR and VBR, when an application requests an ABR connection, it negotiates with the network for a PCR. However, it does not request specific cell delay variation tolerance or burst tolerance parameters. Instead, the application and the network agree to a minimum cell rate requirement. This guarantees the application a small amount of bandwidth—typically, the minimum required to keep the application up and running. The ABR user agrees not to transmit at rates above the PCR, and the network agrees always to provide at least the minimum cell rate (MCR).

MCR is calculated in cells per second, based on the application's ability to tolerate latency. For example, if the application needs a 1-Mbyte file (approximately 20,000 ATM cells) to arrive at its destination in no more than 2 seconds, the required MCR for that application is 10,000 cells per second. An application requesting ABR service is not required to specify peak and minimum cell rates, but instead can simply accept the network default settings. In such cases, the PCR defaults to the access rate and the MCR defaults to zero.

Users of ABR receive guaranteed quality of service with respect to cell loss and bandwidth availability within the parameters defined by the traffic descriptors. As to cell delay, although it is kept to a minimum, ABR offers no absolute guarantees. Hence, ABR is meant for non-real-time applications in which data is not extremely delay-sensitive.

CBR, VBR, and UBR make no attempt to control congestion from within the network. CBR and VBR rely instead on the threat of cell loss to keep applications from exceeding their PCR limits. But ABR is able to take advantage of idle bandwidth because it has the intelligence to know when that bandwidth is available. It accomplishes this through *closed-loop congestion management,* a feedback technology that lets end stations know when to transmit and when to slow down. ABR's congestion management system is made possible by the ATM Forum's rate-based flow control specification. ABR gives network users and service providers a great deal of flexibility in defining services. With a service such as VBR, as utilization goes up, the potential for cell loss also increases. With ABR, when increasing use causes congestion, the congestion control mechanism slows transmission into the network until the traffic clears. Delay increases slightly, but there is no increase in cell loss.

The ATM Forum's ABR specification requires a closed-loop congestion control mechanism. However, there are several levels of feedback that switch makers and network service providers can implement (see Fig. 12.4). And there are a number of different feedback loops available for ABR (see Fig. 12.5).

The simplest is an end-to-end control loop that uses explicit forward congestion indication (EFCI) messages from the switches. These

Mechanism	Switch functions	End-station functions
Explicit forward congestion indication (EFCI)	All switches passively forward resource management cells; if congested, switches set EFCI indicator in cell headers	Destination end station returns latest EFCI information in periodic resource management cells; source responds by raising or lowering its rate
Explicit rate marking (ERM)	ERM switches add rate-adjustment information to resource management cells	Same as EFCI end stations, except that source end station may also respond to explicit rate instructions
Segmented virtual source/virtual destination (VS/VD)	Switches act as virtual end stations; the network is segmented into smaller feedback loops	Source end-station functions are the same as for ERM, but network reliance on correct end-station behavior is diminished (creating a firewall)
Hop-by-hop virtual source/virtual destination (VS/VD)	All switches function as virtual end stations; the network is segmented into link-by-link feedback loops	Source end-station functions are the same as for ERM, but network reliance on correct end-station behavior is diminished (creating a firewall)

Figure 12.4   Feedback mechanisms.

messages are piggybacked onto data cells, which notify the destination station of the congested conditions. That end station then sends a message contained in a special resource management cell back through the network to the source station, instructing it to reduce its transmission rate.

In this method, the end stations bear most of the responsibility for flow control, with the intermediate switches playing a passive role in the feedback process. The ATM switch does not itself implement a closed-loop feedback mechanism; it merely sets a congestion indication bit in the ATM cell header of a resource management cell going in the forward direction. The feedback loop is closed by the destination end station.

Section 6.   Simple Problems

In any heterogeneous network environment, especially a public WAN, there are significant problems with this simple feedback method:

- If either the source or the destination station does not support ABR (and as yet no end-station ATM equipment or application does, because the specification is too new), the end-to-end feedback loop will not work.

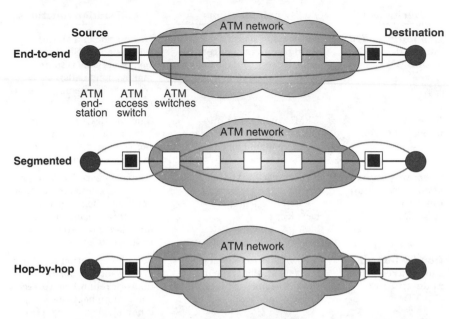

Figure 12.5 Getting into the ATM feedback loop. Three levels of congestion control are available for ATM networks in end-to-end schemes, the destination end station sends a message to the transmitting station when congestion arises. With segmented control, specially equipped switches in the ATM network can close the feedback loop, acting as a network firewall. Hop-by-hop control, in which each switch has congestion-control intelligence, provides the most thorough form of control.

- If either of the end stations is malfunctioning, the end-to-end feedback loop will not work.

- Network switches must buffer incoming packets until congestion information can travel from the switch to the destination station; the instruction to throttle down transmission then travels back through the network to the source station. The larger the feedback loop, the more buffer space each switch will have to allocate for packets that arrive between notification and reduced transmission.

A more sophisticated feedback mechanism called explicit rate marking (ERM) allows switches to participate to a greater degree in the feedback control loop. In an ERM scheme, switches can add to the feedback instructions provided by the destination end station. As resource management cells containing flow control information travel from the destination station back to the source, the switches can use ERM to "mark" these cells, indicating that even greater traffic reductions are needed.

ERM somewhat improves the performance of the feedback loop, but the switches are still partially dependent on the end stations to implement congestion control. And although switches that use ERM can be combined in the same network with those that use only EFCI, the overall performance of the feedback loop will not improve much unless all switches can use ERM and indicate their congestion levels to the network as a whole. Ending the reliance on end stations for end-to-end congestion control requires the creation of smaller feedback control loops within the switched network. To achieve this, the ATM Forum's ABR specification also defines a rate-based feedback scheme known as a segmented virtual source/virtual destination (VS/VD) control loop. Switches equipped with VS/VD capability are positioned in strategic locations throughout the network, breaking the feedback loop into smaller segments.

In the virtual destination function, switches can respond to EFCI notification as an ordinary destination station would, thereby closing the congestion control feedback loop. Acting as a virtual source end station, which can send its own resource management cells to either real or virtual end stations, the switches create a second feedback loop that can exert additional control over traffic flow. VS/VD switches also can use and respond to ERM to improve performance further.

VS/VD does more than solve the problems caused by depending on end stations to close the ATM network's end-to-end feedback loop. When placed at the interface between a private ATM network (such as a campus LAN) and a public ATM WAN, a VS/VD switch acts as a firewall, insulating the public network from non-ABR-compliant end stations, and from end stations that disobey feedback instructions from resource management cells. In the process, it creates smaller, more manageable feedback loops, enabling switches to handle more traffic with fewer buffers.

By placing VS/VD-compliant switches at various points within the network, designers can create smaller segments. This is important, because smaller feedback control loops reduce the delay in reporting congestion to transmitting end stations. If every switch in the ATM network has VS/VD capability, the feedback loop can be closed at every node. This approach, called hop-by-hop VS/VD, offers the greatest control, but it also requires each switch to contain a fair amount of intelligence, adding to network expense.

Section 7.   The Buffering Challenge

The second means by which ABR traffic manages to tolerate delay, avoid cell loss, and implement efficient flow control is through extensive cell buffering. Not surprisingly, the size of the buffers on an ATM switch has a significant impact on the switch's performance. The more data a switch can buffer in memory (up to a certain measure), the less likely it is that cell loss will occur and retransmissions will be required. But buffering must be structured in an efficient way that enables priority traffic to get through without other, less time-critical data being discarded.

The theoretical minimum buffer size required for a single source, or port, on a WAN switch supporting ABR is determined by the amount of bandwidth multiplied by the round-trip transmission time. This formula simply expresses in arithmetic terms the obvious fact that an ATM switch must be able to buffer incoming cells for as long as it takes for flow control information to reach the source end station and reduce the flow of traffic into the network.

Section 8.   Separate But Equal

A VS/VD switch should also have separate buffer queues for each virtual connection. This focuses traffic management on specific connections and prevents virtual circuits operating within their predetermined specifications from slowing down. For example, if an end station fails to respond to a resource management cell requesting slower transmission, it will not deprive others connected to that same switch of their requested bandwidth. When buffering is handled on a per-circuit basis, the excess cells fill up and overflow only the misbehaving connection's buffers. Other connections have enough space in their buffers to avoid cell loss, provided they comply with flow control information in the resource management cells.

Many ATM switches now available have too little buffer space to support ABR, or use common buffers for all virtual circuits rather than offer per-circuit buffering. Others use first-in, first-out buffering schemes. These place traffic from many virtual connections in one common memory pool, which can cause applications that have not violated their traffic management parameters to be unnecessarily penalized.

Section 9.   The Bandwidth Police

Service policing prioritizes an application's access to network bandwidth according to the class of service it uses. Up to now, most ATM switches implemented a simple, one-pass service policy scheme that gave CBR traffic first priority, placed VBR second, and left UBR for last. Under this type of scheme, the combination of CBR and VBR can potentially freeze out traffic using the other classes of service. But such prioritization will not work with ABR, which requires at least its minimum cell rate guarantee. Some bandwidth must be allocated for ABR traffic.

For ABR to work properly, the ATM switch or network must implement a two-pass service policing algorithm that can meet the requirements of CBR, VBR, and ABR. In this scheme, the switch delivers a certain amount of bandwidth to each class of service. CBR traffic receives the bandwidth necessary to meet its peak cell rate limit; VBR traffic receives the bandwidth necessary to fulfill its sustained cell rate specification—the average demand for VBR connections; and ABR receives the bandwidth necessary to meet its minimum cell rate requirement. This ensures that each connection can remain up and running without cell loss, but does not deliver ABR traffic at the expense of CBR or VBR. On the second pass of this two-stage algorithm, CBR and VBR traffic can consume all the network bandwidth if necessary, since the ABR connection will have met its minimum cell rate guarantee.

The ATM Forum's traffic management subworking group has been laboring over ABR since mid-1993, but only recently has the group settled on the rate-based congestion control that makes ABR possible. While the group does not have a final draft of the ABR specification, the bulk of its work is complete. Note: This topic is still under debate. Also on the horizon is another service class, now known as VBR+. This service class promises not only a closed-loop feedback control system but also guarantees about cell delay. The ATM Forum is considering this specification, but no timetable has been set for its development.

ABR can provide fast, fair access to large amounts of ATM bandwidth. In doing so, it promises to make good on one of ATM's long-standing promises: available bandwidth on demand. The way a given switch or network implements the ATM Forum's specified ABR functionality will determine just how well it delivers on this promise. ABR gives switch makers some leeway in implementing traffic management techniques. A successful ABR implementation is one that provides users with a high rate of successful data throughput, low cell loss, minimal cell delay, quick access to excess network bandwidth, fair allocation of available bandwidth, and minimum cell rate guarantees.

13

25-Mbit/s ATM

Section 1. Overview

Back at the start of the 1990s, when the internetworking industry first started talking seriously about employing ATM in local area networks, conventional wisdom had it that the technology would thrive on the campus backbone before it arrived on the desktop. But that was when everyone assumed that ATM would run at 155 Mbit/s or faster. In 1993, some vendors started talking up the benefits of building lower-speed (and lower-cost) ATM switches and adapters which would be designed and priced to jump-start the uptake of end-to-end ATM. The ATM Forum initially threw out a 25-Mbit/s blueprint in favor of a 51-Mbit/s proposal, but subsequently reversed its decision—triggering a wave of 25-Mbit/s product announcements.

Several vendors now ship 25-Mbit/s ATM switches and adapters including: ATML (Cambridge, UK), Connectware Inc. (San Jose, CA), First Virtual Corp. (Santa Clara, CA), IBM Corp. (Armonk, NY), and Whitetree Network Technologies Inc. (Palo Alto, CA). Additionally, in 1995 Optical Data Systems Inc. (Richardson, TX) announced a line of products based on 25-Mbit/s ATM technology from IBM, promising to develop its own line of low-speed ATM hardware at a later date. Such products have made small but significant inroads into the high-speed LAN market, and caused market forecasters to rejig their predictions for ATM usage in LANs upward. Electronic Trend Publications (San Jose, CA) predicts that total U.S. ATM LAN market revenue will jump from $807 million in 1995 to $2404 million in 1998.

Price is the main selling point for these products: a 25-Mbit/s network can be had for as little as $750 per node. That's roughly a third of the price of a 155-Mbit/s network. It's also competitive with Ethernet switches, and is actually less than the price of token ring switch solutions—its chief competitors. Of course, upgrading to ATM is more of a hassle. LAN switches replace LAN hubs in the wiring closet but work with the adapters already installed in users' workstations. Moving to ATM means swapping out all the adapters, and that means lots of work and considerable network downtime.

Other than price, 25-Mbit/s ATM owes its popularity to its ability to make the migration to high-speed networking easy for net managers: 25-Mbit/s adapters typically come with free LAN emulation software, which lets net managers run current applications unaltered over ATM. And the products work with low-cost Category 3 UTP (unshielded twisted pair), which accounts for over 50 percent of the cabling installed in U.S. corporations. Further, 25-Mbit/s ATM has some significant advantages over Ethernet switches and token ring switches, allowing net managers to leverage the benefits of a scalable, connection-oriented, virtual circuit technology that is equally adept at handling time-sensitive multimedia as it is at carrying asynchronous data. It also delivers more bandwidth—25-Mbit/s to each and every network node—and does so easily enough to handle mainstream applications (see Fig. 13.1).

This chapter describes how 25-Mbit/s ATM became a standard and how it works, and then gives detailed descriptions of the offerings from some of the vendors selling 25-Mbit/s ATM products today.

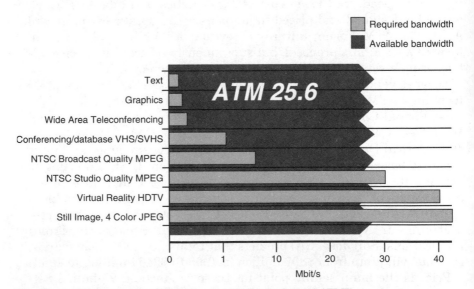

Figure 13.1 Applications and their bandwidth needs. Source: ATML.

Section 2.   The Origins

The first moves to create a low-speed ATM specification took place in March 1993, when IBM first presented a 25.6-Mbit/s proposal, and AT&T countered with a 51.8-Mbit/s spec. In September of that year, the ATM working group looking into the proposals gave the thumbs-down to the 25-Mbit/s spec and voted to proceed only with the faster version. Proponents of the scheme refused to take no for an answer. Some 25 of them banded together in an industry body called the DeskTop ATM25 Alliance, which reproposed the 25-Mbit/s spec in November 1994. However, just to make things interesting, PMC-Sierra Inc. (Burnaby, British Columbia) countered with a 25.9-Mbit/s alternative which used Sonet encoding. Members of the physical layer subcommittee voted it down 35 to 12, and the 25.6-Mbit/s proposal was finally approved in 1995. While 51-Mbit/s ATM still has an ATM Forum stamp of approval, products have yet to appear.

One of the beauties of the 25.6-Mbit/s ATM proposal is that it allows equipment vendors to reuse some existing LAN components— and so keep equipment costs down. Specifically, the physical media-dependent (PMD) transceivers used in 25-Mbit/s ATM cards are typically identical to the ones vendors already use in their token ring adapters and hubs. However, instead of token ring's Manchester encoding methodology, the ATM products use new silicon that uses a 4b5b transmission control layer encoding scheme to send and receive data at 25.6 Mbit/s.

Section 3.   Whitetree's WS3000 Work Group Switch

As mentioned, there are currently several vendors shipping 25-Mbit/s ATM hardware. Each has its own value-added take on the technology. Whitetree's is easy to spot: Its WS3000 switch is the only one which supports both Ethernet and ATM on every port. By supporting either 10-Mbit/s switched Ethernet *or* 25.6-Mbit/s ATM on each port, the WS3000 enables net managers to migrate their networks from switched Ethernet to ATM via a single switch platform, and eliminates the need for two equipment upgrades—one when the Ethernet switch goes in, another when it gets trashed to make way for an ATM switch.

To make the segue to ATM even sweeter, the ports on the WS3000 automatically detect if they are connected to ATM or Ethernet equipment—dynamically switching to the right protocol and speed without the need for any reconfiguration by the net manager.

Even though it's equipped to play two network roles, the WS3000 is priced to compete against conventional Ethernet work group switches. It costs $650 per 10/25-Mbit/s port. The average price of Ethernet work group switches is roughly $500 per port. In addition to its switch, Whitetree is shipping a 25-Mbit/s ATM adapter for PCI workstations costing $395. In standard configuration, the WS3000 ($7795) is supplied as a standalone switch equipped with twelve RJ-45 ports. For larger configurations, up to twelve WS3000s can be stacked on top of each other for a total capacity of up to 144 ports. Modules in the same stack are connected over short drop cables using Whitetree's Stacking Bus Module, which carries traffic between the switches using two 622-Mbit/s bidirectional rings. The Stacking Bus Module ($995) fits into one of two available "option" slots on the back of the WS3000. The other option slot can be used for a 155-Mbit/s ATM module supporting either fiber ($1395) or copper ($995) cabling. This high-speed ATM link can be used to connect the switch over a backbone campus connection to a variety of devices—including ATM routers, switches, servers, workstations, or remote WS3000s. The switch supports both permanent virtual circuits (PVCs) and switched virtual circuits (SVCs).

The WS3000 switches both ATM and Ethernet packets as cells, using ASICs developed in house by Whitetree. Here's how that works. As traffic arrives at the WS3000, the switch exploits the fact that ATM and Ethernet use different pins on the RJ-45 connectors on each switch port to detect whether it is receiving cells or packets; 53-byte

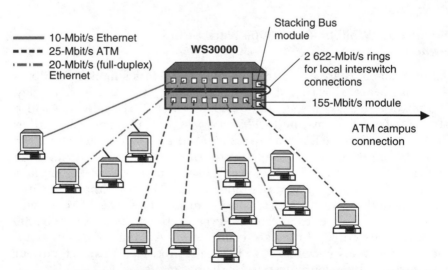

Figure 13.2 Whitetree's two-timing switch. Each port on a Whitetree WS3000 Workgroup Switch can be configured to handle either 10-Mbit/s Ethernet, full-duplex (20-Mbit/s) Ethernet, or 25.6-Mbit/s ATM traffic. Up to a dozen of the 12-port switches can be stacked via drop cables attached to Stacking Bus modules.

ATM cells are forwarded in native format directly over the WS3000's switching matrix. Ethernet packets are first stored in a memory buffer (where off-kilter packets are trashed) and then converted into ATM cells by a segmentation and reassembly (SAR) ASIC before being switched. The cells are reconverted to Ethernet packet format by another ASIC at the outgoing Ethernet port. (The WS3000 also can transfer traffic between ATM and Ethernet links, in accordance with ATM Forum LAN emulation specifications.) With ATM-to-ATM connections, the latency (network delay) for each 53-byte cell is 5 microseconds. For Ethernet-to-Ethernet traffic delay increases in proportion to packet size. Latency for a 64-byte packet is 40 microseconds. Latency for a 1500-byte Ethernet packet is 1.24 milliseconds.

The WS3000 comes with a 1024-entry MAC address table, enabling net managers to attach multiple Ethernet devices to each port. Alternatively, for maximum performance, net managers can opt to connect only one device to each port and transmit traffic at 20 Mbit/s using full-duplex Ethernet technology. For full duplex to work, however, the node at the other end of the connection must also be equipped with a full-duplex adapter. Each WS3000 is equipped with its own SNMP agent. The agent supports MIB I, MIB II, the SNMP bridge MIB, and a proprietary Whitetree MIB. It also comes with a prestandard version of the ADAM MIB (designed to allow SNMP management of ATM equipment). The switch can be monitored and configured using Whitetree's WM1000 Configuration Management System ($995) management software package, which runs under Microsoft Windows. The WM1000 can be used to assign ports on different WS3000s in the same stack to different virtual LANs.

A flaw with the WS3000 is that it doesn't provide a way to analyze switched traffic. Unlike some LAN switches, Whitetree's box lacks RMON (remote monitoring) agent software, and it doesn't have a port-mirroring facility that allows traffic to be copied to an external analyzer. Net managers in the mood to monitor have only two approaches open to them: either shift an analyzer from port to port (inconvenient), or buy an RMON agent for each Ethernet segment attached to the switch (pricey).

Section 4.   IBM's Turboways Adapter

IBM thinks it can jump-start 25-Mbit/s ATM by making net managers an offer they can't refuse: 25.6-Mbit/s Turboways ATM adapters for ISA workstations at $405 a pop—$30 less than it charges for its 16-Mbit/s token ring ISA cards. The Turboways adapter comes with free LAN emulation software also. IBM was due to ship a 25-Mbit/s switch to go with its adapter by the end of 1995. In the meantime, the vendor

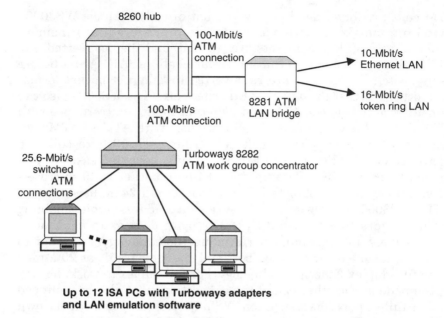

8260 hub

100-Mbit/s
ATM
connection

10-Mbit/s
Ethernet LAN

16-Mbit/s
token ring LAN

8281 ATM
LAN bridge

100-Mbit/s
ATM connection

25.6-Mbit/s
switched
ATM
connections

Turboways 8282
ATM work group concentrator

Up to 12 ISA PCs with Turboways adapters
and LAN emulation software

ISA = Industry Standard Architecture

Figure 13.3 ATM to the desktop. IBM's Turboways 25-Mbit/s ATM adapter card slots into ISA PCs and works in conjunction with other ATM gear from Big Blue or other vendors.

also offers an interim solution: The Turboways 8282 ATM Workgroup Concentrator allows up to twelve 25-Mbit/s workstations to share a 100-Mbit/s Taxi (transparent asynchronous transmitter/receiver interface) port on an ATM switch module in its 8260 hub. IBM also sells the 8281 ATM LAN Bridge, which is used to link conventional Ethernets or token rings to an ATM network through the 8260 (see Fig. 13.3). IBM also says its adapter can be used in conjunction with the products from other vendors supporting the 25.6-Mbit/s proposal. The Turboways adapter supports both PVCs (permanent virtual circuits) and SVCs (switched virtual circuits) in accordance with the ATM Forum UNI (user network interface) Version 3.0. In the absence of a LAN emulation spec, IBM has gone ahead and implemented a proprietary scheme. The vendor says its cards will be upgraded in software when the ATM Forum finishes up its spec.

IBM implements two types of flow control between the adapter cards and concentrator: buffering and direct control of data transmission. Both the adapters and the concentrator are equipped with 4- to 8-kbyte buffers, which serve to even out bursty LAN traffic and avoid congestion. Further, if the concentrator buffer fills up, it can signal the adapter to stop transmitting using X-on/X-off. IBM says it is working on 25-Mbit/s adapters for MCA (microchannel architecture), PCI (peripheral component interface), and S-Bus machines.

Section 5.   ATML's Virata Product Family

Instead of developing just a switch or an adapter, ATML has gone all out—creating a suite of 25-MBit/s ATM products that deliver 25 Mbit/s to the desktop, 155 Mbit/s to the backbone, and support for multimedia applications.

The family consists of the Virata switch, the Virata Link ATM PC adapter card, and the Virata Store server. ATML says its products are designed to allow an incremental move to ATM. That means that net managers don't need to rip out their existing hardware and soft-ware—they hook their current Ethernet to the ATM switch with an interface furnished by the vendor. Ethernet applications continue to run via the vendor's LAN emulation software. On the downside, the single 10-Mbit/s link used to connect the ATM side of the network with the Ethernet side creates a traffic bottleneck, adversely affecting performance. (In its defense, ATML says that Ethernet bandwidth would be freed up when big users are shifted from Ethernet to ATM, thus reducing the chances of a bottleneck.) Another glitch—ATML sells only an ISA adapter.

The Virata switch has 12 RJ-45 ports for 25-Mbit/s ATM connec-tions to PCs and three expansion slots that can be used for expansion cards. Three cards are available. The ATM155 Switch Expansion Card adds two 155-Mbit/s ATM ports for making a high-bandwidth connection to the corporate backbone, to the Virata Store server, or to another stacked Virata switch. The Ethernet Switch Expansion Card can be used for a 10-Mbit/s connection to the Ethernet hub or switch, and the ATM25 Switch Expansion Card furnishes 4 additional 25-Mbit/s ports. Support for multimedia applications sets the Virata family apart from most other 25 Mbit/s ATM offerings. According to ATML, the Virata Store multimedia server differs from normal servers in using mechanisms to guarantee smooth picture quality when handling up to 25 simultaneous streams of video over the LAN. The Virata Store comes with 8 Gbytes of storage—enough to store up to four compressed feature-length films. It is connected to the Virata switch via a 155-Mbit/s connection.

In its next batch of 25-Mbit/s peripherals, ATML is planning to include ATM video cameras and display screens as part of an inte-grated videoconferencing system. A 16-Gbyte version of the Virata Store is also in the works. ATML has priced the Virata switch at about $500 per port, although users will need the Virata Link card if they're moving from Ethernet, and that pushes the price to $900 per port (a basic 12-port Virata switch costs $6500, and the Virata Link costs $395). The ATM155 Switch Expansion Card, containing two high-bandwidth ports, costs $3000. The Ethernet Switch Expansion Card, providing a 10-Mbit/s connection to the Ethernet, costs $1500. The ATM25 Switch Expansion Card costs $1200. The PCI bus version of Virata Link is expected to cost $550. The 8-Gbyte Virata Store costs $25,000.

Section 6.   First Virtual Corp.'s Product Family

ATML's product line bears a remarkable likeness to the one from First Virtual Corp. (FVC). That's actually no coincidence. At one time the two companies collaborated, and used common silicon technology developed by Olivetti.

Like ATML, VFC offers three primary components—a switch, an adapter, and a media server, which is actually a network-attached RAID (redundant array of inexpensive disks). It also supplies the media operating system (MOS), a middleware package that buffers the application from the network and shields programmers from the underlying complexities of the hardware. Also like ATML, FVC's family of products creates an ATM work group that's linked to an Ethernet. End users have 25-Mbit/s ATM links to the switch, which also connects to both the LAN file server (through an Ethernet interface) and the media server via a 155-Mbit/s connection (see Fig. 13.4).

The client portion of MOS resides on the end user's PC between the applications and the LAN emulation software, where it sets up real-time calls for voice, video, and audio. MOS also has a component that runs on the media server. MOS allows video to be stored to the work group's ATM media server. Users can then download the data from their desktops, thanks to the video applications they're running. These programs include any that use OLE (object linking and embedding) object libraries, as well as any written to Video for Windows. OLE and Video for Windows are APIs (application program interfaces) developed by Microsoft.

The MOS client requires a 25-MHz 486 PC running Windows 3.1 with 8 Mbytes of RAM and a 160-Mbyte hard drive. MOS costs $2000 for 10 users; $12,000, for 30 users (not counting hardware). A 4-Gbyte media server sells for $15,000; $20,000 buys 8 Gbytes. The media server is the work of First Virtual and Conner Peripherals Inc. (San Jose, CA). The switch costs $5300 with eight 25-Mbit/s ports, two 155-Mbit/s ports, and one 10-Mbit/s Ethernet port. Adapter cards list for $330 to $1200 apiece.

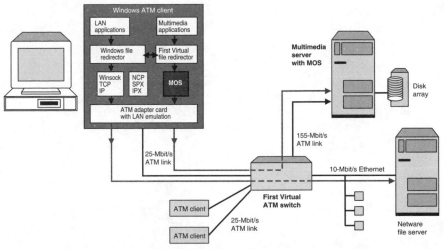

Figure 13.4 FVC's multimedia ATM network. First Virtual's Media Operating System makes it possible to run PC-based multimedia packages over ATM. In essence, MOS redirects real-time data streams to a multimedia server while fooling the PC into thinking it's working locally. Requests to the LAN file server are handled by the LAN emulation card.

Section 7.   Connectware's Cellerity Product Family

Connectware has 10 products in its 25-Mbit/s range. They include three types of network interface cards: EISA bus ($595), PCI bus ($495 to $839), and Silicon Graphic GIO-32 bus ($1695 to $1795). Connectware also sells a 16-port 25-Mbit/s ATM switch ($550 per port), the Cellerity 6100, which can be extended to 32 ports with an expansion unit ($8500). To provide a connection from the ATM network to legacy LANs, Connectware sells the Cellerity 6210 ATM/LAN Bridge ($5495)—a stackable module which connects to the switch and allows up to four Ethernet or token ring LANs to exchange traffic with the ATM network. Rounding out Connectware's portfolio is the Cellerity 3300 Remote ATM/LAN Bridge Router ($5995), which allows the 6100 switch to up to four remote Ethernet and token ring LANs.

All Connectware products are based around its single-chip segmentation and reassembly chip (SAR chip), one of the first to support the ATM Forum's available bit rate (ABR) flow control specification. Connectware currently OEM's IBM's LAN emulation software, with support from both PVCs and SVCs.

14

Assessing the ATM State of the Art

Section 1. Overview

Networking vendors are notorious for exaggerating the abilities of their products—even when, in some cases, those products have yet to make it off the whiteboard and onto the network. Nowhere is the gulf between technology and reality wider than in the world of ATM. The only way to determine what today's ATM products are truly capable of is to plug them in and find out. Fortunately, that's exactly what *Data Communications* magazine teamed up with the European Network Laboratories (ENL, Paris) to do in 1995.

The goal was simple: find out if ATM switch boxes have really got what it takes to deliver delay-sensitive multimedia traffic while being buffeted by bursty data. After all, that's what ATM is all about. Overall, the tests demonstrated that ATM switches still have a way to go before they justify their manufacturers' hyperbole. The ENL/Data Comm test focused on the switching engine. The original plan also called for tests of UNI 3.1 signaling, rate-based flow control, and LAN emulation. But the testers soon discovered that most vendors haven't yet implemented these features. Until they do, their ATM switches are limited to single-vendor, ATM-only networks and ATM-specific applications. Just getting the goods on ATM switching engines meant asking—and answering—a lot of tough questions:

This chapter first appeared as an article in *Data Communications* magazine and was written by Robert Mandeville at European Network Laboratories (ENL, Paris).

How quickly and consistently can these switches move ATM (asynchronous transfer mode) traffic? What sorts of latency and jitter are inherent in their architectures? How well can this gear stand up to the barrage of traffic that's going to be common on campus and enterprise backbones?

That's just for starters. Effective ATM switching means more than shunting cells at top speed. The ability to cope with different types of traffic, at different data rates and under different loads, is what separates the leading switches from the also-rans. That's where traffic management and buffering come in. A switch must be able to strike a balance between consistently low latency (the time it takes a cell to pass through a device) and efficient cell buffering (the memory and queueing required to handle congestion and bursty traffic). To make sure all the products were given a complete workout, ENL designed its own suite of ATM benchmarks, ATM Perform. It consists of seven tests that measure latency and jitter and determine how well a box contends with bursts and protects delay-sensitive traffic

Section 2.   The Methodology

Fourteen vendors were invited to participate in the ATM test: Bay Networks Inc. (Santa Clara, CA), Cisco Systems Inc. (San Jose, CA), Digital Equipment Corp. (DEC, Maynard, MA), Fore Systems Inc. (Warrendale, PA), Fujitsu Network Switching of America Inc. (Raleigh, NC), General Datacomm Inc. (Middlebury, CT), Hughes Network Systems Inc. (Germantown, MD), IBM, Lightstream Corp. (Billerica, MA), NEC America Inc. (San Jose, CA), Network Equipment Technologies Inc. (Redwood City, CA), Newbridge Networks Corp. (Herndon, VA), Northern Telecom Ltd. (Mississauga, Ontario), and 3Com Corp. (Santa Clara, CA). Seven accepted the challenge, and the lab tested the following switches: the Lattiscell from Bay, Hyperswitch A100 from Cisco, Gigaswitch ATM from DEC, Forerunner ASX-200 from Fore, Lightstream 2020 from Lightstream, Mainstreet 36150 from Newbridge, and Cellplex 7000 from 3Com. All vendors submitted switches configured with a minimum of four 155-Mbit/s OC3c ports, supporting either single-mode or multimode fiber.

ENL's ATM Perform evaluates the performance and traffic management capabilities of ATM switches. The test suite was run on an ATM-100 analyzer from Wandel & Goltermann (Eningen, Germany). ATM Perform's four performance and three traffic management tests share a common format. One virtual circuit serves as the basis for all the measurements. Cells on this circuit are switched either twice or four times by the device under test. This is achieved by feeding traffic out of one port and back into the switch a second (or a third and fourth) time via an OC3c 155.52-Mbit/s fiber link to two ports. The technique, known as *tromboning,* takes advantage of ATM's full-duplex capabilities and makes it possible to fully load a switch from a single source. The ATM-100 analyzer matches incoming and outgoing cells, records cell delay and cell interarrival times, and calculates standard deviations. It also verifies the integrity of the cell headers and payload field and reports cell loss and cell sequence integrity errors.

- Performance Test 1 produces baseline values for cell delay and cell delay variations. The traffic generator transmits a single 7.488-Mbit/s stream across a single virtual circuit. Cells are transmitted at regular intervals of one cell every 20 cell times, which effectively makes the traffic behave like a CBR (constant bit rate) stream. Traffic on the virtual circuit is switched through two of the switch's four ports; no other traffic is run through the switch while the test is performed.

- Performance Test 2 verifies whether cell delay per hop stays constant when the number of hops through the switch increases. The generator transmits the same 7.488-Mbit/s stream, but the virtual circuit traverses all four switch ports.

- Performance Test 3 checks for any degradation in transit time when all the ports under test are fully loaded. In this test, the generator transmits 100 sources of 1.498-Mbit/s traffic over a single virtual circuit, for a total throughput of 149.8 Mbit/s. SDH (synchronous digital hierarchy) framing uses the remaining 5.72 Mbit/s in the 155.52-Mbit/s interface, so the virtual circuit is fully loaded. The virtual circuit is switched in and out of all four full-duplex switch ports, so the total load on the switch is 1.244 Gbit/s.

- Performance Test 4 checks for cross talk between fully loaded and lightly loaded switch ports. The tester generates two parallel streams of traffic, with each stream running through the switch twice on separate ports. The first stream is generated by a single CBR source at 7.488 Mbit/s. The second stream consists of VBR (variable bit rate) traffic generated at loads ranging from 1.498 Mbit/s to a full 149.8 Mbit/s.

- Traffic Management Test 1 verifies the ability of a switch to protect delay-sensitive CBR traffic when it is sent to an overloaded port. Two streams of traffic, a CBR stream at 7.488 Mbit/s and a VBR stream ranging from 0 to 149.8 Mbit/s, are sent to the same port. The analyzer records the effects of congestion on the performance of the 7.488-Mbit/s CBR stream.

- Traffic Management Test 2 attempts to initiate a buffering and queuing problem known as *head-of-the-line blocking*. This term refers to instances in which high-priority traffic is inadvertently delayed in a switch buffer because low-priority traffic is in the queue ahead of it. In this test, two CBR streams running at 7.488 Mbit/s and 74.9 Mbit/s are switched from a single port to two different ports, one of which is overloaded by a stream of 149.8 Mbit/s. The test verifies whether the CBR stream, which is not switched to the overloaded port, slows down or loses cells.

- Traffic Management Test 3 examines the buffer size of the switches under test. The generator sends 192-cell bursts of VBR traffic, corresponding to the 9-kbyte maximum permitted by Classical IP over ATM, to a port already saturated by a 149.8-Mbit/s traffic stream.

Section 3.   The ATM Balancing Act

When all the cells were counted and the test results tabulated, Fore's ASX-200 showed itself to be the top performer. The ASX-200 offered more than adequate switching speed, along with the traffic management and buffering needed for tomorrow's internetwork backbones. The Lightstream 2020 also offers strong traffic management and enormous input and output buffers.

Fore Systems Inc.

As the follow-up to the popular ASX-100, Fore's ASX-200 has some big shoes to fill and a lot to offer. It consistently outpaced most products in the ATM Perform benchmarks. The ASX-200 is remarkably well balanced, able to handle bursty LAN data and high-volume CBR streams. It also boasts interfaces galore, including T1 (1.544 Mbit/s), E1 (2.048 Mbit/s), E3, T3 (45 Mbit/s), 100-Mbit/s Taxi, 140-Mbit/s Taxi, and 155-Mbit/s OC3c. The Taxi and OC3c interfaces accommodate Category 5 STP copper and optical fiber. Like Bay's Lattiscell switch, the ASX-200 supports virtual path switching. It also offers two traffic management schemes and standard UNI 3.1 signaling.

Bay Networks' Lattiscell is well balanced but slow. Cell delays are nearly six times those of the Forerunner, although it's important to note that latency doesn't increase markedly with load. The Lattiscell is no speed demon, but it should be very reliable. Cisco's Hyperswitch A100 handles light traffic with tolerable delays. Latency, however, increases dramatically with volume. Of these two switches, Cisco's is more burdened by buffering schemes that slow processing as ports become congested. Some switches were not nearly as balanced. DEC's Gigaswitch ATM, 3Com's Cellplex 7000, and Newbridge's Mainstreet 36150 demonstrate latencies only slightly higher than Fore's when lightly loaded. But this power trio had a tendency to dump cells when bombarded with large bursts. The Cellplex's small buffers and unsophisticated traffic management make it fast but unreliable under bursty conditions. Similarly, Newbridge's Mainstreet 36150 proved to be a solid performer on low-volume latency tests but doesn't have the buffers needed to handle bursts.

Section 4.   Testing Traffic Management

The traffic management portion of the test suite had two goals. The first was to see if a switch can guarantee delivery of delay-sensitive voice or video while also contending with less time-critical traffic. The second was to ascertain whether congestion on one switch port would affect virtual circuits on other ports. Once again, the ASX-200 took the top spot. Even when ports were overloaded, it continued to allocate the bandwidth required for voice and video. The Lightstream 2020 also did a good job. Its extensive buffers protected CBR (constant bit rate) traffic. Bay Networks' Lattiscell safeguarded CBR cells as well, while showing the lowest proportional increase in latency. Newbridge's Mainstreet 36150 and 3Com's Cellplex 7000 could not fully protect delay-sensitive traffic. With the exception of the Hyperswitch (Cisco) and the Gigaswitch (DEC), all the switches could shield an uncongested virtual circuit when traffic backed up at another port. The Hyperswitch and the Gigaswitch defaulted to backpressure congestion control mechanisms that slowed virtual circuits using uncongested ports. The two switches did manage to deliver delay-sensitive traffic, but neither did a particularly good job.

Section 5.   New Networks, New Metrics

Because ATM networks operate at wire speed at all times, measuring throughput is not a true test of performance. ATM always delivers the bandwidth specified by the physical interface, whether it's 155 Mbit/s, 51 Mbit/s, or some other rate. If the virtual connections don't need all the available throughput, end stations and switches simply transmit enough idle cells to fill up the pipe. For example, if an application needs only 10 Mbit/s, a 155-Mbit/s switch interface will transmit 145 Mbit/s of idle cells. Because these cells have no payload, they're simply dropped when they reach the end station.

Bay Networks Inc.

Bay's Lattiscell implements a sophisticated switching fabric that the vendor says ensures cells always have alternative paths under congested conditions. Unfortunately, Bay pays a performance price for these extra lanes: considerably higher latency than competing switches. There's also an upside to delivering throughput at any cost. The latency gap between the Lattiscell and other switches narrows significantly when bursty traffic is encountered. Lattiscell also offers multiple-priority output queues that help guarantee bandwidth for CBR traffic. Bay Networks is slightly ahead of the field in offering UNI 3.0 signaling and switched virtual circuits—both of which are essential building blocks for a scalable ATM network. Bay also supports 155-Mbit/s interfaces using Category 5 STP (shielded twisted-pair) copper cabling. Virtual path switching is planned.

That's why the ATM Perform benchmark measures latency and jitter. *Latency,* or the amount of time required to establish a virtual connection and transmit cells between end stations, should ideally be minimal and constant. *Jitter,* or cell delay variation, refers to the differences in transit time for a given series of cells. Like latency, it should be minimal and constant. The wide range of applications that ATM is designed to handle makes latency and jitter critical metrics. Too much latency—although no one knows precisely how much—will skew the timing of voice and video and cause data sessions to time out. Likewise, too much jitter will cause voice and video to perform erratically (although it may have relatively little effect on data). What's more, latency and jitter could cause problems with ATM signaling in multiswitch environments. The ATM Forum's UNI (user network interface) 3.1 uses standard 53-byte cells to set up virtual circuits. Too much latency and jitter will lengthen setup times. It also can delay flow control messages on their way through the network, which in turn can make congestion worse.

Section 6.   Latency Testing

ENL's basic latency test switched a single virtual circuit carrying a 7.488-Mbit/s stream of CBR traffic across two ports (see Fig. 14.1). An ATM-100 analyzer from Germany's Wandel & Goltermann (W&G) was used to generate traffic and count cells. The ATM-100's backplane can accommodate multiple analyzer modules; only one was slotted in for this test. Traffic management was disabled on all switches except the Lattiscell, which does not allow this feature to be turned off.

Fore's ASX-200 delivered the lowest latency, exhibiting a cell delay of only 10.57 microseconds (see Fig. 14.2). 3Com's Cellplex came in a close second at 10.87 microseconds, and DEC ranked third with 11.75

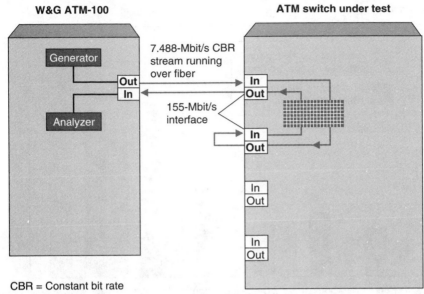

CBR = Constant bit rate

Figure 14.1 Switching across two ports. The basic latency test generates a single 7.488-Mbit/s CBR stream that's switched across two ports. Cell delay through the switch is measured.

microseconds. These are remarkably low latencies—virtually one-third those of the fastest 100-Mbit/s Ethernet switches.

Cisco Systems Inc.

Cisco's Hyperswitch A100 is actually the result of a reseller agreement with NEC America Inc. (San Jose, CA). NEC makes the underlying hardware; Cisco developed the software. Hyperswitch incurred relatively high latency, but Cisco claims that 5000 switches could be strung together before exceeding the 200-millisecond latency of a standard voice call. Hyperswitch supports full UNI 3.0 signaling. It features a back-pressure flow control scheme that slows traffic on inbound ports when outbound ports are jammed. Tests revealed a head-of-the-line blocking problem. The switch can be configured with E3 (34 Mbit/s), 100-Mbit/s Taxi (transparent asynchronous transmitter/receiver interface), and 155-Mbit/s OC3c interfaces.

Latency rose noticeably for the rest of the pack. Newbridge clocked in with 19.01 microseconds, while Lightstream hit 24.50 microseconds. Cisco's Hyperswitch A100 was a more substantial 39.90 microseconds, and Bay Networks' Lattiscell recorded a surprisingly high 61.90 microseconds. For the second round of latency tests, the lab increased the load to 1.07 Gbit/s across four full-duplex 155-Mbit/s interfaces, again with traffic management disabled (see Fig. 14.3).

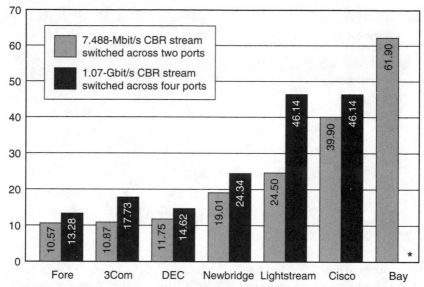

Microseconds

Legend:
- 7.488-Mbit/s CBR stream switched across two ports
- 1.07-Gbit/s CBR stream switched across four ports

Fore	3Com	DEC	Newbridge	Lightstream	Cisco	Bay
10.57	10.87	11.75	19.01	24.50	39.90	61.90
13.28	17.73	14.62	24.34	46.14	46.14	*

*Traffic management could not be disabled on Bay's Lattiscell. Switch could not handle 155 Mbit/s on all four ports with traffic management enabled.

CBR = Constant bit rate

Figure 14.2   Latency per port. Switching across two and four ports.

Once again, the W&G ATM-100 was used to generate and measure traffic.

This time out, cell delay for most of the switches increased marginally, typically by about 20 percent. The Fore switch was once again the top performer, with a latency of 13.28 microseconds. DEC took second place, with a latency of 14.62 microseconds, and 3Com's Cellplex took third, with a latency of 17.73 microseconds. When switching full speed on four ports, it dropped 8 percent of the offered traffic—unacceptable performance for a switch supposedly headed for the enterprise.

Section 7.   Performance Jitters

But latency is only part of the story for real-time applications. Switches have to forward cells not only quickly but also consistently. To gauge if they can do so, ENL measured two related types of jitter: cell delay variation and cell interarrival variation. When cells take different amounts of time to pass through a switch, the difference in

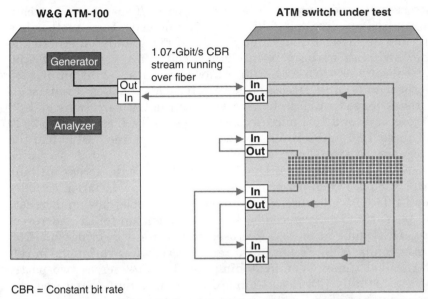

Figure 14.3 Switching across four ports. In the second series of latency tests, a 1.07-Gbit/s CBR stream is generated and switched across four ports using a technique known as tromboning. Again, cell delay through the switch is measured.

latency is known as cell delay variation. This fluctuation can play havoc with CBR traffic, which depends upon cells being delivered at precise intervals. It's simple: When latency remains constant, cells arrive at the end station at constant intervals. But when latency varies, cell interarrival times fluctuate.

Digital Equipment Corp.

DEC's Gigaswitch ATM arrived at the test site accompanied by three Alpha workstations and all the software needed to make a convincing display of DEC's proprietary credit-based flow control scheme. Unfortunately, when it came time to connect the switch to the lab's analyzer, DEC's flow control mechanism had to be shut down. It doesn't operate outside an all-DEC environment.

That's too bad, since without flow control, the Gigaswitch tended to bog down under heavier loads. Like Cisco's Hyperswitch, the Gigaswitch also exhibited signs of head-of-the-line blocking. Although DEC has positioned its switch for the campus backbone, it's probably better suited to high-performance work groups—using Alpha AXP workstations.

ATM Perform measures cell delay variation by taking the standard deviation of cell delay over a sampling of 2.5 million cells. The lab generated a 7.488-Mbit/s stream containing one data cell every 54.6

microseconds and switched it across two ports. Thus, the test stream transmitted one live cell, followed by 19 idle cells, then another live cell, and so forth. 3Com's Cellplex 7000 marginally outscored the other switches with an infinitesimal cell delay variation of 0.96 microsecond. Fore's ASX-200 followed with a variation of 1.25 microseconds, and DEC's Gigaswitch ATM and Bay's Lattiscell switches logged in close behind with cell delay variations of 1.39 microseconds and 1.41 microseconds, respectively. Lightstream's 2020 registered 1.66 microseconds; Newbridge's Mainstreet 36150 had the widest spread at 2.03 microseconds.

When the lab switched the 7.488-Mbit/s stream across all four ports, 3Com's switch performed even better. Delay variation actually dropped to 0.95 microsecond. All the other switches saw an increase. Bay posted 2.17 microseconds, and Cisco crept up to 3.27 microseconds. DEC jumped to 3.95 microseconds, while Newbridge hit 4.83 microseconds. ATM Perform also recorded very low variations in cell interarrival times when switching 7.488 Mbit/s across two ports. 3Com's virtually jitterless Cellplex 7000 marginally outscored the other switches with a variation of 1.01 microseconds on two ports (see Fig. 14.4). Fore exhibited a variation of 1.54 microseconds; Lightstream, 1.99; Bay, 2.01; DEC, 2.06; and Cisco, 2.81. Newbridge showed the highest interarrival variation, logging in at 2.92 microseconds.

Section 8.   Extreme Loads

Out on the enterprise, ATM switches will have to contend with both delay-sensitive traffic and bursty data. Thus, any real-world evaluation must gauge how well these boxes handle different types of traffic and stand up to heavy loads. ENL's test suite does both—evaluating a switch's ability to manage and protect traffic types and measuring how effectively it buffers data when ports are swamped. To do so, the lab switched a single 7.488-Mbit/s stream across two ports with each product's traffic management mechanism enabled. Broadly speaking, first-generation ATM switches use four different mechanisms to ensure that delay-sensitive traffic will get the bandwidth needed to guarantee cells are not discarded:

- Separate buffer queues for high-priority traffic
- Usage parameter controls (UPCs) to reserve bandwidth
- Cell-loss priority (CLP) bits to mark traffic that can be dumped
- Proprietary fairness algorithms to dedicate bandwidth to specific circuits

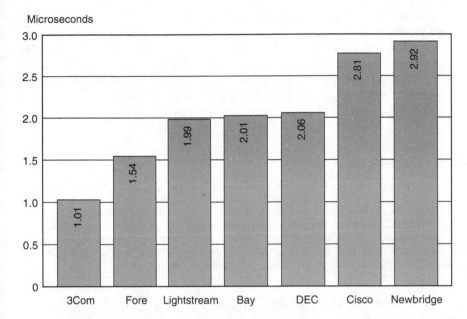

Microseconds

Switching one 7.488-Mbit/s CBR stream across two ports
CBR = Constant bit rate

Figure 14.4 Variation in cell interarrival time. Switching across two ports.

With separate buffer queues, a switch systematically places CBR cells in a high-priority output queue and assigns VBR (variable bit rate) traffic, such as bursty data or packetized voice and video, to a lower-priority queue. This guarantees that CBR cells will be handled ahead of less time-critical data. Bay, Cisco, Fore, and Lightstream all implement this sort of scheme. Newbridge relies on circuit queues rather than output buffers. These can be partitioned so that high-priority traffic always has enough circuits available, with low-priority traffic taking whatever's left.

UPCs, which are part of UNI 3.0 signaling, are algorithms that work together to prevent virtual circuits from getting more than their share of available bandwidth. The so-called single leaky bucket algorithm works with CBR traffic, detecting and discarding any cells that surpass the specified throughput. Fore and Lightstream use this approach, as do Cisco and Newbridge. The dual leaky bucket algorithm applies to VBR cells. It checks for violations of both the peak rate and the sustained rate. VBR traffic is inherently bursty: The peak rate defines the maximum legal burst; the sustained rate specifies the highest throughput a circuit is allowed to maintain for a particular interval (say, 75 Mbit/s for 3 seconds). Fore and Lightstream also implement this algorithm. The CLP bit is contained in the header of ATM cells. When set to 1, it tells the switch that this traffic should be dropped first. When set to 0, which is the case with CBR cells, it indicates that the traffic should never be dropped. All the switches tested recognize the CLP bit; 3Com's Cellplex 7000 relies on this scheme as its sole traffic management mechanism.

Lightstream Corp.

The latest addition to the Cisco Systems family of companies, Lightstream brings some impressive ATM technology to the party with its 2020—a big, powerful box full of interfaces, including E3, T3, and 155-Mbit/s OC3c. Although not the fastest switch, the 2020 held its own when congestion began to mount. Its huge buffers contributed some additional latency, but they also cut down on delay when handling bursty traffic on overloaded ports. Lightstream's buffering capacity comes at a price, however. At $61,700, the 2020 carries the highest price tag of any switch tested.

Finally, two of the switches implement proprietary fairness algorithms—Cisco's Hyperswitch and DEC's Gigaswitch ATM. Although the two schemes are not identical, they achieve the same end. Essentially, specific amounts of bandwidth are allotted to virtual circuits as soon as the switch starts to junk cells. By default, each virtual circuit running through the same port is allocated a share of the available bandwidth on that port. The fairness mechanism allows any circuit to trespass its predefined bounds, as long as it doesn't encroach on the bandwidth requirements of the neighboring circuit.

Section 9.   Traffic Mismanagement?

By and large, ENL found that all the foregoing traffic management mechanisms did a first-rate job. But a toll must be paid: They also added significantly to switch latency. The one exception was Newbridge's 36150, the only switch whose latency actually improved with traffic management turned on. The 36150's cell delay fell to 16.50 microseconds, a 13.2 percent drop from the 19.01 microseconds it scored when switching across two ports without traffic management. For all its improvement, though, Newbridge was not able to match Fore's latency of 12.10 microseconds—an increase of only 12.6 percent from its original score of 10.57 microseconds. Bay's Lattiscell exhibited a modest increase in cell delay from its very high 61 microseconds to 70.03 microseconds. DEC jumped from 11.75 to 27.18 microseconds, while Cisco went from 39.90 to 81.49 microseconds. The poorest performer was 3Com's Cellplex, which paired very shallow buffers with its ability to recognize the CLP bit. Latency took an

81 percent jump with traffic management invoked, coming in at 19.67 microseconds. What's more, the Cellplex dropped 1.1 of the cells. Clearly, CLP is the least effective of the management schemes.

Newbridge Networks Corp.

The Newbridge Mainstreet 36150 has been tried and tested in telecom environments, and it shows. The box supports virtual path switching and boasts a range of interfaces, including E3, T3, 100-Mbit/s Taxi, and 155-Mbit/s OC3c.

Although the 36150 turned in fairly low latencies on some tests, it dumped 8 percent of the cells when heavily loaded—a big problem for a switch that's headed for the enterprise. What's more, cell delay variation and cell interarrival variation were not particularly impressive. Newbridge is working on a new 155-Mbit/s interface card that's supposed to address its troubles with bursty traffic.

Section 10.   Introducing IP

ENL also took a look at how well these switches can handle the sort of traffic mix they're likely to encounter in the real world. To do so, a 7.488-Mbit/s CBR stream and IP traffic were sent to the same port (see Fig. 14.5). This time out, W&G's ATM-100 was equipped with two

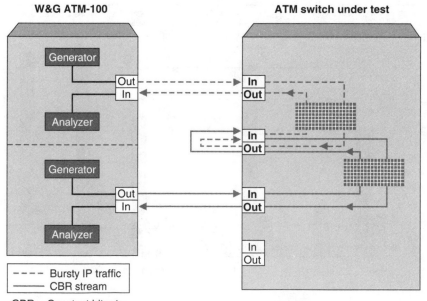

Figure 14.5 Switching delay-sensitive and bursty traffic across one port. By generating a 7.488-Mbit/s CBR stream and bursty IP traffic and switching both across one port, ENL determined how congestion affects latency.

modules: one generating and counting delay-sensitive cells; the other, bursty traffic. The IP traffic consisted of 9-kbyte frames, the largest allowed by the Classical IP over ATM specification from the IETF (Internet Engineering Task Force). The goal was to see if the switch could protect the CBR stream without introducing additional latency, which could disrupt voice and video. In the first round of tests, the data was allowed to burst to 10 percent of the available bandwidth on the ATM interface (once the CBR cells were accounted for). In the second round, the data was allowed to burst to roughly half the remaining bandwidth. Not surprisingly, when the IP traffic hit the ATM port, latency for the CBR stream jumped significantly. This is a good indicator of the sort of trouble that flow control mechanisms and buffering schemes run into when fielding unpredictable data traffic.

Fore, which exhibited the lowest latency for most of the foregoing tests, once again was out in front of the pack. Latency went from 10.57 microseconds on the lightly loaded switch to 27.19 microseconds, with data bursting to 10 percent of capacity (see Fig. 14.6). Under the heaviest loads, Fore's latency took a steep climb to 77.89 microseconds. DEC's Gigaswitch ATM showed one of the severest increases in latency, going from a lightly loaded 11.75 microseconds to

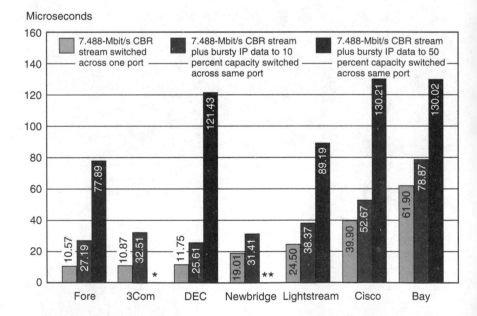

Figure 14.6 Latency per port under heavy loads.

a fully loaded 121.43 microseconds. Lightstream climbed from a low of 24.50 microseconds, when switching across two ports, to 89.19 microseconds under the heaviest load. The lightly loaded Cisco Hyperswitch exhibited a latency of 39.90 microseconds; when data was allowed to burst to 50 percent capacity, latency increased to 130.21 microseconds, the highest recorded. At 130.02 microseconds, Bay's fully loaded latency was almost as high. Still, that represents only a 110 percent increase for the switch—the smallest proportional increase of any vendor.

3Com and Newbridge both ran into trouble with this part of the ATM stress test. Latency for the Cellplex climbed to 32.51 microseconds when data burst to 10 percent of capacity. When bursts reached 50 percent of capacity, however, the Cellplex dropped 12 percent of the cells. Similarly, latency for the Mainstreet 36150 came in at 31.41 microseconds with the 10 percent bursts. When the bursts hit 50 percent, though, the 36150 dumped 8 percent of the cells.

3Com Corp.

The Cellplex 7000 is very much the new kid on the block. 3Com's newly acquired ATM switch division (formerly Nicecom Inc.) had just initiated its first production run when ENL began testing. Cellplex is very fast, delivering very low latency—second only to that of Top Performer Fore Systems—and minimal jitter. Despite these strengths, the switch wound up dumping 12 percent of the traffic under heavy loads—an unacceptably high level of cell loss.

ENL also ran into some technical troubles during these trials—among them, a clocking problem and a CLP (cell loss priority) trigger that was set too high. The latter had a direct effect on the first traffic management test: Cellplex did not begin discarding low-priority cells until it reached 80 percent saturation. By that time, it was too late to avoid losing some high-priority cells as well.

3Com says these problems have been corrected. The vendor is not a big believer in deep buffers. It is currently trying to implement rate-based flow control, which 3Com believes will keep buffers shallow and allow bare-bones designs.

Section 11.   Head-of-the-Line Blocking

ENL also wanted to find out if congestion on one output port would affect throughput on an uncongested port—a phenomenon described earlier as head-of-the-line blocking. This phenomenon can indicate architectural weaknesses that may pose problems when traffic starts to back up. Head-of-the-line blocking results from the way buffers are managed. Essentially, traffic destined for the congested port sits in a queue ahead of traffic headed for the uncongested port. Because the stream bound for the congested port cannot get through, it gets in the way of the traffic bound for the uncongested port. Both wind up losing cells. This time around, the lab sent two streams of traffic to a single input port—both consisting of data. The two streams were then switched onto different output ports—one uncongested, one tied up with data traffic from another source (see Fig. 14.7). Five of the seven switches handled this situation admirably. The data that hit the congested port lost cells, but the congestion did not affect traffic on the uncongested port. Cisco's Hyperswitch and DEC's Gigaswitch ATM, however, ran into some problems. Cell loss spilled over from the congested port to the uncongested port.

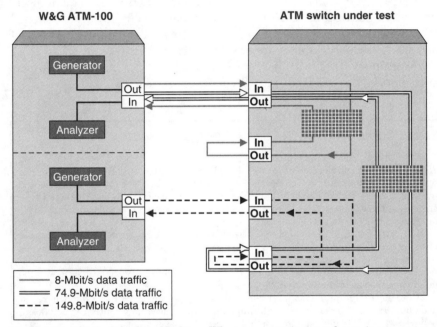

Figure 14.7 Head-of-the-line blocking. When one port is maxed out, it can cause cells to be junked on an uncongested port—a problem known as head-of-the-line blocking. ENL switched two data streams across one heavily congested port and checked to see if latency increased on the lightly loaded port.

An ATM Glossary

Every high-speed LAN has a language all its own—replete with arcane acronyms and bewildering buzzwords. But the vernacular for ATM is more diverse than most. This chapter provides an explanation of ATM terminology with definitions of everything from *asynchronous transfer mode* itself all the way through to *virtual path identifier.*

asynchronous transfer mode (ATM)   A high-speed, connection-oriented switching and multiplexing technology that uses 53-byte cells (5-byte header, 48-byte payload) to transmit different types of traffic simultaneously, including voice, video, and data. It is asynchronous in that information streams can be sent independently without a common clock. ATM can be described logically in three planes. The user plane coordinates the interface between user protocols, such as IP or SMDS (Switched Multimegabit Data Service) and ATM; the management plane coordinates the layers of the ATM stack; the control plane coordinates signaling and setting up and tearing down virtual circuits.

ATM adaptation layer (AAL)   A set of four standard protocols that translate user traffic from the higher layers of the protocol stack into a size and format that can be contained in the payload of an ATM cell and return it to its original form at the destination. Each AAL consists of two sublayers: the segmentation and reassembly (SAR) sublayer and the convergence sublayer (see Fig. 15.1). Each is geared to a particular class of traffic, with specific characteristics concerning delay and cell loss. All AAL functions occur at the ATM end station rather than at the switch.

AAL 1 addresses CBR (constant bit rate) traffic such as digital voice and video and is used for applications that are sensitive to both cell loss and delay and to emulate conventional leased lines. It requires an additional byte of

The information in this chapter first appeared in *Data Communications* magazine, and was written by Donald R. Marks, senior technology editor at Data Comm.

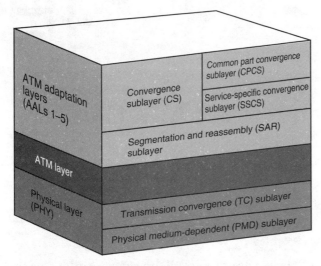

Figure 15.1 ATM layers and sublayers.

header information for sequence numbering, leaving 47 bytes for payload. AAL 2 is used with time-sensitive, VBR (variable bit rate) traffic such as packetized voice. It allows ATM cells to be transmitted before the payload is full to accommodate an application's timing requirements. The AAL 2 spec has not been completed by the ATM Forum.

AAL 3/4 handles bursty connection-oriented traffic, like error messages, or variable-rate connectionless traffic, like LAN file transfers. It is intended for traffic that can tolerate delay but not cell loss; to ensure that the latter is kept to a minimum, AAL 3/4 performs error detection on each cell and uses a sophisticated error-checking mechanism that consumes 4 bytes of each 48-byte payload. AAL 3/4 allows ATM cells to be multiplexed. AAL 5 accommodates bursty LAN data traffic with less overhead than AAL 3/4. Also known as the simple and efficient adaptation layer (SEAL), AAL 5 uses a conventional 5-byte header. It does not support cell multiplexing.

ATM address   At 20 bytes long, ATM addresses scale to very large networks. Addressing is hierarchical, as in a phone network, using prefixes similar to area codes and exchanges. ATM switches share address information with attached end stations and maintains end-station addresses in routing tables. ATM source and destination addresses are not included within each cell but are used by the switches to establish virtual path and virtual channel identifiers (VPIs/VCIs). This is in marked contrast to some LAN protocols, like TCP/IP and IPX, which pack destination addresses into each packet.

ATM API (application program interface)   Although several vendors have written proprietary code, no standard ATM API yet exists. The ATM Forum is working on an API that will let application developers take advantage of ATM's quality-of-service and traffic management features; some forum members are pushing for a single API that supports other network interfaces when ATM is not available.

ATM CSU/DSU (channel/data service unit)   Segments ATM-compatible information, such as DXI (data exchange interface) frames generated by a router, into ATM cells and then reassembles them at their destination.

ATM Forum   The primary organization developing and defining ATM standards. Principal members participate in committees and vote on specifications; auditing members cannot participate in committees but receive technical and marketing documentation; user members participate only in end-user roundtables. Formed in 1991 by Adaptive Corp. (Redwood City, CA), Cisco Systems Inc. (San Jose, CA), Northern Telecom Ltd. (Mississauga, Ontario), and Sprint Corp. (Kansas City, MO), the ATM Forum currently consists of about 700 manufacturers, carriers, end users, and other interested parties.

ATM layer   ATM protocol stack that handles most of the processing and routing activities. These include building the ATM header, cell multiplexing/demultiplexing, cell reception and header validation, cell routing using VPIs/VCIs, payload-type identification, quality-of-service specification, and flow control and prioritization.

audio/visual multimedia services (AMS)   Specifies service requirements and defines application program interfaces (APIs) for broadcast video, videoconferencing, and multimedia traffic. AMS is being developed by the ATM Forum's Service Aspects and Applications (SAA) working group. An important debate in the SAA concerns how MPEG-2 video applications will travel over ATM (asynchronous transfer mode). Early developers chose to carry MPEG-2 over ATM adaptation layer 1 (AAL 1); others found AAL 5 a more workable solution. Recently, some have suggested coming up with a new video-only AAL using the still-undefined AAL 2. At the moment, there's no consensus on which approach will become the standard.

available bit rate (ABR)   A class of service in which the ATM network makes a "best effort" to meet the traffic's bit-rate requirements. ABR requires the transmitting end station to assume responsibility for data that cannot get through and does not guarantee delivery.

broadband integrated services digital network (B-ISDN)   A technology suite geared to multimedia. There are two transmission schemes: STM (synchronous transfer mode) and ATM.

broadband intercarrier interface (BICI)   A carrier-to-carrier interface similar to PNNI (private network-to-network interface) but lacking some of the detailed information offered by the latter. The difference arises because carriers are less likely to let their switches share routing information or detailed network maps with their competitors' gear. BICI now supports only PVCs (permanent virtual circuits) between carrier networks; the ATM Forum's BICI working group is currently addressing SVCs (switched virtual circuits).

cell   An ATM cell consists of 53 bytes or "octets." Of these, 5 constitute the header; the remaining 48 carry the data payload.

cell delay variation (CDV)   Measures the allowable variance in delay between one cell and the next, expressed in fractions of a second. When emulating a circuit, CDV measurements allow the network to determine if cells are arriving too fast or too slow.

cell interarrival variation (CIV)   "Jitter" in common parlance, CIV measures how consistently ATM cells arrive at the receiving end station. Cell interarrival time is specified by the source application and should vary as little as possible. For constant bit rate (CBR) traffic, the interval between cells should be the same at the destination and the source. If it remains constant, the latency of the ATM switch or the network itself (also known as cell delay) will not affect the cell interarrival interval. But if latency varies, so will the interarrival interval. Any variation could affect the quality of voice or video applications.

cell loss priority (CLP) field   A priority bit in the cell header; when set, it indicates that the cell can be discarded if necessary.

cell multiplexing/demultiplexing   An ATM layer function that groups cells belonging to different virtual paths or circuits and transmits them in a stream to the target switch, where they are demuxed and routed to the correct end points.

Classical IP and ARP over ATM   An adaptation of TCP/IP and its address resolution protocol (ARP) for ATM defined by the IETF (Internet Engineering Task Force) in RFCs (requests for comment) 1483 and 1577. It places IP packets and ARP requests directly into PDUs (protocol data units) and converts them into ATM cells. Classical IP does not recognize conventional MAC (media access control) layer protocols like Ethernet and token ring.

common part convergence sublayer (CPCS)   The portion of the convergence sublayer of an AAL that remains the same regardless of the type of traffic.

congestion control   Mechanisms that control traffic flow so switches and end stations are not overwhelmed and cells dropped. ATM defines several simple schemes—among them GFC (generic flow control) and CLP (cell loss priority) fields in cell headers and the EFCI (explicit forward congestion indicator) bit in the PTI (payload type identifier). More sophisticated mechanisms are needed to deal with congestion in large ATM networks carrying different types of traffic. The ATM Forum recently ratified a rate-based traffic management strategy that counts on switches and end stations throttling back when congestion is encountered; a credit-based scheme also was considered, which relied more heavily on switch buffers. Other means of congestion control include UPC (usage parameter control) and CAC (connection admission control).

When confronted by congestion, many ATM switches discard cells according to CLP. Since voice and video are not tolerant of cell loss, this can make it difficult to achieve quality of service parameters. Data traffic is more tolerant of loss and delay, but if cells containing information from a higher-level packet are dropped, the entire packet may have to be transmitted. Considering that IP packets are 1500 bytes long and FDDI packets 4500 bytes long, the loss of a single cell could cause significant retransmissions, further aggravating congestion.

connection admission control (CAC)   Two mechanisms used to control the setup of virtual circuits. Overbooking, which allows one connection to exceed permissible traffic limits, assumes that other active connections are not using the maximum available resources. Full booking limits network access once maximum resources are committed and adds only connections that specify acceptable traffic parameters.

connectionless communications   A form of cell switching or packet multiplexing that identifies individual channels on the basis of global addresses rather than predefined virtual circuits. Used by shared-media LANs like FDDI and token ring.

connection-oriented communications   A form of cell switching or packet multiplexing characterized by individual virtual circuits based on virtual circuit identifiers. ATM is a connection-oriented technology.

constant bit rate (CBR)   Digital information, such as video and digitized voice, that must be represented by a continuous stream of bits. CBR traffic requires guaranteed throughput rates and service levels.

convergence sublayer (CS)   The portion of the AAL that prepares information in a common format—a convergence sublayer protocol data unit (CS-PDU)—before it is segmented into cells and returns it to its original form after reassembly at the destination switch. At the destination switch an ATM cell goes through reassembly in the SAR layer, then is passed up to the convergence sublayer in the form of a CS-PDU. The CS then converts the PDU to whatever the traffic was in its original form.

convergence sublayer protocol data unit (CS-PDU)   Information contained within a PDU that conforms to the specifications of the ATM convergence sublayer and is ready to be segmented into cells.

customer network management (CNM)   Allows users of ATM public networks to monitor and manage their portion of the carrier's circuits. Thus far, the ATM Forum has agreed that the CNM interface will give users the ability to monitor physical ports, virtual circuits, virtual paths, usage parameters, and quality-of-service parameters.

cyclic redundancy check (CRC)   A mathematical algorithm used to ensure accurate delivery on the basis of actual contents of the data.

data exchange interface (DXI)   Defines a format for passing data that has gone through the ATM convergence sublayer (a CS-PDU) between a router and a CSU/DSU or other device with ATM SAR capability.

early packet discard (EPD)   A congestion control technique that selectively drops all but the last ATM cell in a Classical IP over ATM packet. When congestion occurs, EPD discards cells at the beginning of an IP packet, leaving the rest intact. The last cell is preserved because it alerts the switch—and the destination station—of the beginning of a new packet. Because IP packets from which cells have been discarded receive no acknowledgment from the destination, they are automatically retransmitted from the source. Most vendors expect EPD to be used in conjunction with unspecified bit rate (UBR) service. Switches simply junk UBR cells when congestion occurs, without regard for application traffic. By discarding cells selectively, so that whole IP packets are resent, EPD makes UBR a safer option.

E1   European standard for digital transmission service at 2.048 Mbit/s.

E3   European standard for digital transmission service at 34.368 Mbit/s (transports 16 E1 circuits).

flow control   See **congestion control.**

generic flow control (GFC) field   The 4 priority bits in an ATM header. The default setting—four 0s—indicates that the cell is uncontrolled; thus, it does not take precedence over another cell when contending for a virtual circuit. Setting any of the bits in the GFC field tells the target end station that the switch can implement some form of congestion control; the end station echoes this bit back to the switch to confirm that it can set priorities. The switch and end station could use the GFC field to prioritize voice over video, for example, or indicate that both voice and video take precedence over other types of data.

header   The 5 bytes in an ATM cell that supply addressing and control information, including generic flow control, virtual path identifier, virtual circuit identifier, payload type, and cell loss priority.

header error control (HEC) field   A single byte containing the information needed for the transmission convergence (TC) sublayer of the ATM physical (PHY) layer to perform error detection on the cell header. If errors are found, the cell is dropped before processing moves up to the ATM layer, where routing takes place.

interim interswitch signaling protocol (IISP)   Formerly known as PNNI Phase 0, this limited, temporary routing scheme requires net managers to establish PVCs between switches from different vendors. Unlike PNNI Phase I, which will automatically distribute routing information, IISP relies on static routing tables. Routing is done hop by hop.

interim local management interface (ILMI)   Furnishes a pro tem basic simple network management protocol (SNMP) management interface for ATM. ILMI requires each user network interface (UNI) 3.0 end station or ATM network to implement a UNI management entity (UME). The UME functions as an SNMP agent that maintains network and connection information specified in an ILMI MIB (management information base). It responds to requests from SNMP management applications. Standard SNMP management frameworks can use AAL 3/4 or AAL 5 to encapsulate SNMP commands in ATM protocol data units (PDUs).

jitter   See **cell interarrival variation.**

LAN emulation   A way for legacy LAN MAC layer protocols like Ethernet and token ring, and all higher-layer protocols and applications, to access work transparently across an ATM network. LAN emulation retains all Ethernet and token ring drivers and adapters; no modifications need to be made to Ethernet or token ring end stations.

LAN emulation network-to-network interface (LNNI)   Enables one vendor's implementation of LAN emulation to work with another's. This spec is essential for building multivendor ATM networks and is currently under development at the ATM Forum.

LAN emulation user network interface (L-UNI)   Defines how legacy LAN applications and protocols work with ATM. Currently in development at the ATM Forum, L-UNI adapts layer 2 LAN packets to AAL 5 PDUs, which can then be divided into cells. L-UNI uses a client-server architecture to resolve LAN-to-ATM addresses, the most complex aspect of LAN emulation. A LAN emulation client (LEC) resides in each ATM-attached device; a LAN emulation server (LES) and a broadcast and unknown server (BUS) reside anywhere on the ATM network. When a legacy LAN end station sends a message across the ATM network to another legacy end station, the LEC requests ATM address and routing information from the LES and BUS, which correlate the MAC layer LAN address of the destination with the ATM addresses needed to traverse the backbone.

leaky bucket algorithm   A form of flow control that checks an arriving data stream against the traffic-shaping parameters specified by the sender. Cells arriving at a switch are placed in a "bucket" (memory buffer), which is allowed to fill up but not overflow. The bucket is "leaky" in that it allows cells to flow out to their destinations—permitting more to be added. Incoming cells that would cause the bucket to overflow are considered "nonconforming" (exceeding bandwidth allocations) and are dropped.

multiprotocol encapsulation over ATM   Allows higher-layer protocols, such as IP or IPX, to be routed over ATM by enabling an ATM-aware device or application to add a standard protocol identifier to LAN data.

multiprotocol over ATM (MPOA)   A proposed ATM Forum spec that defines how ATM traffic is routed from one virtual LAN to another. MPOA is key to making LAN emulation, Classical IP over ATM, and proprietary virtual LAN schemes interoperate in a multiprotocol environment. At this point, it's unclear how MPOA will deal with conventional routers, distributed ATM edge routers (which shunt LAN traffic across an ATM cloud, while also performing conventional routing functions between non-ATM networks), and route servers (which centralize lookup tables on a dedicated network server in a switched LAN).

network-to-network interface (NNI)   Interface between ATM network nodes (switches) defined in the ATM Forum's UNI (user network interface).

operations, administration, and maintenance (OAM)   A range of diverse network management functions performed by dedicated ATM cells, including fault and performance management (operations); addressing, data collection, and usage monitoring (administration); and analysis, diagnosis, and repair of network faults (maintenance). OAM cells do not help segmentation and reassembly.

optical carrier (OC-n)   The fundamental unit in the Sonet (synchronous optical network) hierarchy. OC indicates an optical signal and n represents increments of 51.84 Mbit/s. Thus, OC-1, -3, and -12 equal optical signals of 51, 155, and 622 Mbit/s.

payload information   The portion of an ATM cell exclusive of the header. ATM cells typically have 48-byte payloads, but size can vary depending upon type of data and AAL.

payload-type indicator (PTI) field   A 3-bit field in the ATM cell header. The first bit indicates which AAL was used to format the data in the payload; the second provides explicit forward congestion indication (EFCI), which alerts the application of possible delays by informing it of congestion behind the cell; the third indicates whether the cell contains data OAM information.

peak cell rate (PCR) The maximum rate at which cells can be transmitted across a virtual circuit, specified in cells per second and defined by the interval between the transmission of the last bit of one cell and the first bit of the next.

permanent virtual circuit (PVC) A virtual link with fixed end points that are defined by the network manager. A single virtual path may support multiple PVCs.

physical layer (PHY) The bottom layer of the ATM protocol stack, which defines the interface between ATM traffic and the physical media. The PHY consists of two sublayers: the physical medium dependent (PMD) sublayer and the transmission convergence (TC) sublayer.

physical layer convergence protocol (PLCP) A protocol specified within the TC sublayer that defines how cells are formatted within a data stream for a particular transmission facility, such as T1, T3, or OC-n.

physical medium dependent (PMD) sublayer Defines the actual speed at which ATM traffic can be transmitted across a given physical medium. The ATM Forum has approved three Sonet interfaces for UNI: STS-1 at 51.84 Mbit/s, STS-3c at 155.52 Mbit/s, and STS-12c at 622.08 Mbit/s, as well as DS-1 (T1) at 1.544 Mbit/s, E1 at 2.048 Mbit/s, E3 at 34.368 Mbit/s, and DS-3 (T3) at 44.73 Mbit/s. The ATM Forum also has adopted a number of specifications for LAN environments, including a 100-Mbit/s interface using FDDI encoding, a 155-Mbit/s interface using Category 5 UTP (unshielded twisted pair), and 51-Mbit/s and 25-Mbit/s interfaces using Category 3 UTP.

private network-to-network interface (PNNI) A routing information protocol that allows different vendors' ATM switches to be integrated in the same network. PNNI automatically and dynamically distributes routing information, enabling any switch to determine a path to any other switch.

protocol data unit (PDU) A discrete piece of information (such as a packet or frame) in the appropriate format to be segmented and encapsulated in the payload of an ATM cell.

quality-of-service classes Five broad categories outlined by the ATM Forum's UNI 3.0; implementation details and precise characteristics are to be determined in the future. Class 1 specifies performance requirements and indicates that ATM's quality of service should be comparable with the service offered by standard digital connections. Class 2 specifies necessary service levels for packetized video and voice. Class 3 defines requirements for interoperability with other connection-oriented protocols, particularly frame relay. Class 4 specifies interoperability requirements for connectionless protocols, including IP, IPX, and SMDS. Class 5 is effectively a "best effort" attempt at delivery; it is intended for applications that do not require a particular class of service.

segmentation and reassembly (SAR) sublayer Converts PDUs into appropriate lengths and formats them to fit the payload of an ATM cell. At the destination end station, SAR extracts the payloads from the cells and converts them back into PDUs, which can be used by applications higher up the protocol stack.

segmentation and reassembly protocol data unit (SAR-PDU)   Information that has passed through SAR and been loaded into ATM cells that is ready to be forwarded to the TC (transmission convergence) sublayer of the ATM physical layer for actual transmission.

service-specific convergence sublayer (SSCS)   The portion of the convergence sublayer that is dependent upon the type of traffic that is being converted, such as the frame relay service-specific convergence sublayer (FR-SSCS) or the switched multimegabit data service service-specific convergence sublayer (SMDS-SSCS).

signaling   The standard process, based on CCITT Q.93B, used to establish ATM point-to-point, point-to-multipoint, and multipoint-to-multipoint connections.

simple and efficient adaptation layer (SEAL)   See **ATM adaptation layer (AAL 5)**.

sustainable cell rate (SCR)   Maximum throughput that bursty traffic can achieve within a given virtual circuit without risking cell loss.

switched virtual circuit (SVC)   A virtual link, with variable end points, established through an ATM network. With an SVC, the user defines the end points when the call is initiated; with a PVC, the end points are predefined by the network manager. A single virtual path may support multiple SVCs.

synchronous digital hierarchy (SDH)   An international form of Sonet (synchronous optical network). SDH is built on blocks of 155.52 Mbit/s; Sonet, on 51.84 Mbit/s.

synchronous optical network (Sonet)   An international suite of standards for transmitting digital information over optical interfaces. "Synchronous" indicates that all component portions of the Sonet signal can be tied to a single reference clock.

synchronous transfer mode (STM)   A B-ISDN communications method that transmits a group of different data streams synchronized to a single reference clock. All data receives the same amount of bandwidth. STM is the standard method carriers use to assign time slots or channels within a T1/E1 leased line.

synchronous transfer module (STM-n)   The basic unit of SDH (synchronous digital hierarchy), defined in increments of 155.52 Mbit/s, with n representing multiples of that rate. The most common values of n are 1, 2, and 4.

synchronous transfer signal (STS-n)   The basic unit of Sonet (synchronous optical network), defined in increments of 51.84 Mbit/s, with n representing multiples of that rate. The most common values of n are 1, 3, and 12. STS uses an electrical rather than an optical signal.

T1   A digital transmission service with a basic data rate of 1.544 Mbit/s.

T3   A digital transmission service with a basic data rate of 44.736 Mbit/s for transport of 28 T1 circuits.

traffic management (TM)   See **congestion control**.

traffic shaping   Allows the sender to specify the throughput and priority of information entering the ATM network and to monitor its progress to ascertain if service levels are met.

transmission convergence (TC) sublayer   Part of the ATM physical layer, it defines a protocol for preparing cells for transmission across the physical media defined by the physical media dependent (PMD) sublayer. The function of the TC sublayer differs according to physical medium.

usage parameter control (UPC)   Prevents congestion by not admitting excess traffic onto the network when all resources are in use. UPC changes the CLP (cell loss priority) bit of cells that exceed traffic parameters so they are dropped.

user network interface (UNI)   The protocol adopted by the ATM Forum to define connections between ATM user (end station) and ATM network (switch). UNI version 3.0, published in 1993, specifies the complete range of ATM traffic characteristics, including cell structure, addressing, signaling, adaptation layers, and traffic management.

variable bit rate (VBR)   Information that can be represented digitally by groups of bits (as opposed to streams) is characterized by a variable bit rate. Most data applications generate VBR traffic, which can tolerate delays and fluctuating throughput.

virtual channel   A defined route between two end points in an ATM network that may traverse several virtual paths.

virtual channel identifier (VCI)   The unique numerical tag used to identify every virtual channel across an ATM network, defined by a 16-bit field in the ATM cell header.

virtual circuit (VC)   A portion of a virtual path or a virtual channel that is used to establish a single virtual connection between two end points.

virtual path   A group of virtual channels, which can support multiple virtual circuits.

virtual path identifier (VPI)   An 8-bit field in the ATM cell header that indicates the virtual path over which a cell is to be routed. A virtual connection established using only the VPI is known as a virtual path connection (VPC).

Proprietary
LAN Switches

Back in the early 1990s it was the standards-based high-speed LANs from ANSI and the IEEE that were getting all the attention from the networking industry. Most pundits agreed that it was technologies like FDDI, 100Base-T, and 100VG-AnyLAN that would one day corner the lion's share of the desktop market. But around 1994 a funny thing happened: The networking industry caught onto the power of the switching paradigm. All of a sudden, standards-based shared-media LANs were overshadowed by proprietary LAN switch technologies.

Proprietary LAN switches all work the same way, increasing the performance of shared-media LANs (such as Ethernet, FDDI, and token ring) by dividing them into dedicated, switched network segments. Ethernet switches are now firmly established as the de facto way to pump up the performance of the installed 10-Mbit/s LANs. Meanwhile, token ring LANs also are getting some much-needed relief, thanks to the arrival of several switches geared toward that technology. FDDI switches have also proved to be a surprise success. And as this book goes to print, the first switches that work with 100Base-T are being installed in corporate networks. A recent survey shows that 56 percent of corporations believe that by 1997 between 25 and 75 percent of their workstations will be hooked up to LAN switches; 20 percent put the number of switch-attached nodes at more than 75 percent (see Fig.1).

Generally speaking, proprietary LAN switches owe their popularity to two factors: they're cheap, and they're easy to install. Ethernet switches can be had for less than $500. Token ring and 100Base-T switches go for less than $1000. The exceptions here are FDDI switches. Like FDDI technology

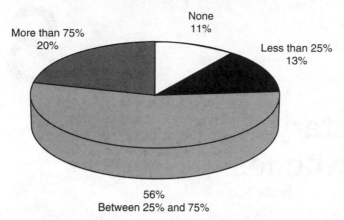

Figure 1   Percentage of computers likely to be attached to switched LANs by 1997. (From a survey of 102 *Fortune* 5000 companies.) Source: Sage Research and Brook Trail Research (Natick, MA).

generally, these products are expensive—typically costing more than $10,000 per port. And proprietary LAN switches have an advantage which neither standards-based shared-media LANs nor standards-based switched LANs can boast: They work with the interface cards which typically are already in place in the workstations in corporate LANs. This makes the migration path to high-speed networking far easier for the net manager, because there is no need to open up desktop equipment and upgrade it with new hardware and software.

However, for all their ability to provide huge amounts of affordable bandwidth, these products are not without their drawbacks. Unlike standards-based technologies, proprietary switching technologies remain for the most part steadfastly outside the standards process (despite some halfhearted efforts to bring them within the official jurisdiction of bodies like the IEEE). This has had some unpleasant side effects. For one thing there are no compulsory flow control schemes defined for proprietary LAN switches, leaving net managers with no way to guarantee that the device they install won't make performance worse by dropping an inordinate number of frames. Also, the virtual LAN and management implementations from different switch vendors currently will not interwork.

Chapters 16–19 describe Ethernet, token ring, FDDI, and 100Base-T and 100VG-AnyLAN switches. Chapter 20 examines "enterprise switching hubs"—a new category of internetworking device designed to support both legacy shared-media and new switched technologies in a single platform. Finally, Chaps. 21 and 22 discuss full-duplex switch technology and the flow control problems with proprietary switches.

Ethernet Switches

Section 1. Overview

In the ongoing battle to supply LAN users with the bandwidth they need, the good guys—i.e., net managers—finally have some momentum in their favor. Ethernet switches are now firmly established as the most popular way to breathe new life into sagging LAN segments. Ethernet switches take the place of the conventional Ethernet repeater in the wiring closet—vastly increasing throughput by switching traffic between 10-Mbit/s Ethernet segments. The feature sets, performance numbers, and prices of this technology category are improving at a stratospheric pace.

Ethernet switches have replaced bridges and routers as the preferred way to boost performance when Ethernet segments start to slow down. Switches are hot for three basic reasons. First, they're less expensive than either of these alternatives: Ethernet switches cost an average of $730 per port, compared with $1000 per port for Ethernet bridges and $4000 per port for Ethernet routers. Second, they're simpler to manage and support. Third, they introduce far less delay every time traffic is sent between segments.

Sure, there are other ways to boost performance; ATM, fast Ethernet, and 100VG-AnyLAN come to mind. Some of these technologies are priced to compete with Ethernet switches. Low-cost 25-Mbit/s ATM products can now be had for about $750 per node. 100Base-T equipment costs an average of $450 per node. 100VG-AnyLAN kit goes for about $650 per node. However, none of these alternatives can match the ability of Ethernet switches to boost performance without making changes to the network interface cards (NICs) already installed in PCs and servers. It is the combination of performance, cost, *and* convenience that is making Ethernet switches a hands-down winner with net managers today (see Fig. 16.1).

In 1993 about five vendors were selling Ethernet switches; by the end of 1995 that number had gone up to more than 100. Given the wide range of choices, it's easy for prospective buyers to get confused over what's available. In essence, there are three key factors to consider when choosing an Ethernet switch: how it processes frames, its underlying hardware design, and whether it is equipped to serve in the work group, department, or backbone.

Section 2.   Frame Processing

Ethernet switches process frames using one of four methods: store-and-forward switching, true cut-through switching, fragment-free cut-through switching, and adaptive cut-through switching.

As their name suggests, store-and-forward switches *store* each frame in a buffer before *forwarding* it to the outgoing port. While a

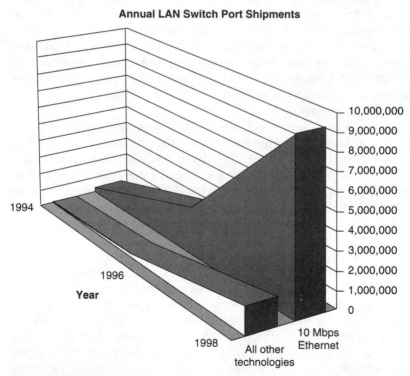

Figure 16.1 10 Mbps Ethernet vs. all other switch ports, 1994–1998. Market researchers predict phenomenal growth for switched 10-Mbps Ethernet. Source: Infonetics Research, Inc.

frame is in the buffer, the switch measures it and then runs a CRC (cyclic redundancy check) to see if it's OK. If the frame is too small or too large, or fails the CRC, it's discarded (see Fig. 16.2). Otherwise, the switch forwards the frame to the destination port. By assuring error-free operation, store-and-forward mode improves network reliability. By filtering out bad packets, it also reduces network overhead and provides more available bandwidth for applications.

Nevertheless, store-and-forward switching also introduces an unavoidable latency delay equal to the time it takes to store, error-check, and forward each packet. This latency increases with the size

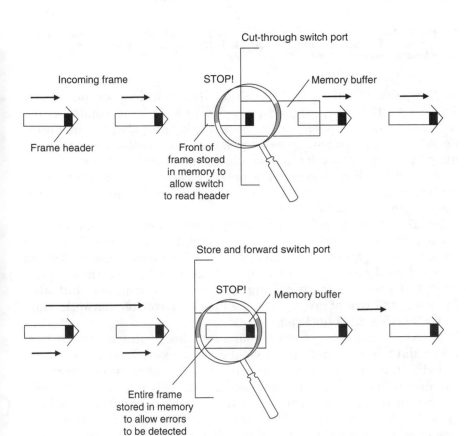

Figure 16.2 The inside story on switching. Ethernet switches process incoming frames in one of two ways. With cut-through switching, the frame is forwarded as soon as the header has been read. This keeps delays to a minimum, but also means that the switch propagates errored packets. With store-and-forward switching, the entire frame is stored into a memory buffer before being forwarded, giving the switch chance to scrutinize incoming data and discard faulty frames. The tradeoff is that the buffering process means that latency increases in proportion to frame size. Grand Junction, Kalpana, and Netwiz sell switches that operate in either mode.

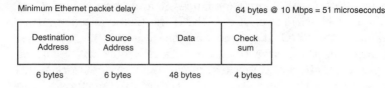

Minimum Ethernet packet delay   64 bytes @ 10 Mbps = 51 microseconds

Destination Address	Source Address	Data	Check sum
6 bytes	6 bytes	48 bytes	4 bytes

Minimum Ethernet packet delay   1518 bytes @ 10 Mbps = 1,214 microseconds

Destination Address	Source Address	Data	Check sum
6 bytes	6 bytes	1502 bytes	4 bytes

Figure 16.3 Buffering delays. Store-and-forward switches buffer the entire frame before forwarding it. The amount of time it takes to buffer the frames increases in proportion to its length. Source: AmberWave Systems Inc.

of the packet. For 64-byte packets (the smallest supported by Ethernet), the total latency is typically 91 microseconds, which includes 51 microseconds for the packet delay plus about 40 microseconds for switch processing. For the largest Ethernet-supported packets of 1518 bytes, the latency is 1254 microseconds, 14 times longer (see Fig. 16.3). High and variable delays have an adverse effect on the performance of applications, particularly those that include a time-sensitive multimedia element.

In an attempt to reduce the delay problems of store-and-forward switching, some switches operate in cut-through mode. Here, the switch reads a minimal amount of the packet header then makes its forwarding decision, ensuring the packet a quick time through the switch. Cut-through switching improves performance, but also increases the risk of propagating bad packets over the network, such as CRC errors and broadcast storms.

There are two types of cut-through switches, distinguished by how much data is read before forwarding a packet. True cut-through switches minimize latency by reading only the destination address—the first 6 bytes of data in the packet. With this procedure, the only latency incurred is that caused by the switch's internal processing—typically, 40 microseconds. However, by reading only the first 6 bytes of a packet, the cut-through switch will not detect packet "runts," the partial data created by normal packet collisions. Runts are very common on busy Ethernet LANs, and if the cut-through switch forwards the runts, 15 to 20 percent of network bandwidth can be wasted. Actual lost bandwidth depends on the network load—the higher the load, the more collisions, and the more runts with the potential to slip through the switch undetected.

The second type of cut-through switching is designed to increase available bandwidth by eliminating runts. It's called fragment-free cut-through mode. Here, the switch always reads the first 64 bytes of a packet before making a forwarding decision. Fragment-free operation eliminates packet fragments from propagating across the network, because 64 bytes is the minimum packet size permissible on Ethernet. This switching mode typically adds 91 microseconds to the forwarding latency, which includes the time to receive the packet's first 64 bytes plus the switch processing delay. Fragment-free operation slows performance compared with straight cut-through processing, but it ensures that the minimum bandwidth will be wasted by errors, boosting the overall network performance. Compared with the delays caused by reading and error-checking large packets in store-and-forward mode, fragment-free cut-through latency is far smaller, and it is a fixed delay that does not increase with packet size.

Recently, several vendors have started to ship Ethernet switches that circumvent the need to decide between cut-through and store-and-forward switch processing in a simple and ingenious fashion: they support both. Switches which process packets in adaptive cut-through mode support both cut-through and store-and-forward modes on a per-port basis, allowing net managers to choose between performance gains and reliability.

Vendors offering this facility include Amber Wave Systems Inc. (Acton, MA), Grand Junction Networks Inc. (Fremont, CA), Kalpana Workgroup (Sunnyvale, CA), Netwiz Ltd. (Haifa, Israel), and Xedia Corp. (Wilmington, MA). With some of these switches, such as the ones from Grand Junction and Netwiz, network managers use traffic statistics on the net management console to decide whether to manually set the box in store-and-forward mode. Amber Wave and Kalpana automatically switch modes. When a frame arrives at the switch, the silicon at the incoming port stores just enough of it to read its address and then immediately forwards it to the appropriate outgoing port. As the end of the frame passes through the incoming port, the switching silicon, operating in cut-through mode, assesses the CRC on the fly. If too many bad frames are clocked at any one port, the switch automatically reverts to store-and-forward mode. Once the number of flawed frames drops to an acceptable level, the switch returns to cut-through mode.

It's a good bet that most other vendors will eventually follow these dual-mode pioneers. Given that cut-through switches already come with buffers, there's very little reason for them not to.

Section 3.   Hardware Design

Another key factor to consider when shopping for a LAN switch is hardware design. Some switches use an off-the-shelf CPU (such as a reduced instruction set computing, or RISC, processor) to process packets; others use switching ASICs (application-specific integrated circuits) custom-made to handle the task. In general, ASIC-based switches drop fewer frames under congested conditions and they deliver frames at lower latencies. This is because they make packet forwarding decisions on the spot at each switch port, rather than handing that task off to a shared processor.

Some of the ASIC-based gear, in fact, performs so well that it could actually change the underlying assumptions made about Ethernet switches. Currently, companies buy (and vendors sell) these products as stopgaps until ATM (asynchronous transfer mode) comes of age. But some ASIC-based boxes actually offer lower latencies than ATM switches. Given this sort of performance, ASIC-based Ethernet switches could conceivably play a key role in corporate networks for a long time to come.

Despite their advantages, the cost and time involved in developing switch ASICs has meant that most switch vendors started out using general-purpose CPU designs—even though they're less efficient. Now that's changing. Most major vendors—including Bay Networks Inc. (Santa Clara, CA), Cabletron Systems Inc. (Rochester, NH), IBM (Armonk, NY), and 3Com Corp. (Santa Clara, CA)—are now delivering ASIC-based Ethernet switches.

CPU-based products do have some advantages over their ASIC-based counterparts. They can be enhanced with new features via simple software downloads (vendors of ASIC-based switches have to reforge silicon to add significant new features). Also, about a half-dozen vendors now sell CPU-based switches that can route traffic as well as forward it at the MAC (media access control) layer. These products reduce the need to rely on more expensive, slower routers to furnish features like security and firewalls, or to hand off traffic between different virtual LANs (VLANs). That's a trick that most ASIC-based switch manufacturers have yet to master, although Cisco Systems Inc. (San Jose, Calif.) and 3Com do sell ASIC-based products that handle IP routing.

Section 4.   Work Group Versus Departmental Switches

Performance (or the lack of it) may be the reason corporate networkers install switches in the first place, but they also need to consider a variety of other switch attributes before shelling out for one particular product. Ethernet LAN switches can be divided into two categories: fixed-configuration work group switches and departmental or backbone switches (see Fig. 16.4). Companies need to ensure that

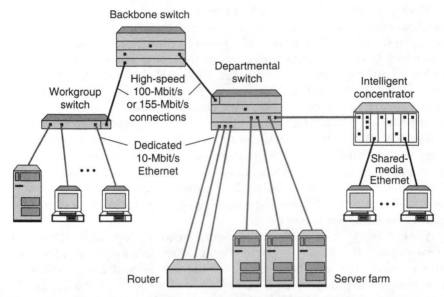

Figure 16.4 Work group, departmental, and backbone switches. Today's Ethernet switches are designed to serve either in the work group, department, or backbone. Most now support high-speed ports and full-duplex connections for use on busy network connections. Net managers can use switches to design hierarchical topologies, in which a backbone switch interconnects several smaller switches, which in turn support their own population of workstations, servers, or shared media hubs.

their switch comes with both the performance attributes *and* the feature sets commensurate with their needs. As a rule of thumb, buying a work group switch and installing it at the center of a large network is not recommended—these switches lack the requisite features. Buying a high-end switch for a work group is simply a waste of money.

In fact, the term *work group switch* has misleading connotations, implying that these switches are designed *only* to support small work groups in which each PC or workstation gets its own personal connection to the switch. A better definition of a work group switch is a device that is designed to split a large shared-media LAN into smaller work-group-size LANs.

Switch vendors say that the commonest configuration for work group products is in a network that has 10 to 20 PCs connected on each port (usually via a small hub or Ethernet repeater). To enable that configuration, work group switches typically come with a table that can hold multiple MAC addresses (often more than 1000). Grand Junction's Fastswitch 10/100 is the only one of today's switches which actually prevents the connection of more than one node. In some configurations it is supplied with only one MAC address per switch port.

Work group switches are easy to spot. They are delivered as fixed-configuration boxes with a set number of Ethernet ports—typically between 6 and 16. The Series 1800 switch from Xnet Technology Inc. (Milpitas, CA) represents a departure from this form factor. It comprises a card that slots into an EISA, ISA, or PCI bus workstation.

Along with 10-Mbit/s Ethernet ports, most work group switches now support faster connections which can be used to relieve traffic congestion on busy interswitch or switch-server links. For instance, roughly half of today's work group switches come as standard with support for full-duplex transmission—a technique which allows the throughput of dedicated connections to be doubled to 20 Mbit/s. Full-duplex-capable switches can be set to disable the collision detection part of Ethernet's CSMA/CD protocol, allowing traffic to flow in two directions simultaneously.

Alternatively, most work group switch vendors now offer either one or two optional 100-Mbit/s ports. Two-port models are especially useful, because they can be used to handle server and LAN backbone connections separately and simultaneously (see Fig. 16.5). Bay's 28000 switch takes this flexibility to the max: Each of its 16 ports can be configured as either a 10-Mbit/s or a 100-Mbit/s connection.

The commonest varieties of high-speed port available are FDDI and 100Base-T (fast Ethernet). Only Plaintree Systems Corp. (Waltham, MA) and Proteon Inc. (Westborough, MA) support 100-Mbit/s 100VG-AnyLAN. No fewer than 10 switch vendors are also planning to implement 155-MBit/s ATM—giving users the option to connect it over a high-speed, switched campus network.

Work group switches are the best bet for net managers planning to pull time-sensitive multimedia applications onto their LANs. These products are built for speed—typically providing better latency numbers than their departmental/backbone counterparts. They also cost less. That's an important consideration, given that the best way to improve the quality of multimedia applications is to decrease the number of nodes attached to each port—thereby adding to the number of switches required in the network, and its overall cost. Work group switches typically cost around $500 per port. Departmental switches go for about $900 per port and up.

The tradeoff with work group switches is in features. In an effort to economize on costs, some work group switch vendors—like Networth Inc. (Irving, TX) and Network Peripherals Inc. (Milpitas, CA)—include only partial support for the 802.1D spanning tree algorithm in their products. 3Com's 1200 product omits it altogether. This leaves net managers with an extra job: designing their way around traffic loops (something which requires net managers to know their network by heart) or installing bridges or other internetworking kits to eliminate them. In contrast, all the departmental/backbone switch-

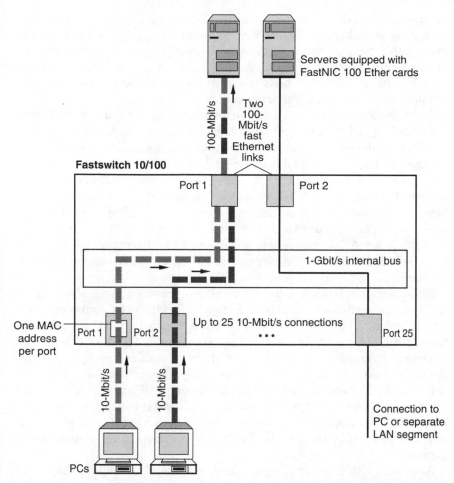

Figure 16.5 Grand Junction's Fastswitch 10/100 switch. Grand Junction's Fastswitch 10/100 is one of many Ethernet switches that supports two 100-Mbit/s connections for use on congested connections. But the 10/100 is also the *only* switch that comes with only one MAC address per switch port. In this configuration it is impossible to use it in departmental or backbone applications where more than one device is hooked to each port.

es support 802.1D. Similarly, reliability features like hot-swappable components and optional redundant power supplies are the exception for work group switches, and the rule for the departmental/backbone switches.

The most obvious difference between the two categories of switch is in capacity. Departmental/backbone switches are supplied as chassis loaded with interchangeable switching modules. Exceptions include the Etherswitch Pro16 from Kalpana, the NV7500 from Netvantage Inc. (Santa Monica, CA), and the Switchstak from Retix (Santa

Monica, CA). All three use a stackable design in which multiple Ethernet switching modules are connected by a high-speed proprietary cable bus to form a single logical switch. The extensible chassis architecture allows net managers to start small and then scale up switch capacity incrementally (some of these switches can be set up to support more than 100 Ethernet ports).

Most departmental/backbone switches can be configured with multiple high-speed ports—a prerequisite for serving in high-speed campus backbones. Some vendors are readying switches which can be configured as fully fledged ATM, FDDI, and token ring switches. This eliminates the need to buy switches from multiple sources to obtain different flavors of switched connectivity, and lets net managers enjoy benefits like one-stop convenient support and unified network management. Xylan Corp.'s OmniSwitch LAN switch supports any-to-any switching for ATM, Ethernet, FDDI, and token ring networks. The EliteSwitch ES/1 from SMC supports Ethernet, FDDI, and token ring switching.

Most Ethernet work group switches operate at the MAC layer, just like conventional two-port Ethernet bridges. In contrast, some departmental/backbone switches [like those from Alantec Corp. (San Jose, CA), and Xylan Corp. (Calabasas, CA)] offer filtering or network-layer routing facilities. Filtering enables them to provide firewalls between different parts of the switched network, preventing broadcast storms and enforcing security. Without higher-layer intelligence, net managers must use traditional routers to get those jobs done—an approach which is more expensive, adds stratospheric levels of latency to network traffic, and makes management more complex.

About 10 Ethernet switches take the firewall concept a stage further, offering virtual LAN facilities which allow net managers to allocate nodes attached to different switches to common virtual work groups using mouse commands from a management console. Vendors offering this service include Alantec, Bay, Lannet Data Communications Ltd. (Irving, CA), Retix, SMC and Xylan.

Section 5.   Backpressure Flow Control

An increasing number of both work group and departmental/backbone switches come equipped with a flow control feature known as backpressure that helps curb frame loss. Light frame loss isn't usually a problem for asynchronous data applications; the protocol stack or application running on the end station times out and resends lost frames. Similarly, a small number of dropped frames typically goes unnoticed by end users when multimedia traffic is being carried. But severe frame loss can cause a variety of problems with async applications, ranging from wasted bandwidth (as frames are resent) to session time-outs and lost connections. With multimedia, heavy frame loss is manifest as discordant sound and jerky picture quality.

Backpressure leverages the collision detection part of Ethernet's CSMA/CD (carrier-sense multiple access with collision detection) protocol. Each time a buffer on a switch port starts to fill up, the switch spoofs the devices attached to that port, sending a false collision detection signal that causes the devices to back off and pause before trying to transmit data again.

Backpressure is a powerful weapon in the fight against lost frames. But it also can misfire. Backpressure's fake collision detection signals can cause frames to be lost at the sending device. When this happens, the protocol stack or application redirector on the transmitting node will time out and resend the frames. Delays will result, even though the switch itself dropped no frames. This happens for two reasons. First, the Ethernet standard dictates that if a node receives 16 back-off notifications in a row, it has to dump the frame it is sending. Second, frames can be knocked off the wire by collisions as they leave the sending station. Either way, net managers need to be careful when setting time-out parameters. Too long, and the time spent waiting for confirmations leads to session loss. Too short, and there's a chance that frames that haven't been lost will be resent.

There's another problem. Each time a switch sends out a backpressure collision detection signal it stops *all* the traffic on the segment attached to that port—not just the traffic destined for the switch itself. The safest and easiest way to ensure that backpressure doesn't interfere with other traffic is to use it only when there is one device attached to each switch port—in a work group, for instance. Ironically, the low volume of traffic generated on one-node segments is least likely to cause buffer overflows in the first place. Another safe way to deploy backpressure switches is hierarchically, with each switch port connected to a bridge, router, or switch that doesn't use the flow control mechanism. Those devices, in turn, are connected to the workstations and servers.

Section 6. Limiting Latency

It's also important to keep latency numbers in perspective when choosing between different switch designs. It's true that latency numbers provide a good way to gauge the overall efficiency of a switch; the lower and more constant a switch's latency numbers are, the better the switch design. And in some configurations, low latency also can improve the quality of asynchronous data applications.

Likewise, when cut-through switches that exhibit low and constant delay are deployed with only one device attached to each port, it's possible to establish a multimedia network with close-to-guaranteed service levels. But that's hardly a representative network. Most companies are looking for switches that can boost the performance of LANs carrying async data. Switches will typically be configured with multiple nodes on each port. And once that's done, all devices on one switched segment contend for bandwidth using the same CSMA/CD scheme as shared-media LANs, a situation that adds far more delay than the switches themselves. Thus, the high levels of latency found on some switches may well be acceptable, and variable delays irrelevant.

The best latency numbers come from ASIC switches handling packets in cut-through mode. However, it's important to note that cut-through switches don't always live up to their names. Switches with 10-Mbit/s and 100-Mbit/s ports must use memory buffers to account for speed mismatches when passing frames from higher- to lower-speed connections. In this situation, latency increases in proportion to frame size, exactly as it does with store-and-forward switches. The same thing can happen under extreme traffic conditions, when cut-through switches fall back to store-and-forward mode.

The next-best performers as far as latency goes are ASIC switches operating in store-and-forward mode; CPU-based switches running in store-and-forward mode deliver the worst latency numbers. These products typically refer all switching decisions to a central processor. As traffic levels increase, and more decisions have to be made, response time falls and latency rises.

Section 7.   Design Issues

Ethernet switches can work wonders out on the enterprise; miracles are beyond their grasp. Installing the wrong switch (or the right switch in the wrong part of the network) will lead to worse performance, not better. It's the proprietary nature of Ethernet switch designs that makes them especially hard to handle. Unlike the standards-based switch technologies (ATM, Fibre Channel, HIPPI) there are no specifications defining how Ethernet switches can control traffic flow—and thus no easy way to tell which ones won't drop frames. Without standards to help them, net managers need to be guided by switch architectures when designing their LAN. Net managers who need to deliver time-sensitive multimedia to the desktop should be looking at cut-through switches with low, constant delay. Similarly, if a switch is headed for a busy backbone, it better have substantial memory buffers. Here are seven pointers on how to get the best performance from LAN switches.

Avoid the straight swap

Ignore vendor marketing blurbs which advocate simply swapping out shared-media Ethernet hubs for switches—it's a recipe for traffic mayhem. On a shared-media Ethernet everyone communicates over the same segment, so it doesn't matter if a PC on a hub in the east wing of a building exchanges files with a server hooked up to a hub in the west wing. But on a switched Ethernet it's much better to connect equipment such as printers and servers to the same switch as the users that access them. Connecting PCs to one switch and their server to another will cause a bottleneck (and possible frame loss) when files try to squeeze over the interswitch connection.

Go with the flow

Tune throughput by analyzing traffic flow, working out who's talking to whom (and how often), and then reallocating switch ports accordingly. Of course, analyzing switched traffic is easier said than done. Very few switches support the RMON (remote monitoring) MIB. Without it, net managers with more money than sense can try installing a standalone RMON agent on every port. Others will have to lug an analyzer around from port to port.

Play some one-on-one

Thinking about running real-time multimedia? There's really only one way to ensure requisite response times and that's to implement "desktop switching," in which each workstation gets its very own dedicated connection to the switch. (If more than one PC is connected per port, contention between nodes on the same port will stymie timely delivery of audiovisual data.) Also, install cut-through switches. They keep delays low and constant, unlike their store-and-forward cousins.

Count the errors of your ways

Use an analyzer to help decide between cut-through switches and store-and-forward switches. If the level of runts, jabbers, and other network garbage is below 3 percent on the preswitched, shared-media LAN, it's generally OK to go with the speedier cut-through switch. Anything approaching 10 percent and it's better to install store-and-forward switches to filter out the problem frames.

Safe six

Tests show that CPU-based switches tend to run out of steam and drop frames when more than six ports are in service. One way to avoid the problem is simply to buy six-port switches. Alternatively, try putting lightweight users on ports seven and up.

Keep it down

Aim to keep traffic activity on each switch segment at around 50 percent. Almost all switches can juggle multiple 5-Mbit/s streams without dropping frames. But when traffic is red-lining at 100 percent, most switches lose frames. Use an analyzer to measure the flow of traffic on each port; if it's peaking regularly at over 50 percent, reassign the attached devices to more than one switch port.

Back off from back off

Backpressure flow control schemes stop switches from dropping frames. Unfortunately, they also shut down *peer-to-peer* communications between nodes attached to the switch port. There are two configurations in which backpressure switches can be installed safely: in networks where only one device is attached to each port, or in a backbone where workstations and servers are insulated from the effects of backpressure by conventional bridges and routers.

Token Ring Switches

Section 1.   Introduction

Good things come to those who wait. For corporations looking for an affordable and easy-to-implement way to boost the performance of their 4-Mbit/s and 16-Mbit/s token ring networks, the wait has been a long one. Net managers with Ethernet networks have had the option to install a LAN switch to help them out of the performance hole since 1992, and there are now almost 100 Ethernet LAN switches to choose from; but token ring switches took much longer to hit the market.

Just as Ethernet switches emerged to extend the lives of Ethernets, token ring switches are now being offered to net managers as a way to augment the performance of their LANs. This approach boosts aggregate throughput, reduces latency, and simplifies network management—all without incurring any network disruption or expensive adapter upgrades. Segmentation with switches improves performance by reducing the number of devices contending for bandwidth on a given ring. For servers and power users, dedicated bandwidth may be desired to ensure adequate performance. For other users, ring segments with fewer devices (e.g., 10–40 users) may be necessary to support high bandwidth applications.

Token ring switches are fast becoming a hot item with corporate networkers. A recent survey shows that more than 60 percent of Fortune 5000 companies are either somewhat or highly likely to implement token ring switching before the end of 1996 (see Fig. 17.1). This chapter examines how the need for token ring switches has come about, then details the architectural differences among the switches available today.

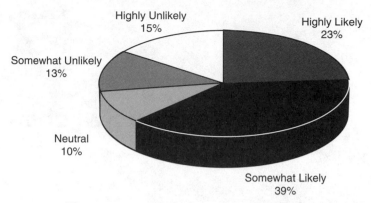

Figure 17.1 Plans to use switched token ring by Q4 1996. From a sample of 74 *Fortune* 5000 companies. Source: Sage Research.

Section 2.   Background

Token ring is often perceived as the poor relation of Ethernet in the internetworking industry, but the numbers don't justify that view. As token ring enters its second decade of service, it now plays a critical part in the information systems infrastructure of a huge number of corporations. And while it's true that token ring systems may constitute less than 30 percent of today's local area networks, that still means there are more than 12 million nodes attached to token ring LANs—and those networks are growing at an annual rate of over 20 percent.

More importantly, if we ever bothered to work out the dollar value of the applications running over those token ring networks, we'd find that they represent a disproportionate level of corporate revenue. It is known that token ring is present in virtually every Fortune 500 company. And those organizations are using it to carry mission-critical data—not merely to support their file and print and e-mail services.

Deterministic behavior, predictable behavior under high load, and the IBM stamp of approval are what have garnered token ring its fan club. And until recently token ring has served them well. When Ethernet networks reached their breaking points in the early 1990s, token ring networks kept on ticking. But today many of these networks are finally approaching a practical limit in throughput, latency, and scalability. A variety of LAN-based applications—including e-mail, software distribution, and imaging—are driving token ring network growth. As these client-server applications are deployed, more users are added to networks, causing network administrators to add rings to maintain fault domains at comfortable levels (typically between 50 and 80 users).

Traditionally, the most common method for subdividing token ring is to deploy two-port bridges. These devices are simple to install and require little maintenance. However, they consume expensive floor space and often lack important internetworking features, such as fault tolerance and SNMP management. The price per port for two-port bridges depends on the platform but typically runs from $1500 to $3000.

Segmenting the network with more and more bridges provides temporary relief to performance problems in departmental rings. Unfortunately, it typically gives rise to a new problem—in the backbone. Most token ring networks are connected, via their two-port bridges, to a single 16-Mbit/s token ring backbone. When too much network traffic attempts to cross the backbone, the result is a bandwidth bottleneck. Fueling this backbone crunch are centralization trends, such as consolidating departmental servers into super-servers—to which everyone needs access. And the performance problem is set to get really ugly when high-bandwidth, time-sensitive multimedia applications start making it onto corporate networks.

As an alternative to the two-port bridge solution, some corporations are turning to routers—using their multiport bridge capabilities to support collapsed backbone topologies. Here again there are problems. Routers logically segment routable protocols (e.g., TCP/IP and IPX) to reduce broadcast propagation. However, for SNA and NetBIOS, routers simply support local bridging within the building or campus; broadcasts are not prevented. And as bridging devices, routers are expensive to implement, in terms of both hardware costs and demand on management resources. Further, configuring routers is not a trivial operation (particularly in comparison with the source-route bridges they replace). Routers also add relatively high latency delays to traffic—something which has an adverse effect on user performance, particularly when the router is providing many functions (such as filtering) at the same time.

Section 3.   Late Arrivals

They may have been a long time coming, but token ring switches have finally started to appear in numbers. More than 10 token ring switches are scheduled to ship by the start of 1996—including the first switches from token ring maven IBM Corp. (Armonk, NY) and Madge Networks Inc. (San Jose, CA). (See Table 17.1.)

As noted, one reason for the dearth of token ring switch solutions to date is that token ring LANs held up under the ever-increasing pressure of traffic crossing corporate LANs better than their Ethernet counterparts. It's not just that a 16-Mbit/s token ring runs that much

TABLE 17.1 Token Ring Switch Vendors

Vendor	Product	Mode	Source route or transparent bridging	Broadcast caching	Ports/ price per port
Centillion Networks Inc. Mountain View, CA 415-969-6700	Speed Switch 100	Store and forward	Both	NetBIOS and source route	24/$1,800
IBM Contact local sales office	LANstreamer 8272	Cut-through with buffering on outbound port	Transparent, source route planned	None	12/$600
Madge Networks Inc. San Jose, CA 408-955-0700	Smart Ringswitch	Cut-through with buffering on outbound port	Source route	NetBIOS	8/$2,000
Nashoba Networks Inc. Littleton, MA 508-486-3200	Concord TR Switch	Store and forward	Both	NetBIOS	16/$1,500
Netedge Systems Inc. Research Triangle Park, NC 909-361-9000	ATM Connect Edge Router	Store and forward	Both	None	16/$3,000
Netvantage Inc. Santa Monica, CA 310-828-9898	Blue Ox	Store and forward	Both	NetBIOS	8/$1,800
Cabletron Systems Inc. Rochester, NH 603-332-9400	Eliteswitch ES/1	Store and forward	Both	None	20/$3,150
3Com Corp. Santa Clara, CA 408-764-5000	LANplex 6000 switch module	Store and forward	Both	None	80/$1,625
Xylan Corp. Calabasas, CA 818-880-3500	Omniswitch	Store and forward	Both	None	48/$1,700

faster than the 10-Mbit/s top speed of Ethernet. More importantly, under heavy traffic conditions, the token passing access method used on token ring sustains much more efficient levels of network utilization than the CSMA/CD technique used on Ethernet. Ironically, the token passing scheme which has helped keep token ring LANs happy and humming also has been the number 1 impediment to the development of token ring switches. It's taken time for switch vendors to design ways to deal with the token.

As with Ethernet LAN switches, the premise underlying token ring switches is that they pump up network bandwidth by switching traffic between nodes using dedicated LAN segments (see Fig. 17.2). It follows that some of the selection criteria used when shopping for an

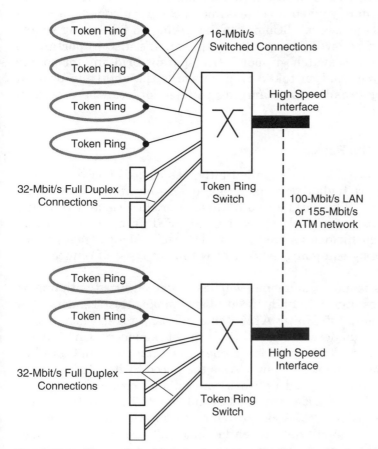

Figure 17.2 The switched token ring network. Source: Madge Networks Inc.

Ethernet switch can be reused when casting around for a token ring device. Price, port density, routing and filtering facilities, virtual LAN capabilities, ATM or FDDI high-speed uplinks, and the ability to support SNMP management and RMON analysis all must be factored into the buying process.

There are also some crucial differences between the checklist for Ethernet and the one for token ring switches. For instance, it turns out that most of the token ring switches on the market actually are based on modified versions of CPU-based, store-and-forward LAN Ethernet switches. Only IBM and Madge have gone back to the whiteboard to develop new silicon especially designed for token ring switching. This should give them two advantages—high packet per second (pps) rates, and low latency (something that will come in particularly handy when it comes time to carry multimedia applications over the network). 3Com also is working on token ring switch silicon. Its first switch has yet to appear. It's also important to check whether a switch supports transparent bridging, or source route bridging. And on token ring networks the ability to prevent unnecessary broadcasts swamping the network can be a critical requirement.

Section 4. The Basics

Token ring switches are supplied either as chassis-based products (which support higher port densities) or fixed-configuration stand-alone switches. The ports on both kinds of product come with either DB-9 connectors for shielded twisted-pair (STP) cable or RJ-45 connectors for unshielded twisted-pair (UTP) cable. Madge leaves users' options open by equipping every port with both types of connector as standard.

Both chassis and standalone switches can be outfitted with one or, in some cases, multiple high-speed fiber uplinks. Most vendors offer uplinks to both 155-Mbit/s ATM (for connecting token rings over a switched campus network) and FDDI (so net managers don't have to can their existing high-speed backbone). One example from Centillion Networks Inc. (Mountain View, CA) is the Speed Switch 100 (see Fig. 17.3). These higher-speed network connections serve two purposes: (1) to extend network coverage beyond the 100-meter limitation imposed over copper cable on switch-to-workstation token ring connections and (2) to alleviate potential bandwidth bottlenecks on busy network links (e.g., between switches or on server connections). Netedge also gives net managers the option of equipping their switches with wide-area network interfaces.

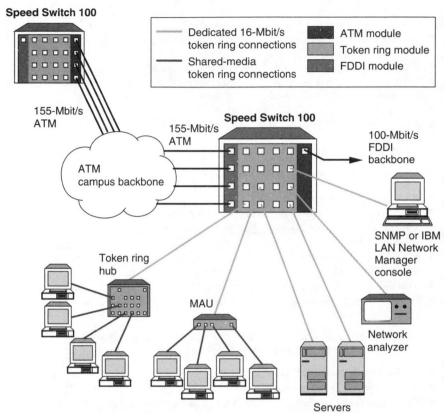

Figure 17.3 ATM and FDDI connectivity. Centillion's Speed Switch 100 accommodates switching modules for token ring, ATM, and FDDI traffic. The token ring modules come with four ports, each of which provides 16 Mbit/s of bandwidth. ATM modules are available with two or four 155-Mbit/s ports for campus connections, and the FDDI module offers a single 100-Mbit/s port for a backbone link.

Preparing a Request for Proposal

The following list of questions are important to ask when putting together an RFP for token ring switches. Switches provide different levels of functionality depending on where they are intended to fit in the network. It follows that certain questions are important to ask when buying a switch for the work group, but are less relevant when buying a departmental/backbone product (and vice versa).

When shopping for a work group switch some key questions are:

- Does it support full-duplex token?
- Does it support cut-through switching, store-and-forward switching, or both?
- What latency numbers does the switch deliver?

Pertinent questions when shopping for a departmental or enterprise backbone switch are:

- How many devices can be connected to each port?
- Does the switch support virtual network groups, or is every user on the switch a part of a single logical network?
- What redundancy and reliability features are supported?
- What level of throughput does the switch support, and how many packets does it drop under extreme traffic conditions?
- Does the switch filter all bad frames?
- What is the mean time to failure?

Regardless of whether a switch is being selected for the work group or the backbone, it's important to assess whether the device will fit into the current network environment easily. That can be done using these questions:

- Does the switch support source routing?
- If not, does the switch have filters to prevent it forwarding discovery frames?
- Will the switch support common configurations such as dual backbones and duplicate MAC addresses?
- Will the switch support a spanning tree to maintain a single route for single-route broadcast frames?
- Does the switch support transparent bridging?
- What token ring speeds are supported by the switch (i.e., does it support both 4-Mbit/s and 16-Mbit/s speeds)?

In addition to token ring, it's important to assess which high-speed LAN technologies the switch supports. Some questions to ask are:

- Will the switch support FDDI connections?
- Will it support ATM connections?
- If yes, what speed, and are ATM LAN emulation standards supported?

It is also obviously important to ask about price. Switch pricing is typically related to the function provided; thus, a work group switch should come with a lower price tag than a backbone switch. The questions to ask are:

- What is the price per port?
- What is the incremental cost of adding additional ports?
- What is the cost of high-speed ports?

Most internetworking equipment today supports SNMP management, but in the token ring world bridges are often managed by LAN Network Manager, an OS/2 LAN management application from IBM. RMON, which allows analysis of traffic flow, is another key differentiator to look for. Ask:

- Does the switch support SNMP management?
- Does the switch support LAN Network Manager?
- Does the switch support RMON?
- Can the switch provide port-by-port monitoring?

Section 5.   Cost Considerations

Token ring switches now on the market or in the pipeline cost an average of $1900 per port—around three times as much as the average price of Ethernet equivalents. That price point isn't surprising. With the exception of IBM and Netwiz (Horsham, PA), all the token ring switch vendors say that their products will first be installed to alleviate bandwidth shortfalls in token ring backbones. Consequently, most vendors are pricing their switches to undercut the two categories of equipment that traditionally have been used to pump up token ring backbone performance: routers ($5000 per port) and two-port bridges ($2000 per port).

Big Blue, in contrast, wants to kick-start the deployment of token ring switching in the work group, and is pricing (or underpricing) its switch LANStreamer 8272 Model 108 accordingly, at a mere $600 per port. The IBM switch was developed via a collaboration with switch pioneer Kalpana Inc. (Santa Clara, CA), which was acquired in 1995 by Cisco. IBM has exclusive rights to the switch. Netwiz says it will charge between $500 and $900 for its switch.

Section 6.   Performance Parameters

When it comes to performance, token ring switch vendors all claim that their products can switch token ring packets at wire speed on each port. Closer questioning reveals that such pedal-to-the-metal performance levels are possible only in best-case scenarios. In less utopian circumstances (such as when larger packets are present, specialized filtering functions are invoked, or traffic is being passed between token ring and other LAN media), switch performance can deteriorate.

Without the benefit of independent testing, it's still too early to say for sure how much of a hit performance each switch will take, but a look at the internal architectures of the switches in Table 1 (Part 4) reveals that the products from IBM and Madge are likely to hold up best. That's because their products perform switching in hardware, using silicon. In contrast, the other products in the table switch packets with CPUs and shared memory. If the hardware-versus-CPU debate sounds familiar, that's because it's already been hashed out in the world of Ethernet switches. In fact, the token ring switch market's development is mirroring that of the more mature (and much larger) Ethernet switch market.

Faced with the challenge of developing Ethernet switch solutions, the vast majority of R&D departments opted for CPU-based designs—mainly because they could be brought to market faster and less expensively than products which switch packets in silicon. The same thing is now happening with token ring switches. All three of the token ring switches now shipping, and four of the ones on the way, use CPU architectures.

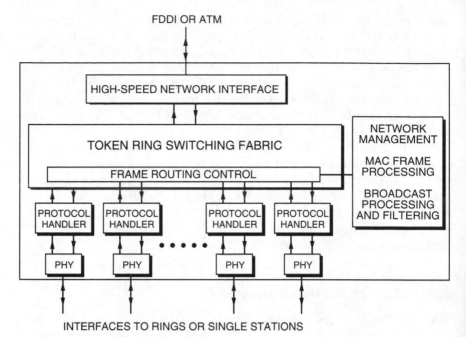

FDDI OR ATM

HIGH-SPEED NETWORK INTERFACE

TOKEN RING SWITCHING FABRIC

FRAME ROUTING CONTROL

PROTOCOL HANDLER   PROTOCOL HANDLER   PROTOCOL HANDLER   PROTOCOL HANDLER

PHY   PHY   PHY   PHY

NETWORK MANAGEMENT

MAC FRAME PROCESSING

BROADCAST PROCESSING AND FILTERING

INTERFACES TO RINGS OR SINGLE STATIONS

Figure 17.4 Madge's token ring switch silicon.

Section 7.   Silicon Solutions

IBM and Madge, in contrast, have opted to take the higher ground by developing their own specialized switch silicon (see Fig. 17.4). This is one reason that their products have taken longer to come to market. 3Com also plans to take the hardware path; it says it will follow the release of a CPU-based LANplex 6000 token ring switch module with a silicon-switching module for its SuperStack range of stackable hubs, due to hit the market in the second half of 1996. Hardware switching delivers consistently higher pps rates than CPU-based switching because it allows packet-forwarding decisions to be made by a chip set at the incoming switch port, without the need to refer to a centralized CPU.

Developing their own silicon has allowed IBM and Madge to attain a second advantage over CPU-based products: the ability to support low-latency cut-through switching. Both the IBM and the Madge chip sets feature a streaming protocol that allows them to begin forward packets as soon as the packet header has been read. The other switches in the table all enter packets into a memory cache before forwarding them—a restriction that means they can support *only* the slower store-and-forward mode. Their inability to support cut-through switching can be traced to their use of conventional token ring silicon (either made by Texas Instruments or coproduced by IBM and National Semiconductor). The older silicon chip sets cannot stream packets.

Cut-through switches are a good fit for networks requiring very low delay—in particular, for those carrying multimedia applications. With a cut-through token ring switch, the time that elapses between when a packet arrives at the switch and when the packet arrives at the outbound port remains constant—at around 30 microseconds—regardless of packet size. With store-and-forward switches, the process of storing packets into memory means that latency increases in proportion to packet size. With small packets, such as 32- or 64 bytes, that isn't a problem—delays are usually kept to within 60 microseconds. With larger packets, latency can be more than 100 times higher, and is measured in milliseconds. For instance, Netvantage says that it takes its Blue Ox switch 4 milliseconds to process a 4-kbyte packet. (Note that the maximum size frame handled on most token ring networks is 4500 bytes. This means store-and-forward latency problems are more likely to occur on token ring networks than on Ethernet LANs—where the maximum packet size is 1512 bytes.)

Until now, cut-through switches have come with a significant drawback. Because they read only the packet header, they propagate bad packets over the network. In contrast, the buffering stage in a store-and-forward switch provides the opportunity to examine and discard faulty frames. IBM, via its codevelopment agreement with Kalpana, claims to have come up with a technique called Adaptive Cut Through which eliminates the problem. The patent-pending process allows the switch to begin processing packets as soon as it has read the packet header, yet still allows it to read the cyclic redundancy check (CRC) checksum at the end of each packet to ensure frame integrity. CRCs are read "on the fly," without requiring additional buffering, says IBM. If too many bad frames are clocked at any port, the switch automatically sets that input to process packets in store-and-forward mode. The switch comes with a default error threshold, or net managers can configure their own choice of level from a net management console.

Madge's box has no equivalent to Adaptive Cut Through. Instead, it relies on higher-level protocols like IP and IPX to spot faulty packets once they have arrived at the workstation or server and to request retransmissions—a procedure that takes longer than stopping the errors in the first place. Madge argues that error propagation isn't a problem because there are far fewer errors on token ring networks than on Ethernet LANs.

It's important to realize that while IBM and Madge eliminate the need to buffer packets at incoming ports, their products—like all token ring switches—hold up packets on the way out. The additional buffering is necessary because of the token-passing scheme used on these networks. As a token travels around the ring, it stops at each station to give it the chance to transmit. This means the outgoing switch port usually must hold up packets until the token circulates back to the switch. Madge says that if no nodes are transmitting on the receiving ring, the switch will have to wait an average of 20 microseconds—an insignificant delay. But if nodes are transmitting, delays can easily stretch into milliseconds. This problem isn't exclusive to token ring switches. Ethernet switches also have to buffer outgoing traffic if a node on a receiving Ethernet segment is transmitting.

One way to reduce delays on outbound ports—for both token ring and Ethernet switches—is to limit the number of nodes on each port. Madge and IBM say they've got a better answer: Configure the receiving ring so that the switch port gets the token more often than the other nodes. Both companies are implementing a little-known part of the IEEE 802.5 token ring spec, called token priority, which makes it possible to assign different levels of access rights to different nodes. By assigning the highest priority to the switch port, net managers can guarantee that it will have access to the token at least 50 percent of the time. Centillion also supports token priority. 3Com says it will implement it on the first release of its LANplex 6000 switch.

Section 8.   Full-Duplex Efficiency

There's a third option available—one that eliminates the problem altogether by eliminating the token. It's called *full-duplex token ring*. With this technology, network nodes get their own dedicated switch connections; the token is disabled. This allows traffic to flow in both directions, doubling the speed of the connection to 32 Mbit/s. Because the switch no longer has to wait for the token to arrive back on the outgoing port, there's no need to buffer outgoing traffic.

The IEEE 802.5 committee is still working on a draft standard defining dedicated token rings. The specification calls for full backward compatibility with the installed token ring network base. IBM says its token ring switch will support full duplex out of the box when it first ships—whether or not IEEE 802.5 has finished up its spec by then. The rest of the token ring players say they will send customers a software or firmware upgrade enabling their switches to support the standard once it is complete. IBM also says that the first release of its switch will support an "autodiscovery protocol" that allows it to automatically step into full duplex mode by sensing whether the adapter at the other end of the connection is full-duplex-capable.

Section 9.   Transparent and Source Route Switches

Most of today's token ring switches support two different ways to direct packets to their destination:

- Transparent (or MAC layer) bridging
- Source route bridging—a bridging algorithm developed for token ring internetworks

Usually the decision over which bridging technique to use will depend on where the switch is being installed. Source route bridging is the best choice for backbone switches installed on large networks. The source route standard defines a way for network devices to forward packets on the basis of ring numbers, rather than MAC addresses. In source route mode, each port on a switch is given its own ring number. Source route bridging enables switches to choose the fastest route for traffic of multiple paths available, and provides better security. Switches make forwarding decisions on the basis of the source route RIF (routing information filed) carried in packet headers.

In contrast, transparent bridging is a better choice for switches installed in the work group. Transparent switches allow the work group to appear to the rest of the network as a single token ring— even though the switch has actually physically divided the work group into multiple rings. This provides two benefits. First, it means less work for net managers at network setup, because they don't have to go around and assign each port on the switch a new ring number. Second, transparent bridged networks are not affected by the "seven hop" limitation imposed on source-route-based networks.

The Madge switch supports only source route bridging, which means that its switch cannot be installed in token ring networks which use a combination of transparent bridging and routers. But that's only a fraction of the token ring market, according to Kevin Tolly, president of The Tolly Group (Manasquan, NJ), a strategic consulting and testing organization. Tolly estimates that 99 percent of token rings use source route SRB. Madge says it left out support for transparent bridging in order to bring its product to market faster, and points out that its switch is not designed for installation in work group environments anyway. The vendor says it plans to launch a switch that supports both source routing and transparent bridging at a later date.

In its first release, IBM's token ring switch did not support source route bridging, a significant disadvantage that limited it to just two applications: working in transparent bridging work groups, or enhancing the performance of an installed source routed LAN by installing it cheek by jowl with old-style two-port, source-route-compliant bridges. (IBM plans to send customers a source route upgrade for the switch free of charge.)

Three-Step Migration

Once a decision to purchase token ring switches has been made, net managers can decide how much of their network they want to migrate to switching, and how fast. Many will follow a three-stage process.

Stage 1: Replace the local bridges with token ring switching. Here, one or more switches are used to provide multiport bridging functionality between attached segments. Depending on the configuration, a switch can sometimes be added in parallel with the existing bridges for testing. If testing is satisfactory, the bridges are removed from the network. Busy devices, such as servers and mainframes, can be moved to dedicated ports on the switch for optimal performance. Benefits include simplified management of fewer devices, reduced maintenance costs, higher LAN-to-LAN throughput, space savings, and lower latency delays.

Stage 2: Add high-speed technologies where required for better performance. In this stage, the campus/building backbone is upgraded. The primary choices for a backbone upgrade are ATM and FDDI. The upgrade is achieved by adding high-speed ports to connect the switch to servers and other switches on the new high-speed backbone. Since the faster ports are an upgrade to the switch, the new technology can be completely tested before migrating production users. A key benefit of this step is relieving congestion for busy devices (e.g., servers).

Stage 3: Augment shared hub technology with switching technology on the horizontal (departmental) floors. This stage involves taking token ring switching out to the desktops. Benefits are low latency, more aggregate throughput, and reduced impact of power users on other network nodes.

Section 10:   Caching and Filtering

Devices implementing source route bridging broadcast "explorer" packets to discover the optimum route for token ring packets. On large networks these packets can create a broadcast storm which can destroy network throughput. The switches from Centillion, Madge, Netvantage, and Nashoba all prevent this from happening by caching source route information. Each time these switches see a packet from a new node, they open it and read the source route information fields. This information is stored in a memory cache in the switch. This means that when the switch receives a Source Route or NetBIOS discovery packet, it sends it only to the destination node—rather than broadcasting it out over all its ports. Centillion has even gone a stage further—its switch performs caching for NetBIOS broadcasts, which are used by NetBIOS nodes to discover the location of other devices on the LAN.

In addition to supporting different bridge standards, the switches from Cabletron, Netedge, SMC, and 3Com all are equipped with network layer intelligence that allow them to route IP and IPX protocols. Netedge also routes Appletalk, and Cabletron has plans to add this facility to its product. All three vendors use their routing facilities to allow net managers to assign nodes on different switches to the same virtual LAN domain. Without the benefit of network layer intelligence, Nashoba and Xylan have resorted to proprietary schemes to allow them to support virtual LANs across multiple switches, using encapsulation (or packet tagging) to carry information between switches about which ports belong to which virtual LANs. The switches from Centillion, IBM, and Netvantage support virtual LANs on a switch-by-switch basis, by allocating ports on the same switch to different logical domains (see Fig. 17.5).

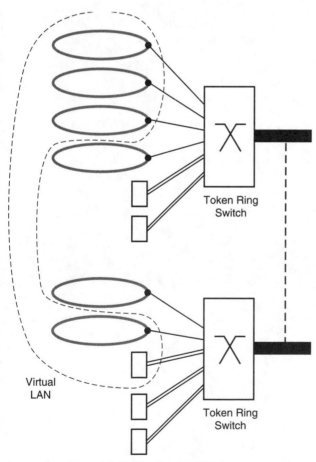

Figure 17.5 Virtual LANs in a switched token ring environment. Source: Madge Networks Inc.

Section 11.   Management Issues

As with Ethernet switches, management capabilities are another crucial differentiator to look for in token ring switches. All the products
in Table 17.1 are equipped with an SNMP management agent that
allows them to report basic diagnostic and status information to a
network management platform. Most all vendors also sell a graphical
user interface–based application which can run under one of the leading management consoles—such as HP Openview, Sunnet Manager,
or IBM Netview 6000.

Only four of the vendors implement (or are planning to implement)
RMON analysis in their switches: Nashoba, Cabletron, 3Com, and
Xylan. Without integral RMON, net managers must resort to add-on
analyzers or RMON probes—an inefficient and expensive alternative.

18

FDDI Switches

Section 1. Overview

The bad thing about buying FDDI switches is that it means investing in an old technology. The good thing is that they work. Corporate networkers looking for a way to pump up capacity on congested LAN backbones are set to learn all about this FDDI switching double-whammy.

For several years, 100-Mbit/s shared-media FDDI has been the number 1 backbone network. In fact, until recently, it was the *only* high-speed backbone available. But as the LANs connected to backbones get bigger and faster, a growing number of corporations are finding that 100 Mbit/s of shared bandwidth is not enough to go around. According to industry hype, the technology which is supposed to come to the rescue in this situation is ATM. But the reality is that interoperable, fully featured ATM switches are years away. Corporations that can't afford to wait are turning to FDDI switches to boost the capacity of their backbone networks.

The first users of FDDI switches report that in most cases they boost the performance of backbones by at least 50 percent. And a large number of companies are choosing FDDI over ATM: FDDI switches currently outnumber ATM switches in Fortune 1000 networks by almost two to one, according to market researcher Sage Research Inc. (Natick, MA).

With FDDI switches now available from eight equipment vendors, there's no shortage of products to choose from. Digital Equipment Corp. (DEC, Maynard, MA) pioneered FDDI switching back in 1993 with its Gigaswitch/FDDI product, and currently accounts for about 70 percent of FDDI switch revenues. The Gigaswitch/FDDI is still the only product which supports low latency cut-through switching and 200-Mbit/s full-duplex FDDI switching.

The seven other FDDI switch vendors are Alantec Corp. (San Jose, CA), Cabletron Systems Inc. (Rochester, NH), Cisco Systems Inc. (San Jose), Lannet Data Communications Ltd. (Irvine, CA), Netedge Systems Inc. (Research Triangle Park, NC), Network Systems Corp. (NSC, Minneapolis, MN), and Xylan Corp. (Calabasas, CA). Most of these companies are looking to challenge Digital's dominance by offering value-added features such as support for other types of LAN or WAN connectivity in the same FDDI switch chassis, or the ability to route frames instead of just bridging them at layer 2.

Bells and whistles aside, all FDDI switches have two things in common. First they dramatically improve the performance of shared-media FDDI networks by dividing them into dedicated, switched network segments; just like the Ethernet LAN switches which preceded them (see Fig. 18.1). Second, and unlike Ethernet switches, FDDI switches are expensive. The average price of the FDDI switches now shipping is $10,640 dollars per port. This guarantees that—even with their five-figure price tag—the vast majority of FDDI switches will end up installed in backbones (where CFOs can amortize the expense across all the nodes in the network) rather than in work groups providing desktop connectivity. Using a switch to segment the FDDI ring is both cheaper and faster than the traditional alternative: installing a router. For instance, a Cisco 7000 Series router equipped with five FDDI interfaces costs $21,620 per port, and adds milliseconds of delay to every frame it handles. In contrast, FDDI switches cost half as much, and add only microseconds of delay to the network.

Because FDDI switches are based on the established FDDI standard, they will interwork with the FDDI products (including adapters, concentrators, routers, and analyzers) now shipping from over 100 manufacturers. Corporations already running shared-media FDDI rings can boost backbone performance easily—and without making changes to installed FDDI internetworking hardware—by simply hooking up their FDDI equipment to the FDDI switch.

FDDI switches are easily distinguishable from another category of LAN switch: fixed-configuration Ethernet switches which come equipped with one or two FDDI ports. These devices are designed to switch traffic between 10-Mbit/s and 100-Mbit/s connections (e.g., between client workstations and a server), not between 100-Mbit/s backbone links.

Section 2.   FDDI Versus ATM

Installing a switched FDDI backbone is a whole lot easier than installing an ATM backbone (an operation which requires corpora-

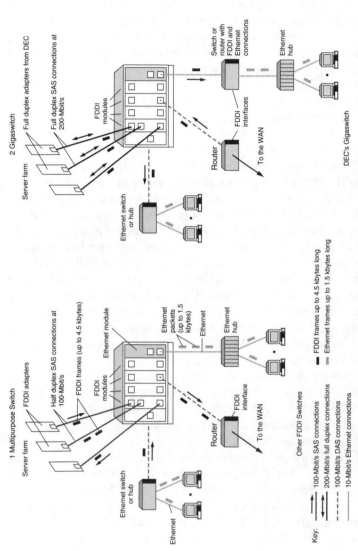

Figure 18.1 Look, no ATM. When it comes to FDDI switches, the products fall into two categories: Digital's Gigaswitch (2), and everything else (1). The Gigaswitch is designed from the ground up for FDDI, making it the only switch able to support very fast cut-through switching, and 200-Mbit/s full duplex connections to nodes equipped with DEC's full duplex adapters. On the downside, unlike its general-purpose switch counterparts, it can't support other LANs like Ethernet or Token Ring, meaning some net managers will have to buy additional switches and routers equipped with FDDI interfaces in order to hook their legacy LAN equipment into the Gigaswitch backbone.

tions to make wholesale changes to the network infrastructure, and to retrain their IS staff with the skill set to deal with a virgin technology). Nevertheless, ATM's status as the only scalable high-speed networking technology that spans both LAN and WAN means that almost all corporations are still planning to implement it at some point down the road. Consequently, before they even start evaluating FDDI switching products, net managers have an important decision to make: whether it's possible to sidestep FDDI switches altogether by holding out for ATM.

That's a question that can be answered only on a network-by-network basis, and depends on two factors. First, how much money has already been invested in FDDI equipment? For many corporations, the answer is a lot: 41 percent of Fortune 1000 companies now feature an FDDI backbone, according to Sage. FDDI switches provide corporations with a way to preserve this investment. Second, corporations need to factor in how bad backbone performance is now, how much worse it's expected to get, and whether its feasible to put up with a backbone bottleneck until ATM is ready for prime time. Judging from sales of FDDI switches, an increasing number of corporations figure the wait will be too long. Revenues from FDDI switches were expected to grow from $62 million (14,400 ports) in 1995 to $129 million (30,000 ports) in 1996, according to market researcher the Dell'Oro Group (Menlo Park, CA). ATM vendors are also taking longer than expected to get their products to work together. That's a big problem on enterprise backbones, which typically embrace equipment from multiple sources.

Of 15 ATM switches tested in 1995 at the University of New Hampshire, only five could communicate using switched virtual circuits (SVCs). Most ATM vendors are not yet implementing the ATM Forum's LAN emulation standard for carrying legacy LAN traffic over ATM backbones, and the ability of rate-based flow control schemes from different vendors to work together is a complete unknown. What all this means is that it will be years before net managers can build interoperable multivendor ATM networks or take advantage of the quality-of-service attributes in ATM, which are largely designed to ensure that multimedia applications are delivered on time.

Fortunately for today's net managers, the vast majority of the applications now running over corporate networks still comprise asynchronous data—and do not contain a multimedia element. What asynchronous applications require is bandwidth, and plenty of it. That's a prescription that FDDI switches are well equipped to fill, analysts reckon. According to market researcher Forrester Research Inc. (Cambridge, MA), between 1995 and the year 2000, most corporations will simply dish out raw bandwidth to satisfy users' demand for speed. A few will implement priority and reservation schemes, but most will ignore all services except fatter pipes.

FDDI switches may only deliver 100-Mbit/s of switched capacity compared to the 155-Mbit/s of ATM switches, but they use that bandwidth more efficiently. ATM cells are 53 bytes long. Five of the 53 bytes (9.5 percent) are used by a header containing addressing information. FDDI frames, on the other hand, can be up to 4,500 bytes in length, of which only 23 bytes (0.05 percent) are used for addressing information. Further, the short cell sizes used on ATM also mean that LAN packets have to be broken up (or segmented) before passing over the ATM backbone, and then reassembled on the other side. FDDI does away with this overhead because the maximum length of an FDDI frame is longer than those found on Ethernet or token ring networks.

Section 3. Which Switch?

The need for switching is being driven by several factors, including more users and faster desktop systems. Also, the trend is for IS departments to consolidate applications on centrally located "superservers" accessed by users all over the company premises. (The side effect of this centralization trend is that far more traffic travels between clients and servers over the backbone than is the case in distributed client-server networks.) However, recognizing what's causing the bandwidth problem is a lot simpler than working out which switch is best equipped to solve it.

Although nine equipment vendors now offer FDDI switches, only one has designed its product from the ground up for FDDI: Digital. Its Gigaswitch/FDDI product features specialized FDDI switching silicon that sits on every port, making forwarding decisions as each frame reaches the switch. The FDDI-oriented design of the Gigaswitch/FDDI gives it several advantages over the other FDDI switches available: It is the only FDDI switch to support cut-through switching; it is the only FDDI switch to support full-duplex operation; it supports more FDDI ports than any other switch; and—at $6955 per port—it's the second least expensive FDDI switch out there. The cheapest is sold by Xylan.

When the Gigaswitch is running in cut-through mode, the port receiving a frame starts to transmit it to the destination port as soon as the first 60 bytes of the frame have been received—keeping delay to 15 microseconds, according to Digital. The downside to cut-through mode is that the switch loses the opportunity to inspect frames and discard errored traffic. Net managers who want to keep errors to a minimum can opt to run the Gigaswitch/FDDI in store-and-forward mode. In this configuration, each frame is buffered as it enters the switch, and latency increases in proportion to frame size. The delay with a 4478-byte frame goes up to 720 microseconds, Digital says. Only one other FDDI switch comes close to matching the Gigaswitch/FDDI's cut-through capabilities: NSC's Enterprise Routing Switch can be set to start forwarding frames after the first 200 bytes have been received, keeping latency to between 50 and 60 microseconds, regardless of frame size. The other products all mandate store-and-forward mode, and can take more than a millisecond to forward full-size frames.

Section 4. Full-Duplex Switching

The ability to support full-duplex switching is another Gigaswitch/FDDI differentiator. Full-duplex operation allows throughput on point-to-point FDDI connections (e.g., between two switches, or between a switch and a single end node) to be doubled to 200 Mbit/s. It works by disabling the FDDI token, which circles the ring allowing stations to send data, so that traffic can travel in two directions at once on dedicated connections.

Digital calls its full-duplex implementation FFDT (FDDI full-duplex technology). Because Digital is the only vendor offering the feature, corporations are limited to using full-duplex FDDI between Gigaswitch/FDDI's, or between Digital's switch and a workstation or server equipped with one of its FFDT-enabled adapters. Digital's attempts to standardize the technology have so far been stymied by the fact that ANSI does not have a committee to deal with enhancements to the FDDI standard, and Digital is not currently planning to pursue standardization.

Cabletron also plans to implement full-duplex FDDI. In the absence of a standard defining full-duplex FDDI, it was not known at press time if the products from the two vendors would work together. Other equipment vendors are proving slow to pick up on full-duplex FDDI's benefits, a fact that ultimately stands to limit FDDI switching's window of opportunity.

Section 5. Filling Up

Capacity is another criterion to consider when scoping out FDDI switches. Again, Digital is the leader in this category. Its Gigaswitch/FDDI can support up to 22 dual-attach station (DAS) ports; the average maximum number of DAS ports supported by FDDI switches is 13. DAS ports come with twin connectors, allowing the switch to be connected to both of the redundant rings in an FDDI network. This way, if the primary ring fails, the switch can take advantage of FDDI's fault-tolerant construction, which "wraps" the primary ring onto the secondary ring, bypassing the fault. Given that most FDDI switches are headed for service in enterprise backbones— where reliability is of a key consideration—most corporations are opting for DAS ports, vendors report.

There is an alternative to DAS ports, however. Instead, net managers can choose to configure switch ports as single-attach station (SAS) ports. In this setup, the switch is physically connected to only *one* of the rings. SAS connections are typically used for work group applications, in which only one device is connected per switch port. Alantec, Cabletron, and Xylan offer a neat feature which allows users to double the capacity of their switches for no extra cost when they are configured for SAS connections. These vendors equip each port on their switches with two MAC addresses. This allows net managers to use both twin connectors on each port (which are required for the dual-attach connections) as two SAS ports. With other switches, ports serve as either one SAS or one DAS connection.

Digital's Gigaswitch/FDDI, NSC's Enterprise Routing Switch, and Cisco's Lightstream 2020 (which actually comprises an ATM switch with FDDI interfaces) all use an internal matrix (or crossbar) to connect different ports. The other products connect FDDI ports either by installing a high-speed TDM backplane along the back of the switching chassis or by using shared memory. Both solutions offer lower aggregate throughput than matrices—a characteristic which means that they are more likely to become a bottleneck when configured to support multiple FDDIs.

Section 6.   Multiservice Switches

Given the dominance of Digital in the FDDI switching market, newcomers are having to find new ways to differentiate their products. The most obvious is the ability to support other types of switched network connectivity from the same switch chassis. Digital's Gigaswitch supports FDDI, and can also be configured with an interface card containing an ATM bridge that allows the switched FDDI network to be connected to an ATM network.

All seven of Digital's competitors handle Ethernet switching. Five of them support token ring ports (not surprising given the prevalence of FDDI in token ring sites). Four support ATM (making the eventual migration to ATM easier). Four of them support serial interfaces to wide-area network services such as T1 lines and frame relay. Four vendors also support 100Base-T (fast Ethernet). Such "multiservice" switches convert the headers in Ethernet and token ring packets into

FDDI addresses in accordance with the IEEE 802.1h standard for translational bridging. Additionally, they support the IP fragmentation specification defined in the IETF's RFC 791 standard, enabling them to segment FDDI frames into shorter Ethernet packets, and vice versa.

Multiservice switches have several potential benefits: They economize on equipment costs by reducing the need to buy separate FDDI and LAN switches; they simplify administration by eliminating the need to use separate management consoles to oversee the network (one from the vendor of the FDDI switch and another from the supplier of the LAN switches); they conserve room in the computer room; and they allow LAN switch modules to leverage high-end FDDI switch redundancy features—such as dual power supplies and extra fans. Also, because multiservice switches handle the transfer of traffic between dissimilar networks themselves, they reduce the need to buy additional equipment in order to hook legacy Ethernet or token ring LAN equipment into the FDDI backbone. For instance, with Digital's Gigaswitch/FDDI, some net managers with installed Ethernet hubs and repeaters will have to purchase switches or routers equipped with both Ethernet and FDDI interfaces to interconnect older repeaters to the switched FDDI backbone.

Section 7.   Multilayer Switches

Another difference between Digital's offering and some others is routing. Digital's Gigaswitch/FDDI operates only at the MAC (media access control) layer and cannot read network-layer information. The switch appears to the network as an IEEE-802.1d-compliant bridge. In contrast, the switches from Alantec, Netedge, NSC, and Xylan can route protocols—most commonly IP and IPX. This reduces the need for corporations to use expensive, slow routers to furnish features like security and firewalls, or to hand off data between virtual LANs.

Cabletron's MMACplus FDDI switching module does not support routing code itself. However, it can forward IP and IPX traffic at the network layer when it is installed in the same chassis as the Securefast Virtual Network Server, a $30,000 route server which hands down routing decisions to the FDDI module. Cisco says it next plans to add routing facilities to its Lightstream 2020 in 1996.

19

100Base-T and 100VG-AnyLAN Switches

Section 1. Overview

Switches that convert 10-Mbit/s shared-media Ethernet LANs into switched networks are the hottest item in the networking industry. Now the first vendors are starting to bring out switches which perform the same function for 100Base-T fast Ethernet *100-Mbit/s* shared-media networks.

The same principle underlies these products as lower-speed Ethernet switches: By dividing the network into dedicated segments, 100Base-T switches vastly increase the amount of bandwidth available to networked users. At press time, only two companies had launched products which were designed from the ground up for 100Base-T switching: Bay Networks Inc. (Santa Clara, CA) and NBase Switch Communications (Chatsworth, CA). Each of the 16 ports on Bay's Lattiswitch System 28000 switch can be configured as either a 10-Mbit/s or 100-Mbit/s connection. Nbase's product supports up to seven 100-Mbit/s ports. Both products process packets using a store-and-forward technique, and operate at the MAC layer.

Additionally, a handful of other vendors—such as Madge Networks Inc. (Palo Alto, CA)—now sell chassis-based products that can be converted to act as 100Base-T switches by outfitting them with multiple 100Base-T modules. Still, compared with the 100-plus Ethernet switches on the market, there are few products available. The shortage of 100Base-T switches has to do more with the technological challenges involved in creating a switch that handles multiple 100-Mbit/s segments than with a lack of demand, and more vendors are expected to join this market. Designing from the ground up for 100Base-T switching makes the products from Bay and Nbase far cheaper than converted chassis-based switches. The Bay/Nbase switches cost around $1000 per port. That's twice as much as Ethernet switches (which deal with connections that are 10 times slower) and less than a fifth of the average cost of 100-Mbit/s FDDI switches. Also, $1000 per port is about $500 less than the cost of 155-Mbit/s ATM switches. In contrast, a single one-port 100Base-T module for the Multinet switching hub from Madge costs $3995—almost four times as expensive.

In contrast to 100Base-T switches, 100VG-AnyLAN switches have yet to arrive. There are two reasons. First, silicon for implementing the IEEE 802.12 100VG spec has taken longer getting to market than that for 100Base-T. Second, fewer vendors support the standard. Hewlett-Packard Co. (HP, Palo Alto, CA), which is easily the largest supplier of 100VG, has announced plans to ship a 100VG switch. But when pressed, HP admits that work has not yet started on the project. Consequently, the switch is unlikely to be available until 1997.

Section 2.   Applications

Vendors see three applications for their 100Base-T switches: (1) in client-server LANs, (2) in power work groups (e.g., supporting engineering design departments), and (3) in the network center, as a backbone device supporting connections to concentrators, routers, and Ethernet switches equipped with 100Base-T ports. It is this last application which actually holds the most promise for 100Base-T switches. Currently, supplying dedicated 100 Mbit/s to the desktop is overkill for all but the fraction of network users equipped with high-end workstations. Today, a more useful function for this power is in improving the overall performance of a network by switching traffic between concentrators and switches. Because Bay's switch can be set to support either 10-Mbit/s or 100-Mbit/s ports, it allows net managers to use lower-speed 10-Mbit/s connections to network devices that do not support a 100Base-T connection (see Fig. 19.1).

Section 3.   Bay's Lattiswitch

The first vendor to ship a 100Base-T switch was Bay. Its Lattiswitch System 28000 was initially delayed for over a year while its designers sorted out frame-loss problems. With reforged silicon, the 28000 now comes equipped with 256 kbytes of buffering on each port (about four times as much as the average buffer size on 10-Mbit/s Ethernet switches). Each of the 16 ports on the switch can be selectively configured as either a 10-Mbit/s or a 100-Mbit/s full- or half-duplex connec-

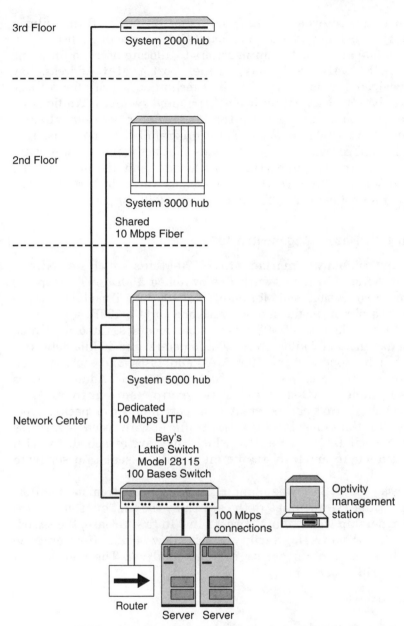

3rd Floor

System 2000 hub

2nd Floor

System 3000 hub

Shared
10 Mbps Fiber

System 5000 hub

Dedicated
10 Mbps UTP

Network Center

Bay's
Lattie Switch
Model 28115
100 Bases Switch

Optivity
management
station

100 Mbps
connections

Router

Server   Server

Figure 19.1   100Base-T in the network center. Bay's Lattiswitch allows net managers to choose whether to connect devices over 10-Mbit/s on 100-Mbit/s links.

tion. Ports are internally connected using Bay's Fastframe silicon technology, which provides an internal 2-Gbit/s switching fabric.

Bay's 28000 allows net administrators to allocate users to the same virtual LAN (vLAN) on the basis of their port or MAC address. Bay has developed a proprietary signaling technique which allows these vLANs to be set up across multiple distributed switches. Traffic must still be sent to a separate router for transfer *between* vLANs. Currently, the 28000 does not support integral fiber connections. This is a significant drawback, since it means that net managers who want to use the switch for supporting runs longer than 100 meters must invest in separate (and costly) fiber transceivers which convert the switch ports for fiber cable. The 28000 costs $940 per port.

Section 4.   NBase's Megaswitch 100

The second company to market with a 100-Mbit/s switch was NBase. Its Megaswitch 100 comes with five switched 100Base-TX (copper) ports, and two "option" slots for additional 100Base-T modules. Nbase offers four different modules (each with one port): a 100Base-TX module, and three flavors of 100Base-FX fiber modules, rated for transmission distances of 2 kilometers, 20 kilometers, and 40 kilometers.

The switch supports up to 4096 MAC addresses, and each port can be set to operate in either full- or half-duplex mode. Administrators can use those MAC addresses to group users into vLANs. Alternatively, vLANs can be created on port number or packet type. Users within the same vLAN transfer traffic at wire speed, regardless of the physical LAN segment to which they are attached. As with Bay's product, inter vLAN traffic must still be sent to a separate router.

At press time, NBase was planning to add RMON (remote monitoring) traffic analysis facilities to the switch by the first quarter of 1996 via a partnership with Axon Networks Inc. In first release, the switch supports a port-mirroring facility which allows traffic from any one port to be copied to a separate network analyzer. The Megaswitch costs from $1370 per port.

20

High-End
Enterprise
Switching Hubs

Section 1. Overview

Call them enterprise hubs, call them switching hubs, call them super-hubs. Whatever name they go by, there's a new category of LAN hardware that is destined to play a pivotal role in enterprise-size high-speed LANs.

The need for net managers to migrate from 10-Mbit/s or 16-Mbit/s shared-media LANs to 100-Mbit/s shared-media or switched networking has given rise to a new type of internetworking device, described here by the name *enterprise switching hub*. These high-end hybrids are based on a chassis that holds two types of slot-in devices: conventional hub modules that connect multiple devices to a single LAN segment, and switching modules that comprise autonomous LAN switch supporting multiple LAN segments.

Unlike work group switches, which are designed to split a large shared-media LAN into smaller work group size LANs, enterprise switching hubs are designed to serve in the data center at the core of the enterprise LAN—interconnecting conventional hubs and smaller switches. They are also typically put to work providing dedicated switched connectivity for devices like servers and high-end workstations.

Enterprise switching hubs enable net managers to put all their switching and shared-media network connections in a single box. In a multifloor building, for instance, enterprise switching hubs can be configured to interconnect PCs on one floor using conventional shared-media network modules, while connecting stackable and modular hubs on other floors using switching modules. The hub also acts as a central management point, allowing the entire network to be monitored from a single console.

Buying a hub that supports both legacy LANs and switched LANs within one chassis is the best way to ensure an economical and smooth migration to higher-performance networking. Such equipment allows users to meet their networking requirements today using affordable shared-access legacy networks, and then incrementally upgrade to the faster and more expensive switching technology later on—without having to trash installed equipment.

Products announced to date which fall in this category include:

- The System 5000 from Bay Networks Inc. (Santa Clara, CA)

- The MMACplus from Cabletron Systems Inc. (Rochester, NH)

- The Network 9000 from Xyplex Inc. (Littleton, MA).

- The GeoLAN/500 from UB Networks Inc. (Santa Clara, CA)

- The Oncore from 3Com Corp. (Santa Clara, CA), which acquired the product when it purchased Chipcom Corp. (Southborough, MA) in 1995; the hub is also available from IBM Corp. (Armonk, NY)

As well as supporting both shared-media and switched connections, enterprise switching hubs have several other characteristics that differentiate them from other hubs and switches. As befits their central position in the network, they come with reliability features like hot-swappable components and optional redundant power supplies. Capacity is another feature; these products' extensible chassis architectures allow net managers to start small and then scale up switch capacity incrementally—in most cases, to more than 100 ports.

All the devices can be configured with multiple high-speed ports—a prerequisite for serving in high-speed campus backbones. And while most vendors offer only Ethernet switching today, most are also readying modules which allow their chassis to be configured as fully fledged ATM, FDDI, and token ring switches. This eliminates the need to buy switches from multiple sources to obtain different flavors of switched connectivity, and lets net managers enjoy benefits like one-stop convenient support and unified network management.

Unlike smaller and cheaper work group and departmental switches, which mostly operate at the MAC layer, some enterprise switching hubs offer network-layer filtering and routing facilities. Along with routing, Cabletron offers the option of adding a route server facility to its hub which allows it to act as a centralized repository of routing information for distributed LAN switches. Both approaches enable the switching hubs to provide firewalls between different parts of the switched network, preventing broadcast storms and enforcing security. Without higher-layer intelligence, net managers must use traditional routers to get those jobs done—an approach which is more expensive, adds stratospheric levels of latency to network traffic, and makes management more complex. Some vendors plan to take the firewall concept a stage further, offering virtual LAN facilities which allow net managers to allocate nodes attached to different switches to common virtual work groups using mouse commands from a management console.

Section 2.   Treading Carefully

For all that's good about enterprise switching hubs, picking one product from the mix available is a tricky business. In an effort to get their foot in the door at corporate networks, some equipment vendors are guilty of ridiculous specmanship when describing their offering's feature sets. Typically, most vendors describe as currently available features which are still on the whiteboard in their R&D departments.

In particular, it's absolutely crucial to examine the claims being made about backplanes with a fine-tooth comb. The backplane is the most crucial element in an enterprise switching hub. Its capacity (or speed) dictates not only how many shared-media Ethernet or token ring networks can be connected to the hub, but also how well it will scale to the task of handling high-speed LANs like ATM (asynchronous transfer mode) and 100Base-T. Unfortunately, switching hub vendors often wildly exaggerates the capacity of their backplane.

The purpose of this chapter is to provide guidance on how to choose a switching hub. The first part of the chapter describes a methodology that can be used to debunk vendors' backplane claims. The rest of the chapter provides descriptions of the five leading enterprise switching hubs—including their main advantages and drawbacks.

Section 3.   Crunching the Numbers

When it comes to backplane performance, some vendors are claiming speeds that will be real when faster network modules ship. Others boast bandwidths that no one is going to catch sight of before some promised backplane upgrade actually makes an appearance. Corporate networkers who don't want to be duped best remember some old advice: Believe half of what you hear and less of what you see. The best thing to do is forget the fabulous numbers on the data sheets and figure out for yourself how much *usable* capacity it's possible to wring out of that supersonic backplane.

Broadly speaking, there are three kinds of backplanes: ones with multiple LAN segments, ones that use TDM (time division multiplexing) to shunt data on and off a high-speed bus, and ones built around a switching matrix. To get the goods on a LAN segment backplane, add the speed of each LAN together. If the backplane comes with four 10-Mbit/s Ethernets, four 16-Mbit/s token rings, and two 100-Mbit/s FDDI segments, the aggregate available throughput is 304 Mbit/s. With a TDM backplane, multiply the number of bits (or lines) on the bus by the speed at which the bus operates (measured in megahertz). Thus, a 64-bit bus running at 20-MHz delivers 1.28 Gbit/s. And if it's a switching matrix, multiply the number of connections the switch has to handle by the speed they're running at. An ATM matrix with 16 connections running at 155-Mbit/s delivers 2.48 Gbit/s.

Using these calculations, net managers can easily debunk the figures boasted by hub vendors. At press time, Cabletron Systems Inc. (Rochester, NH) advertised that the internal network bus (INB) in its MMACplus smokes along at 4 Gbit/s. Since the INB consists of two 64-bit buses running at 25 MHz, top speed is actually 3.2 Gbit/s. Cabletron says the missing 800 Mbit/s will be there when it ships new 40-MHz modules. The vendor isn't the least bit embarrassed about the shortfall. In fact, it believes it's being modest because in 1996 it intends to launch 66-MHz modules, giving a (highly) theoretical throughput of 8.448-Gbit/s.

Ask about backplanes at Bay Networks Inc. (Santa Clara, CA) and you might hear how the System 5000 chassis claims a sizzling 12 Gbit/s. Since the backplane actually comes with 52 Ethernet, 26 token ring, and 5 FDDI LAN segments, the true total is 1.436 Gbit/s. When pressed, the company admits that the extra 10.5 Gbit/s won't be available until Bay rolls out its 2-Gbit/s Ethernet switching modules. Yes, 12 Gbit/s *could* be achieved—if multiple switching modules were slotted into the hub and their ports used to link network modules. But the resultant configuration surely stretches the definition of *backplane*.

Very few companies can even make a dent in the multimegabit capacities claimed for the latest hubs *today*. But net managers looking to future-proof their networks are forking out big bucks for these products. If performance isn't there when they try to migrate to higher speeds, they'll pay for it three times: when they bring the network down to install new hardware, when they get the bill for the new equipment, and when they try to explain to the boss what went wrong.

Section 4.   Difficult Upgrades

Debunking vendor claims about backplane performance is only one part of choosing a switching hub. Some of the backplane designs now in use make it difficult to upgrade to high-speed LAN technologies. In particular, switching hubs which use multiple Ethernet, FDDI, or token ring LAN segments on the backplane are at a disadvantage—for two reasons. First, these segments are protocol-specific. In order to carry another packet or cell format, the module traffic must first be converted—adding to the cost of the modules that are connected to the backplane. Second, if the traffic being pushed over the backplane comes from a network faster than the backplane segment (as is the case when net managers try to move to faster networking standards), the backplane itself will become a bottleneck. The only way to alleviate the crunch is to multiplex multiple backplane segments together—a procedure which also will add to equipment costs.

TDM backplanes are a better solution; but again, it pays to look closely at the vendor's implementation. Some TDMs carry packets over the backplane in a proprietary frame format. The additional processing involved in converting packets and cells as they pass on and off the backplane may have a detrimental effect on switch performance. A better approach is to use ATM cells on the backplane. This way, traffic passing from a packet-based LANs to ATM needs to be converted just once, as it's passed onto the backplane.

Another problem with TDM backplanes is capacity. Regardless of what vendors may claim, the maximum capacity of TDM designs is limited to around 1 Gbit; beyond that, levels of radiation and heat on the backplane become impractically high. That is not the case with matrix-based backplanes, which represent the most promising solution to carrying traffic between switching hub modules. Because the amount of capacity on a matrix backplane increases in proportion to the number of connections, these devices can easily offer throughput in the multigigabit range.

Bay and Cabletron are among the leading internetworking vendors now working on matrix-based backplane solutions, but one vendor that has beaten them to it is Fibronics International Inc. (Haifa, Israel). Its Gigahub comes with a matrix backplane made up of 40 independent 300-Mbit/s buses, giving it a total capacity of 12 gigabits. Fibronics' backplane is designed around a so-called generic architecture which allows all protocols to be passed in native format—without modification or conversion. This gives Fibronics a lot of leeway in reacting to trends in networking. To support a new type of network, the vendor has to produce only a new slot-in module. Currently, the Gigahub supports Ethernet and FDDI switching. Token ring switching and ATM are planned.

Section 5.   The System 5000 from Bay

Product Summary

Product name: Bay System 5000

Description: High-end LAN hub that supports Ethernet, token ring, and FDDI network connections

Vendor: Bay Networks Inc., Santa Clara, CA; (408) 988-2400

Price: Chassis costs $2495 to $3995. Supervisory modules cost $1000. Power supplies cost $1000. Cluster modules cost $4495. Management modules cost from $5395 with one DCE; 6-port and 2-port FDDI modules cost $7795 and $10,995, respectively; 24-port Ethernet or token ring modules cost $4495 each.

Advantages: Interconnects System 3000 and System 2000 hubs, and also allows them to access centralized network resources, at an affordable price. Provides scalable network management. Allows reconfiguration of the network in software. Saves space.

Snags: Poor availability of switch modules.

Bay was one of the first equipment vendors to grasp the nettle of switching hub development. The result of its labor is the System 5000 concentrator—its third-generation hub, which is designed to let users build distributed hub networks *and* provide a migration path to switched LAN technologies. The 5000 has really taken off with Bay's customer base; ironically, the vendor shipped about 5000 System 5000s in the first year it was available. However, on the downside, Bay is proving slow in shipping high-speed LAN modules for the hub.

In the past, Bay (formerly Synoptics) users who wanted to provide a single point of connection for distributed LAN hubs in a campus environment usually used another LAN hub as the axis point. But old-style LAN hubs are primarily designed for providing connections to desktop devices—not for supporting connections to other hubs.

Consequently, configuring them for service as a "hub of hubs" is both expensive and tricky to manage.

Bay's System 5000 targets exactly this application, and is designed for installation in a computer room or network center at the heart of a distributed hub network—interconnecting its existing (smaller) System 3000 modular hubs and existing (even smaller) System 2000 stackable hubs (see Fig. 20.1). Remote System 3000/2000 hubs—located up to 2 kilometers away—are attached over fiber cable to the System 5000 using devices called *cluster modules* that slot into the System 5000 chassis. Each cluster module supports either three or four remote hub connections. Net managers dictate which remote hubs can exchange traffic by issuing commands from a net management console loaded with Bay's Optivity management software.

Remote hubs that are connected to different cluster modules in the System 5000 chassis are allowed to communicate by assigning them to one of the internal backplane buses that run along the back of the System 5000 chassis. Alternatively, remote hubs that are attached to the same cluster module can exchange packets via an internal bus within the slot-in cluster module itself—thus freeing up backplane capacity and helping improve overall LAN performance.

Before the System 5000 came along, net managers who wanted to interconnect Bay's earlier hubs used a System 3000 hub to get the job done. According to Bay, the System 5000 delivers four advantages over this solution. First, the cluster modules allow the System 3000 and System 2000 hubs to be interconnected far less expensively. Second, the cluster controllers provide a much higher density of port connections, and thus interconnect hubs using a fraction of the space in the computer room. Third, the System 5000 allows users to configure connections between remote hubs in software, rather than having to go through the protracted process of physically reconfiguring the network in the wiring closet. Finally—in order to make managing complex, and distributed LANs easier—the System 5000 can be configured to report different levels of network management information—from basic performance statistics right up to protocol analysis.

Note that the System 5000 is significant for one other reason. Bay is due to launch an ATM backplane upgrade for the System 5000 hub, plus ATM (155 Mbit/s), switched Ethernet (10 Mbit/s), and switched Ethernet/fast Ethernet (10/100 Mbit/s) modules that fit into the device—allowing users to migrate their networks from a traditional shared-media design to a switched, dedicated bandwidth architecture. Bay's System 5000 is delivered as a 14-slot chassis, into which users slot interchangeable hardware modules. The System 5000's cooling system, redundant power supplies, and a supervisory module for system management all are built into the back of the hub, without tak-

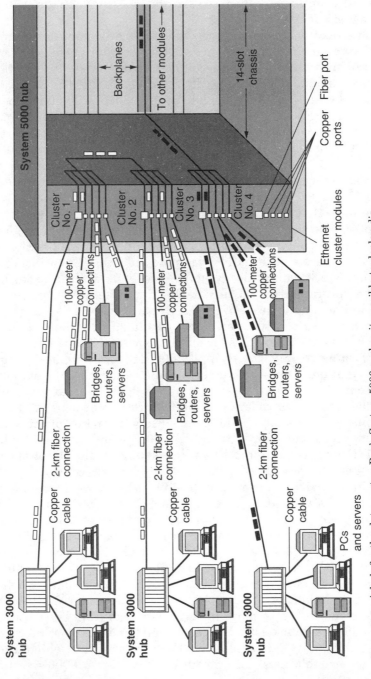

Figure 20.1 A hub for the data center. Bay's System 5000 makes it possible to deploy distributed hubs as far as 2 km away from the central computer center. Remote hubs connect to cluster modules and communicate either over the hub backplane or via a module's internal bus.

ing up valuable slot spaces. All components in the System 5000 are hot-swappable.

The hub is available in three versions, each of which features a different combination of backplanes. The first version supports twelve 10-Mbit/s Ethernet backplanes. The second supports both twelve Ethernet backplanes and nine 16-Mbit/s token ring backplanes. The third supports twelve Ethernet backplanes, nine token ring backplanes, and five 100-Mbit/s FDDI backplanes, simultaneously.

Bay is launching a number of network modules for the hub. As mentioned, the most significant are the cluster modules. Two are available. The first module is the Model 5378-F, which supports four Ethernet "clusters." Each cluster is made up of one fiber port, which supports a 10-Mbit/s Ethernet connection over multimode fiber cable to a remote System 2000 or System 3000 hub up to 2 kilometers away, plus four RJ-45 copper ports, which are used to connect the remote hub to locally attached equipment—such as bridges, routers, and servers—in the network center. The second module, the Model 5575-F, supports two token ring clusters. Each cluster features a pair of fiber ports, which are used to support a 16-Mbit/s token ring ring-in/ring-out connection to a remote hub, plus three RJ-45 sockets for local equipment.

Depending on how the net manager configures them, each cluster either can act as an independent LAN segment or can be joined with another cluster (or clusters) to make a bigger LAN.

According to Bay, cluster modules allow net managers to interconnect remote hubs (and to connect remote hubs to centralized resources) much less expensively and using much less space than with System 3000 hubs. For example, a net manager needing to support and manage 20 Ethernets could buy one System 5000 hub equipped with 5 cluster modules (each supporting 4 Ethernets), plus 4 net management modules for $61,310. To support the same configuration, with management, using Bay's System 3000 would require the manager to make room for 4 hubs, costing a total of $174,880. (Space savings become more advantageous in proportion to the complexity of the network; it would require 10 System 3000s to support the maximum of 52 Ethernets supported by a single System 5000 hub.)

Bay is also announcing a variety of other network modules for the System 5000. They include modules providing up to a maximum of 24 Ethernet or 24 token ring ports to PC nodes attached locally over unshielded twisted-pair (UTP) or shielded twisted-pair (STP) copper cable. Also, two-port and six-port FDDI (fiber) modules are in the works. Bay points out that the System 5000 is less expensive than the System 3000 only when configured for service in the network center, using the cluster modules. When only conventional to-the-desk network connections are required, the System 3000 works out cheaper.

By either manually setting a switch at the chassis itself, or by using a console loaded with Bay's Optivity software, the net manager can isolate each module from the hub backplane to create independent LAN segments. Alternatively, the manager can assign these modules to any of the LAN backplane segments in the chassis, thus enabling them also to communicate with cluster modules and the equipment attached to them.

The System 5000 can be configured for two modes of network management, one of which provides a more detailed level of information than the other. In the simpler mode, all the network modules in the hub send statistics about subjects like network utilization to a single net management module (Model 5310/5510). The net management module processes the information from all the network modules and then forwards it to a workstation loaded with Bay's SNMP-compliant Optivity management software. The connection between the network modules and the management module is provided via a dedicated 32-Mbit/s internal common management bus (CMB). The connection between the net management module and the console can be made either "in band" over a LAN connection, or "out of band" via a dial-up telco line.

In the second mode of management, the net management module is enhanced with daughterboards, called data collection engines (DCEs). Each DCE is dedicated to monitoring a single Ethernet or token ring on the chassis backplane. (All network modules connected to that backplane also are managed by the DCE.) In this configuration more detailed diagnostic information is provided, and net managers can use the Optivity management console for advanced functions like decoding protocol packets and automatically building pictures of LAN topology. Each net management module in the 5000 can be equipped either with two token ring DCEs, or three Ethernet DCEs. To obtain in-depth monitoring of more LANs on the backplane, more network management modules must be added to the chassis.

When picking modules for their System 5000, users must weigh their need for management against their need for network capacity, because every management module added to the chassis reduces its capacity to support network connections. When configured for the maximum number of network connections, the System 5000 can support 52 Ethernet connections (13 Ethernet cluster modules plus one net management module), or 26 token ring connections (13 token ring cluster modules plus one net management module).

At press time, Bay had yet to offer switched LAN modules for the System 5000. When they finally appear, they are expected to include a two-slot ATM switch, a one-slot Ethernet switch (delivering 10-Mbit/s of dedicated bandwidth to each network node), plus an Ethernet switch that also can be configured with 100-Mbit/s fast Ethernet connections to bandwidth-hungry nodes such as servers or high-end workstations. A token ring switch is planned, as are switches which operate at the MAC layer. Bay also is planning to develop multilayer switches (which operate at both layer 2 and layer 3) for the 5000. The conversion between ATM cells and conventional LAN packets will be undertaken by daughterboards attached to switch modules, and will not require a module occupying a whole slot in the chassis.

Section 6.   The MMACplus from Cabletron

Product Summary

Product name: MMACplus

Description: Modular LAN hub that can handle both shared-media LANs and switched dedicated connections

Vendor: Cabletron Systems Inc., Rochester, NH; (603) 332-9400

Price: Per-port prices are as follows: $500 for shared-access Ethernet or token ring and $1000 for shared-access FDDI. Dedicated Ethernet, $1200 to $1500; dedicated token ring, $2000 to $2500; dedicated FDDI, $10,000.

Advantages: A single platform that offers a migration path to higher-performance networking. Both shared-media and switched networks can be managed from a central platform. Switch modules support layer 2 switching and layer 3 routing. A route server also is available.

Hitches: Some of the hub's most significant features won't be available for some time; per-port price is high.

In the last couple of years, Cabletron has gained ground and ultimately overtaken arch rival Bay in terms of the number of hubs it is shipping. Its latest platform, the MMACplus, is designed to drive the final nail into Bay's coffin. It features a number of highly innovative and advanced features, including integral SNMP/RMON and bridge/routing capabilities in every slot-in module.

As with other switching hubs, the basic tenet underlying the design of the MMACplus is its ability to support dedicated high-speed switched connections and shared-media LANs from a single hardware platform. The 14-slot modular hub can simultaneously accommodate shared-access and switched versions of Ethernet, token ring, and FDDI. It also supports links to ATM networks (see Fig. 20.2).

The hub is configured by sliding interface modules into the chassis (each occupies one slot). The vendor says WAN interfaces and a fully fledged ATM switch module are in the works. Every interface module manufactured for the hub contains an SNMP agent and an RMON analysis agent, and is able to perform bridging, routing, and call setup. A significant benefit is that users will be spared the cost of separate modules to handle these tasks; also, the scheme is inherently fault-tolerant.

On the drawback side of the ledger, loading modules with such sophisticated capabilities is an expensive proposition. Configured for switched Ethernet connections, for example, the hub costs about $1200

MMACplus hub

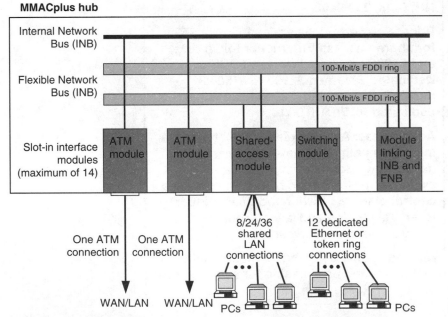

Figure 20.2 One box, many connections. The 14-slot MMACplus hub contains two separate buses. The Flexible Network Bus (FNB), for shared-access LANs, comprises two redundant 100-Mbit/s FDDI rings. The Internal Bus (INB) supplies an aggregate 4 Gbit/s of throughput to switched connections.

to $1500 per port—$200 to $500 more than the average cost of an Ethernet switch. Alternatively, configured for shared-access Ethernet connections, it costs $500 per port—$200 to $250 more than the average cost of a conventional, managed modular hub. Consequently, the appeal of the MMACplus may be limited to only those net managers who must have end-to-end management and integral bridging and routing, and who are able to offset the hub's high sticker with the savings that accrue from not having to buy an extra kit.

The hub features a separate-but-equal bus architecture. It contains two buses: one geared to shared-access LANs and the other geared to switched connections. The flexible network bus (FNB) comprises two 100-Mbit/s FDDI rings for transporting traffic between shared LAN segments. The internal network bus (INB) uses time division multiplexing and offers 4 Gbit/s of aggregate, nonblocking throughput to switched connections.

Cabletron sells a variety of interface modules that link shared-access LANs to the FNB. Versions are available supporting 24 or 36 10Base-T Ethernet ports over UTP cabling, 24 or 36 10Base-FL Ethernet ports over fiber, 24 token ring ports over UTP or STP, or 8 FDDI ports. The vendor also offers a 12-port FDDI concentrator that can use either STP or UTP cabling and a repeater module that connects the FNB to both redundant rings of an external FDDI backbone network.

Each interface module for the INB bus contains an autonomous LAN switch in the form of a Securefast Packet Switch (SFPS) application-specific integrated circuit (ASIC), a recent Cabletron development. Each SFPS ASIC is able to forward 400,000 packets per second (pps); a fully SFPS-loaded chassis has an aggregate processing rate of more than 5.6 million pps, according to the vendor. Modules offered for the INB include a 12-port Ethernet switch using either UTP or fiber cabling. A 12-port token ring switch is planned, that will use STP, UTP, or fiber cabling. Each switched link runs at the full speed of the LAN: 16 Mbit/s for token ring or 10 Mbit/s for Ethernet.

Cabletron says that Ethernet throughput can be doubled to 20 Mbit/s by enabling a full-duplex Ethernet feature. With full-duplex Ethernet, the "collision detection" part of Ethernet's CSMA/CD protocol is disabled so that traffic can flow up and down switch connections at the same time. In addition, the vendor sells a two-port FDDI switch that connects the INB as a dual-attach station (DAS) to one or two external FDDI rings. This module also can be used to connect the INB with the FNB, so that switched nodes can send traffic to shared access nodes, and vice versa. When set up solely for switching, the MMACplus is designed to accommodate 168 dedicated Ethernet or token ring connections or 28 FDDI links, or an amalgam.

Cabletron has ambitious plans for the MMACplus. In the pipeline is an ATM switching module, courtesy of a partnership with Fore Systems Inc. (Pittsburgh). It will occupy two slots in the chassis and supply 16 ports with dedicated connections ranging from 51 to 155 Mbit/s; it will offer an internal nonblocking aggregate switching capacity up to 2.5 Gbit/s. The ATM module will exchange traffic with other modules via the INB.

Modules forward traffic across the buses one of three ways: routing (IP, IPX, Appletalk, and DECnet Phase IV protocols), MAC-layer bridging of all other protocols, or setting up a connection using the Connection Services spec defined by the ATM Forum. Individual interface modules are configured to use one of the techniques during system setup from a management console. Either bus can exchange packets from dissimilar LANs. Modules attached to the INB convert all traffic into a proprietary 56-byte cell format. It is reconverted to the appropriate format when it reaches its destination. The FNB converts all traffic into FDDI frames for bus transport.

As noted, each interface module contains an SNMP agent with RMON MIB. When setting up the hub, managers select one module to act as the hub's master unit. Its job is to collect statistics from agents in other modules and pass them to a net management console. Users can gather management information out of band over a 10-Mbit/s dedicated management bus inside the chassis. The MMACplus features redundant power supplies. Owners of the earlier MMAC hub should note that interface modules for the MMACplus come in a different form factor than MMAC modules and are not interchangeable.

The latest addition to the MMACplus is a route server module that allows the switching hub to act as a centralized store of routing information to other, distributed MMACplus chassis. This provides a central point of control for the entire network.

Section 7.   Xyplex's Network 9000 LAN Hub/Switch

Product Summary

Product name: 600 Series Switching Modules

Description: Ethernet and FDDI switching modules which fit inside Xyplex's existing Network 9000 modular LAN hub

Vendor: Xyplex Inc., Littleton, MA; (508) 952-4700.

> **Price:** 601/603 Ethernet (copper) switching modules cost $7995; 604 Ethernet (fiber) switching module costs $11,995; 641 FDDI switching module costs $9,995.
> SwitchPlane upgrade for existing Network 9000s costs $1500. Network 9000 chassis with the SwitchPlane costs from $2400. 500 Series router modules cost from $8990 to $17,990, depending on configuration.
>
> **Advantages:** Allows migration from shared-media to switched networking via a single platform. Centralized management. Inexpensive. Allows switched traffic to be analyzed.
>
> **Hitches:** Doesn't support virtual networks. Requires an external router to interconnect the new Ethernet and FDDI switching modules to Xyplex's old token ring modules.

When it came time to develop enterprise switching hubs, most of the internetworking industry's brightest opted to go back to the drawing board to come up with a new hardware design. Not Xyplex Inc.; its ability to support both shared-media and switched connections comes courtesy of an upgrade to its existing Network 9000 modular LAN hub (see Fig. 20.3). The upgrade consists of a new family of slot-in Ethernet and FDDI switching modules (called the 600 Series) and a new backplane (called the SwitchPlane). The only other vendor offering a similar upgrade approach is Whittaker (Mountain View CA). Like the Xyplex product, Whittaker's Enterprise hub is based on its existing modular hub—making the migration to switched networking easier for its installed base of users.

According to Xyplex, adding switching into an existing LAN hub has four advantages over tacking a standalone switch onto the hub network—the standard MO of net managers today:

1. It is cheaper than forking out for a separate, standalone switch.

2. It eliminates the need to use two management consoles to oversee the network (one from the vendor of the Ethernet hubs, another from the supplier of the Ethernet switch).

3. It takes up less room in the wiring closet.

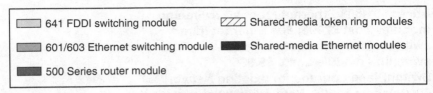

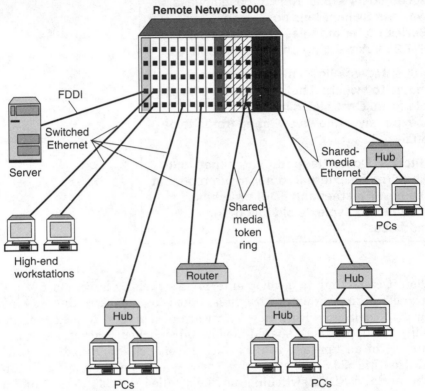

Figure 20.3 A mix of modules. Thanks to a field-upgradable backplane, Xyplex's Network 9000 hub now supports both switched and shared-media connections in the same chassis. An external router is needed to link the switching modules with their shared-media token ring counterparts.

4. It allows the switch modules to leverage hub redundancy features, such as dual power supplies and extra fans.

What's more, Xyplex's switching solution has an important price benefit which should sway managers who aren't presently using the Network 9000. Even when the cost of buying a new Network 9000 chassis is taken into account, Xyplex's products cost from $500 per switched Ethernet port. That's half the industry average of about $1000 per port for a typical Ethernet LAN switch. Xyplex's switching technology offers another advantage: It allows the net manager to analyze traffic on all switched ports simultaneously.

On the downside, Xyplex's Network 9000 does not yet support the ability to allocate different switched ports to virtual LANs. The only way to subdivide the switched network is by using Xyplex's new 500 Series slot-in router module. The added cost ($8990 to $17,990) could defray the product's price advantage. Further, using a router to support vLANs provides less granular control over traffic flow and produces more network delay than competitive switches from vendors such as Agile Networks Inc. (Concord, MA), Alantec Corp. (San Jose, CA), and Xylan Corp. (Calabasas, CA), which allow switched ports to be allocated to different virtual work groups from a net management console. Xyplex has plans to add virtual networking capabilities to the 9000, but has not set a date.

Another glitch is that Xyplex has not yet worked out a way for its new switching modules to communicate with its earlier shared-media token ring modules installed in the same chassis. To facilitate this link, the Network 9000 must be installed along with yet another router, this time from a third-party. Surprisingly, Xyplex's new Series 500 router has not been outfitted to handle this task.

There are three new switching modules in the Xyplex rollout. The 601/603 Ethernet switching module comes with sixteen 10-Mbit/s copper Ethernet ports and costs $7995. The 604 Ethernet switching module comes with twelve 10-Mbit/s 10Base-FL fiber Ethernet ports and costs $11,995. The 641 FDDI switching module comes with two 100-Mbit/s multimode fiber FDDI ports and costs $9995. Xyplex predicts that its more expensive and less numerous FDDI ports will mainly be pressed into service to alleviate traffic bottlenecks on heavily used interswitch and switch-to-server connections.

Each 600 Series module comprises an autonomous LAN switch with an integral SNMP agent and an 8000-entry address table. Up to seven of the switch modules can be installed in the 15-slot Network 9000 modular hub chassis, for a maximum switch capacity of 112 dedicated Ethernet connections. The other eight slots can be filled with Xyplex's old line of shared-media Ethernet and token ring modules.

As with the other enterprise switching hubs, the new Network 9000's ability to support switched and shared-media modules simultaneously means that net managers can add performance to their networks incrementally, by selectively swapping out shared-media modules for switched modules in the parts of their network that need higher performance, while leaving the rest of the LAN untouched.

To support nonblocking internal communications between switch modules linked to locally attached LAN segments, Xyplex also is announcing a new bus for the Network 9000 called the SwitchPlane.

Xyplex says upgrading existing Network 9000 hubs is a simple operation that can be accomplished in the field; the new backplane bus simply screws into the hub. The new bus features a hardware-based crosspoint matrix with an aggregate throughput of 8 Gbit/s. Currently, the SwitchPlane handles all packets in native format, but in the future the backplane could be upgraded to handle cell-based ATM traffic.

Xyplex's Series 600 Ethernet and FDDI switching modules can communicate with its older shared-media Ethernet modules over the SwitchPlane. However, Xyplex currently does not support a way for packets to be exchanged between the Series 600 switch modules and its earlier token ring modules. Users requiring this capability must install the 9000 in conjunction with a third-party standalone internetworking device that will support Ethernet/token ring connectivity. This could add significantly to the cost of the network.

Each Series 600 switching module port stores incoming packets in a memory buffer before forwarding them to the relevant outgoing switched port. This store-and-forward approach gives the module a chance to examine traffic and root out runts, jabbers, and other problem packets. However, it also makes the switch much slower than products which are based on so-called cut-through switching (where the switch reads only the destination address in the header at the front of each packet before forwarding it). It takes a 600 Series switch 54 microseconds to process a 64-byte packet. The buffer delay increases in proportion to packet size; thus, it takes about 1.2 milliseconds for its switch to handle a 1500-byte packet. In contrast, cut-through switches offer delays of roughly 50 microseconds—regardless of the size of the packet. (Of course, the flip side to cut-through switches is that net managers must pay extra to buy and install a bridge or router to serve as an adjunct technology for removing errored packets from the network.)

Along with the Series 600 switching modules, Xyplex is introducing a Series 500 router module. The device serves two main duties. First, it connects the Network 9000 to the wide-area network. Second, it tunes performance by segregating traffic between devices attached to the 9000 on the basis of layer 3 subnet addresses. The router supports AppleTalk, DECnet Phase IV, IP, and IPX protocols.

By allowing existing users to upgrade their modular hub to switching functionality, Xyplex clearly makes net managers' lives easier. 3Com's product (see below) requires its existing users to tear out their hub chassis and replace it with a new one—a major aggravation. Further, while the slot-in network modules from 3Com's old product can be plugged into its new product, following this course wastes port capacity because each of the old modules requires an entire slot, even though it takes up only half the slot space available. Even that's preferable to Cabletron's new hub, which presents a case of "out with the old, in with the new." Not only does the MMACplus require Cabletron users to undertake a forklift upgrade, since its chassis is different from the older MMAC product; it also is incompatible with Cabletron's older hub modules.

Conversely, Cabletron is one of the few enterprise switching hub vendors other than Xyplex to address the issue of how to analyze switched traffic efficiently. Its modules feature built-in RMON. In contrast, Xyplex's Series 600 modules come with components which can be set to copy switched packets and forward them to a network analyzer (not included) attached to a dedicated port. The components can be set to copy either a small proportion of the traffic on all the ports or all the traffic on one port. With other switching hubs, the only way to look at traffic is to haul an analyzer from port to port, or shell out loads of cash to give each port its own analyzer.

Section 8.   The GeoLAN/500 from UB

Product Summary

Product name: GeoLAN/500

Description: Chassis-based hub holding Ethernet switch modules, and shared-media Ethernet, token ring, and FDDI modules.

Vendor: UB Networks Inc., Santa Clara, CA; (408) 496-0111.

Price: The cost is $234 per port for a 144-port shared-media hub containing six 24-port shared-media Ethernet modules with RJ-45 connectors, a management agent, and one power supply.

Advantages: Multiple redundancy and reliability features; easy to service. Allows migration from shared-media to switched networking using a single hub platform. Enables net managers to economize on equipment costs by reusing shared-media modules from earlier UB hubs in the new chassis.

Hitches: Many features are not available in first release; switch modules are based on CPUs rather than ASICs.

UB was one of the last of the major hub vendors to announce a switching hub, and in its first iteration its GeoLAN/500 is thin on switching capabilities and sports a mediocre backplane architecture. Nevertheless, UB's offering does have at least one attribute that could guarantee it favorable market share: reliability. UB's GeoLAN/500 is replete with fault-tolerant features, including hot-swappable and redundant slot-in modules. It features a management agent that prevents broadcast storms from crashing the network, as well as a chassis that can be quickly and easily serviced in the event of a component failure.

These are significant features. The high price of network failure is no secret, and nowhere is an equipment breakdown more expensive than at the LAN hub that ties the network together. In addition, the GeoLAN/500 makes life simpler and less expensive for network managers by allowing them to reuse modules from the vendor's previous-generation hub in the new chassis. An Ethernet repeater and an optional switching module called the Center Switch are also available with the hub.

For all of that, however, prospective customers should keep the GeoLAN/500's shortcomings in mind. ATM, FDDI, and token ring switching modules won't be available until 1996 at the earliest (for now the hub can be fitted with shared-media Ethernet, FDDI, and token ring modules, or with Ethernet switching modules). And, despite UB's claim that the GeoLAN/500 has a 10-Gbit/s backplane, the actual amount of usable bandwidth is 440 Mbit/s. The hub will get a boost in 1996 when UB ships an ATM switching matrix upgrade, but even then usable backplane bandwidth will total only 5 Gbit/s, since the other 5 Gbit/s is offered for backup purposes only.

Given UB's reputation for delivering technology later than promised, planners whose network designs really rely on being able to use any of these features (make that futures) might be better off looking at a switching hub that has already made the transition from whiteboard to real world.

The key to the GeoLAN/500's management features is the Access/EMPower module, an SNMP agent that also supports the RMON traffic analysis MIB (management information base) and occupies a single slot in the chassis. It comes with a roving feature so that it can analyze traffic on either of the two buses that are used for connecting the slot-in modules: a 320-Mbit/s bus and a bus comprising twelve 10-Mbit/s Ethernet channels. The Access/EMPower also can prevent broadcast storms by automatically seeking out and disconnecting ports that are connected to faulty LAN devices. Meanwhile, the GeoLAN/500 has an advantage over hubs with cables that plug straight into the network modules: It features a telecommunications patch panel that separates the cables from the modules. When a module fails, a technician can swap in another one in seconds, without having to unhook and reconnect all the cables.

The vendor is also offering a rack system in which up to four GeoLAN/500s can be mounted. The rack can pivot on a single axis, giving engineers easy access to modules, or it can be locked in place against a wall. The UB switching hub also comes with dual power cords for connection to different power sources. All the hub modules—including fans and power supplies—are hot-swappable, which adds to the GeoLAN/500's ability to furnish uninterrupted service. Some modules, including the ATM switch fabric (when it becomes available), can also be duplicated for redundancy.

With the GeoLAN/500, UB is also giving net managers a way to reuse parts from its previous-generation Access/One hub. Companies that own Access/One hubs can save on equipment costs by removing modules from the older device and slotting them into the GeoLAN/500. There are four types of Access/One modules: Ethernet switch, shared-media Ethernet, FDDI, and token ring. Both the new modules and the old modules take up a single slot in the 12-slot GeoLAN/500 chassis. So that those previous-generation modules can exchange traffic within the hub, the GeoLAN/500 is also equipped with the 320-Mbit/s TDM (time division multiplexing) bus from the Access/One. (3Com is currently the only other vendor engaging in such recycling; its Oncore switching hub makes use of parts from earlier products.)

One of two new modules that UB is introducing with the GeoLAN/500 is the Port Mobility Ethernet Concentrator, a 24-port shared-media Ethernet repeater. The concentrator features an electronic patch panel that allows ports to be individually assigned to any of the twelve 10-Mbit/s Ethernet channels. The other is the Center Switch, an optional slot-in component that boosts performance by providing switched connections internally among the twelve 10-Mbit/s channels. The GeoLAN/500 has two dedicated slots for the Center Switch, in case net managers want to add another for redundancy.

The Center Switch also can be used to connect the 320-Mbit/s TDM bus with the Ethernet channels, allowing devices attached to each to exchange traffic. But using it this way could cause serious problems for net managers. Because the switch runs at 10 Mbit/s, the connection could easily turn into a bottleneck if a host of devices attached to one bus attempted to communicate with nodes attached to the other. The Center Switch (as well as the Ethernet switch modules) is based on a design that uses a general-purpose reduced instruction set computing (RISC) processor with shared memory for processing packets. But many switch manufacturers have abandoned CPUs and are making the move to designs based on ASICs (application-specific integrated circuits), which are less prone to dropping packets in heavy traffic conditions.

The GeoLAN/500 costs $234 per port when configured with 144 10Base-T Ethernet ports, one Access/EMPower management module, and a single power supply. In the same configuration, the MMACplus from Cabletron Systems costs $496 per port, the System 5000 from Bay Networks costs $185 per port, and the Oncore from 3Com (see below) costs $181 per port.

Section 9.   The Oncore from 3Com

Product Summary

Product name: Oncore

Description: modular hub

Vendor: 3Com Corp., Santa Clara, CA (408) 764-5000

Price: from $240 per switched Ethernet port, and from $181 per shared-media Ethernet port

Advantages: fault tolerant, high capacity

Disadvantages: some traffic carried over sluggish shared-media backplane

3Com's Oncore switching hub originally was the product of a codevelopment project with IBM. Big Blue itself sells the Oncore under the name 8260. Like other switching hubs, the device is designed to address the requirements of very large LANs—providing high bandwidth, excellent fault tolerance, and support for a variety of different network types.

The Oncore backplane comes as standard with five Ethernet, four token ring, and eight FDDI segments on the backplane. Net managers can also upgrade the hub with ATM facilities, via a backplane module with 8 Gbit/s of capacity. The Oncore chassis comes with 17 slots. All are available for hot-swappable network modules. The hub can be configured to support five different types of connectivity: shared-media Ethernet, switched Ethernet, shared-media FDDI, shared-media token ring, and switched 100-Mbit/s ATM. Token ring switching is now in development.

Another point to note: Each module features distributed management capabilities. Also, the hub allows net managers to reuse shared-media Ethernet and token ring slot-in modules from 3Com's earlier hubs in the new chassis and so economize on costs. The Oncore hub costs from $240 per switched Ethernet port; and from $181 per shared-media Ethernet port.

21

Full-Duplex Technology

Section 1. Overview

Proprietary LAN switches—such as those which support Ethernet, 100Base-T, FDDI, or token ring connections—can massively torque up the throughput of today's installed networks by allowing up to the full bandwidth of the LAN to be dedicated to an individual node. Some switch and adapter vendors have hit on a way to double the performance of dedicated switch connections—via a technology called *full duplex*. There's usually no price penalty for full duplex. Many of the switch vendors that offer it do so as part of their standard feature set. And suppliers of full-duplex adapters say their cards are priced to compete aggressively with their half-duplex counterparts.

Double the bandwidth without paying twice the price? If that sounds as if customers should be lining up for full-duplex technology, think again. Three factors currently dull full duplex's allure.

First, only multithreaded workstation operating systems like OS/2 and Windows NT and Windows 95 can take full advantage of this hardware. Second, full duplex can function only on dedicated, point-to-point links, where only a single node is attached per switch port (currently, the vast majority of LAN switches are being installed as backbone devices, with multiple devices connected per port). Third, enabling full-duplex traffic flow vastly increases the potential for traffic flow problems—leading to frame loss, retransmissions, and generally poor performance. The standards now in the works defining full-duplex transmission have yet to address or eliminate this snafu.

Despite these drawbacks, around 30 vendors are delivering—or planning to deliver—full-duplex switches and adapters. Most of the products available implement full-duplex Ethernet (see Fig. 21.1). Around five vendors are shipping full-duplex 100Base-T products.

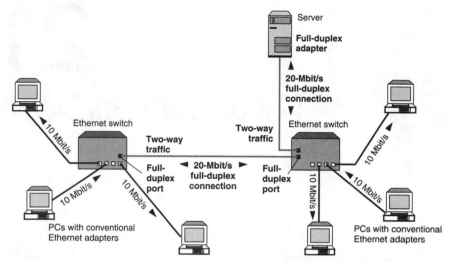

Figure 21.1 Putting LAN data on a two-way street. Full-duplex Ethernet can double the throughput of switch-to-switch and switch-to-server connections. The technology disables the collision detection portion of the CSMA/CD protocol, allowing for two-way traffic.

Bay Networks Inc. (Santa Clara, CA) offers a 28000 LAN switch that comes with 16 ports; each can be configured as either a full- or half-duplex 10-Mbit/s Ethernet or 100-Mbit/s fast Ethernet connection. Currently only IBM Corp. (Armonk, NY) and Madge Networks Inc. (San Jose, CA) offer full-duplex-capable token ring switches. Digital Equipment Corp. (DEC, Maynard, MA) is the only vendor offering a full-duplex FDDI switch.

Section 2.   How It Works

Broadly speaking, full-duplex works by disabling the access control mechanism which comes built into shared-media standards like Ethernet and token ring, so that traffic can flow in two directions over the switch connection at once. Take Ethernet as an example. The way Ethernet LANs are usually set up, only one node on any network segment can transmit data at any time. If two nodes try to send data simultaneously, the collision detection part of Ethernet's CSMA/CD protocol (which controls access to the network) automatically tells one of the stations to back off and try again.

This mechanism is the reason that bandwidth is normally restricted to 10 Mbit/s on switched Ethernet connections, because attempts by the end node to send and receive data at the same time are foiled, since they are interpreted as collisions. But with full duplex, the collision detection feature is disabled, and the end node is free to transmit and receive data at the same time—bringing aggregate throughput to 20 Mbit/s. Conveniently enough, 100Base-T (fast Ethernet) uses exactly the same access mechanism as its 10-Mbit/s cousin. By using the same procedure (disabling collision detect), full-duplex 100Base-T switches and adapters double throughput to 200-Mbit/s.

Full-duplex works in a similar way with token ring. By definition, traditional token ring operates in half-duplex mode. Information flows in one direction only and the media can be used (at any given time) only by a single transmitting station, which must wait until it receives the token before it can send data. But when a node is hooked directly to a switch, token ring's shared-media protocol ceases to be relevant. Thus, it becomes feasible to disable the token-passing access mechanism and run token ring in a full-duplex fashion—doubling the speed of the link to a healthy 32 Mbit/s.

Workaday FDDI networks also use a token-passing mechanism to control ring access. By disabling the token on dedicated switched connections, full-duplex FDDI links can run at 200 Mbit/s.

Section 3.   Primary Applications

Full-duplex vendors see two primary applications for their equipment—switch-to-switch connections and switch-to-server connections. In both cases, the idea is to use full duplex to break the bandwidth bottleneck that can occur when a number of nodes try to send data simultaneously over the same switched connection. PC and workstation clients rarely (if ever) need to transmit *and* receive at the same time. Thus, providing dedicated full-duplex ports for clients is usually both expensive and pointless.

In the area of full duplex, switches outshine (much more expensive) routers. That's because even the most sophisticated router still treats each of its LAN ports as a standard, half-duplex, shared-media environment. Thus, a server farm, or even dedicated server ports, hung directly off a router can never provide the effective throughput of a full-duplex switch.

Not everyone is a believer in full duplex. Some critics doubt that the twofold increase in performance it offers is adequate to eliminate the squeeze on busy connections. Instead, many switch vendors favor a different approach: Use a higher-speed technology like ATM, FDDI, or 100Base-T for switch and server links and switch Ethernet or token ring between network nodes.

Even so, there's no denying that full duplex can sometimes provide a noticeable increase in response times on client-server networks. On a traditional token ring, for instance, a server may need to transmit and receive at the same time, but cannot. Data on the transmit queue simply must wait until received data is processed before it can be shipped out across the network. Thus, even when high-performance CPUs and expensive disk caches are utilized, effective end-user performance can suffer simply because the transmit queue is not being serviced often enough by the network. Assuming adapter and network operating system (NOS) support, a switch-connected server can be reconfigured to run in full-duplex mode. In such a mode, a single server network interface card (NIC) can theoretically deliver a combined 32 Mbit/s of transmit/receive traffic. The result: an instant improvement to end-user response times.

Critics of full duplex are quick to point out that for end nodes to take full advantage of the technology, they must be running a multithreaded operating systems (OS). In essence, this type of OS divides tasks into multiple threads (streams of instructions) that run concurrently. The key is that the OS must be capable of handling traffic streams in and out at the same time. OS/2, Windows NT, and Netware 3.11 and 4.x (server versions) are all multithreaded operating systems, as are different varieties of Unix, including SCO Unix and IBM AIX. Nodes running under DOS and Windows will at best see a marginal performance increase from full-duplex hardware.

Section 4.   Upgrade Path

Full-duplex Ethernet has one big advantage over other bandwidth-boosting schemes: It's a lot cheaper. Most of the vendors now shipping full-duplex switches say that full duplex is standard on their boxes. Similarly, vendors of full-duplex adapters like Cogent Data Technologies Inc. (Friday Harbor, WA), Compaq Computer Corp. (Houston), Digital Equipment Corp. (DEC, Maynard, MA), and IBM Corp. (Armonk, NY) indicate that their products are priced to sell against half-duplex cards.

A small minority of users will even be able to upgrade installed adapters to full-duplex capability rather than swapping in new ones. It all comes down to whether the controller on the adapter card features dual FIFO (first-in, first-out) paths that can send and receive traffic at the same time. If that's the case, upgrades can be accomplished via software downloads, which can translate into very big savings. First off, no new adapters need be purchased. Then, there's no need to open up the PC and install a new adapter—a task that can take anywhere from a few minutes to several hours. With the average cost of labor running at about $45 per hour, hardware upgrades can mean big bucks at large sites.

In the case of Ethernet, cards carrying the 82596 Ethernet controller from Intel Corp. (Santa Clara, CA) or the Super Eagle Ethernet controller from Texas Instruments Inc. (Dallas) should be upgradable. Unfortunately, none of the Ethernet controllers from Advanced Micro Devices Inc. (AMD, Sunnyvale, CA) or National Semiconductor Corp. (Santa Clara, CA) can be upgraded. National Semi's silicon represents by far the largest percentage of the controllers now in place on Ethernet adapters. Both manufacturers have full-duplex chips on the drawing board.

Section 5. Auto Sensing

The task of developing full-duplex specifications is being undertaken by three committees—one within ANSI and two from the IEEE. A preliminary specification covering full-duplex Ethernet and 100Base-T was finished up by the IEEE 802.3 committee in 1994, within 12 months of the first appearance of full-duplex technology. Observers say that's no surprise, since full-duplex mainly involves disabling existing Ethernet access control mechanisms—rather than adding something new.

The specification is largely the work of National Semiconductor (Santa Clara, CA). It calls for software running on both network interface cards and switches, and defines an autodetection (or autonegotiation) option that allows full-duplex Ethernet adapters and switches to sense the presence of a full-duplex device at the other end of a connection and automatically move into full-duplex mode.

At power-up, a protocol automatically negotiates a connection at the highest speed supported by the devices at each end of the link. (The process is conceptually similar to that used by multispeed modems during handshaking.) Along with undertaking full-duplex negotiations, the technology can be used to allow multispeed Ethernet equipment to sense the speed of a link and automatically adjust to it. This should eliminate outages caused by users unwittingly plugging 10/100-Mbit/s adapters into the network at the wrong speed (the number 1 cause of downtime on 4/16-Mbit/s token ring LANs).

At press time, the IEEE 802.5 committee was still working to standardize a full-duplex specification for token ring switches and adapters. Similarly, Digital Equipment Corp. (DEC) is pushing to have its FFDT (FDDI full-duplex technology) adopted as an addendum to the ANSI FDDI standard. FDDT requires changes to SMT software in adapters and switch, and has been patented by DEC. Finally, the IEEE 802.12 committee is working on a full-duplex scheme for use with 100VG-AnyLAN—despite the fact that 100VG-AnyLAN switches are not expected to ship until 1997 at the earliest.

Section 6.   Flow Control

A point to note is that none of these specifications yet addresses the problem of how to control the flow of traffic on full-duplex links. Half-duplex switches rely on the contention that occurs naturally on shared-media segments to slow down the amount of traffic arriving on the switch and prevent buffer overflows. But full-duplex switches eliminate this contention by canceling the shared-media access control schemes. This means that the potential for buffer overflows is much higher.

At a plenary meeting of the IEEE in mid-1995, the 802.3 committee took its first tentative steps in the direction of standardizing a flow control scheme for use with full-duplex switched Ethernet and full-duplex switched 100Base-T (fast Ethernet) connections, but its work was not expected to be finished until mid-1996 at the earliest. None of the three full-duplex committees—802.5, 802.12, or ANSI—has yet started to look at the problem of flow control. Further, all full-duplex standards are being made optional, to prevent vendors having to rejigger their current full-duplex switch offerings. This means that hardware vendors can choose not to implement them. Net managers who want to implement full-duplex now, or think they might in the future, would be well advised to check that the switches and adapters they buy support the full specifications.

22

Flow Control in LAN Switches

Section 1. Background

LAN switch vendors may have spent the first half of the 1990s touting their products as little short of a miracle cure for the bandwidth crisis plaguing today's Ethernet and token ring LANs, but these products also come with an inconvenient (and little publicized) drawback. Under extreme traffic conditions, they can drop packets.

Take the experience of Adnet Technologies Inc. (East Granby, CT), an equipment reseller. Back in 1994, a client asked Adnet to cure a performance problem on a Netware LAN. The vendor thought it had the perfect remedy: install LAN switches on the corporate backbone. But switching turned out to be bad medicine for Adnet's customer. According to Adnet, the performance was actually worse after the switches were installed. The reseller says the switches couldn't process the traffic coming off the backbone quickly enough, and ended up dropping packets. To resolve the problem, Adnet had to resort to a traditional remedy. It pulled out the switches and replaced them with multiple FDDI rings hooked up to a router.

Adnet isn't alone in getting burned by switching. As more and more corporations convert their LANs to a switched infrastructure, it's becoming clear that the rapid rise in the popularity of switching has also served to camouflage the fact that under certain traffic conditions LAN switches will drop packets. What's even more worrying is that those traffic conditions aren't found only on high-end networks, such as those at scientific research establishments. Given the right (read wrong) circumstances, they can occur during the day-to-day operation of any busy commercial LAN—especially if the LAN switch is installed without careful planning. The net (or network) result of traffic losses is that packets have to be resent. In the most catastrophic cases, that procedure can result in worse performance for the applications that LAN switches are being installed to speed up; which these days include everything from file transfer to e-mail to heavy-duty graphics to number crunching. All this is distressing news for net managers who were counting on LAN switches to pep up the performance of their current networks until ATM comes of age.

A large part of the traffic flow problem comes down to the fact that while shared-media Ethernet and shared-media token ring are covered by IEEE standards, Ethernet and token ring *switching* are still proprietary technologies. Without an official flow control scheme, net managers installing today's LAN switches are working without a safety net, with no way to guarantee that the device they install won't make performance worse by dropping an inordinate number of frames.

The lack of switch standardization has nothing to do with technology, and even less to do with the best interests of the companies that buy LAN switches. It comes down to vendor self-interest. For one thing, switch vendors don't want to spend the R&D dollars to add a flow control feature to their existing switches (especially if it means forging new silicon). For another, admitting that there's a need for a flow control standard would mean admitting that there's a problem—and that could put a dent in sales.

Instead, switch vendors have been guilty of teaming up to keep flow control off the standards agenda. The IEEE 802.3 committee has already taken its first tentative steps in the direction of standardizing a flow control scheme for use with *full-duplex* switched Ethernet and 100Base-T (fast Ethernet) connections. (The spec is due to be finished up in 1996.) However, it has already been decided that the flow control scheme will not be applied to the half-duplex Ethernet switches that currently make up the bulk of switch sales. The IEEE 802.5 committee responsible for token ring has no plans to look at flow control.

In contrast, standards-based switch technologies—such as ATM, Fibre Channel, and HIPPI—all come with flow control built in. Similarly, dropped packets are not an issue with shared-media high-speed alternatives such as FDDI. Ironically, networks like FDDI owe their immunity to traffic flow problems to the very shared-media design that switch proponents have always criticized for its inability to provide scalable capacity. FDDI uses a token-passing scheme to send traffic onto the network. A token travels around the FDDI ring, stopping at each station to give it the chance to transmit frames.

Section 2.   Different Solutions...

While most Ethernet and token ring switch vendors are now beginning to acknowledge that their products can potentially lose packets, the question of how to solve the dilemma has split them into two conflicting camps. On one side are vendors who have geared up the ports on their switches with extra-large memory buffers. The theory is that the economy-size buffers will hold any excess traffic until traffic congestion in the switch can clear. In the opposing group are vendors who claim that no amount of buffering is sufficient to guarantee that traffic losses won't occur. These companies have developed (or are working on) several proprietary flow control techniques designed to prevent switch congestion from occurring in the first place. These enhancements restrict the amount of traffic that gets onto the LAN when it starts to busy up.

While hardware vendors have been bickering about which approach works best, Sunsoft (Mountain View, CA) and Novell Inc. (Provo, UT) have gradually been improving the existing flow control capabilities of the protocols used in their network operating systems (NOSs) to ameliorate losses. However, on their own, neither set of enhancements will put a stop to packet outages.

Section 3.   ...Same Problem

The potential for packet loss is present in all LAN switches. For instance, if seven of the 10-Mbit/s ports on an eight-port Ethernet switch continuously try to transmit data to the switch's eighth port simultaneously, packets will be dropped. Switch vendors rely on three things to prevent this from happening. First, statistically the odds are against this traffic pattern occurring for a sustained period of time. Second, memory buffers on switch ports are supposed to deal with transitory traffic surges by temporarily storing excess packets until the outgoing switch port is free to process them. Third, contention between nodes attached to the same switch segment has the effect of slowing down the amount of traffic arriving on the switch port.

When all the ports on a LAN switch are running at the same speed, the risk of traffic losses is highest on the connection to the server, as multiple client PCs attempt to pull down files or request applications from a server over a single 10-Mbit/s Ethernet or 16-Mbit/s token ring connection at a given time (typically, 80 to 90 percent of LAN traffic comprises client-server traffic).

To alleviate this problem, more than a dozen vendors have announced products which support not just Ethernet or token ring ports, but also one or two high-speed FDDI or ATM links for server connections. Adding a high-speed link to a switch may uncork the bot-tleneck to the server, but this speed mismatch also serves to shift the point of contention to the remaining low-speed ports (see Fig. 22.1).

Imagine a network in which the marketing department's PCs are all connected to one 10-Mbit/s switch port. In the morning, several staffers get to work at the same time and simultaneously send file requests to their network server. Their requests get to the server just fine, thanks to its 100-Mbit/s connection to the switch. But then the server's responses arrive back at the switch in a high-speed stream. If the switch buffers aren't big enough, or the stream continues for too long, traffic loss will occur on the outgoing 10-Mbit/s port.

Avoiding traffic losses when adding just one high-speed port to a LAN switch is tricky enough. But when multiple low-speed and multiple high-speed connections are invoked, preventing buffer overflows gets even harder. That's a lesson that Bay Networks (Santa Clara, CA) learned the hard way with its 28000 LAN switch. A version of the 28000 with 16 ports (each configurable for either 10-Mbit/s or 100-Mbit/s operation) was due to ship to beta test sites in June 1994.

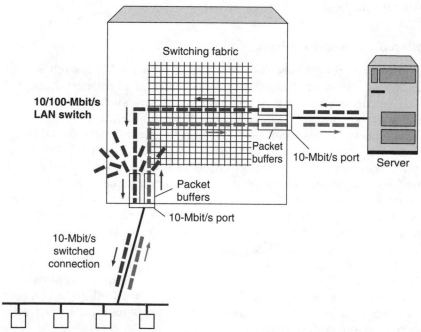

Figure 22.1 Switch congestion. Adding a high-speed connection to a LAN switch merely shifts the bottleneck from the server side to the client side of the device. Several endusers on the shared-media segment can simultaneously ship requests to the server, but when the server blasts files and applications back in a high-speed stream, packets pile up at the low-speed port and data gets deep-sixed.

Buffer overflows stymied that schedule. The permutations of multiple 10 megabit ports with multiple 100 megabit ports were what caused the problem, according to Bay Networks. The vendor had to go back to the drawing board to reengineer its switching ASIC with additional memory to eliminate the obstacle, and it finally shipped in 1995.

Section 4.   Dealing with Design

One of the best ways to avoid traffic losses is to carefully design the switched LAN. There are three ways to do so. First, analyze the traffic flow between the various devices attached to the switch—using RMON probes (costing $4000 and up), protocol analyzers ($10,000 and up), or a specialized network simulation package ($3000 or more). The twin downsides to this approach are that none of these tools are cheap and that all of them are time-consuming—since they require the net manager to get involved in gauging traffic flow over a period of time. A second approach is to follow the rules of thumb used by switch vendors and resellers themselves. According to 3Com Corp. (Santa Clara, CA), it's usually OK to put up to 70 lightweight PC users who just need apps like e-mail and terminal access on the same port, but for power users you probably don't want more than eight per port, and for users with high-end Unix workstations the limit is more like one or two.

Of course, this still leaves a lot of room for error. A more certain and even easier way to prevent problems is to strictly limit the number of devices connected to any switch port to just one. This shortens the odds that multiple incoming streams of traffic will arrive at one port simultaneously and exceed buffer capacity. For this reason, switches that are installed in work groups in which just one PC or workstation is connected to each port are far less likely to suffer from traffic loss than switches which are installed on the corporate backbone.

Finally, in the absence of flow control standards, it's best to use full-duplex connections cautiously. Half duplex switches bank on the contention that takes place naturally on shared-media segments to slow down the amount of traffic arriving on the switch, and so prevent buffer overflows. But full-duplex switches gets rid of this contention by eliminating the shared-media access control schemes, thus making the potential for buffer overflows much higher.

Section 5.   Lessons Learned

Reseller Adnet learned its design lessons the hard way when it installed three PowerPipes Ethernet/FDDI LAN switches from Networth Inc. (Irving, TX) on a customer's LAN. The network was running a variety of protocols (including Netware) and applications (including database access and imaging). In the first configuration used by Adnet, several hundred desktop and server devices connected to the Ethernet switch ports communicated over a 100-Mbit/s FDDI backbone ring. Adnet found that the sheer volume of traffic coming off the FDDI backbone overwhelmed the switches' buffers—leading to unacceptably high levels of traffic loss.

Adnet went back to the whiteboard and came up with two ideas to reduce the amount of backbone traffic. First, it attached devices in the same department or work group LAN to the same switch, and limited the number of devices attached to each switch to about 45. Second, it installed a router to interconnect the switches via multiple FDDI rings. The plan worked. Once the switches were put in the work groups, they worked just fine, according to Adnet.

Section 6.   Backbone Configurations

Grand Junction Networks Inc. (Fremont, CA) guarantees that its Fastswitch 10/100 LAN switch can function in a work group environment solely by providing a single media access control (MAC) address on each of its 26 ports. However, Grand is currently the only switch vendor that takes this approach. All the other products now shipping can handle multiple MAC addresses on each port. This facility is included so that net managers can install switches either in the work group or on the corporate backbone.

In a backbone configuration, each installed hub on the network is given its own port on the LAN switch (the hub ports are in turn used to connect to PCs). By using a switch to segment the network and thereby improve performance, net managers can save themselves a huge amount of money on the cost of buying a router to do the same thing. Some of today's Ethernet switches go for less than $500 per port. Typically, routers cost about $5000 per port. Of course, the downside to using a switch on the backbone is that the possibility of buffer overflows (created by traffic patterns) increases in proportion to the number of devices attached to each port. But that isn't stopping some vendors from encouraging users to install their products in highly ambitious backbone configurations. For one thing, most LAN switches come with gigantic MAC-address tables—usually capable of holding thousands of entries. A fully loaded Multinet Hub from Madge Networks Inc. (San Jose, CA) can handle 1,024,000 MAC addresses—enough for a switched Ethernet the size of Detroit.

Trying to connect anything like that many devices to a single switch is asking for trouble. Despite this fact, many switch vendors make no recommendations as to the maximum number of devices that it is advisable to connect per port. Net managers should be aware that indiscriminate installation of LAN switches on the backbone is a recipe for disaster. As a rule of thumb, switches make network design more complicated, not less.

Section 7.   Switch Buffers

Even a switch in a well-planned network can still run into problems should a fluke traffic pattern occur. To cope with these instances, all switches come with a certain amount of memory buffering on each port, which is supposed to temporarily store packets until the device's switching fabric can get around to processing them. Buffer size varies immensely from product to product. For example, the Netswitch/16 Ethernet switch from Matrox Electronic Systems Ltd. (Quebec, Canada) comes with 32 kbytes of memory on each of its sixteen 10-Mbit/s ports. That's enough to buffer twenty-one 1512-byte packets (the maximum size permissible on Ethernet). In contrast, the Etherswitch EPS2015 RS from Kalpana Workgroup (Sunnyvale, CA) sports 15 times as much buffering as the Matrox device—0.5 Mbytes on each of its 15 ports, or enough to buffer more than 330 maximum-size packets.

The question of exactly how much memory is enough can be answered only on a site-by-site basis, and depends on a variety of factors (including which applications are being run, over what type of NOS, by how many devices, and how often). However, the obvious rule of thumb applies: The bigger the buffer, the less likely a problem is to occur. Vendors implement buffering in one of two ways. Some allocate a fixed amount of memory on a port-by-port basis. Others outfit their switches with a shared-memory buffer pool. The shared-memory approach has the advantage that if one port needs all the buffering, it can grab it. With dedicated buffering, the memory is tied up at each port even if it is not in use.

On the other hand, allocating buffering from a pool has a downside. If the allocation is 100 percent dynamic, there is a possibility that a conversation between two ports will hog all the available memory. Some vendors—including Chipcom, Madge, and Matrox—also allow net managers to assign priority levels to different types of traffic. Prioritization is implemented by equipping the switch buffers with multiple FIFO (first-in, first-out) paths. If overflows occur, preset traffic priorities can be used to dictate which packets are dumped first.

Section 8.   Software Solutions

Both Novell and Sunsoft are currently modifying their NOS protocols to alleviate traffic flow problems. But neither vendor is claiming to be able to vanquish packet losses completely. That's because high-level protocols like NCP (the protocol used by Netware clients and servers to exchange information) and NFS (a distributed client-server file system implemented within the Solaris NOS) can react to traffic congestion only after it has occurred. This means that long-term solutions to the traffic loss problem must come from switch vendors rather than software developers.

Sunsoft's high-level network file system (NFS) protocol already comes with flow control algorithms to deal with network congestion, but at the end of 1994 the vendor reengineered the protocol so that it can use TCP/IP as a transport protocol instead of UDP (user datagram protocol). This allows it to take advantage of the superior congestion control mechanisms present in TCP, including the ability to retransmit lost packets individually (previously, traffic was resent in 8-kbyte blocks containing multiple packets).

With Netware, packets can be sent in two modes. In Single Acknowledgment mode, the sending device waits for an acknowledgment after each packet is transmitted. This procedure slows throughput and helps avoid congestion. Problems are far more likely to occur in Packet Burst mode, where a stream of packets can be sent before the sender looks for an acknowledgment. Packet Burst comes with two flow control features that are supposed to prevent network congestion. The adjustable window lets the net manager alter the number of packets sent without an acknowledgment. Further, a mechanism called Packet Pacing is designed to automatically assess the bandwidth available on the network and adjust the rate of transmission accordingly.

Section 9. Preventive Measures

Careful design, big buffers, and improved protocols are three things that can help prevent traffic loss. But a growing number of vendors believe that the only way to prevent traffic losses in the long term is by implementing flow control. They point out that switch problems are set to get worse as more vendors bring out products with multiple high- and low-speed ports. Likewise, they argue that adding huge buffers is an unnecessary expense. (It's no coincidence that most of the companies arguing for buffers tend to be larger cash-rich outfits; buffers rank alongside pro-baseball salaries in terms of outrageous expenditure.) Amber Wave (Acton, MA) says a key reason its Ethernet switch costs just $175 per port is that it comes with a pool of only 250-kbytes of buffering for every eight ports.

Necessity is proving the mother of invention for outfits that either cannot stump up the funds to throw expensive buffering at the overflow problem or are unwilling to lose their switches' budget price points. Matrox and Xnet Technology (Milpitas, CA) have independently developed the same methodology for preventing overflows. Their technique leverages the form factor of their switches. Instead of using a standalone configuration, both vendors supply their products as adapter cards which slot into the file server itself. Xnet and Matrox have written special software drivers for their cards which allow their switches to communicate with Netware and Windows NT operating systems running on the server. When the queue in the switch gets full, it sends a message to the driver which slows down the send rate over the server's bus.

Networth has come up with an alternative solution to the problem. Its Flow NLM ($1695) software package runs as a netware-loadable module (NLM) on the LAN's Novell Netware file server. The Flow NLM communicates with an SNMP agent in Networth's LAN switch in order to keep tabs on how full each of the switches' buffers are. When any of the buffers approach capacity, the NLM sends a message to the server telling it to stop sending traffic to that port. When the buffer flushes, the transmission is restarted. Essentially, the NLM makes the server switch-aware.

One drawback to the Matrox/Xnet driver and the Networth NLM solutions is that they work only with specific operating systems (neither of them addresses the needs of NFS users, for instance). That isn't the case with the so-called backpressure flow control mechanism being implemented by Madge and Onet Data Communication Technologies Corp. (Cambridge, MA). Backpressure uses the collision detection part of the Ethernet CSMA/CD MAC-layer protocol to prevent traffic loss. When a buffer on a port approaches capacity, the switch reacts by sending a collision detection signal to all the devices on that port to stop them from sending any more packets to the switch. Devices receiving the signal wait for a while before attempting to transmit again. Supporters of backpressure allege that it works 10 times faster than retransmitting lost packets.

But backpressure also has two big drawbacks. First, it can cause frames to be destroyed at the sending station. Second, every time a switch port sends out a collision detection signal, it stops all communications on the network segment attached to that port—not just the traffic which is being sent to the switch. In other words, all the peer-to-peer conversations between devices on the segment are jammed for as long as the switch is congested, even though the traffic they are sending is not destined for the switch itself. When only one device is attached to each port, that isn't a problem. Then again, buffer overflows are unlikely to occur in that configuration anyhow. But when the switch is serving in the backbone, the problem will be a lot worse.

Some vendors, such as Cabletron and Matrox, are planning to take the flow control work which is being undertaken in the ATM Forum and modify it for use on switched LANs. Even if Cabletron and Matrox succeed in implementing ABR over switched LANs, they will still have to wait until file transfer applications arrive which can read congestion notification messages and react to them by changing rate. In order for flow control to be implemented properly, the application on the client side has to be aware of the messages and be able to slow down. In the meantime, ABR will be able to work fully with audio and video applications that support different rates of transmission.

Section 10.   Back to the Future

Ultimately, there may prove to be more than one way in which LAN switch vendors can learn from the world of ATM. When the first evidence emerged that ATM switches tend to drop packets, some major ATM switch vendors went on record as saying that flow control was unnecessary. They reckoned the problem was best solved with a combination of (you guessed it) careful network design and deep buffers. Shortly after, the same vendors had embraced flow control on ATM networks wholeheartedly. Some observers reckon it is only a matter of time before LAN switch vendors must do the same.

Cross-Comparison Tables

*This book's charter is to provide enough information about
each high-speed LAN's strengths and weaknesses to enable
readers to make an intelligent decision about which technologies
to implement. To achieve that end, it is important not only
to discuss the various technologies individually, but also
to contrast them with one another. Part 4 of this book delivers a
cross-comparison of all the different high-speed LANs (standard
and nonstandard), via a series of tables accompanied by
explanatory text. These tables provide an "at a glance"
comparison of the different technologies.*

*Table 1 sets the scene by detailing each LAN's origins, status,
and time in existence. It also indicates whether the technology
can be used in the wide-area network (WAN) as well as the LAN.*

*Table 2 deals with the issue of latency, or network delay. The
amount of latency incurred when sending traffic over a LAN
(and whether that latency is variable or fixed) is the most critical
factor in determining if a network is capable of supporting time-
sensitive multimedia applications—or, conversely, if it is
equipped to shunt only high-speed asynchronous traffic.*

*Table 3 summarizes how much support each technology is
receiving within the networking industry today. It also leans on
analysts' predictions to forecast how widely the various
technologies will be implemented in the future. Regardless of
their technological merit, industry support will turn out to be a
crucial factor in deciding the fates of each of the high-speed
LANs, since corporations tend to shy away from technologies
that have failed to garner a significant level of interest and
backing among equipment vendors.*

*Table 4 describes each LAN from an architectural viewpoint.
Issues covered include whether the network implements a
shared-media or a switched architecure and, in the case of
switched architectures, whether each switch port can handle*

multiple devices (as is the case with Ethernet switches) or only one (as with ATM). The table also deals with questions such as network coverage (how far nodes can transmit data), throughput rates (how fast they can carry data), and network overhead (how efficiently they carry data).

Table 5 details how easy it is for net managers now running conventional Ethernet and token ring networks to migrate to each of the high-speed LANs. For instance, it indicates how token ring switches will work over existing cables and with the adapters already in place in user's workstations, whereas HIPPI will require an expensive and time-consuming change of cable and cards. Equipment prices are also covered.

Table 1: A Little History

Table 1 provides some historical perspective on the high-speed LANs. One of the reasons that network managers now have so many high-speed LAN technologies to sort through is that the IEEE (Institute of Electrical and Electronics Engineers) seems to be working overtime to define them; three of the technologies in the table come from IEEE. That's a curious turn of events, given that ANSI (the American National Standards Institute) was originally supposed to take care of *all* standards operating above 20 Mbit/s.

History has overtaken that decision. In fact, the IEEE's newfound responsibilities illustrate the fact that standards have become big business. Put simply, companies that invest in a proprietary technology and then get it standardized can recoup that investment. In fact, some venture capitalists are now making standardization a condition of further investment in products, vendors report.

The financial factor has spurred vendors to push hard to get their technologies stamped with an IEEE seal of approval—a procedure that has proved ludicrously easy, since standards committees are made up almost exclusively of vendor representatives. This can spell trouble for network managers, who lack an official ombudsman to voice their opinions and concerns. 100Base-T and 100VG-AnyLAN are a good example of the standards approval process gone awry. The IEEE was originally supposed to give the nod to *one* new 100-Mbit/s technology. In 1993, however, it announced that it couldn't decide between the two and would ratify both.

Four of the high-speed LANs come out of ANSI: FDDI, FDDI II, Fibre Channel, and HIPPI. These standards are also the oldest on the books. FDDI, in particular, first debuted way back in 1983; it's been a fully ratified LAN standard since 1988.

When it comes to standards bodies, ATM is the odd LAN out. ATM specifications get an official seal of approval from the Internet Engineering Task Force (IETF) and the ITU-TSS. But the standards are actually hashed out and brought to life within the ATM Forum—a coalition of equipment manufacturers, software developers, and other interested parties. Membership is expensive. For the record, it costs $10,000 to join the ATM Forum as a principal vendor (with voting rights). And that's only the tip of the iceberg. The cost of sending staffers to six technical committee meetings a year can easily scale to a six-figure sum for each person.

The ITU-TSS is a telecom organization. Its involvement in the development of ATM provides a heavy hint that asynchronous transfer mode has a different charter than the other technologies in the table. ATM is the only standard which targets service in both the local- and wide-area network domains equally; though FDDI II and

IsoEnet also feature some low-speed wide-area network capabilities. The extra distances covered by FDDI means this technology is suitable for deployment in both LANs and metropolitan area networks (MANs). The rest of the technologies target only LAN applications.

Table 1 also covers five categories of high-speed LAN that fall outside the responsibility of standards organizations: Ethernet switches, FDDI switches, 100Base-T switches, 100VG-AnyLAN switches, and token ring switches.

TABLE 1   A Little History

	Standards group	First sighted	Status	Suitable domains	Unsuitable domains
Standards-Based Technologies					
ATM	ATM Forum, IETF, ITU-TSS	1989	half ratified; rest due by 1997	all	none
FDDI	ANSI	1983	ratified since 1988	LAN, MAN	WAN
FDDI II	ANSI	1987	ratified in 1994	LAN, MAN, some WAN	most WAN
Fibre Channel	ANSI	1988	ratified in 1993	LAN	MAN, WAN
HIPPI	ANSI	1986	ratified in 1993	LAN	MAN, WAN
IsoEnet	IEEE	1992	ratified in 1995	LAN, some WAN	most WAN
100Base-T (fast Ethernet)	IEEE	1992	ratified in 1995	LAN	MAN, WAN
100VG-AnyLAN	IEEE	1992	ratified in 1995	LAN	MAN, WAN
Proprietary Switching Technologies					
Ethernet switches	n/a	1992	n/a	LAN	MAN, WAN
FDDI switches	n/a	1993	n/a	LAN, MAN	WAN
100Base-T switches	n/a	1995	n/a	LAN	MAN, WAN
100VG-AnyLAN	n/a	1995	n/a	LAN	MAN, WAN
Token ring switches	n/a	1993	n/a	LAN	MAN, WAN

MAN: Metropolitan area network.

Table 2: Multimedia Capabilities

Table 2 summarizes the multimedia capabilities of the different high-speed LAN technologies. To accurately assess each network, net managers need to look at three different attributes: latency (column 2), available bandwidth (column 3), and packet or cell size (column 4).

Of this trio, latency (or network delay) is the most critical. Time-sensitive multimedia applications—such as interactive voice and video—are best served by a technology which delivers low, predictable (or fixed) node-to-node latencies. Fluctuations cause video images to appear jerky, and distort the quality of audio signals; the higher and more varied the delay, the lower the quality of the interactive application. (Bear in mind that not all multimedia traffic is interactive: Stored video and still images, for example, are not displayed until the receiving station has gotten the entire file. Variable or even high latency will not affect the quality of these applications.)

One way to lessen the problem of variable latency is to equip desktop multimedia gear with memory buffers that collect video and voice frames as they arrive and deliver them in a smooth stream. But even then, some loss of quality will be apparent to users. And the extra memory adds to the cost of running multimedia applications.

Shared shame

As the table indicates, shared-media LANs like FDDI, 100Base-T, and 100VG-AnyLAN are inherently unsuitable for carrying interactive applications because they implement mechanisms to ensure that only one station can access the network at any time, forcing other nodes to queue up until it's their turn to transmit. This results in variable and high levels of latency, which in turn lead to poor-quality multimedia. In the worst case (when one node hogs the network for a sustained period of time by sending a lengthy file), the delay can become so long that it actually crashes the multimedia application.

One way to limit this problem on shared-media networks is to drastically restrict the number of devices on each network segment to a small handful by adding bridges and routers. But this only ameliorates the problem—it doesn't make it go away. What's more, highly segmented networks are a headache to manage, can become fantastically expensive, and introduces irksome levels of delay every time traffic is sent between segments, as opposed to within them.

Priority service

Both FDDI and 100VG-AnyLAN incorporate prioritization schemes that can be activated in order to improve multimedia quality.

Synchronous FDDI uses a timer to reserve a portion of the bandwidth for delay-sensitive communications. 100VG-AnyLAN uses a mechanism called demand priority protocol (DPP). With DPP, network access requests from workstations are forwarded to a central hub. Workstations can signal the hub to indicate whether they're sending high- or low-priority packets. If two or more stations transmit high-priority traffic simultaneously, access is allocated in a round-robin fashion in the order that the requests are received. The latency for traffic transmitted by the first workstation is 121 microseconds; this delay increases by 120 microseconds for every workstation that subsequently accesses the network. Thus, traffic from the fifth station to request priority access will be delayed by 601 microseconds.

Both of the foregoing schemes help make shared-media FDDI and 100VG-AnyLAN networks better suited to multimedia traffic. But switched LANs are a better vehicle for time-sensitive traffic, since they allow managers to eliminate contention entirely and establish multiple paths between workstations.

Switch superiority

Along with eliminating contention, ATM and Fibre Channel switches come with facilities that further improve their multimedia dexterity. Both networks have multiplexing facilities which allow them to carry data and time-sensitive multimedia traffic simultaneously by interleaving them on the same links. Quality-of-service parameters—such as guaranteed data rate and maximum delay—can be set on a link-by-link basis, allowing users to run their diverse applications without incurring a tradeoff with quality. Both ATM and Fibre Channel should deliver latency of less than 30 microseconds in a well-crafted network.

Multiplexing sets ATM and Fibre Channel apart from HIPPI, the other standards-based switching technology. HIPPI's designers architected it entirely toward servicing very large asynchronous data transfers, and omitted to outfit the standard with the ability to multiplex traffic from different nodes onto a single connection. On a HIPPI LAN, if one node is transmitting to another, there's no way for a third node to interject traffic onto the link; instead, it must wait until the first two nodes have finished before it can transmit its message. This means that while latency added by the HIPPI switch itself is extremely low (less than 2 microseconds in a best-case scenario), latency measured from the moment a node first attempts to access a LAN to the moment delivery is complete can be extremely high (hundreds of milliseconds), depending on traffic flow.

Proprietary approaches

The latency characteristics attributed to the proprietary LAN switches in the table assume that only one network device is attached to each switch port; attaching multiple devices to each port is a bad idea when the switches are being used for multimedia, since it immediately reintroduces the risk that network contention will stymie timely delivery of audiovisual data. (Hooking up multiple devices to a port isn't even an option with standards-based switches based on ATM and HIPPI, which will work only when one device is connected per port.)

Proprietary LAN switches can operate in one of two ways: using cut-through switching (in which packets are forwarded as soon as they've read the MAC header) or store-and-forward switching (where packets are stored in a memory buffer before being forwarded). Cut-through switches are a far better fit for multimedia networks because their on-the-fly approach to packet processing keeps latency low—at between 20 and 60 microseconds, depending on the type of network being switched.

With store-and-forward switches, on the other hand, the act of storing incoming packets into memory means that latency increases in proportion to packet size. With small packets (32 or 64 bytes), that isn't a problem. Delays are usually kept to 60 microseconds or less. With larger packets, latency can be more than 100 times higher and is measured in milliseconds. Bear in mind that the maximum size of the frames found on FDDI and token ring is usually kept at 4478 bytes; for Ethernet, it's 1512 bytes. This means store-and-forward latency problems are likely to be more severe on FDDI or token ring networks. Some switch vendors now offer products that allow users to select one or other mode of operation, depending on the application being handled.

Also, tests show that store-and-forward switches which rely on a RISC processor to handle packets feature worse latency characteristics than store-and-forward switches which use custom ASICs to process packets. With almost all the CPU-based devices, latency increases when the switches are under load (i.e., handling traffic from multiple different sources simultaneously). The extra delay is caused by switch ports having to wait for a forwarding decision from the shared CPU. As traffic levels increase, response times worsen. ASIC switches are immune to this overhead because they perform forwarding decisions locally, at the incoming port.

Contrary to popular belief, there are three circumstances when cut-through switches must also buffer traffic in exactly the same way as their store-and-forward counterparts:

- When traffic is being transferred between ports running at different speeds

- When the switch is sending packets out onto a segment where a node is already transmitting
- When outgoing traffic arrives at a port already busy handling traffic from another port.

In these instances, cut-through switches automatically buffer traffic, and latency increases.

Hybrid approaches

FDDI II and IsoEnet both take a different approach to minimizing latency—by defining hybrid networks which allow simultaneous packet transfer of traditional asychnronous data, as well as circuit-switched transfer of time-sensitive multimedia data. By using circuit-switching (also called isochronous) services, FDDI II and IsoEnet can deliver low and constant delays for time-sensitive signals.

FDDI II uses a multiplexing technique to divide FDDI's 100-Mbit/s bandwidth into sixteen 6.144-Mbit/s circuits, each of which can be allocated to carrying *either* asynchronous data *or* isochronous traffic. Each of the sixteen circuits is in turn subdivided into ninety-six 64-kbit/s channels. IsoEnet also uses a multiplexing approach, this time to separate 16 Mbit/s of total network bandwidth into two logical parts: 6.144-Mbit/s is parceled off into ninety-six 64-kbit/s multimedia circuits; the other 10 Mbit/s handles the old data applications.

Bandwidth reservations

By implementing circuit switching, both standards guarantee fixed latency for multimedia traffic—an achievement that none of the other LAN technologies can match. Even ATM (the alleged multimedia champion) experiences some latency fluctuations.

But this advantage is almost completely outweighed by the fact that FDDI II and IsoEnet are shared-media networks, meaning that available bandwidth decreases in proportion to the number of nodes added to the network. After latency, bandwidth is the next most important criterion to look at when assessing a multimedia LAN. The bandwidth problem is most acute with IsoEnet, which has only 6 Mbit/s of pipe available for multimedia applications in any event. Reasonable-quality compressed video requires about 1 Mbit/s per stream. Net managers who choose to implement IsoEnet leave themselves with only two choices—either implement low-quality, kilobit-speed, low-bandwidth applications or strictly limit the number of multimedia users on the network. FDDI II suffers from the same problems—though to a lesser extent.

All the switched networks in Table 2 are immune to this problem. Take Ethernet switches, the slowest type of LAN switch in the table.

When only one device is attached to each port of an Etheret switch, each multimedia user has access to the full 10 Mbit/s of network bandwidth—enough to service the vast majority of multimedia applications. More powerful technologies—such as 155-Mbit/s ATM—can handle much faster streams, enabling them to support applications such as movie special effects and medical imaging.

Packet size

The third criterion to check when assessing multimedia LANs is packet or cell size. As a simple rule of thumb, the smaller the packet, the better the network is able to transport time-sensitive multimedia.

Most of the networks in Table 2 have been designed primarily for carrying data—and use large packet sizes. FDDI and token ring, for instance, permit packets up to 4.5 kbytes in length. HIPPI is even more datacentric in design, allowing 2-kbyte frames to be combined into streams measuring more than 1 Gbit in length. The additional overhead incurred in filling and processing these very large packets adds to network delay. ATM goes to the other extreme, using 53-byte cells which can be prepped and processed in a fraction of the time.

Summary

In conclusion, while all the networks in Table 2 manage to fulfill at least one of the requirements for a high-quality multimedia network (latency, bandwidth, packet size) only one network meets them all. It is ATM's combination of low latency with very high bandwidth and cell switching that promises to make it the multimedia network of choice into the twenty-first century

TABLE 2 Multimedia Capabilities

	Latency characteristics	Bandwidth characteristics	Maximum cell/packet size	Suitable applications	Unsuitable applications
Standards-Based Technologies					
ATM	variable and low; typically less than 30 microseconds in a well-designed LAN	very high speed, switched	53 bytes	data, time-sensitive multimedia, voice	none
FDDI	variable and high; typically measured in milliseconds	high speed, shared media	4478 kbytes	data	time-sensitive multimedia, voice
FDDI (synchronous)	variable and moderate; typically measured in hundreds of microseconds, or milliseconds	high speed, shared media	4478 kbytes	data, some time-sensitive multimedia	voice
FDDI II	variable and high for data (typically measured in milliseconds), fixed for multimedia	high speed, shared media	4478 kbytes	data, time-sensitive multimedia, voice	high-bandwidth multimedia
Fibre Channel	variable and low; typically less than 30 microseconds in a well-designed LAN	very high speed, switched	2 kbytes (sometimes more)	data, some time-sensitive multimedia	some time-sensitive multimedia, voice
HIPPI	variable; can be very low (less than 10 microseconds) or very high (hundreds of milliseconds)	very high speed, switched	2 kbytes (can be combined into bursts in excess of 1 Gbyte)	data	time-sensitive multimedia, voice
IsoEnet	variable and very high for data (sometimes measured in seconds), fixed for multimedia	low speed, shared media	1512 kbytes	low-speed data, low-speed time-sensitive multimedia, voice	all high-speed traffic
100Base-T (fast Ethernet)	variable and high; typically measured in milliseconds	high speed, shared media	1512 kbytes	data	time-sensitive multimedia, voice
100VG-AnyLAN	variable and high; typically measured in milliseconds	high speed, shared media	1512 or 4478 kbytes	data, some time-sensitive multimedia	some time-sensitive multimedia, voice

TABLE 2 Multimedia Capabilities (*Continued*)

Property	Latency characteristics	Bandwidth characteristics	Maximum cell/packet size	Suitable applications	Unsuitable applications
Switching Technologies					
Ethernet switches (cut through)	variable and low; usually around 40 microseconds	low speed, switched	1512 kbytes	data, time-sensitive multimedia	voice
Ethernet switches (store and forward)	variable; low (microseconds) with small packets, high (milliseconds) with large packets	low speed, switched	1512 kbytes	data, some time-sensitive multimedia	some time-sensitive multimedia, voice
FDDI switches (cut through)	variable and low; around 20 microseconds	high speed, switched	4478 kbytes	data, time-sensitive multimedia	voice
FDDI switches (store and forward)	variable; low (microseconds) with small packets, high (milliseconds) with large packets	high speed, switched	4478 kbytes	data, some time-sensitive multimedia	some time-sensitive multimedia, voice
100Base-T switches (cut through)	variable and low; around 30 microseconds	high speed, switched	1512 kbytes	data, time-sensitive multimedia	voice
100Base-T switches (store and forward)	variable; low (microseconds) with small packets, high (milliseconds) with large packets	high speed, switched	1512 kbytes	data, some time-sensitive multimedia	some time-sensitive multimedia, voice
100VG-AnyLAN switches (cut through)	variable and low; latency not yet measured	high speed, switched	1512 or 4478 kbytes	data, time-sensitive multimedia	voice
100VG-AnyLAN switches (store and forward)	variable; low (microseconds) with small packets, high (milliseconds) with large packets	high speed, switched	1512 or 4478 kbytes	data, some time-sensitive multimedia	some time-sensitive multimedia, voice
Token ring switches (cut through)	variable and low; 30 microseconds	low speed, switched	17,000 bytes	data, time-sensitive multimedia	voice
Token ring switches (store and forward)	variable; low (microseconds) with small packets, high (milliseconds) with large packets	low speed, switched	17,000 bytes	data, some time-sensitive multimedia	some time-sensitive multimedia, voice

Table 3: Level of Industry Support

It's vital that network managers carefully and accurately gauge each LAN technology's chances of long-term survival before investing in it. The networking industry will support only a limited number of LAN technologies. Some of the high-speed LANs being talked up so enthusiastically at IEEE and ANSI meetings are going to end up in the "Where are they now?" file. Technology also-rans don't make for successful long-term implementations; quite simply, nobody wants to end up with a wiring closet full of equipment vendors no longer support.

There are two easy ways to assess a high-speed LAN's chances down the stretch, and thus identify potential no-hopers. One is to look at how widely the LAN is being implemented today by corporations, and how many equipment vendors are selling products which support it. The other is to look at analyst and vendor forecasts for how popular the LAN will be in the future.

Table 3 summarizes this information. Columns 2 and 3 detail whether an industry group has been formed to lobby for a technology and, if so, how many members belong to it. Column 4 shows how many nodes* of each LAN technology had been installed worldwide at the time of going to press in 1995. The other columns give predictions for the number of new nodes of each technology being installed annually through 1998. The figures shown were culled from a variety of market forecasters and consultancies—including Dataquest (San Jose, CA), Forrester Research Inc. (Cambridge, MA), and Rising Star Research (Van Nuys, CA).

Support organization

In terms of organized backing, ATM is way out in front. The ATM Forum—the organization responsible for developing ATM and foisting it on the rest of the world—now boasts over 700 members, and that number is climbing. ATM's popularity is also evidenced by the number of equipment vendors jumping into the market. Already, more than 150 companies are supplying ATM equipment or software—a huge number for such an immature market. Together, these factors demonstrate that—barring unforseen disasters—ATM is a safe bet for long-term investment.

Similarly, the numbers in columns 2 and 3 show that FDDI, Fibre Channel, HIPPI, and 100Base-T have attracted healthy levels of

---

*When applied to shared-media technologies, the term *node* describes the number of network devices (hubs, printers, servers, workstations, and so on) being attached to that LAN technology in any given year. When used in reference to switched technologies, it describes the number of new switch ports installed.

industry support. FDDI doesn't have an official body to lobby for it. However, 70 vendors are shipping products that support it, and they're unlikely to drop the technology like a hot potato any time in the foreseeable future. Likewise, equipment vendors are getting into Fibre Channel and HIPPI technologies in relatively large numbers, considering the somewhat niche nature of both technologies.

Not all high-speed LAN standards have garnered this level of support: The FDDI II and IsoEnet vendor fan clubs don't exactly have a waiting list at the moment. Only one vendor now supplies FDDI II equipment; with IsoEnet the number is at least in double figures. To a certain extent, 100VG-AnyLAN also is suffering from the same lack of enthusiasm.

When it comes to proprietary LAN switching technologies, the situation is a little different. For one thing, LAN switch vendors don't go around forming clubs to talk up the benefits of their products. That's because whereas vendors supporting standards-based technologies want to be seen as team players conforming to a common set of rules, with the LAN switch market differentiation is actually a key selling point. Even so, column 3—showing the number of vendors implementing each type of switching in 1995—speaks volumes about the long-term outlook for the different LAN switching technologies.

At least 100 vendors are now involved in manufacturing Ethernet switches—an indication that they will be a mainstay of corporate networks for a long time to come. Meanwhile, support for token ring switching is growing fast—eight vendors are playing in that market. Eight vendors now sell FDDI switches. Conversely, there is less enthusiasm for 100Base-T switching, and no one yet sells a 100VG-AnyLAN switch.

Future tense

Analyst and market researcher forecasts for how well different technologies will fare typically enforce the enthusiastic reception that vendors are giving to some technologies, and the tepid reaction they are bestowing on others. The technology category in which forecasters expect to see the most growth is Ethernet LAN switches, with the number of new switch ports installed growing from 1,061,000 in 1995 to a gargantuan 7,150,000 in 1998. Clearly, network pundits expect Ethernet switches to become a de facto way to boost the performance of both installed Ethernet networks, and new Ethernet LANs, as they come on line.

The numbers predicted for the token ring switch market are lower, but for a reason. Analysts expect token ring switches to be mainly installed in corporate backbones, rather than providing desktop, work group, or departmental connectivity. Consequently, while most token ring networks will end up having a switched component in them by 1998, the actual number of ports shipped will remain lower than for Ethernet switches—which will be widely installed at every level of the network hierarchy.

Although starting slowly, sales of 100Base-T switches are eventually expected to gain momentum—climbing to an anticipated 760,000 ports in 1998. This is mainly as a result of support from leading industry names like Bay Networks Inc. and 3Com Corp. (both of Santa Clara, CA). Conversely, industry observers say that FDDI and 100VG-AnyLAN switches will never account for more than a small slice of the internetworking pie. Analysts see the popularity of shared-media FDDI continuing to climb, slowly, until 1996, and then starting to fall away rapidly as it loses market share to the other, cheaper and (in some cases faster) LANs.

Of the standardized high-speed LAN technologies ATM is—unsurprisingly—predicted to go gangbusters toward 1998. However, it's interesting that in that year Ethernet switches will still outsell ATM in terms of ports shipped by a factor of more than eight—putting the lie to claims by some equipment vendors that ATM is poised to sweep through corporate networks at any moment.

100Base-T is expected to experience fairly rapid growth, mainly at the expense of its main competitor—100VG-AnyLAN. Fibre Channel and HIPPI are supposed to experience moderately healthy growth rates. In contrast, predicted shipments of IsoEnet and FDDI II are so low that many of the vendors who are now promising support for these LANs may well bail out in favor of other technologies—leaving net managers who have invested in them in a very sticky situation.

TABLE 3 Level of Industry Support (Worldwide)

	Industry body; number of members	Number of equipment vendors implementing in 1995	New nodes installed in 1995	New nodes in 1996 (predicted)	New nodes in 1997 (predicted)	New nodes in 1998 (predicted)
Standards-Based Technologies						
ATM	ATM Forum; more than 700	more than 150	33,000	93,000	440,000	840,000
FDDI	none	more than 100	87,000	93,000	80,000	75,000
FDDI II	none	one	3000	2000	1000	1000
Fibre Channel	Fibre Channel Systems Initiative; 3	50	5000	15,000	35,000	70,000
HIPPI	HIPPI Networking Forum; 18	30	5000	10,000	20,000	30,000
IsoEnet	none	10	less than 1000	15,000	30,000	60,000
100Base-T (fast Ethernet)	Fast Ethernet Alliance; 73	20	750,000	3,200,000	6,500,000	8,400,000
100VG-AnyLAN	100VG-AnyLAN Forum; 40	10	40,000	165,000	250,000	500,000

TABLE 3 Level of Industry Support (Worldwide) (*Continued*)

	Industry body; number of members	Number of equipment vendors implementing in 1995	New nodes installed in 1995	New nodes in 1996 (predicted)	New nodes in 1997 (predicted)	New nodes in 1998 (predicted)
Proprietary Switching Technologies						
Ethernet switches	none	more than 100	1,061,000	2,505,000	4,480,000	7,150,000
FDDI switches	none	8	20,000	30,000	39,000	42,000
100Base-T switches	none	1	5,000	110,000	330,000	760,000
100VG-AnyLAN switches	none	none	none	12,000	35,000	50,000
Token ring switches	none	8	30,000	112,000	320,000	1,120,000

Table 4: Architecture

High-speed LAN designers have come at the problem of how to deliver more bandwidth from very different angles. Table 4 summarizes their varied approaches by dissecting the design, or architecture, underlying each high-speed LAN technology.

Switch versus shared

If life were simple, assessing high-speed LAN technologies would merely be a matter of comparing their data rates. Unfortunately, there's a lot of confusion as to what throughput figures really indicate about performance. On shared-media LANs such as FDDI and 100Base-T, line speed decreases in proportion to the number of nodes contending for a portion of the total available bandwidth (100 Mbit/s in both cases). Thus, line speed (the throughput to any single node) is going to equal total throughput only when there is a single node being serviced. On a 10-node FDDI installation, for example, each node on average gets no more than one-tenth the available bandwidth, or 10 Mbit/s.

With standards-based switched LANs, such as ATM and HIPPI, every node is attached to a dedicated segment. Thus, line speed is no longer proportional to the number of nodes. On a 155-Mbit/s ATM installation, each link runs at full line speed, as does every link that is added. On a HIPPI network, each node can get up to 3.2 *Gbit/s* of bandwidth—320 times more than the maximum amount of bandwidth available on a 10-Mbit/s Ethernet.

Most of the high-speed LAN standards—100Base-T, FDDI, FDDI II, IsoEnet, and 100VG-AnyLAN—retain the shared-media architecture of the original Ethernet and token ring. Performance increases come thanks to new signaling and encoding schemes, which boost total available bandwidth. But that bandwidth still must be divided among every node on the network. A net manager who replaces a 10-Mbit/s Ethernet supporting 40 PCs with a 100-Mbit/s FDDI network boosts the average bandwidth available to each user tenfold, from 250 kbit/s to 2.5 Mbit/s—not to 100 Mbit/s.

A far larger increase in throughput is realized by going with any of the switched architectures. If an ATM switch were added to the aforementioned 40-node Ethernet, the bandwidth to each user would jump to 155 Mbit/s—620 times that available with 10-Mbit/s Ethernet and 62 times that furnished by 100-Mbit/s FDDI. If a HIPPI network were installed, each node could get 3.2 *Gbit/s* of bandwidth—1280 times more than the maximum amount of bandwidth available on the old network (and, coincidentally, a level of capacity which only Sbus or PCI workstations could make a real dent in).

One or more

Almost all the standards-based switching technologies dicate that only one device is connected to each switch port (Fibre Channel LANs can optionally be architected in a shared-media configuration). But the proprietary switching technologies, such as switched Ethernet and switched token ring, give net managers the option to attach a segment containing multiple users to each port. However, in this configuration, the amount of bandwidth available to each user decreases in the same way as it does on a shared-media network segment.

There's another drawback to attaching multiple devices to a proprietary switch port—it removes their ability to operate in full-duplex mode. Full duplex works by disabling the access control mechanism which comes built into shared-media standards like Ethernet and token ring, so that traffic can flow in two directions over the switch connection at once. This effectively doubles the throughput on the switched connection—to 20 Mbit/s for switched Ethernet, 32 Mbit/s for switched token ring, and 200 Mbit/s for switched 100Base-T, FDDI, and 100VG-AnyLAN.

Max headroom

How much bandwidth is available is only part of the story. How efficiently a network uses that bandwidth also is an important consideration when evaluating high-speed LAN technologies. Network overhead—the amount of information shipped relative to frame size—is a good indicator of efficiency. The lower the overhead, the more effective the transport.

ATM, for all its reputation as a top performer, actually uses its bandwidth less efficiently than any of its high-speed rivals. Each ATM cell is 53 bytes long: 5 bytes are used by a header containing addressing information; the remaining 48 go for payload. (Unlike conventional LAN frames, ATM cells are not rounded off with a trailer incorporating error-checking information).

To determine network overhead as a percentage of total bandwidth, divide 100 by the total frame size and then multiply by the size of the header. For ATM, that's 100 divided by 53 multiplied by 5, for a network overhead of 9.5 percent (9.43396 percent, to be more precise). In contrast, the network overhead for FDDI, FDDI-over-copper, and FDDI II, all of which have a payload of 4478 bytes and 23 bytes-worth of header and trailer, is 0.5 percent. Fibre Channel, which has a 2112-byte payload and a 36-byte header, has a network overhead of 1.7 percent.

Go with the flow

Bear in mind that all the high-speed LAN standards are affected by another kind of network overhead. Each comes with a flow control methodology that prevents too many users from transmitting data at the same time (an event that causes packet loss when network capacity is exceeded). Some of these techniques work more efficiently than others.

Take 100Base-T and IsoEnet. Both rely on the carrier sense multiple access with collision detection (CSMA/CD) scheme used on 10-Mbit/s Ethernet to resolve contention problems. When more than one station tries to send data over the network simultaneously, the collision detection scheme tells each node to stop transmitting. It then runs an algorithm that allows one station to access the network ahead of the other. Tests by LANquest Labs (San Jose, CA) show that collision detection reduces available bandwidth on a 10-Mbit/s Ethernet (with 4 servers and 12 PCs) to 6.8 Mbit/s (by 32 percent). The same levels of overhead can be expected on the high-speed LANs that use CSMA/CD. High-speed LANs that employ a token-passing scheme to assign access are far more efficient. In tests conducted by The Tolly Group (Manasquan, NJ), FDDI delivered 96 Mbit/s, or 96 percent of available bandwidth.

The developers of switching standards use three different methods to control network access:

- ATM uses a rate-based scheme. The transmission rate available to a given node depends on how many other nodes are transmitting data at the same time. The rate changes dynamically, from almost zero right up to the maximum speed of the network.

- Fibre Channel has a sliding-window approach something like that found in TCP/IP.

- HIPPI uses a credit-based approach. Usage is monitored on links connecting every node in the network. "Credit" messages are exchanged between network nodes to ensure that frames are passed from one node to the next only if there is capacity available at the next node.

Obviously, the amount of overhead which each of the three schemes adds will vary depending on the number of nodes communicating over the network at any time. If few nodes are trying to send data, the flow control schemes will remain inactive, and overhead is nonexistent. If many are transmitting, the flow control schemes will kick in—causing noticeable degradation in performance as the effective amount of bandwidth available to each node goes down. In any case, it's safe to say that the schemes used in ATM, Fibre Channel, and HIPPI provide far more efficient methods for controlling packet flow than those used in CSMA/CD-based networks.

Further, its much better to put up with the overhead caused by flow control than to run the risk of losing traffic when too many nodes send data at once. That's precisely the problem faced by designers of networks based on proprietary LAN switching technologies. Because they are proprietary, there is currently no standard specifications defining how flow control can be implemented on LAN switches. A few Ethernet switch vendors have come up with proprietary approaches; but their usefulness is in doubt. In the absence of flow control schemes, net managers have to design their way around the problem, installing enough switches with sufficient memory to prevent traffic flow from reaching capacity.

Run along

Cabling compatibility is another architectural issue to consider. Choosing a high-speed LAN that can work with the copper cables, patch panels, and connectors already installed—rather than requiring better-grade copper or fiber—is an easy way for network managers to eliminate one of the biggest expenditures on the path to higher performance: 62.5/125-micron multimode fiber can cost four times as much as copper, depending on factors such as union labor rates. But just working over copper isn't always enough. Net managers also need to ensure that the LAN they choose can drive data for sufficient distances over their network, or risk having to install an excess of hubs and switches to attain requisite coverage.

Of the technologies listed in Table 4, only FDDI and FDDI II cannot run over copper cable of any type. Fibre Channel works with a variety of copper cables, though transmission distances depend upon the combination of line speed and media. Thus, the standard defines a maximum distance of 25 meters for 1-Gbit/s traffic over thick coaxial cable but extends that to 100 meters for data traveling at 133 Mbit/s. The spec also states that STP (shielded twisted pair) can be used for distances up to 50 meters. HIPPI is even more finicky—requiring use of a huge 50-pair copper cable for a maximum of 25 meters. The remaining technologies (standards-based and proprietary switching) can all run over Category 3 or Category 5 UTP for distances of 100 meters.

Vendors of 100VG-AnyLAN equipment claim that their adapters and hubs can drive data for 200 meters, though network managers who opt for that configuration will be violating TIA-568A standards defining the topology of premises wiring schemes in North America.

TABLE 4 Architecture

	Data rates	Switched or shared media	Devices per switched connection	Full-duplex-capable	Maximum packet or cell size	Network overhead	Flow control	Internode distance over copper cable	Topologies supported
Standards-Based Technologies									
ATM	25 Mbit/s, 51 Mbit/s, 155 Mbit/s, 622 Mbit/s	switched	one	yes	53 bytes	9.5%	rate-based	100 meters	mesh, point-to-point, star
FDDI	100 Mbit/s	shared media	n/a	no	4478 Kbytes	0.5%	token passing	n/a	point-to-point, ring, star
FDDI-over-copper	100 Mbit/s	shared media	n/a	no	4478 Kbytes	0.5%	token passing	100 meters	point-to-point, ring, star
FDDI II	100 Mbit/s	shared media (some traffic carried in circuits)	n/a	no	4478 Kbytes	0.5%	token passing	n/a	point-to-point, ring, star
Fibre Channel	100 Mbit/s, 200 Mbit/s, 400 Mbit/s, 800 Mbit/s, 1 Gbit/s, 2 Gbit/s	shared media or switched	one	yes	2112 Kbytes	1.7%	sliding window	50 meters (STP)	mesh, point-to-point, ring, star
HIPPI	800 Mbit/s, 1.6 Gbit/s, 3.2 Gbit/s	switched	one	yes	2000 Kbytes	1.6%	credit-based	25 meters (proprietary cable)	mesh, point-to-point, star
IsoEnet	16 Mbit/s	shared media (some traffic carried in circuits)	n/a	no	1512 Kbytes	1.6%	collision detection	100 meters	point-to-point, ring, star
100Base-T (fast Ethernet)	100 Mbit/s	shared media	n/a	no	1512 Kbytes	1.6%	collision detection	100 meters	point-to-point, star
100VG-AnyLAN	100 Mbit/s	shared media	n/a	no	1512 or 4478 Kbytes	1.6 or 0.5%	demand priority	200 meters (Category 5 UTP)	point-to-point, star

TABLE 4 Architecture (*Continued*)

	Data rates	Switched or shared media	Devices per switched connection	Full-duplex-capable	Maximum packet or cell size	Network overhead	Flow control	Internode distance over copper cable	Topologies supported
Proprietary Switching Technologies									
Ethernet switches	10 Mbit/s	switched	multiple	yes	1512 Kbytes	1.6%	available on some	100 meters	mesh, point-to-point, star
FDDI switches	100 Mbit/s	switched	multiple	yes	4478 Kbytes	0.5%	no	100 meters	mesh, point-to-point, star
100Base-T switches	100 Mbit/s	switched	multiple	yes	1512 Kbytes	1.6%	no	100 meters	mesh, point-to-point, star
100VG-AnyLAN switches	100 Mbit/s	switched	multiple	yes	1512 or 4478 Kbytes	0.5%	no	100 meters	mesh, point-to-point, star
Token ring switches	16 Mbit/s	switched	multiple	yes	17,000 bytes	0.5%	no	100 meters	mesh, point-to-point, star

Table 5: Migration Strategy

When planning a journey, it's a good idea to consider not only the destination but also how difficult it is to get there. So it is with network managers moving from one LAN technology to another. While equipment vendors place much emphasis on the level of performance their products will deliver once they are installed, streetwise administrators also will want to consider how easy their technologies are to implement.

Table 5 summarizes the migration path offered by each network using four different criteria: whether the LAN works with the network interface cards (NICs) already installed in users workstations; whether it will run over the cable that is already installed in corporate buildings; if it can carry the applications that currently are running over corporate networks; and how much the LAN hardware itself costs.

The adapter angle

A quick glance at the table reveals that all the high-speed LANs are easily divisible into two categories: proprietary LAN switches (which work with the adapters installed in users workstations), and standards-based technologies (which require companies to install new NICs).

Proponents of the second network category often refer to the process of replacing the NIC in user workstations as "a simple adapter upgrade"— a euphemism which is designed to downplay the complexity of the operation. But net managers on the front line of corporate networking tell a different story. It's true that the act of unplugging the PC, opening it up, replacing one adapter with another and then putting it back together again can be achieved in as little as 10 minutes. But that's usually less than half the battle. Sorting out contention problems between the adapter and other devices (such as mice and modems) that compete for the system CPU's attention means this task can take hours. A new driver also must be downloaded; something which can also cause system conflicts.

The plug-and-play de facto standard is designed to make installation a no-brainer. Version 1.0 was finalized in June 1993. Plug-and-play is sponsored by a variety of leading PC players—most notably Intel Corp. (Hillsboro, OR) and Microsoft Corp. (Redmond, WA). The spec defines two lots of software. One runs on the adapter—or any other PC peripheral such as modems, mice, and serial ports. The second can run either as a part of the PC's basic input/output system (BIOS), or as part of the operating system (OS) running on the PC. However, it will take years before the new specification is widely adopted by workstation and adapter vendors; currently, none of the high-speed LAN adapters now on sale are plug-and-play-compliant. In the meantime, network managers who let themselves in for this adapter aggravation will pay two times: in the bill for labor, and in lost productivity caused by downtime while the user's workstation is out of commission.

Copper comfort

Changing out NICs is tough enough, but having to upgrade or alter cabling in order to run a new network can be an even more daunting and expensive task. Market researchers point to the average cost of installing new UTP copper cable at around $200 to $1000 per seat—depending on factors such as the cost of labor, the difficulty of the installation, and the type of cable used. In some cases, that's more than the cost of the LAN hardware that is itself connected to the cable.

The good news for net managers is that the developers of most of the high-speed LAN standards have worked hard to include specifications that allow their products to work over copper cable. ATM, IsoEnet, 100VG-AnyLAN, and 100Base-T all are available in flavors that will work over any of the common copper cable types now found in corporate networks—namely, Category 3 UTP, Category 4 UTP, Category 5 UTP, and STP.

While the original FDDI standard worked only over fiber, a later addition has enabled it to run over Category 5 UTP as well. Category 3 and 4 UTP may not be used for carrying FDDI traffic. That leaves two other standards-based technologies: Fibre Channel and HIPPI. Both are less easy to migrate to. As its name suggests, Fibre Channel runs over fiber cable. Coaxial copper cable or STP cabling also is an acceptable substitute—though very few networks already have this cabling in place. HIPPI is even more awkward, calling for use of either fiber or an outlandish and hard-to-install 50-pair shielded copper cable.

When it comes to cabling, the proprietary LAN switches again offer an easy upgrade. Ethernet, token ring, 100VG-AnyLAN, and 100Base-T switches all operate over existing network wiring. An exception here is FDDI switches, which currently operate only over fiber. Although it is technologically feasible to build an FDDI switch which operates over Category 5 UTP, no vendors have yet chosen to do so. (One reason is that they see their products playing best in the backbone, where the extensive drive distances offered by fiber cabling are required.)

Net managers also need to think about whether the technology they are moving to will work not only over their existing cabling but also over their current network topology. For instance, even though the 100VG-AnyLAN and 100Base-T standards can operate over copper cable, they drive data over shorter distances than older, slower Ethernet or token ring equipment; the reason is that their designers had to reduce drive distances in order to keep radiation to within acceptable levels at the higher speeds. The upshot is that net managers moving from one of the older 10-Mbit/s or 16-Mbit/s technologies to one of these new 100-Mbit/s LANs will have to perform some rewiring, adding new wiring closets and rerouting cable to close the gaps in their network coverage.

Both Fibre Channel and HIPPI also restrict the length of cable runs to much less than the 100-meter de facto distance usually prescribed for local-area networks. For instance, the physical layer of the HIPPI standard defines a maximum drive distance of just 25 meters. Such restrictions do not apply to ATM, IsoEnet, or any of the proprietary LAN switch technologies; these networks can be installed without changes being made to the existing wiring plant topology.

Application layer

Applications may reside at the other end of the ISO seven-layer network model from cabling, but they are also something to consider when selecting a high-speed LAN. Most of the networks in Table 5 can run today's applications without any modifications at all. That's because they are based on existing packet formats. The ATM Forum has now defined LAN emulation standards which allow current applications to run unaltered over ATM networks by spoofing them into thinking that they are running over a traditional connectionless LAN. Fibre Channel and FDDI are different; currently, they are capable of running only IP-based applications.

Sticker price

Price, the last migration criterion considered in Table 5, is also one of the most critical. Most analysts agree that the price point which LAN technologies must reach if they hope to attain mainstream popularity is $1000 per node.

Note that it's much easier for proprietary LAN switches to reach that magic number than for standards-based technologies. High-speed networks are basically built on two pieces of hardware: a NIC (network interface card) in the user's workstation, and a switch in the wiring closet. Proprietary LAN switches can work with the adapters that net managers already have installed in their users' workstations.

Accordingly, the only piece of equipment the net manager usually has to fork out for is the switch itself. Networks based on the new LAN standards, on the other hand, require the net manager to purchase both new NICs and new switches or hubs.

Table 5 reflects this; the prices given for the LAN standards include the cost of a port on the hub or switch *and* the NIC in the workstation. With the proprietary LAN switches, the price given is for the switch port, and it's assumed that the net manager already has the NIC in place.

By far the most expensive LANs in the table are Fibre Channel ($3600 per node) and HIPPI ($4000 per node), price points which will severely limit uptake of both technologies. At the other end of the scale, both 100Base-T and Ethernet switches are priced to sell, costing half the $1000-per-node benchmark mentioned above. A glance at the table also quickly shows that the FDDI-based technologies are too expensive to make a big dent on the high-speed LAN market: FDDI ($2400), FDDI II ($2600), and FDDI switches ($10,640) need to come down in price or remain in the category of exclusive, boutique technologies.

Prices vary widely for products in each category, and those shown are intended to provide only a guideline as to the price that net managers should be able to attain if they shop around. In some cases, prices will be much lower. For instance, the ATM price of $2250 per node ascribed here describes for cost of a 155-Mbit/s EISA adapter and a port on a 155-Mbit/s switch. (Note that it's possible to get 155-Mbit/s ATM for about $1000 less by shopping around.) If 25-Mbit/s ATM was selected, the price would be a lot lower—at roughly $750 per node. The same goes for token ring switches; while the typical cost of a token ring switch today is around $1900 per port, net managers who opt to buy IBM's switch pay a mere $700 per port.

TABLE 5 Migration Strategy

	Works with installed adapters	Works with installed copper cable	Works with existing applications	Cost per node
Standards-Based Technologies				
ATM	no	yes; Category 3 and 5 UTP, STP	yes; all, using LAN emulation	$750 (25 Mbit/s) $2250 (155 Mbit/s)
FDDI	no	no; fiber only	yes; all	$2400
FDDI-over-copper	no	yes; Category 5 UTP, STP	yes; all	$1500
FDDI II	no	no; fiber only	yes; all	$2600
Fibre Channel	no	yes; STP, coaxial	yes; IP applications only	$3600
HIPPI	no	no; fiber only	yes; IP applications only	$4000
IsoEnet	no	yes; Category 3 and 5 UTP, STP	yes; all	$1400
100Base-T (fast Ethernet)	no	yes, Category 3 and 5 UTP, STP	yes; all	$550
100VG-AnyLAN	no	yes, Category 3 and 5 UTP, STP	yes; all	$650
Proprietary Switching Technologies				
Ethernet switches	yes	yes; Category 3 and 5 UTP, STP	yes; all	$500
FDDI switches	yes	no; fiber only	yes; all	$10,640
100Base-T switches	yes	yes; Category 3 and 5 UTP, STP	yes; all	$1000
100VG-AnyLAN switches	yes	yes; Category 3 and 5 UTP, STP	yes; all	not yet priced
Token ring switches	yes	yes; Category 3 and 5 UTP, STP	yes; all	$1900

High-Speed LAN Design Issues

So far, this book has described and compared each of the high-speed LANs. Part 5 has a different aim: providing design guidelines for implementing these networks in the real world.

There are seven chapters in Part 5:

- *Chap. 23 is intended for net managers on a limited budget who are looking to build a LAN that can handle multimedia applications. It describes three low-cost multimedia alternatives, each of which can be installed without making wholesale changes to the existing LAN infrastructure.*

- *Chap. 24 offers a tutorial on how to design and implement virtual LANs (vLANs) in switched networks. It describes the different approaches available, their pros and cons, and details the products offered by the key players in this market.*

- *Chap. 25 describes the alternative methods available for adding routing capabilities to a high-speed LAN. This is a crucial issue; most of the high-speed LAN technologies are based on switching and create a flat network architecture. The only way to break up these networks (and so enforce security and improve performance) is by using routing.*

- *Chap. 26 and Chap. 27 deal with the design issues involved in building switched Ethernet and switched token ring LANs, respectively.*

- *Chap. 28 uses the results of extensive industry tests to describe how best to implement an FDDI backbone between Ethernets (the number 1 application for FDDI technology today).*

- *Chap. 29 describes the methods available for analyzing traffic on switched LANs. Analyzing traffic flows is a crucial part of switched network design.*

23

Designing an Affordable Multimedia LAN

Section 1. Overview

Most observers agree that multimedia applications will one day sweep corporate networkers off their feet. The question is when. Initially, some observers questioned whether multimedia applications would take off on LANs before the end of the 1990s—citing the lack of a "killer application" to drive the market.

More recently, the latest market research points to multimedia being driven by a host of different uses, rather than a single irresistible application. Consequently, researchers reckon, multimedia is hitting mainstream networking sooner than originally anticipated. In a report on the growth of multimedia networking, Infonetics Research Inc. (San Jose, CA) predicts that by 1998 corporations will have equipped an average of 45 percent of their LAN desktop systems for multimedia (see Fig. 23.1). If growth in LANs continues as expected, that amounts to as many as 20 million desktop computers equipped with multimedia capabilities.

Not all multimedia applications are the same. Multimedia apps which don't feature time-sensitive video or voice components can, with a little care, run over today's Ethernet and token ring LANs. This category includes image retrieval and document conferencing (or whiteboarding). Unfortunately, it's *video-based* applications (either playback or videoconferencing) that are generating the most excitement among corporate users. While video is the most prepossessing multimedia application, it is also the hardest and the most costly to

Note: Some parts of this chapter were contributed by Starlight Networks Inc. (Mountain View, CA).

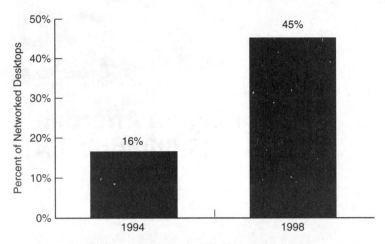

Figure 23.1 Growth of networked multimedia desktop. Source: Infonetics Research, Inc.

implement. Shared-media Ethernet and token ring networks cannot hope to provide a suitable medium for time-sensitive video traffic, or its associated audio component. This chapter is devoted to an examination of how network managers can successfully deploy a multimedia LAN on an affordable budget.

Broadly speaking, net managers who want to make the move to audio- and video-based (or audiovisual) multimedia have two choices. One is to completely overhaul their network infrastructure and move to one of the new technologies—such as ATM—which are especially designed to support multimedia. Of course, that involves a forklift upgrade of network hardware. Hubs, switches, bridges, routers, and adapter cards all must be swapped out. In some instances, cabling will have to be replaced. Network operating system software also must be changed. Understandably, many net managers are leery of spending the time and labor months required to undertake such an upgrade—particularly if they are still undecided as to whether multimedia will be essential to their bottom line.

Fortunately, the all-out upgrade is not the only option open to network professionals. A less expensive and less time-consuming alternative is to leverage the network infrastructure already in place. Broadly speaking, there are three ways in which net managers can do so:

- By enhancing an existing LAN with an Ethernet or token ring LAN switch

- By enhancing an existing Ethernet with IsoEnet equipment
- By enhancing an existing Ethernet with 25-Mbit/s ATM equipment

This chapter explains each of these three alternatives. But first, it's important to understand the different categories of multimedia applications, and the challenges involved in networking them.

Section 2. The Video Star

Of all the multimedia applications, it's those that feature video that are causing the most excitement. Desktop video is an emerging technology that over time will come in many flavors. Here are some examples:

- Training applications are a natural for incorporating digital video on the computer. Many large businesses and other institutions are developing so-called performance support systems that revolutionize the way that employees learn their jobs and perform their tasks. Instead of large amounts of classroom training, performance support systems provide training on demand at the desktop. In theory, this training method increases the amount of information which students retain, since they learn new information in context, rather than in classrooms. Many major office productivity software packages can already be outfitted with VHS videotape options today. In addition, some developers are taking the next step—linking digital video directly to their software's on-line help resources. For example, Microsoft Corp. (Redmond, WA) offers a CD-ROM version of Office Works with multimedia on-line help and reference. Video help for spreadsheet or word processing programs is in the cards.

- Businesses can use networked video presentation systems to instantly send corporate resources to employees' desktops. Sales videos and employee data can be viewed on the spot or captured to create customized sales presentations. By putting the video on a server, businesses enable many people to access centralized resources without having to travel to an audiovisual facility, buy a VCR/television, or even rent an editing suite.

- Networked video documentation systems will allow institutions of all kinds to maintain multiuser audiovisual databases. Advertising agencies, for example, have hundreds of hours of video which they need to use in a random, on-demand basis. Today, these agencies use hundreds of VCR tapes that must be located, copied, and then delivered to account executives or clients. A video database would allow easier and quicker access to this information.

Other potential users include health care institutions, which have extensive audiovisual records; travel agencies, which show videos about vacation destinations; and public utilities, which need to maintain records of power generation facilities and equipment. Several state highway departments have still-video databases of every mile of their highways, allowing employees to instantly view any stretch of road.

Section 3.   Service Levels

Broadly speaking, video applications require three different levels of network service: video file services, video object services, and stream management services. The simplest service level, video file services, provides elementary store-and-play file service for video. A video file service gives users the capability to store video and retrieve it for viewing. With this type of application, a high degree of delay may be tolerable. A system offering video file services operates essentially like a conventional LAN with a ho-hum network file server. A good example of this level of complexity is simple playback of training or on-line help videos.

The next step up in video sophistication consists of video object services. These allow the user to combine objects (either video or audio files) to produce a new video stream, to edit the video, or to instantly add video and audio to another document type. This application requires fast access to the video objects and the ability to change their relationships to one another. Users need to access many objects at the same time. For example, an advertising agency would require this level of video service to combine many video clips to provide a quick look at a rough cut of a new ad concept.

The third service category, stream management services, is required when many simultaneous users need access to live video. Desktop videoconferencing falls into this set of video applications. Video stream management service often involves sending live video from a variety of sources to many simultaneous users, and managing the video streams on the network. Users may require different data rates. Some may need to record a teleconference for later viewing.

Section 4.   Matching the App to the LAN

Provided that proper care is taken in the design and implementation of the network, today's Ethernet and token ring LANs can be used to support video file services. To a very limited extent, they may also be used for video object services. But the one thing they can't hope to do is support stream management services.

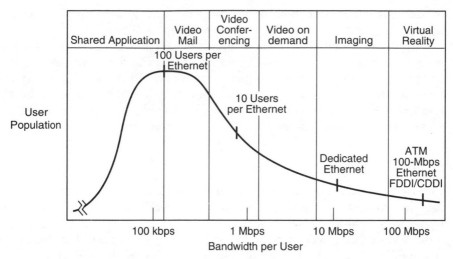

Figure 23.2 Applications and their bandwidth requirements. Source: Cisco Systems, Inc.

The problem isn't just bandwidth. Without compression, it would take 200 Mbit/s of bandwidth to carry a 30-frame-per-second, full-color video stream to one VGA screen. But the compression algorithms implemented in today's multimedia equipment reduce this bandwidth requirement to around 1 Mbit/s (see Fig. 23.2). This doesn't mean that a 10-Mbit/s LAN can support 10 streams of 1-Mbit/s data. Far from it. Today's Ethernet and token ring LANs are optimized for the bursty data traffic generated by asynchronous mainstream business applications—not for the large, continuously flowing streams of data necessary to play compressed digital video. The streaming nature of digital video is at odds with the contention schemes used in Ethernet and token ring, which are designed to share network access equally among attached nodes. Consequently, when an Ethernet or token ring LAN becomes busy, everything slows down, creating bottlenecks for audio and video real-time data.

Streaming audiovisual data also conflicts with the way that LANs and multitasking network operating systems allow applications to take turns to access network resources. With this democratic process, no data has priority over any other. If the network is busy, everything slows down. The inefficiency of democratic resource-sharing schemes is compounded by the overhead required to detect errors and correct them. These functions are important for typical software applications, but are not as important for audiovisual media. In asynchronous data networks, response times grow as more users request bandwidth. The delay is annoying, but not catastrophic. In contrast, audiovisual information, which is time-sensitive, looks and sounds terrible if it slows down and speeds up according to network traffic flow.

Essentially, audiovisual data demands a kind of Federal Express attitude toward data: It "absolutely, positively" has to arrive at the client computer on time. Thus, the important network function for video isn't fair allocation of resources or error checking; it is to make sure that data flows at the proper rate between the server and client, or between client and client, and to guarantee that data arrives on time.

Section 5.   Limited Applications

The easiest way to move multimedia onto a LAN is to implement only certain types of multimedia applications. Specifically, tests show that image retrieval and document conferencing (whiteboarding) can run quite comfortably over current LANs. In an evaluation of both image retrieval and whiteboarding software applications, The Tolly Group (Manasquan, NJ) concluded that both could operate quite happily over today's LAN internetworks—provided certain precautions are taken.

In the case of image retrieval applications, that means keeping file sizes small. The Tolly Group succeeded in transferring a 175-kbyte image of a newspaper column from an application based on Microsoft's object linking and embedding (OLE) technology in under a second. (Engineers transferred the file from an NT server on an FDDI network to a 486 PC on an Ethernet LAN.) When larger images were used, performance became unacceptable.

The Tolly Group advises that the easiest way to keep image files small is to be cautious about the ways in which images are scanned. When the engineers working on the test tried a larger object (two pages from a magazine, including some color), they found out that the scanning period has a dramatic effect on the amount of bandwidth required by a networked OLE app. For instance, using technology to increase the scan density of a stored image by 50 percent—from 200 dots per inch (dpi) to 300 dpi—increased file size sixfold: from around 150 kbytes to more than 950 kbytes. At 400 dpi the file size grew to nearly 1.8 Mbytes—more than 10 times the size of the 200 dpi file.

When it comes to whiteboard applications, The Tolly Group's advice is—again—proceed with caution. Whiteboarding (also known as document conferencing) allows two or more network users to see and update a common image contained in a shred Windows or OS/2 client. A number of vendors are now shipping whiteboard products—including IBM Corp. (Armonk, NY), Intel Corp. (Santa Clara, CA), and Fujitsu Ltd. (Tokyo). After testing IBM's Person to Person for Windows product, The Tolly Group concluded that whiteboarding can cause some bandwidth problems if it is used carelessly. In particular, the seemingly innocuous function of moving the cursor has the potential to chew up enormous amounts of bandwidth.

Section 6.   Three (Poor) Alternatives

While most corporations will be content to cut their teeth on non-time-sensitive applications, eventually they're going to want to start running applications featuring audiovisual data. That means addressing the bottlenecks confronting networked multimedia data.

One solution is to throw away all the installed software and hardware, and replace it with new software and hardware that keep each stream running at the proper rate—for example, by installing ATM switches, adapters, and associated application software. This works, but it means trashing something of great value to users (the network software that allows access to the applications currently running on their servers) and something of great *fiscal* value to the company itself (the expensive LAN hardware).

Another extreme solution is to simply restrict the number of users who have access to each network segment. The big problem with this approach is that it requires the corporation to buy bridges and/or routers in unrealistically large numbers. What's more, there's still no way to guarantee the quality of multimedia applications; a fluke moment of traffic contention can still lead to undue delay.

A third approach is to install a parallel video network. By running video traffic over separate, dedicated cabling connections, net managers can certainly ensure that multimedia applications deliver the quality they want. But installing parallel networks is an expensive and time-consuming task—few network managers will want to install a whole new premises-wiring scheme just so that they can satisfy their multimedia needs.

Section 7.   The Switch Solution

A less problematic way to proof a corporate network for multimedia is to install an Ethernet or token ring LAN switch. These devices are relatively easy to install, for two reasons. First, they can operate over the star topology networks in place in many existing corporate networks, and over the cabling that net managers have already laid under floors and in ceiling spaces. Second, they communicate with the network interface cards (NICs) that net managers already have installed in their users' workstations. Further, the switches themselves aren't that expensive. Expect to pay between $500 and $1000 per port for an Ethernet switch and between $700 and $2000 per port for a token ring switch.

Today's LAN switches are typically installed as backbone devices (in place of a hub or router) with multiple devices attached to each port. But when multimedia applications are being carried, the best way to ensure requisite response times is to implement "desktop switching," in which each workstation gets its very own dedicated connection to the switch. (If more than one PC is connected per port, then contention between nodes on the same port will stymie timely delivery of audiovisual data.)

Note that some vendors, notably Chipcom Corp. (Southborough, MA) and Madge Networks Inc. (San Jose, CA), have instituted priority schemes in their switches which allow net managers to assign priority levels to different types of traffic. Prioritization is implemented by equipping the switch buffers with multiple FIFO (first-in, first-out) paths. If overflows occur, preset traffic priorities can be used to dictate which packets are dumped first. Vendors claim that these schemes allow several asynchronous devices to be allocated to the same switch port as a multimedia station without the risk that time-sensitive traffic will be squeezed out.

Section 8.   Which Switch?

When it comes to handling multimedia traffic, it's important to remember that not all switches are created equal. One of the biggest differentiators among LAN switches is the method they use to process packets. There are two basic types of switches now in use: cut-through switches and store-and-forward switches. In cut-through switches, the receiving switch port reads only the MAC address in each packet's header before forwarding the packet to the outgoing switch port. With store-and-forward switches, the entire packet is stored in a memory buffer at the incoming port before it is forwarded.

Cut-through switches process packets faster than store-and-forward methods. According to tests conducted for *Data Communications* magazine, switch latency—the time that elapses between when a packet arrives at the switch and when the packet begins to leave the switch—typically ranges from 40 to 50 microseconds with cut-through switches. (Some vendors claim even faster performance, but these claims have yet to be verified independently.) The delay remains constant regardless of packet size, because the switch starts to forward the packet as soon as it reads the packet header.

With store-and-forward switches, latency increases in proportion to packet size. Tests conducted for *Data Comm* show that it usually takes about 110 microseconds for a store-and-forward switch to process a 64-byte packet. That latency increases to more than a millisecond for a 2000-byte packet.

The key advantage to store-and-forward switching is that holding the entire packet in memory before forwarding it enables the switch to scrutinize incoming traffic to root out errored packets like runts and jabbers. Because they read only packet headers, cut-through switches simply send errored packets along. To root out errored packets, users must install devices like conventional bridges or routers to scan the network and grab errored packets—thus adding to network costs.

Clearly, these differences make cut-through and store-and-forward switches better suited to different types of applications. Net managers running (or planning to run) multimedia applications like interactive videoconferencing will be better off opting for low-latency cut-through switches, such as those from Ornet Data Communications Technologies (Carmel, Israel). That's because multimedia applications typically comprise very large packets and are time-sensitive, but can tolerate a higher number of errored packets.

This is not to say that store-and-forward switches are *completely* unsuitable for audiovisual data. Provided that only one device is connected to each port, LAN switches certainly have the megabit muscle to deliver time-sensitive multimedia traffic. Likewise, they have sufficiently low latency to provide reasonable quality.

Section 9. Better Reception

With both cut-through and store-and-forward designs, jitter (variance of average latency) can still be caused by CSMA/CD (carrier sense multiple access with collision detection) or token-passing "traffic cop" protocols. These emphasize data integrity through error control protocols, and leave flow control and timeliness of delivery as secondary considerations. Some vendors have developed ways to fine-tune traffic delivery on both store-and-forward and cut-through switches for better performance. Several alternatives are available. All involve either changing or adding to the network access schemes found in Ethernet and token ring LANs.

For example, 3Com Corp. (Santa Clara, CA) has developed a technology for Ethernet switches called PACE (priority access control enabled). PACE monitors traffic and ensures that bandwidth is allocated equally among Ethernet nodes sharing multimedia information—thus keeping latency constant and low. PACE is loaded into the driver on the Ethernet adapter in the user's workstation, and also runs as software on the switch. The driver supports two virtual MAC (media access control) addresses—one for delay-sensitive traffic, the other for ordinary data (see Fig. 23.3). The switch software guarantees that network access is allocated evenly among devices.

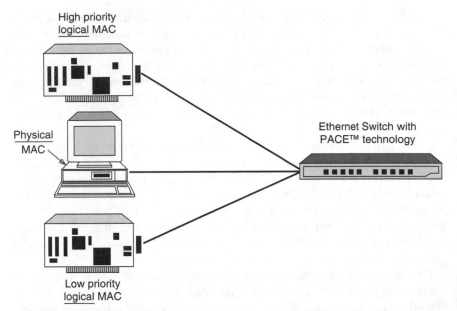

Figure 23.3 3Com's PACE technology. PACE software runs on the driver on the Ethernet adapter in the user's workstation, and on the Ethernet switch itself. Source: 3Com Corp.

Some switch vendors may be put off from implementing PACE because it involves modifying the CSMA/CD network access protocol defined in IEEE 802.3. Despite this, 3Com is hoping to license the technology to other switch vendors (at about $1 per port) in addition to including it in its own products. 3Com also says it will distribute PACE free to any makers of network operating systems or applications that are working on time-sensitive applications.

Another approach comes from Starlight Networks Inc. (Mountain View, CA). Starlight has developed the equivalent of a video protocol stack, called MTP (media transport protocol), that works with switched Ethernet (see Fig. 23.4). MTP ensures that there is a highly reliable connection for lengthy streams of audiovisual data. It also adds a number of multimedia-oriented features to Ethernet, including the ability to allow users to send control messages (such as Stop Stream and Start Stream) during the transmission of very large audiovisual files. Significantly, MTP runs alongside (and does not interfere with) the CSMA/CD protocol found on Ethernet. Nonaudiovisual data continues to use the standard Ethernet protocol. MTP is featured as part of the vendor's StarWorks and StarWare suites of video networking tools.

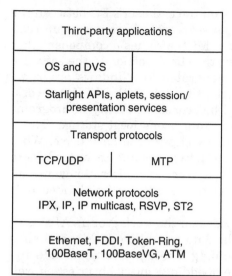

| Third-party applications |
| OS and DVS |
| Starlight APIs, aplets, session/ presentation services |
| Transport protocols |
| TCP/UDP | MTP |
| Network protocols IPX, IP, IP multicast, RSVP, ST2 |
| Ethernet, FDDI, Token-Ring, 100BaseT, 100BaseVG, ATM |

Figure 23.4 Starlight's video protocol stack. Source: Starlight Networks, Inc.

Section 10.   The ATM Add-On

Enhancing an Ethernet LAN with a switch is one way to handle multimedia. But a company called First Virtual (Santa Clara, CA) has an alternative. It posits enhancing the shared-media Ethernet with low-cost 25-Mbit/s ATM equipment and software. First Virtual Corp.'s offering comprises an ATM switch, LAN adapter cards for Windows PCs, and a media server—a network-attached RAID (redundant array of inexpensive disks). It also supplies a media operating system (MOS)—a middleware package that buffers the application from the network and shields programmers from the underlying complexities of the hardware.

Most ATM vendors assume that the high-speed switched technology will be used to create a backbone that links LANs. First Virtual takes the opposite tack, creating an ATM work group that's linked to an Ethernet. End users have 25-Mbit/s ATM links to the switch, which also connects to both the LAN file server (through an Ethernet interface) and the media server (through a 155-Mbit/s connection). In essence, FVC's scheme allows ATM to be added to an Ethernet LAN where and when it's needed to accommodate real-time multimedia. That means companies don't have to scrap their current hardware and software—or even reconfigure it—to gain the benefits of ATM. Users on ATM-attached PCs still run the same Netware and TCP/IP applications, and they access the LAN server as before. The only difference is that they can now run networked multimedia.

The client portion of MOS resides on the end user's PC between the applications and the LAN emulation software, where it sets up real-time calls for voice, video, and audio. MOS also has a component that runs on the media server. Basically, the client portion of the software redirects real-time data streams generated by Windows programs from the local disk drive to a destination across the ATM network. That may not sound very exciting, but consider: Plenty of programs can send and receive real-time data to a user's local storage. That's fine if all a user wants to do is save TV clips to the hard drive. What happens when everyone else on the network wants to watch? More relevantly, what happens when the system administrator wants all the users in the work group to review the informational video that just arrived on disk?

MOS makes it possible to store video on the work group's ATM disk server. Users can then download the data from their desktops, thanks to the video applications they're running. These programs include any that use OLE (object linking and embedding) object libraries, as well as any written to Video for Windows. OLE and Video for Windows are APIs (application program interfaces) developed by Microsoft.

Simply speaking, MOS redirects application calls, thus fooling applications into thinking they're executing locally. For example, when a DOS or Windows program requests a file, MOS knows whether or not the file is stored locally, on the LAN server, or on the media server. It knows because it maintains a map between virtual drives and types of files. When the client requests a file that's stored on the LAN server, the request is processed normally, through the appropriate protocol stack (TCP/IP, SPX/IPX, and so forth). The LAN emulation software on the adapter sets up an ATM call to the LAN server and segments the IP or IPX packets into cells and fires them off. They're reassembled by the ATM-to-Ethernet adapter at the far port of the switch and passed on to the LAN server.

When the client requests a file that's stored on the media server, however, MOS sets up an ATM call to the media server and passes the request along to it. As noted, a portion of MOS runs on the media server (on the vendor's Stream Processor board that controls the RAID). Its chief function is to handle client requests and retrieve data. At the core of this component is a real-time kernel, which performs call-scheduling. This is a critical function, since the server can support up to 80 simultaneous users.

The MOS client requires a 25-MHz 486 PC running Windows 3.1 with 8 Mbytes of RAM and a 160-Mbyte hard drive. MOS costs $2000 for 10 users and $12,000 for 30 users (not counting hardware). A 4-Gbyte media server sells for $15,000; $20,000 buys 8 Gbytes. The switch costs $3400 to $8000; adapter cards list for $330 to $1200 apiece.

Another company offering almost identical products to First Virtual is ATM Ltd. (ATML, London). Like FVC, ATML offers a switch, an adapter, and a media server. The similarity is actually not a coincidence; the two companies were originally partners.

Section 11.   An IsoEnet Alternative

Some companies are beginning to push IsoEnet products as an alternative to add-on ATM and Ethernet switches. The IsoEnet standard defines a 16-Mbit/s network incorporating 6 Mbit/s of circuit-switched bandwidth for carrying multimedia traffic. It is intended as a successor to existing 10-Mbit/s Ethernet LANs.

A pioneer in this market is Incite Inc. (Dallas). Currently, Incite's 12-port Multimedia Hub, which costs $300 per port, uses IsoEnet to transport 10 Mbit/s of Ethernet and 6 Mbit/s of isochronous bandwidth to every desktop. Incite also offers a WAN hub that connects the LAN to switched WAN services via a PBX or public network. Incite's product line includes a server control software, called the Multimedia Manager, which is used to set up and route voice and video calls between users and the switched network.

Section 12.   Playback Changes

Once the LAN itself has been equipped to carry multimedia, net managers need to address attached hardware. Companies that want to implement video playback applications will have to change a number of things—including server software and hardware (see Fig. 23.5). Clearly, these alterations should be budgeted for at the outset to avoid unnecessary cash shortfalls during the course of the multimedia upgrade project.

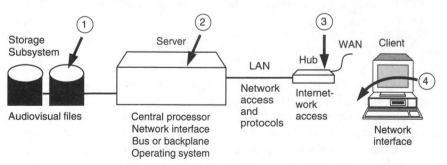

Figure 23.5 Potential bottlenecks. Before they can successfully run multimedia, net managers may have to upgrade hardware in at least four different places to eliminate potential bandwidth squeezes. Source: Starlight Networks, Inc.

At the server, the very minimum the net manager will need to do is modify the network operating system (NOS) software—which uses protocols to allow servers and clients to carry on data conversations. Several vendors now sell applications which run under either Netware (as NLMs) or Unix. These apps modify the NOSs to deal with the real-time nature of video, and incorporate file management capabilities that can handle multiple video streams simultaneously. Changes also may be required to the server hardware to customize it for multimedia applications. In particular, the large file sizes associated with digital audiovisual information usually require additional storage facilities. Even compressed video such as Intel's Digital Video Interactive (DVI) requires 0.5 Gbyte to 1 Gbyte of storage for one hour.

Some observers point out that storage systems based on laser disks and CD-ROM may be inappropriate for multimedia applications—for two reasons. First, they allow access to only one user at a time. Second, they don't allow users to change or update files stored on a disk. A better fit would be an external redundant array of inexpensive disks (RAID).

Adding storage can be an expensive proposition—disk drives today cost around $1 per megabyte. Further, the price tag on a server hard drive or storage subsystem is only the first payment in a never-ending installment plan. The cost of tracking files and shuffling them around to keep LAN storage from falling into complete anarchy can run anywhere from $4 to $9 per Mbyte *per year,* according to estimates from some consultants and suppliers of LAN storage systems. The bigger the network, the bigger the maintenance hit.

Besides having the capacity to store video information, a video server must be able to manage access to video files efficiently. The main requirements are a processor with enough capacity to keep up with the operations required and a backplane bus with enough bandwidth to carry all the video traffic flowing into and out of the storage devices.

Today's average Intel 486-based LAN servers are being used almost exclusively for running file and print services—not multimedia. Generally speaking, they aren't up to the job of servicing playback video. (For maximum performance, vendors recommend that net managers install dedicated audiovisual servers—thus eliminating the compromises that servers have to make between short bursty data and large streams of data.) System requirements for a video server are a minimum of one Pentium CPU. For better performance it is advisable to buy either a symmetric multiprocessor (SMP)server—a server which can divide up and process applications between multiple 486 or Pentium CPUs—or a fault-tolerant, RISC-based minicomputer from a vendor like Stratus Computer Inc. (Marlboro, MA) or Tandem Computers Inc. (Cupertino, CA). Some of these boxes come with specialized video buses that improve performance further. They don't come cheap, however. Intel-based servers with multiple CPUs cost an average of $14,500 and up. RISC systems cost from $90,000.

Since client computers typically need only one or two streams for video, bandwidth is not a problem. The data rate for a typical video stream is 1.5 Mbit/s (the rate used for Intel's Indeo and DVI compression technologies and the MPEG standard). That's slower than the amount of data that comes from a typical hard disk, and also less than the capacity of a dedicated, switched Ethernet or token ring connection. Consequently, no special networking hardware is necessary at client computers.

Video and sound boards are another matter. Video cameras cost $1000 to $2000. Video codec cards (which allow an incoming stream of video to be displayed on the user's screen) cost around $500. Sound cards cost $99 and up. Installing these devices can itself introduce a rat's nest of problems—including hardware interrupts that conflict with those assigned to network adapters, as well as interoperability problems with different compression schemes.

24

Designing
Virtual LANs

The Basics

In the most basic sense, a switched virtual LAN is a broadcast domain that unites any arbitrary group of LAN segments at wire speed. As is the case with a single physical wire, broadcasts travel to all end stations in a virtual LAN.

A single virtual LAN can connect dozens— or in some cases hundreds—of LAN users. The ability to include multiple physical LAN segments gives virtual LANs a distinct advantage over multiport routers. To get more bandwidth to LAN users, network managers often deploy conventional multiport routers to segment LANs, but each physical segment created by a multiport router must be treated as a separate logical subnet. Traffic going between subnets is subject to significant added delay because of processing by routers.

Virtual LANs minimize this problem because they bridge—rather than route— traffic destined for different segments

> within the same network. Multiple segments
> per subnet means fewer routing
> bottlenecks. It also means that end stations
> can be assigned to different virtual LANs
> without having to reconfigure the physical
> network.

Section 1.   Overview

The networking industry is agreed that virtual LANs will be a pivotal feature of next-generation enterprise networks. But until now, real-world virtual LAN implementations have been hard to find. Fortunately for network planners, equipment makers have started to move beyond the vaporware stage to put virtual LANs into real products. Right now, makers of departmental Ethernet switches are furthest along on the road with virtual LAN implementations. More than 10 vendors of departmental Ethernet switches now offer virtual LAN facilities in their products. In contrast, token ring switch vendors are taking longer to add virtual LAN capabilities to their products.

Ethernet switch makers have good reason to take the early lead in deploying virtual LAN technology. By most accounts, Ethernet switches are an interim solution to boosting bandwidth on corporate networks; ATM is the real future of high-speed networking. Once asynchronous transfer mode products and services start rolling out in force, the window of opportunity for Ethernet switch vendors will slam shut. Departmental switches are a logical fit for virtual LANs because they can scale up to provide LAN connectivity at the floor, building, or campus level.

Ethernet switching and virtual LANs both address some ugly side effects that occur when conventional routers are used to segment LAN work groups. Faced with acute bandwidth problems on their networks, many net managers have turned to multiport routers to divide LAN internetworks into smaller units, or segments. Although routers are able to segment LANs in this way, they introduce significant delay when they process packets between LAN segments. Routers also complicate network management, since each physical segment created by a router must exist as a separate logical subnet. Another troublesome side effect is cost: High-end multiport routers can run $5000 or more per port.

Although Ethernet switches by themselves can address some bandwidth performance problems, without virtual LANs their ability to do so is limited. Because of excessive broadcast propagation and other problems associated with bridge topologies, pure Ethernet switches create a flat layer 2 architecture that doesn't scale beyond a few dozen segments. But when virtual LANs are used to subdivide switched traffic into contained areas, Ethernet switching becomes a powerful departmental internetworking method that greatly reduces the role of the router. Each defined virtual LAN can include several physical segments per logical subnet, thus easing the management burden. Finally, Ethernet switches that handle virtual LANs cost around $1000 per port, a significant savings compared with high-end routers.

With virtual LANs, a network administrator can define user groups regardless of the physical LAN segment to which they're connected. Users assigned to the same virtual LAN communicate at wire speeds with low latencies and no routing bottlenecks, no matter what their physical location in the network. Virtual LANs can be extended across multiple switches, provided those switches are linked by a high-speed backbone like FDDI, 100-Mbit/s fast Ethernet, or 155-Mbit/s ATM. Although some smaller work group switches come with virtual LAN abilities, those products typically lack a high-speed backbone port, which prevents them from scaling up to handle campus networks.

Ethernet switching and virtual LANs offer a relatively low-cost way for net managers to boost LAN bandwidth while squeezing another few years out of cabling and end-station adapters already in place. But designing and building virtual LANs is no plug-and-play procedure; right now, there are almost as many approaches as there are products. Some departmental Ethernet switches handle virtual LANs at the data link level (layer 2 of the OSI model), leaving layer 3 (network-layer) functions to routers. Other switches handle virtual LANs at layer 3, which means they perform basic routing chores themselves (see Table 24.1).

Within these two general categories, implementation differences abound. For instance, vendors use different signaling methods to convey virtual LAN information across high-speed backbones, and some switches are more flexible than others when it comes to backbone topologies. Also, performance levels vary hugely depending on the type of virtual LAN scheme implemented. For net managers to get the most out of switched Ethernet virtual LANs, they need to understand the different approaches taken by switch vendors.

Section 2.   Bridged Virtual LANs

Ethernet virtual LANs that function at layer 2 are manually defined by administrative software that lets network administrators group a number of switch ports together into a high-bandwidth, low-latency switched

TABLE 24.1 Ethernet Switches with Virtual LAN Facilities; A Selection

Vendor	Product	Virtual LAN type	Maximum virtual LANs per switch/per network	Virtual LAN backbone signaling method	Backbone topology	Layer 3 protocols built into switching logic	Filtering	Layer 2 switching/IP routing through-put (pps)	Maximum number Ethernet ports/cost per port in maximum configuration
Alantec Corp. San Jose, CA 408-955-9000	Powerhub 3000/5000 **Circle No. 531**	Layer 3	256/unlimited	Subnet	Bus, mesh, ring, star	TCP/IP, IPX, Appletalk, DECnet Phase IV	Intelligent	80,000/79,000	36/$550 (Powerhub 3) 76/$296 (Powerhub 5)
	Powerhub 7000 **Circle No. 532**	Layer 3	256/unlimited	Subnet	Bus, mesh, ring, star	TCP/IP, IPX, Appletalk, DECnet Phase IV	Intelligent	80,000/79,000	216/$358 18/$1,010
Bay Networks, Inc. Santa Clara, CA 408-988-2400	28000 **Circle No. 533**	Layer 2	16/800	Signaling messages	Star	None	None	2.9 million/N/A	
Cabletron Systems, Inc. Rochester, NH 603-332-9400	Emm-E6 **Circle No. 534**	Layer 3	Unlimited/unlimited	Subnet	Bus, ring, star	IP, IPX, DECnet	Media access control	25,000/12,500	8/$1,500
Cisco Systems, Inc. San Jose, CA 408-526-4000	Catalyst Work group Switch **Circle No. 535**	Layer 3	9/unlimited	Subnet (802.10 signaling planned for 2Q95)	Ring	IP	Intelligent	60,000/40,000	8/$1,175
Madge Networks Inc. San Jose, CA 408-955-0700	LANswitch **Circle No. 536**	Layer 2	256/unlimited	Subnet (signaling messages and frame tagging planned for 2Q95)	Bus, mesh, star	None	None	1.9 million/N/A	128/$808
Netedge Systems Inc. Research Triangle Park, NC 919-361-9000	ATM Connect **Circle No. 537**	Layer 3	Unlimited/unlimited	Subnet	Bus, mesh, ring, star	IP, IPX	Intelligent	60,000/60,000	52/$725
Retix Santa Monica, CA 310-828-3400	Switchstak 5000 **Circle No. 538**	Layer 2	8/64	Time-division multiplexing	Ring	None	Media access control	30,000/N/A	8/$499

TABLE 24.1 Ethernet Switches with Virtual LAN Facilities; A Selection

Vendor	Product	Virtual LAN type	Maximum virtual LANs per switch/per network	Virtual LAN backbone signaling method	Backbone topology	Layer 3 protocols built into switching logic	Filtering	Layer 2 switching/IP routing throughput (pps)	Maximum number Ethernet ports/cost per port in maximum configuration
3Com Corp. Santa Clara, CA 408-764-5000	Lanplex 2016/2500 **Circle No. 540**	Layer 2 now; Layer 3 available 2Q95	32/unlimited	Subnet	Mesh, ring, star	IP (IPX planned for 2Q95)	Intelligent	50,000/35,000 (CPU-based); 565,000/100,000 (ASIC-based)	16/$730
	Lanplex 6000 **Circle No. 541**	Layer 2 or Layer 3	32/unlimited	Subnet	Mesh, ring, star	IP	Intelligent	50,000/35,000 (CPU-based); 565,000/100,000 (ASIC-based)	176/$1,925
Xylan Corp. Calabasas, CA 818-880-3500	Omni-5/Omni-9 **Circle No. 542**	Layer 2 available 2Q95	128/65,535	Frame tagging	Mesh, ring, star, tree	None[*]	Intelligent	400,000/40,000	64/$825

Xylan supports IP and IPX routing but does not use them for configuring virtual LANs.
ASIC = application-specific integrated circuit
N/A = not applicable
pps = packets per second

work group. Under the layer 2 approach, each virtual LAN gets a unique number that identifies it for network management purposes.

Layer 2 virtual LANs are based strictly on a bridged architecture that transmits data using media access control (MAC) source and destination addresses. Traffic within virtual LANs is switched using these addresses; traffic between virtual LANs is handled by a router that imposes filtering, security, and traffic management. The router can be either a standalone box or a card integrated into the Ethernet switch; either way, the routing is handled by software that's separate from the virtual LAN switching logic (see Fig. 24.1).

Because the firewalls between layer 2 virtual LANs are not protocol-sensitive, all layer 3 protocols present on the network must adhere to the same set of port-group definitions. Once layer 2 port-group virtual LANs are defined, each switch reads incoming frames and learns the MAC addresses associated with each virtual LAN. If an end station sends broadcast or multicast frames, those frames are then forwarded to all ports in that end station's virtual LAN. The ports can be spread across any number of switches connected to the high-speed backbone. All LAN segments in a port group are bridged together whether they are separated by the backbone or reside in the same switch.

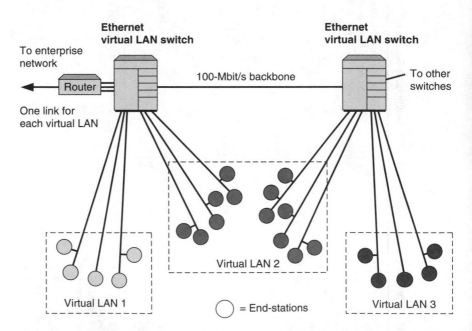

Figure 24.1 Virtual LANs at Layer 2. Ethernet switches that create virtual LANs at Layer 2 use simple bridging to shunt traffic between stations on the same virtual LAN. Traffic between different virtual LANs must be processed by independent routing software.

Supporting layer 2 virtual LAN port groups on a single switch is a straightforward process. Pure Ethernet switches cache MAC addresses and information about which port each MAC address is connected to. With virtual LAN switches, a virtual LAN number is added to the MAC and port information in the switch's forwarding table. But extending this MAC-oriented process across a backbone isn't so simple. Ethernet switch vendors have come up with at least three different methods for conveying information about layer 2 virtual LANs across shared-media backbones: signaling messages, frame tagging, and time division multiplexing (TDM).

Two vendors use signaling messages in their departmental Ethernet switches: Madge Networks Inc. (San Jose, CA) and Bay Networks Inc. (Santa Clara, CA). Under the signaling message approach, when an end station powers up, the local switch learns its virtual LAN number by recognizing which port group the station belongs to. The switch then sends a short, high-priority management frame to other switches attached to the backbone; this frame contains the MAC address and virtual LAN number of the end station. All switches then store the MAC address to a virtual LAN map held in cache memory. Armed with this information, switches can then direct broadcasts to the appropriate ports using the MAC address.

Section 3. Tagging Packets

The signaling message approach is straightforward, but it does create the potential for overhead and synchronization problems for larger networks. Every time an end station powers up and sends its first frame, a signaling message must be propagated to all switches before traffic can flow. To ensure synchronization, switches also send their cache tables to one another every minute or so, using TCP/IP routing information protocol (RIP) updates. These tables can grow to 1000 bytes or more in length.

In addition to message signaling, Madge implements frame tagging for virtual LANs running across its proprietary 200-Mbit/s backbone. With frame tagging, a short tag is appended to the beginning of every frame that crosses the backbone; the tag identifies which virtual LAN the frame belongs to. The tag ensures that switches always know the port group of each frame. Synchronization also is guaranteed, since virtual LAN numbers are carried in each frame.

One obvious downside to frame tagging is overhead—each frame carries a few bytes of extra baggage. But there's a more serious side effect: If a data packet already is at Ethernet's maximum frame length, adding a tag to that packet violates Ethernet's media protocol. Bridges and other forwarding devices usually discard frames that are

too long. Switch vendors can use proprietary techniques to circumvent the rules of frame length, but that means all devices on the
backbone must come from the same vendor—a limitation that does
not apply to switches that use signaling messages for layer 2 virtual
LANs.

One vendor other than Madge is using frame tagging for its layer 2
virtual LANs: Xylan Corp. (Calabasas, CA). Xylan's Omni-5 and
Omni-9 switches use a slightly different approach to creating virtual
LANs. Instead of port groups, the Xylan switches configure virtual
LANs on the basis of user-defined frame fields. Xylan virtual LANs
can be defined not only by groups of MAC addresses but also by common subnet addresses, protocol type, or any other parameter that can
be specified by values in a frame. This flexibility opens up some
intriguing possibilities. Because virtual LANs can be created on the
basis of any frame values, network managers can accommodate nonroutable protocols like NetBIOS. The Xylan scheme thus has a big
advantage over layer 3 approaches to virtual LANs, which can't subdivide nonroutable protocols. And the elimination of port grouping
means users can be moved around the network without concern for
which port they're connected to.

The main problem with using frame fields to configure virtual
LANs is degree of difficulty: Frame fields require an in-depth understanding of protocols, bit masks, offsets, and other routing software
details normally associated with layer 3 virtual LANs.

Section 4.   Multiplexed Traffic

The third approach to sending layer 2 virtual LAN information across
campus backbones involves time division multiplexing. Under the
TDM approach, used by Retix (Santa Monica, CA) in its Switchstak
5000, the backbone is divided into 10-Mbit/s time slots. Each virtual
LAN is assigned one or more of these time slots, to be used by that
virtual LAN only. Switches are configured with the information needed to map port groups to TDM channels.

Segregating virtual LAN traffic into dedicated time slots eliminates the need to use signaling messages or frame tags to identify
packets. This cuts network overhead and improves network stability, because the broadcasts of one virtual LAN don't affect the other
virtual LANs. The flip side of this latter advantage is that unused
bandwidth in any given virtual LAN can't be made available to
other virtual LANs. Getting the most out of TDM backbones
requires constant monitoring of traffic to make sure that time slots
are allocated efficiently.

Section 5. Topology Issues

Switches that handle virtual LANs at layer 2 can use the standard transparent spanning-tree algorithm or a ring design for their switched topologies. Spanning-tree devices converge simple, loop-free daisy-chain and star configurations by sending 802.1d messages to one another. Ring topologies can be based either on FDDI or on proprietary methods. Spanning tree is a low-level protocol that's fine for simple bridge architectures. But spanning tree has trouble scaling up to larger virtual LANs; for this reason, switch vendors are adding proprietary enhancements to the algorithm to make it faster and more robust. Madge puts its bridge topology routines in hardware, claiming a performance advantage over conventional software-based spanning tree implementations.

The maximum number of layer 2 virtual LANs that can be handled per backbone network varies greatly from vendor to vendor. Retix puts its upper limit at 64 virtual nets, while Bay Networks claims its 28000 switches can handle up to 800 virtual LANs in a backbone. Some claims border on overkill. For instance, Xylan says its forthcoming Omni-5 and Omni-9 products will handle more than 65,000 different virtual LANs, and Madge and 3Com Corp. (Santa Clara, CA) claim their switches handle an unlimited number of virtual LANs. Although it's tough to imagine a campus network that requires thousands of virtual LANs, some managers might feel more comfortable with a little extra headroom.

Section 6. Layer 3 Virtual LANs

Ethernet switches that handle virtual LANs at layer 3 bring basic routing functions to the virtual LAN process. Unlike layer 2 virtual LAN switches, layer 3 switches are protocol-savvy devices that understand the subnet fields of IP and other major network-layer protocols.

Layer 3 virtual LANs are configured by assigning ports to subnets that correspond to specific protocols. As with layer 2 virtual LANs, layer 3 ports can be located on the same switch or on multiple switches connected by a backbone. Layer 3 switches use subnet numbers to keep track of virtual LAN traffic across the backbone, in the same way that layer 2 switches use signaling messages, frame tagging, or time division multiplexing (see Fig. 24.2).

In layer 3 vernacular, a collection of ports associated with one subnet is called a virtual subnet. (The terms *virtual LAN* and *virtual subnet* are interchangeable in this context.) Traffic within virtual subnets is switched at layer 2. Traffic traveling between virtual subnets is routed at layer 3—without the need for an external routing device.

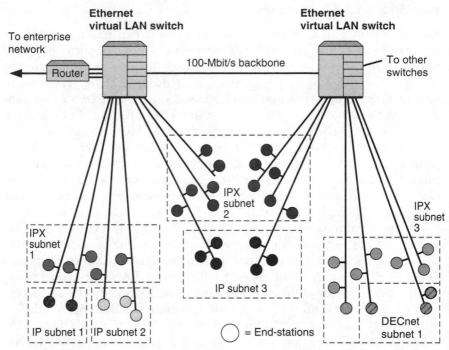

Figure 24.2 Protocol partitioning. Layer 3 Ethernet switches include basic routing functions to create virtual LANs based on network-layer subnet addresses. Traffic within virtual LANs is bridged across the network, just as with Layer 2 switches.

At first glance, layer 3 switches look as though they operate the same way as conventional multiprotocol routers. Layer 3 addresses are read, RIP and ARP (address resolution protocol) messages are generated, and MAC addresses are substituted between subnet hops. But layer 3 switching is not conventional routing. In layer 3 switching, the low-level forwarding logic of the switch is aware of more than just MAC addresses. Layer 3 switches do things on the local backbone topology that routers would never attempt.

In conventional routing, backbone traffic consists of unicast (point-to-point) frames. The routes for these frames are calculated on a hop-by-hop basis using a routing protocol like RIP or OSPF (open shortest path first). Conventional routers normally set up firewalls to limit subnets and their broadcasts to a single LAN. With these firewalls, conventional routers are able to block LAN broadcasts so that they don't reach the backbone and other LANs. TCP/IP, IPX, and similar protocols generally assume that broadcasts will not travel from LAN segment to LAN segment.

With layer 3 virtual LAN switching, however, all LAN segments and backbone links in a virtual subnet are treated like a bridged topology. That means routing protocols like RIP and OSPF no longer apply. If a layer 3 switch receives a frame that it doesn't know how to forward, it typically "floods" the frame out to all the ports of the appropriate virtual subnet, including backbone ports.

When a unicast frame comes back in response to a packet flood, the backbone switches learn which port the return frame comes in on— the same procedure used by learning bridges. And like bridges, layer 3 switches typically use the spanning-tree algorithm to determine the topology for bridging virtual LAN traffic across the backbone. The flood approach is fine for small and medium-size networks. But in larger networks, floods can become excessive, leading to performance problems—a condition often referred to as a *broadcast storm*. The use of high-speed backbones to connect layer 3 virtual LAN switches helps minimize this problem. A number of vendors also allows network designers to deploy manual load balancing to direct traffic across a number of different backbone paths.

Such tweaking of spanning-tree designs can address some of the obvious drawbacks of converging large bridged virtual LANs.

Section 7.   Layer 3 Limitations

Because layer 3 virtual LAN switches can route and bridge, the need for routers in work groups and departments is greatly reduced. But layer 3 switches typically have just enough routing smarts to handle local departmental routing. They still need the services of high-end routers, because they lack the sophisticated internetwork software needed for enterprise connections.

Layer 3 switches can overlay a conventional router topology on their bridged backbones by using RIP or similar protocols. Alantec Corp. (San Jose, CA) is adding OSPF support to its layer 3 Powerhub switches for this reason. Support for network layer protocols varies. The richest protocol mix comes from Alantec; its layer 3 switches handle TCP/IP, Novell IPX, Appletalk, and DECnet Phase IV protocols. 3Com's 2016 and 2500 offerings support IP and IPX. Layer 3 switches from Cisco Systems Inc. (San Jose, CA) handle IP only.

There is one protocol problem that all layer 3 virtual LAN switches share: the inability to handle nonroutable protocols like NetBIOS and LAT (local-area transport), a proprietary protocol from Digital Equipment Corp. (DEC, Maynard, MA). Layer 3 switches cannot subdivide nonroutable protocols into different virtual LANs. In contrast, layer 2 virtual LANs are protocol-independent, making them better suited to subdividing nonroutables. 3Com has come up with a kind of hybrid approach that enables its layer 3 switches to set up virtual LANs for nonroutable protocols.

In addition to layer 3 virtual LANs, 3Com provides an alternative virtual LAN model based on MAC address lists defined by network administrators. These MAC address lists can be used to set up proto- col- and port-independent switched virtual LANs. For instance, a group of end stations using nonroutable protocols could be assigned their own set of virtual LANs, with each LAN corresponding to a MAC address list. 3Com's MAC-based virtual LANs can span switch- es without frame tagging or other proprietary techniques, so they pro- vide a compatible way to partition a large layer 2 switch fabric with- out requiring layer 3 protocols. MAC lists are more sophisticated than layer 2 port groups because users can move to any port in the net- work and be added to the appropriate virtual LAN without reconfig- uring the port.

By themselves, MAC addresses are a somewhat cumbersome, effort-intensive way to configure virtual LANs. But when the approach is used to supplement layer 3 virtual LANs, it offers net managers a solid tool for traffic management.

Section 8.   Sophisticated Filters

Problems with nonroutable protocols aside, layer 3 virtual LAN switches have a lot more intelligence than layer 2 switches. Because of this, layer 3 switches provide a number of useful features that layer 2 products can't match. One of these is advanced filtering.

Filters included with layer 3 Ethernet switches can block or pass traffic by looking at user-defined frame fields. Filters can be used in many different ways to fine-tune traffic control inside virtual LAN firewalls. For example, switches can be set to keep all Netware ser- vice advertising protocol (SAP) broadcasts or all telnet packets off cer- tain segments within a virtual LAN. Net managers also can deploy filters to keep secure servers off-limits to all but a few approved seg- ments on a virtual LAN.

The filtering used by 3Com in its Lanplex switches is based on set- ting up rules that specify the blocking or passing of traffic at any level of the seven-layer OSI protocol stack. Filters can target source and destination addresses, subnet numbers, protocol types, application fields, or any bit values in a frame. Filters can combine multiple rules with boolean logic and up to 16 different parameters, 3Com says.

One big advantage of layer 3 virtual LANs is that they accommo- date not only multiple ports per subnet but also multiple subnets per port. This gives network administrators more leeway in moving, adding, or changing users on a campus network. For instance, with layer 2 switching, if a marketing department user moves to an office that's wired into an engineering department virtual LAN, the end station's subnet number would have to be changed. But because layer 3 virtual LAN switch ports can accommodate multiple subnets, the marketing virtual LAN can be extended to overlap with the engineering virtual LAN. This way, end stations with different subnet addresses can coexist on the same LAN segment. This feature is relevant mainly to IP networks, since IP doesn't assign subnet numbers dynamically. With IPX networks the overlap feature is less important, because IPX does assign subnet numbers dynamically.

Section 9.   Virtual Comparisons

A close comparison of layer 2 and layer 3 virtual LAN architectures reveals the relative strengths and weaknesses of each approach (see Table 24.2). Layer 2 virtual LANs clearly are simpler to configure than layer 3 virtual LANs. Because layer 2 switches don't include routing software, they tend to be less expensive than layer 3 products, although the need for high-end routers in larger networks closes the cost gap somewhat. Because they bridge rather than route traffic, layer 2 switches are inherently faster than layer 3 switches. And because they're protocol-independent, layer 2 switches can accommodate nonroutable protocols that layer 3 products can't handle.

But Ethernet switches that create layer 2 virtual LANs start losing their appeal as the backbone network grows. The signaling messages

TABLE 24.2   The Virtual LAN Matchup

Criteria	Layer 2 virtual LANs	Layer 3 virtual LANs
Ease of configuration	●	○
Low cost	●	○
High speed	●	○
Works for all protocols	●	◐
Separate virtual LAN definitions for each protocol	◐	●
Intelligent filtering	○	●
Built-in routing	◐	●

● Definite strength	○ Partial strength	◐ Definite weakness

and frame tagging used to create layer 2 virtual LANs add overhead that grows in proportion to the size of the network. Further, the proprietary media techniques deployed by some layer 2 switches may not integrate well into existing internetworks.

In contrast, layer 3 switches may be overly complex for handling small virtual LAN installations. But as virtual LANs become larger and more congested, the benefits of layer 3 switch intelligence become clearer. Layer 3 switches forward broadcasts only to those segments that belong to a specific subnet. Broadcast specificity reduces the amount of broadcast traffic on the backbone, giving layer 3 switches a key advantage over layer 2 switches, which send broadcasts to all segments in a given virtual LAN regardless of which subnets or protocols are present. The extensive filtering capabilities of layer 3 virtual LANs also conserve both backbone bandwidth and end-station processing cycles. Filters can provide a high degree of security inside virtual LANs.

Another possible advantage of layer 3 virtual LAN switches is the reduced need for conventional routers: One device handles switching and routing at the work group and departmental levels, providing in the process a backbone that is largely compatible with existing routers, bridges, and servers. But while some organizations may desire combined routing and switching, others may want to stick with their existing routers. For these users, layer 2 switches may be preferable.

In general, if simplicity and protocol independence are needed, network designers should go with layer 2 virtual LANs. With the proper interface software, layer 2 virtual LANs can be administered independently from routers (often by help-desk staffers), thereby conserving networking know-how for use in tackling more complex enterprise issues. On the other hand, if high levels of traffic management and protocol isolation are required, layer 3 virtual LANs are the way to go.

Section 10.   802.10 Secure Data Exchange

A security standard developed by the IEEE holds the possibility of merging some layer 2 strengths into layer 3 virtual LANs. The standard, called 802.10 secure data exchange, specifies a technique that lets end stations negotiate encryption and authentication parameters at the MAC layer. It works by encapsulating each MAC frame in a larger MAC frame that adds a 32-bit group identifier and some other security-related fields. Along with encapsulation, 802.10 specifies a way to automatically fragment and reassemble frames that exceed the maximum frame length of a given medium. Because of this ability, 802.10 could be used to convey virtual LAN information across a number of media types, including FDDI, Ethernet, token ring, and HDLC (high-level data link control) networks. Since it preserves the standard 802 frame spec, 802.10 is transparent to noncompliant intermediate devices, such as spanning-tree bridges.

Cisco is proposing that the 32-bit tag be used as a virtual LAN identifier. Cisco has already built 802.10 into its routers. By adding the spec to its Catalyst switch, Cisco says it will enable users to create interoperable layer 2 virtual LANs that run across Cisco's switching and routing product lines.

Cisco's proposal has yet to win favor with other vendors. One switch maker contends that the same function can be accomplished by using IP encapsulation. IP would bring the advantages of a fully routed protocol, but the overhead would likely approach 40 bytes per frame, compared with the roughly 20 bytes per frame added by 802.10. The 20-byte premium is a lot more than current proprietary frame-tagging methods. But with its 32-bit address space and fragmentation, 802.10 would scale better than the proprietary approaches that typically allocate 8 or fewer bits to virtual LAN addressing.

To complement its layer 2 virtual LANs, Cisco is working on what it calls Autonomous Spanning Tree services that can give layer 2 virtual LANs their own logical topology. With Autonomous Spanning Tree, network designers could create different end-to-end spanning-tree paths for each virtual LAN. For instance, a virtual LAN needing more bandwidth could be assigned its own FDDI links, while other virtual LANs could be made to share links. This could boost the usefulness of spanning tree for larger layer 2 virtual LANs.

Section 11.   Assessing the Field

Clearly, activity on the virtual LAN front is only going to accelerate over the next few years. Some makers of Ethernet switches will continue to focus on building simple, fast layer 2 products, while others move toward intelligent hybrids that combine MAC address lists and multilayer virtual LAN definitions. Given the diverse needs of corporate networks, it's likely that both layer 2 and layer 3 Ethernet switches will thrive. It's also a sure bet that virtual LAN technology will continue to evolve. Vendors are already talking about virtual LANs based on groups of users sharing a common server or application. This ascent from port grouping would require switches that can read well into packets to decode server names, socket numbers, and other application-specific fields. One vendor has even suggested that the ultimate style of virtual LAN membership would be based on user log-in names.

Perhaps the most exciting potential for advancement in the virtual LAN industry lies in automatic configuration. In spite of their advantages over routers, virtual LANs still need a fair amount of ongoing configuration: Ports have to be grouped, backbones have to be monitored, subnet numbers have to be assigned, and so on. Ideally, switches would automatically form virtual LANs according to some common attribute of end users—with little or no operator intervention. For instance, all stations with the same subnet number could be grouped automatically. Then subnets could be assigned to end stations on a departmental basis. This would work for IP, which has permanent subnet addresses, but not for Netware's dynamic services. One possibility in Netware's case is to create virtual LANs according to server access patterns; all stations accessing the same primary server would be placed in the same virtual LAN. Agile Networks Inc. (Concord, MA) is taking this approach with its ATM product.

On the shared-media front, Bay Networks says it is working on automatic virtual LAN configurations that are based on the sensing of subnet information on the network. Bay Networks hopes eventually to extend this service to other criteria, such as servers and application-layer fields. Bay Networks' switches now come with an extended SNMP management information base (MIB) that reports network topology details and statistics on a virtual LAN basis. This information includes MAC addresses, subnets, network names, and broadcast levels.

But even with self-configuring virtual LANs, the network needs to be monitored and tuned. Any automated approach will require robust reporting facilities that send alerts to a management console every time an automated add, move, or change takes place. This information will need to be integrated with real-time and historical statistics about traffic patterns within and between all virtual LANs.

Section 12. Performance Penalties

Net managers considering the different virtual LAN approaches also need to carefully consider another criterion: performance overhead. Ask Ethernet switch vendors how fast their boxes process packets and you're guaranteed to hear some stellar numbers. But the packet per second (pps) rates claimed by switch vendors describe only a best-case scenario: raw filtering rates for 64-byte packets. The truth is, the overhead introduced by virtual LANs can slash those pps rates by 50 percent or more—a hit that can send latency (network delay) through the roof. Two factors dictate how much of a performance penalty virtual LANs impose on Ethernet switches: the way in which virtual LANs are implemented in a given switch, and the hardware architecture used in that switch. As a rule of thumb, throughput decreases and latency increases in proportion to the amount of processing the switch has to perform to forward incoming packets to the appropriate ports. The packet-handling method that involves the least amount of processing is to look up media access control (MAC) addresses, a layer 2 function. For this reason, layer 2 switches that use MAC addresses to form virtual LANs can sometimes offer high performance levels with very low latencies.

The operative word here is *sometimes*. Layer 2 switches can deliver screaming performance only when packets are being shunted between stations that belong to the same virtual LAN. When nodes attached to different virtual LANs need to exchange information, layer 2 switches have to pass those packets through a separate router. Once that happens, net managers can kiss whiz-bang performance good-bye. Simply put, there's no way to send traffic from a layer 2 switch through a network-layer (layer 3) router and maintain switched Ethernet performance levels.

The numbers speak for themselves. When handling 64-byte packets, Ethernet switches typically deliver wire speed rates (14,880 pps per port) and keep latency to under 100 microseconds. Once routers become involved, latency grows to hundreds of milliseconds. That translates to more than a thousand-fold increase in delay. The added delay not only brings down overall performance but also creates the potential for a router bottleneck. If switches overwhelm the router with packets, the router's port buffers can overflow, resulting in lost data and retransmissions. These performance and latency problems apply both to stand-alone routers and to router modules that fit inside a layer 2 switch.

Vendors admit the router performance hit can be devastating. For example, Xylan Corp. (Calabasas, CA) claims that its layer 2 Omni switches deliver performance to the tune of 400,000 pps when switching traffic within virtual LANs. However, once Xylan's routing software gets into the act, performance drops to 40,000 pps—one-tenth that of pure layer 2 switching.

Switch vendors that use routers (either standalone or built-in) to connect virtual LANs assert that trips to the router are the exception rather than the rule. As evidence, they cite the network adage that in a well-designed LAN, only about 20 percent of all network traffic travels *between* work groups. That old saw is getting rusty, some observers say. For one thing, IS departments are consolidating applications on centrally located "superservers" accessed by users on different virtual LANs. Second, the arrival of groupware applications is encouraging corporate users to disregard traditional departmental demarcations in favor of companywide communications.

Section 13.   Layer 3 Delays

Ethernet switches that handle virtual LANs at layer 3 have routing intelligence built into their switching fabrics. Because of this, they offer superior performance over layer 2 switches when it comes to handling traffic sent between virtual LANs. The actual performance benefits depend on two basic factors: how the switch implements routing, and which protocols it routes.

By implementing highly tuned, stripped-down versions of the routing code found on high-end routers, some vendors claim their switches can route IP packets almost as fast as they can bridge them. Alantec Corp. (San Jose, CA) maintains that IP routing reduces the speed of its Powerhub 3000 by only 1.2 percent (from 80,000 pps to about 79,000 pps).

Those numbers have yet to be independently tested, but they are within the realm of possibility says Cisco Systems Inc. (San Jose, CA), the world's leading router maker. According to Cisco, those performance levels could be achieved by implementing a subset of the IP code and optimizing it for use on a particular platform. But it's important not to confuse whittled-down implementations of IP routing with the IP implementations found in high-end routers. The slimmed-down IP is a network-layer function, not a true routing capability; so don't expect to find sophisticated traffic management and security features in layer 3 switches.

Such high levels of performance are possible with IP because it is a public-domain, published stack. To handle proprietary protocols, vendors typically resort to reverse engineering, which results in lower performance. For instance, Alantec says performance for its Powerhub drops by 20 percent when DECnet routing is involved. Other vendors say that the extra processing overhead incurred in looking up network-layer information reduces pps rates more substantially. Cisco says IP routing reduces pps rates by a third for its Catalyst switch (from 60,000 pps to 40,000 pps). 3Com Corp. (Santa Clara, CA) says performance drops by 30 percent (from 50,000 pps to 35,000 pps) when its Lanplex switch routes packets between virtual LANs.

In terms of performance overhead, the intelligent filters included with switches from Alantec, Cisco, Cabletron, 3Com, and Xylan fall halfway between MAC-level switching and network-layer routing. Rather than looking at just MAC addresses, intelligent filters can be programmed to probe more deeply into the information fields in packet headers, where information such as protocol type is stored in special fields. Because intelligent filtering operates at the MAC layer, it works considerably faster than network-layer routing. Cabletron uses intelligent filters to prevent unwanted broadcast packets from traversing virtual LANs and to enforce access rights. Cabletron says filters cut layer 2 performance by 5 to 20 percent.

Section 14.   Route Servers

Making routing or high-level filtering capabilities an integral part of the switch fabric is certainly a more efficient way to implement virtual LANs than adding a router. But the next-generation route servers from vendors like Cisco and Cabletron should work even faster. Route servers act as a centralized repository of routing information and are installed in conjunction with LAN switches. A LAN switch consults the route server whenever it needs to forward a packet to a node that it hasn't heard of before, one that isn't already in its address table. The route server sends a message containing the location of the node back to the switch, which uses that information to update its MAC address list.

Route servers will add about the same amount of latency to the network as sending traffic via a router, their developers say. The big difference here is that the delay occurs only with one packet (the "query" packet sent from switch to route server). Further, the switch talks to the route server only occasionally, on a need-to-know basis, when it sees a packet for a new destination. The rest of the time the network switches forward packets at the MAC layer, maintaining very high levels of performance and low levels of delay.

Section 15.   Alternate Overhead

Layer 2 switches that use either signaling messages or frame tagging to create virtual LANs incur an extra layer of overhead. In both cases, switches exchange virtual LAN information over the LAN backbone— thus effectively reducing network capacity.

Vendors that use these layer 2 techniques—including Bay Networks Inc. (Santa Clara, CA), Cisco, Madge, and Xylan—all claim that the amount of space taken up by their schemes is negligible. Bay says signaling messages add less than 1 percent to its virtual LAN overhead. The frame tagging used by Cisco and Madge adds 32 bits (4 bytes) of data to every frame sent. For larger data frame sizes, that overhead also can be minimal. To avoid problems with lost frames, Madge's switches also send their entire virtual LAN address tables to one another, usually every minute. Again, however, the vendor claims a minimal performance hit. The tables add less than half a percent overhead, asserts Madge.

25

Adding Routing to a Switched Network

Section 1. Overview

Net managers making the move to switched networks may think they've finally said farewell to shared-media LANs, point-to-point WANs, and (at long last) routing and all its attendant aggravations. They'd best be ready to settle for two out of three.

Sure, switches have no trouble delivering huge amounts of afford-able bandwidth. But they also create the sort of flat layer 2 networks that corporate networkers spent most of the 1980s trying to get away from. Flat is fine: as long as broadcast storms, Swiss cheese security, and a host of other headaches are acceptable. Ironically enough, there's a clear way around these problems: Segment the switched net-work into virtual LANs using layer 3 routing.

What's not so simple, though, is deciding how to implement routing on a switched network. Essentially, net managers face three choices. First, they can maintain the status quo by using conventional routers both to divide the network and to tie layer 2 switches into the back-bone. Second, they can migrate to distributed routing. In this sce-nario, they deploy so-called multilayer switches—boxes that support both layer 2 bridging *and* layer 3 routing. A small number of conven-tional routers are used to link these hybrids to the enterprise. Finally, net managers can take a far more radical approach and opt for an entirely new architecture. In this scheme, route servers are used to centralize routing intelligence, while edge switches (LAN switches loaded with enough information to make most routing decisions on their own) are dispersed throughout the enterprise. When an edge switch comes up against a destination address that it doesn't recognize, it queries the route server for assistance.

Right about now, net managers may be thinking that three choices sound like too much of a good thing—especially since they're the ones who'll be spending nights and weekends sorting them out. Actually, making the smart call doesn't mean losing sleep. All that's really involved is applying some familiar yardsticks—like price, performance, and administrative effort—to some unfamiliar technologies.

Mixing layer 2 switches with layer 3 routers allows companies to leverage the products they already own (a sure way to earn points with the CFO). Trouble is, performance on virtual LANs is going to take a hit—particularly when handing off data to an ATM backbone. That's bad news, given that legacy LANs interconnected over ATM are going to dominate into the next century. The distributed approach puts routing exactly where it's needed: everywhere. But it's a bear to manage, and it's not going to come cheap: Pricey routing code has to run on each and every one of those multitalented multilayer switches.

Route servers are optimized for performance, and they take the sweat equity out of administration. But they're strictly proprietary. Product availability also has to be factored in. There are plenty of sources for switches and conventional routers. More than half a dozen vendors now sell multilayer switches, including Bay Networks Inc. (Santa Clara, CA) and Digital Equipment Corp. (DEC, Maynard, MA). Cabletron Systems Inc. (Rochester, NH), Cisco Systems Inc. (San Jose, CA), IBM Corp. (Armonk, NY), and Newbridge Networks Inc. (Kanata, Ontario) are shipping route servers.

Section 2. Strategic Differences

Given the overall flurry of activity (and the sometimes conflicting statements of direction), it's easy to lose sight of what vendors say they'll support. For instance, route servers aren't for everyone: Bay and DEC have drawn the line at multilayer switches. And 3Com Corp. (Santa Clara, CA) argues that routers and switches that work at the MAC (media access control) layer can do the job for the foreseeable future, making it the only major internetworking vendor that isn't championing a new take on routing.

Still, most top internetworking vendors say they'll support two— and sometimes all three—architectures. More important, they're redesigning their product lines so that companies can move from one phase to the next without scrapping their installed equipment. That gives net managers the chance to implement the routing technique that best suits their network, when they need it. Timing, in this case, is going to be very important. Most corporations have only just started installing LAN switches and are years away from deploying switched ATM over the wide area. What's more, net managers need to decide for themselves whether switched networking really demands New Age routing—or whether vendors are simply repackaging conventional technology.

Finally, corporate networkers who decide that new networks merit new routing architectures shouldn't count on much help from standards organizations. The ATM Forum has just gotten started on MPOA (multiprotocol over ATM), which will define how to implement routing on ATM networks. The standard, when it finally arrives, will work for both switched legacy LANs and ATM networks. Still, going it alone should come as no surprise to corporate networkers. They've been there before.

The new routing paradigms also could mean a market shakeup. Vendors like Cisco are going to have to prove that they can deliver the goods for switched networking. Cabletron (known for hubs), IBM (heavy iron), and Newbridge (a mux outfit) see switched networking as their chance to break into the routing market. It's easy to see why they're so eager: Router revenues for 1995 were expected to tip the scale at almost $1.5 billion. And as top dog, Cisco has the most to lose: In 1994 it accounted for 59 percent of the high-end routers shipped, according to International Data Group (IDC, Framingham, MA). In-Stat (Scottsdale, AZ) puts Cisco's number even higher, at 76.5 percent.

Section 3.   Deployment Decisions

Each routing architecture involves different equipment. The most conservative approach requires routers and layer 2 switches (see Fig. 25.1). The former are used to transfer data between different vLANs and establish connections from the switched LAN to the enterprise backbone. Distributed routing deploys multilayer LAN switches. As noted, these hybrids incorporate layer 2 bridging and layer 3 routing in the same box. That sets them apart from switches like the those sold by Kalpana Workgroup (Sunnyvale, CA), which handle traffic only at the MAC layer. Since multilayer switches work at the network layer, they can support virtual LANs—without having to pass traffic off to a separate router or request routing information from a route server.

But multilayer switches don't completely eliminate the need for conventional routers. Typically, these network layer boxes offer a subset of the protocols and security, traffic management, and WAN connectivity found on high-end routers. For example, the Powerhub multilayer switch from Alantec Corp. (San Jose, CA) routes three

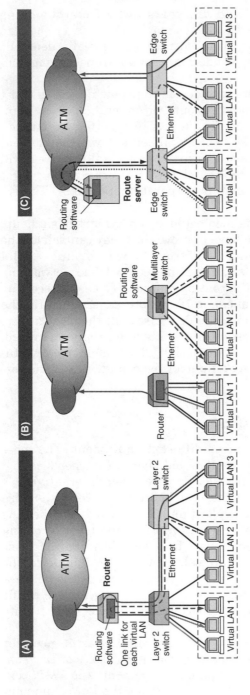

Figure 25.1 Routing's three-way split. When Layer 2 switches and Layer 3 routers are both deployed, the switches transfer traffic between nodes on the same virtual LAN (a). A router gets involved when traffic is sent between virtual LANs or onto the ATM backbone. Distributed routing uses multilayer switches to make the most of the connections between nodes on the same or on different virtual LANs (b). A small number of stand-alone routers are still needed for high-end routing functions. The route server scheme relies on edge switches to make the majority of the routing decisions (c). The route server itself is queried only when an edge switch doesn't know the address of a particular destination node.

Traffic sent to ATM backbone

Traffic transferred between nodes on same virtual LAN

Traffic transferred between nodes in different virtual LANs

Query sent to node server

Response sent by route server

(A) ATM — Router — Routing software — One link for each virtual LAN — Layer 2 switch — Ethernet — Layer 2 switch — Virtual LAN 1 — Virtual LAN 2 — Virtual LAN 3

(B) ATM — Router — Routing software — Multilayer switch — Ethernet — Virtual LAN 1 — Virtual LAN 2 — Virtual LAN 3

(C) ATM — Routing software — Route server — Edge switch — Ethernet — Edge switch — Virtual LAN 1 — Virtual LAN 2 — Virtual LAN 3

324

protocols (DECnet, IP, and IPX) and has no WAN ports. Cisco's 7000 router, in contrast, can handle 12 LAN protocols and supports point-to-point, circuit-switched, packet-switched, and cell-switched WAN communications. Thus, net managers who take the distributed routing approach will wind up installing multilayer switches alongside a (much smaller) number of conventional routers. For instance, a site with 20 multilayer switches might use one router as a gateway to the WAN and for complex routing functions.

Route servers, which centralize some aspects of routing, actually have more in common with distributed schemes than might first be apparent. Underlying this radical architecture is the realization that routing, at its simplest, involves two related functions: packet forwarding and route determination. Conventional routers deliver both functions in a single chassis. Route server networks implement each function in a separate device. Forwarding is the job of edge switches: LAN switches that work with network-layer information, rather than the MAC addresses stored in ordinary Ethernet switches. Route determination is taken care of by the centralized (and more expensive) route server.

An edge switch consults a route server only when it needs to send a packet to a node that it can't find in its address table. The route server sends a message with the correct address back to the switch, which caches the information for a predetermined period. Because route servers use proprietary protocols to communicate with edge switches, products from different vendors can't currently work together. According to route server suppliers, their approach boosts performance and holds down costs.

Section 4.   The Migration Path

Cisco, Cabletron, IBM, and Newbridge all argue that route servers will ultimately be the de facto way to route traffic on switched networks. But that hasn't stopped them from making sure their products support the other two routing strategies.

Ciscofusion, for example, enables companies to begin by installing layer 2 Catalyst 5000 LAN switches in conjunction with Cisco 7000 routers. The network can be upgraded to distributed routing by adding a layer 3 routing card to the Catalysts. Net managers can convert the 7000 to a route server by activating that facility in Cisco's IOS (internetwork operating system). The route server downloads routing information into the layer 3 addressing space in the Catalyst.

In 1995, Cisco announced its next-generation 7500 router. The new box is designed from the ground up with enough performance to run traditional router and route server applications on a single platform.

Cisco's strategy is intended to breathe new life into its old router line and let it compete with vendors like Cabletron and Bay for a share of the switch market. Ciscofusion will give Cisco a way to keep selling high-end routers like the 7000 or new 7500 into customer sites, while taking on hub and switch vendors with its Catalyst. For Cisco customers, it looks like a win-win situation: They can recycle their Catalyst 5000s and Cisco 7000s on distributed routing and route server networks.

Currently, Cisco is the only vendor that plans to run its route server on a converted router. Cabletron, IBM, and Newbridge, are all building their route servers from scratch, arguing that general-purpose routers are too slow for the job. Of course, they don't have an industry-leading router, so they would say that.

- Cabletron's MMACplus switching hub delivers distributed routing via multilayer switch modules. Its Securefast Virtual Network Server route server costs $30,000 and is available as either a standalone box or a module for the MMACplus. Cabletron says one route server will handle 1000 users.

- Under IBM's switched virtual networking (SVN), IBM users can hardware upgrade their 827X Ethernet and token ring switches to support distributed routing. IBM also has a route server module for its 8260 switching hub and 2220 wide-area switch.

- Newbridge, with its Vivid line, was the first vendor to ship a route server. Its Yellow Ridge edge switches can also operate as autonomous multilayer switches in a distributed routing network.

DEC, meanwhile, is delving into distributed routing. Under its EnVISN (enterprise virtual intelligent switched networks) program, it is possible to add IP, IPX, DECnet, Appletalk, and OSI routing to DECswitch 900 layer 2 Ethernet switches via software upgrades that cost from $1500 to $3000.

Several other vendors sell network-layer switches that can be used to implement distributed routing. These include Alantec, Loral Test and Information Systems (San Diego, CA), Netedge Systems Inc. (Research Triangle Park, NC), and Network Systems Corp. (Minneapolis). At press time, Bay had multilayer switch modules for its 3000 and 5000 hubs in the pipeline. As indicated, 3Com is the only top player in the internetworking arena that has not announced a new routing strategy. And it doesn't look as if it will anytime soon. The vendor argues that server farms are actually reducing the need for routing in buildings and across a campus, making route servers and multilayer switches an unnecessary expense.

3Com's line of Lanplex Ethernet switches actually support IP routing, which means they *can* be used for distributed routing. But Geoff Thermond, general manager, says 3Com developed the feature to enable Unix net managers to control traffic flow via subnet IDs. The server farm trend has not taken off in the Unix world, where most networks still feature large numbers of distributed servers and require a high degree of subnetting. 3Com estimates that 20 to 30 percent of its customers run Unix networks.

Vendors that offer both distributed routing and route servers say that network size is a key factor in deciding between the two approaches. Route servers, they suggest, come into their own on very large distributed networks. Companies with smaller networks (in a single building) may prefer distributed routing. This gives them a way to build virtual LANs without having to master the intricacies of route servers.

But distributed routing vendors argue that putting routing intelligence everywhere (in routers and multilayer switches) makes more sense than referring route determination decisions to a centralized server. Distributed routing vendors also claim that their approach is inherently more reliable because route servers can act as single points of failure. Their opponents dismiss that claim out of hand, pointing out that the four route servers announced to date allow for redundant implementations.

Section 5.   The Price Point

Various internetworking vendors were asked to respond to an RFP (request for proposal) which was prepared by *Data Communications* magazine. Participants were asked to cost-out three campus networks: one with 50, one with 250, and one with 500 switched Ethernet ports (see Fig. 25.2). Each network also included an ATM backbone. Newbridge submitted a route server proposal. Cabletron, IBM, and Netedge chose distributed routing. (For the record, DEC also submitted a distributed routing proposal but was disqualified for failing to follow the RFP.) Bay, Cisco, and 3Com went with a combination of layer 2 switches and routers.

Generally, the proposals based on layer 2 switches and routers were the least expensive; distributed routing proposals were the priciest. Newbridge's route server network came in between these two alternatives. IBM's distributed routing network, which is priced to compete against all comers, was a surprising exception. For the two larger configurations, IBM kept equipment costs to less than $1000 per port. Its proposal averaged out at almost 66 percent less expensive than Netedge's bid and about 40 percent cheaper than Cabletron's.

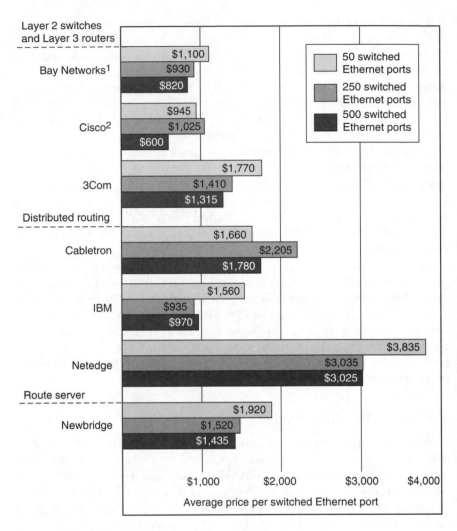

1. Supports IP only; 50-port network does not include ATM backbone.

2. The 50-port network does not include ATM backbone.

Figure 25.2 An RFP for next-generation routing. To reveal the relative costs of three routing schemes, vendors were asked to cost-out three campus networks: one with 50, one with 250, and one with 500 switched Ethernet ports. The RFP specified an ATM backbone for each network. Vendors had to use products that were already shipping.

Per-port prices were established by dividing the total cost of all the equipment on the network by the number of Ethernet ports. When Layer 2 switches and Layer 3 routers are used, per-port prices drop as the network gets larger (and the cost of the expensive component is offset by an increasing number of less costly switches). The same holds for the route server scheme, which adds edge switches to accommodate more ports. Per-port prices for distributed routing tend to remain relatively constant regardless of network size, since each multilayer switch includes its own routing software.

In order to comply exactly with the RFP, some vendors had to supply chassis with only a few ports populated, thus causing price spikes.

The dollar values also show how prices for technologies scale in different ways. Per-port prices both for layer 2 switches and routers and for route servers drop as the network gets larger (as the expensive component of the network is shared by an increasing number of less expensive switches). That typically doesn't happen with distributed routing, since each switch that is added comes with its own routing component. Thus, for distributed routing, per-node prices tend to remain constant regardless of network size. Bear in mind that picking any technology solely on the basis of price could turn out to be a costly mistake. The distributed routing networks all feature redundant capabilities. In contrast, the layer 2 switch and router networks include only one router—a single point of failure, and a potential traffic bottleneck.

Some vendors shaved costs in other ways. Cabletron submitted a bid for an unmanaged network. Bay's network supported only IP routing. And Bay and Cisco went with a hub or proprietary switching, rather than ATM, on their 50-port proposals.

Section 6.   Performance Parameters

Trying to draw a bead on how well multilayer switches and route servers will actually perform is very tough. To date, neither switches nor routers have been independently tested. Even so, it's possible to use known performance characteristics to make some suppositions.

As a rule of thumb, network latency increases (and network performance decreases) in proportion to the amount of processing that devices like switches and routers have to perform before forwarding traffic. Layer 2 Ethernet switches, which execute only a simple MAC address lookup, typically keep latency to less than 100 microseconds per 64-byte packet. Layer 3 routers, in contrast, look deeper into packet headers and then run a variety of algorithms before sending data on its way. That additional processing vastly increases per-packet latency. In fact, it's not unusual for routers to add 5 milliseconds of delay per frame.

Back in the real world what this means is that networks built using a combination of layer 2 switches and layer 3 routers will offer excellent performance some of the time (when traffic is being switched) and poorer performance at other times (when traffic is passed from switch to switch via a router). These sorts of performance hits become critical when virtual LANs enter the picture. Almost all layer 2 switches come with software that allows net managers to improve performance by grouping network nodes into virtual LANs (broadcast domains) on the basis of MAC address or port number. Traffic between nodes in the same virtual LAN is switched at the MAC layer.

But when nodes attached to different virtual LANs need to exchange information, layer 2 switches have to pass the packets off to a router—adding huge amounts of delay. Also, the router itself must be fitted with a separate physical interface for each logical LAN—a procedure that can become fantastically expensive.

Distributed routing eliminates the router as a performance bottleneck by allowing multilayer switches to transfer traffic between virtual LANs on the basis of layer 3 protocol subnet IDs—without getting a router involved. Route servers do the same thing, with the edge switches making the routing decisions. The only routing delay incurred involves the single query packet that is occasionally sent by the edge switches to the route server when they need to know how to find an unknown destination. The rest of the time switches forward packets directly, using a straightforward lookup from their cached address lists. This enables them to deliver the same low levels of latency as today's MAC layer switches.

Critics of distributed routing argue that this scheme will be ponderously slow because it means putting routing functions in every multilayer switch on the network. In their defense, vendors of network-layer switches point out that their products invoke their routing capabilities only when necessary. The rest of the time packets are switched at the MAC layer. Further, distributed routing vendors argue that their products keep latency to a minimum, since they implement stripped-down subsets of the software found on high-end routers—in some cases routing packets at almost the same speed as MAC-layer switches.

Alantec claims that IP routing reduces the performance of its Powerhub 3500 by 1 percent. DEC indicates that the performance of its DECswitch 900 falls by 66 percent when IP routing is enabled, but says it plans enhancements that should reduce the dropoff. Finally, distributed routing proponents say their products will actually deliver higher performance than route servers because they allow switches to make forwarding decisions on the spot, eliminating the risk that the route server will act as a bottleneck.

26

Designing a
Switched Ethernet LAN

Section 1. Overview

Despite what vendors claim, there's nothing plug-and-play about Ethernet switches; plug and *pray* would be nearer the mark. LAN switches may relieve congestion to the desktop, but install them wrong and they can shift the bottleneck to other parts of the LAN. While vendors are more than happy to talk about slam-dunk performance levels, ask them for some granular advice on how to design a switched LAN and the silence is usually deafening. Fortunately, net managers also have access to another—more accurate—source of information: the corporations that have already made the move to switching.

One such company is BSW International Inc. (Tulsa, OK). In 1993, when the architectural and engineering firm wanted to pump up the performance of its network, it decided to deploy Ethernet switches. Two years later, BSW owned a switched network with enough punch to allow its professional staff to collaborate on bandwidth-hungry CAD (computer-aided design) files. Performance has doubled on some portions of its LAN, the company estimates. The switch to switching didn't come cheap. BSW's hardware budget came in at about $500,000—almost $1000 per end user. That includes $50,000 for traffic analysis tools. But the bottom line is only part of the story. The transition itself wasn't easy.

Some of BSW's staff believe the move to switching would have been easier if it had planned more—specifically, by buying a network analyzer and plugging it into the shared-media LAN to work out who was talking to whom. BSW installed its switches without having an exact picture of traffic flow. The company simply plugged all its high-end workstations (the nodes that needed the most bandwidth) into switch ports. That improved performance when traffic was traded between workstations attached to the same switch. But it also created bottlenecks that bogged down the workstations when they tried to send data to other floors over the LAN backbone or access printers and servers connected to the old shared-media LAN. How bad did it get? One bottleneck was severe enough to cause a critical network component to crash on a daily basis. Others caused workstation sessions to time out.

And once the switches were in place, it was too late to go back and use an analyzer or other troubleshooting tools to spot the traffic jams. (LAN switches segment a network; thus, when an analyzer is plugged into the LAN, it sees only the traffic on the port to which it's connected.) So BSW's IS department spent 5 months puzzling out traffic patterns and reconfiguring the network to eliminate congestion. And just to keep things interesting, it also had to resolve a problem with some buggy switch hardware that caused the LAN backbone to run at less than one-tenth of its advertised speed.

Corporate networkers at other companies can learn a great deal from BSW's pioneering venture into switched Ethernet. The factors that prompted the firm to deploy switches (more users, collaborative computing, and a new centralized database of essential company data) can be found on practically all enterprise Ethernets—and many of these are in line for the switch treatment. By 1997, nearly half of all LAN devices will be connected to switched LANs, according to Strategic Networks Consulting Inc. (Rockland, MA).

Lessons Learned at BSW

Believe the Hype

Switches really *can* solve congestion problems on today's Ethernets. BSW's switched network runs about twice as fast as its old shared-media LAN—despite the fact that it now supports a third more users and carries applications that eat up more bandwidth.

Don't Believe the Hype

Despite what vendors claim, there's nothing easy about Ethernet switches. Installed wrong, they can relieve one bottleneck while creating others—in BSW's case at the juncture of switched and shared-media domains and the backbone between the floors.

Planning Is Everything

A happy and humming switched network requires some hard work before the products are taken out of their styrofoam. BSW wishes that preanalysis of traffic flow had been feasible prior to adding switches. That way it would have known which nodes were the big talkers and could have tuned performance by attaching them to the same switch.

Go Farming

When BSW first installed its switches, it didn't give enough thought to where the servers should go. That caused problems when workstations tried to reach servers on other floors—and clogged the backbone. Now it's looking to set up an FDDI backbone that will let it build a server farm, improving performance by connecting all its commonly accessed devices to the fastest part of the network.

Add Analysis

BSW built its switched network before Madge added integral RMON (remote monitoring) analysis to its product. Waiting until the analysis was in would have made life easier. Madge is one of the only switch vendors now offering RMON analysis—few others switch suppliers even have it in the pipeline.

Never Mix, Never Worry

BSW believes that most of its traffic problems can be traced directly to its separate-but-unequal network design— parallel shared-media and switched Ethernets connected via a single switch module. BSW says the best thing net managers can do is bag their repeater-based networks altogether and give each device its own connection to a switch.

Section 2.   In the Beginning

BSW decided to build a switched network in 1993, during the planning stage of a relocation from a two-floor office to six floors in a new building. Rapid growth meant that BSW had outgrown its old office—and its old LAN. So the company decided to give its staff some room to breathe and bump up the bandwidth on its LAN in one push. BSW chose Multinet Ethernet switching hubs from Lannet Data Communications (Huntington Beach, CA), which has since been bought by Madge Networks Inc. (San Jose, CA).

The Lannet/Madge boxes were selected by Dwight Wolf, who was then a CAD and network support manager. Wolf left the company shortly afterward, before the switches were installed. The job of overseeing the installation fell to Rick Mulligan. According to Chip Paul, network manager at BSW, the nod went to Madge switches as much on the basis of availability as of feature set, since there were only three products to choose from at the time. BSW also was swayed by the Multinet's 1.2-Gbit/s cell-based backplane (which it thought would make it easier to migrate to higher-speed LAN technologies) and by Madge's promise to add integral traffic analysis to its switch at some point in the future. When BSW first moved into its new headquarters in July 1993, it had 400 nodes on its Ethernet. Within a year, that number had grown to 550. About 300 of BSW's employees use Macintosh computers; roughly 175 are on Unix workstations; another 75 are PC users.

BSW's rapidly expanding LAN was a big reason behind its decision to become an early adopter of Ethernet switches. As nodes were added to the network, response time slowed noticeably—and end users were complaining. BSW knew things were going to get worse. In fact, the principal motivation for instituting a switched infrastructure was to improve productivity by allowing employees to collaborate on the architecture and engineering projects that are BSW's bread and butter.

Collaborative computing isn't a new concept at BSW. A symbol of the company's commitment can be seen in the Genesys Room, in which up to 16 staffers can brainstorm on projects. Each participant sits behind a terminal (connected over an Ethernet LAN), typing ideas and contributions that appear on a screen at the front of the room. To ensure that ideas flow freely, the collaborators make their comments incognito; the terminal monitors are set into the desktop and protected by a hood.

BSW realized early in the game that its new and ambitious collaborative applications would far exceed the capabilities of its shared-media Ethernet LAN. First, the additional traffic would plunge response times into the deep freeze. Second, collaborations would be carried on companywide, rather than within departments. Unlike many companies, which turn to switching once they're in trouble, BSW saw switches as a way to head off performance problems before they occurred.

Back in 1993, Ethernet switches were on the bleeding edge. Nevertheless, BSW's IS department didn't have a hard time selling the proposal to chief financial officer Harry Lay. One reason is that BSW prides itself on embracing cutting-edge technology as a way to gain competitive advantage.

BSW's Business Case for Switches

BSW's specialty is undertaking high-volume architecture and engineering projects. Clients include Circuit City, Computer City, and Wal-Mart. BSW's strategy has always been to use technology to increase efficiency, in particular by borrowing techniques from high-volume manufacturing. The company's IS staffers like to describe their network as a production line for building drawings.

From the start, BSW relied on CAD software to speed the process of prototyping buildings. The CAD packages allow its architects to design their plans using on-screen palettes, adding and subtracting building items from a menu of building components. Its clients can then reuse the plans multiple times at different sites (with minor modifications to account for site-specific differences).

BSW's hi-tech strategy has paid off, in terms of both productivity and profitability. The company boasts that it can produce design documents in half the time taken by its competitors. And while BSW declined to give revenue numbers, its growth rate (20 employees in 1983, 600 today) bears testimony to its financial good health. Given its previous successes with technology, pitching Ethernet switches to chief financial officer Harry Lay wasn't all that hard.

> Network support manager Rick Mulligan describes it as the equivalent of the site manager at Ford asking to buy a faster conveyor belt. Of course, in BSW's case, the conveyor belt cost half a million dollars.
>
> Not all of BSW's experiments with new technology have been winners. For instance, the company's attempt to use a wireless LAN to connect the workstations in its Genesys brainstorming center had to be abandoned because of woefully slow throughput, Mulligan says.

Besides introducing switches, Mulligan and Paul instituted three other major changes that were necessary to bring collaborative computing to the network:

1. They reorganized the company's multiple Appleshare, Netware, and Unix network operating systems under a single Netware environment.

2. They installed a database from Oracle Corp. (Redwood Shores, CA), running on a server from Hewlett-Packard Co. (HP, Palo Alto, CA). The database holds information that can be shared by employees throughout the building. BSW also uses Filemaker Pro from Claris Corp. (Santa Clara, CA).

3. They introduced a Groupwise e-mail system from Novell Inc. Staffers had previously communicated via a mishmash of voice mail, voice paging, and memos.

> **Out with the Old, In with the Netware**
>
> Aside from increasing bandwidth, BSW's biggest challenge was to find a way to allow its PCs, Macs, and Unix workstations to communicate. When BSW first moved to its new site, its Macintosh users (the majority of its work force) communicated over Appleshare; its PC users relied on Netware LAN; and its Unix operators made up a third, autonomous environment.
>
> That approach caused several headaches. First, the desktop workstations couldn't

exchange files. Second, the Appleshare network was proving unreliable and slow, with at least one of BSW's six Appleshare servers crashing on a daily basis. Further, the generally poor performance of the Appleshare servers meant that the IS department had to restrict the number of users that could log into the servers at the same time.

BSW's solution was to move to an all-Netware environment. Currently, all its users are attached to a Netware 3.12 LAN with four Netserver LS servers from Hewlett-Packard. The servers run network file server (NFS) and Macintosh NLMs (Netware-loadable modules) from Novell Inc. (Provo, UT). This setup allows cross-platform communication throughout the company and also has eliminated the Appleshare downtime.

Ultimately, BSW wants to move to Netware 4.1. It has already bought a license for Novell's new operating system. But its first attempts to install 4.1 had to be abandoned when it discovered that the current edition of Netware NFS (Version 1.2C) causes file servers running Netware 4.1 to crash. Attempts to solve the problem via BSW's local Netware reseller proved unsuccessful. Novell has since told BSW that Version 2.0 of NFS will solve the snafu.

Section 3.   The Cabling Connection

As part of its move, BSW decided to overhaul the wiring and topology at its premises. At the old site, BSW's Macintosh computers were daisy-chained over coaxial cable. At the new site, all nodes are linked over a star-wired UTP (unshielded twisted-pair) cabling plant. Each cubicle in the new building is supplied with two 4-pair Category 5 UTP cables for data and a third Category 5 UTP cable for voice.

Changing the physical infrastructure reduced network downtime. BSW estimates that roughly 30 percent of downtime at the old site was caused by cable-related problems. The two key problems were the size of the wiring closets (not large enough) and the coaxial cable (which had unpredictable shielding). What's more, because the Macs were daisy-chained, it took only one bad connection to cause the whole Appleshare network to crash. At this point, according to BSW, only 5 or 10 percent of network downtime is caused by bad cable and connectors.

BSW also canned its HP Ethertwist repeaters in favor of Madge's 18-slot Multinet hubs. The Multinet chassis can hold two types of slot-in network modules: The LE140XTQ Ethernet repeater connects 10 devices to the shared-media Ethernet LAN. The LSE-808 Ethernet switching modules comprise an autonomous LAN switch that accommodates eight 10-Mbit/s segments. BSW also has a smattering of LSE-108 switch modules, which allow eight devices to be connected to one 10-Mbit/s switch port. The repeater modules communicate internally over any of four shared-media Ethernet segments running inside of each Multinet. Switching modules installed in the Multinet hub communicate via a 1.2-Gbit/s backplane.

Section 4. A Staggered Start

BSW introduced switching onto its network incrementally. When BSW moved into its new site in July 1993, the Madge hubs were first fitted with LE140XTQ shared-media repeaters. A couple of months later, it started to increase network performance by swapping out shared-media repeaters and replacing them with LSE-808 and LSE-108 switch modules in some of the Multinets. BSW technicians connected one Unix workstation running CAD applications to each 10-Mbit/s port. PCs and Macs were left attached to shared-media repeaters.

Each of the wiring cabinets on six floors of BSW's offices now contain two Multinet hubs—one with LSE-108 and LSE-808 switching modules, the other with shared-media modules. (BSW has also installed a few stackable Ethernet shared-media hubs on the first floor, where its reception area and the offices of the three founders are located.) The shared-media hubs on different floors are all part of the same 10-Mbit/s Ethernet and are connected over a 10-Mbit/s fiber Ethernet backbone. In contrast, the switching hubs on different floors are connected by Madge's 100-Mbit/s proprietary LHB fiber backbone.

BSW's side-by-side networks are the result of its staged rollout. At press time, the company is halfway to its goal of going 100 percent switched. In the meantime, the only link between the two networks is furnished by an LSE-208 module in a Multinet hub on the fifth floor. The LSE-208 is a two-port switch module set into so-called I/O mode to allow it to transfer traffic from the switched domain to the shared-media network.

It didn't take long after BSW had activated its switches for staffers to notice the improvement. By switching traffic between CAD stations, the company roughly doubled the speed of file transfers between workstations on the same floor. The files are typically between 1 and 5 Mbytes long. The amount of time it takes to transmit a file containing a building plan has fallen from an average of 3 minutes to about 1.5 minutes, according to BSW.

But for a firm that specializes in design, BSW had more than a few problems designing its switched LAN. It soon found out that switches aren't necessarily a quick fix. The trouble comes down to math. Madge's Multinet hub switches between multiple 10-Mbit/s segments via an internal bus running at 1.28 Gbit/s—enough capacity to ensure that the hub itself doesn't act as a bottleneck. The bottlenecks come when multiple 10-Mbit/s streams attempt to leave the hub and cram onto slower network connections. In BSW's building, this happens in two places: the connection between the switched and shared-media networks on the fifth floor and the 100-Mbit/s backbone between the switching hubs (see Fig. 26.1).

The bottleneck is worse in the LSE-208 switch module. When too many switched devices attempt to communicate with nodes attached to the shared-media network, the traffic swamps the LSE-208 and it crashes. At its worst, the LSE-208 would shut down on a daily basis. The only way to restart the device is to send someone to the wiring closet to reboot the module. Even when the LSE-208 was working, BSW found that the bottleneck between the shared-media and switched networks also caused a problem with the Madge's backpressure flow control scheme. When a switch receives more frames than it can process, it transmits a network "busy signal" to sending stations, letting them know to stop shipping frames. The juncture of BSW's shared-media and switched networks was so congested that the back-off signals caused Unix stations to time out.

What's more, a software conflict between the LSE-208 switch module and the LHB module that establishes the link to Madge's backbone caused the backbone to run at 10 Mbit/s rather than 100 Mbit/s. BSW spotted the problem because users started to complain, and LEDs on the front of the LHB modules started flashing more slowly. On Madge's advice, BSW moved the LSE-208 to a shared-media hub, thus eliminating the conflict. Madge's solution resolved the problem, though it meant that BSW had to use its spare Multinet. But even when the backbone was back at 100 Mbit/s, BSW still found it acted as a bottleneck.

Section 5. Reconstructive Surgery

BSW realized that the only way to relieve the congestion on the backbone and in the LSE-208 was to reconfigure its network, reducing the

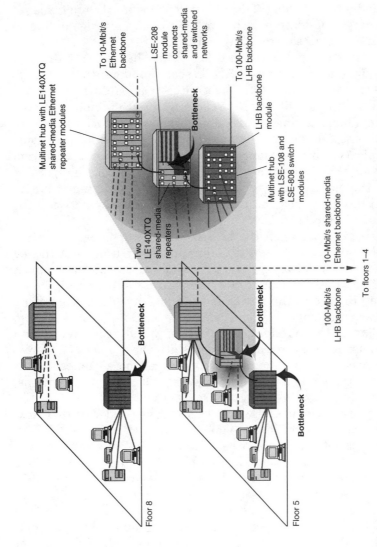

Figure 26.1 Switched Ethernet: Planning makes perfect. BSW's staged switch rollout left is with separate but unequal networks—and a couple of big bottlenecks. The worst traffic jam was in the slot-in module that linked its shared-media and switched networks. BSW also ran into slowdowns when switched traffic piled up on the 100-Mbit/s backbone between floors. Close analysis of traffic patterns and extensive reconfiguration have eased most of the problems.

volume of traffic crossing between floors and from the shared-media to the switched network. That meant doing two things. First, the company had to work out which switched nodes were talking to one another and move them onto the same floors. Second, it had to work out which shared-media nodes were talking to switched devices and shift them onto the switched network.

Easier said than done. It took BSW 5 months of hard work—suggesting that it would have been much easier to design the switched network if RMON analysis tools which work on switched LANs had been available at the time. Plugging a standalone network analyzer into any part of an unbridged shared-media LAN lets a net manager observe all the network traffic. But Ethernet switches work by dividing the network into multiple 10-Mbit/s segments. That means that when an analyzer is plugged into the LAN, it sees only the traffic on the port to which it is connected.

BSW bought a Sniffer from Network General Corp. (Menlo Park, CA) this year. But it uses it to troubleshoot its *shared-media* network. In order to use the Sniffer ($8995) to build a picture of traffic flow on the switched LAN, BSW would have to move it around between 175 switch ports—an approach that is clearly unworkable. Without the benefit of automated analysis tools, BSW's IS technicians had to use deductive reasoning to work out whom each Unix workstation was talking to. That included going to each workstation and checking its system configuration to determine where its print jobs were going and which Unix server it was communicating with. Then they had to lock themselves in a conference room and use a whiteboard to work out what was going on.

To improve performance, BSW made a number of changes to the network. It says that two of them really paid off. First, it moved all the heavily used plotters (for creating diagrams) onto the switched network. Second, it moved all the Unix servers, which already were attached to switch ports, onto the same floors as the users that accessed them. This reduced the amount of traffic crossing the LSE-208 switch module and thinned out the traffic on the backbone. The plan worked. The LSE-208 has gone from crashing once a day during the first month to crashing once a month. The new design also has eliminated the session time-outs, and people have stopped complaining about performance.

Section 6.   More Monitoring

At press time, BSW was about to take delivery of Madge's NMA-RS, a Multinet module that allows net managers to get full RMON traffic analysis of every port at the same time. Madge is one of the first vendors to offer this facility. One NMA-RS is required for each hub. Traffic statistics are displayed on a net management console running SMONmaster, an add-on package for Madge's Multiman network management software application. Buying the NMA-RS management modules has added about $50,000 to the cost of BSW's switch implementation.

BSW also plans to take advantage of the NMA-RS's SNMP capabilities, which can assign nodes to different virtual LANs from the management console. The virtual LAN feature allows BSW to improve security and add firewalls without having to buy and support routers. (Currently it runs a flat network, with no bridges or routers used to segment network traffic.)

BSW has other ambitious plans. While its network is now behaving satisfactorily, the firm is still unhappy with the performance of the LSE-208. Madge claims that replacing the LSE-208 with its new four-port LSE-404S switch module will take care of the trouble. But BSW feels it's safer to eliminate the bottlenecks altogether by replacing the remaining shared-media modules with switches. Establishing a fully switched LAN will enable BSW to connect all its Multinet hubs to the 100-Mbit/s backbone.

BSW also is considering a change of backbone—from Madge's LHB to FDDI. It originally went with LHB because the vendor didn't have an FDDI backbone module in 1993. Changing to FDDI would enable BSW to hook its HP servers directly to the 100-Mbit/s backbone. That isn't an option with Madge's FHB, because the vendor doesn't sell an FHB server adapter.

Currently, the main stumbling block to this scheme is price. Madge charges $10,000 per FDDI port—more than three times as much as the FDDI options from other switch vendors. BSW briefly considered buying Madge's one-port 100Base-T module as an alternative, but abandoned the idea because HP, which makes its servers, is a proponent of the 100VG-AnyLAN standard and does not sell a 100Base-T card. That meant BSW would have to replace its server to be able to work with Madge's 100Base-T Multinet hub cards. At $5995, BSW also thought the 100Base-T module was too expensive. Madge has since dropped the cost of the module to $3995, which is still too rich for BSW's blood.

Designing a Switched Token Ring LAN

Section 1. Overview

The last time IBM boosted token ring bandwidth (from 4 to 16 Mbit/s) was in 1988. A lot has changed since then on corporate networks. High-performance applications and high-cost servers mean that today's token ring LANs are suffering from the bandwidth malaise that first cropped up on Ethernet networks. This chapter describes the bandwidth problems associated with token ring. It also gives granular advice on how to design around the capacity shortfall. Ultimately, token ring switching represents the most promising solution to the problem. Switches are installed in the wiring closet; nothing needs to be touched at the end users' desktops. Specifically, this means that the net manager doesn't have to run or reterminate new cable, or install, test, and tweak new communications drivers in the adapters on network workstations.

From a design perspective, the simplest way to look at token ring switches is as a cost-effective means of collapsing token ring backbones. Most existing token ring backbones consist of a 16-Mbit/s ring off of which hang many dual-port bridges; the bridges connect individual departmental or work group 4- or 16-Mbit/s LANs. As LAN traffic increases, these 16-Mbit/s backbones can become severely congested (see Fig. 27.1).

This chapter first appeared as an article in *Data Communications* magazine and was written by Kevin Tolly, president of The Tolly Group (Manasquan, NJ), a strategic consulting and testing organization.

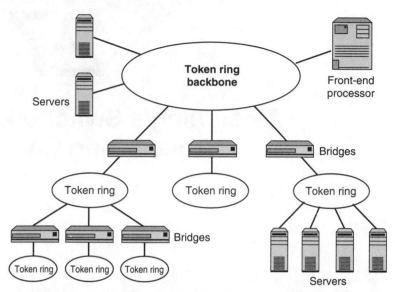

Figure 27.1 Blueprint for a bottleneck. With first-generation token ring designs, servers, mainframe equipment, and bridged departmental LANs in a campus network are connected by a single 4- or 16-Mbit/s token ring backbone. As the campus net grows, the backbone becomes a throughput bottleneck.

Up until recently, the easiest way to improve the speed without affecting the infrastructure of such networks has been to replace the dual-port bridges and 16-Mbit/s backbone ring, and then directly terminate each token ring LAN into a high-performance router backplane (see Fig. 27.2). But high-performance routers from the likes of Cisco Systems Inc. (Menlo Park, CA) usually run about $5500 per port.

In contrast, token ring switches are optimized for token ring backbones (and as such don't have to support every protocol and WAN interface in creation). This means that they typically cost around $1900 per port; IBM has announced a product which goes for as little as $700 per port. Some token ring switches also offer a feature that routers don't—full-duplex operation so that congested server links can actually have dedicated access to 32 Mbit/s of total send *and* receive bandwidth, instead of just 16 Mbit/s of send *or* receive bandwidth.

Certainly there will be break-in problems with token ring switches. The principal one with existing products is network management. Since switches establish point-to-point connections, they eliminate the shared media which form the basis for traditional token ring network analysis. Plugging a Sniffer analyzer into a switch port allows

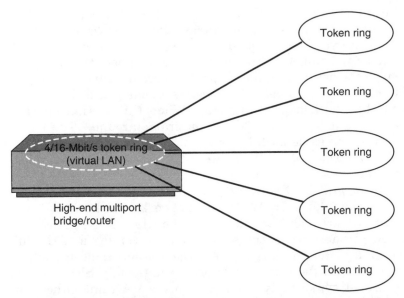

Figure 27.2 Routers to the rescue. Network designers can eliminate the bottleneck problem of first-generation token ring installations by using multiport bridge/routers equipped with high-speed backplanes to replace the physical ring backbone. The main drawback to the bridge/router approach is its high cost.

the net manager to see the traffic only on that one port. This glitch notwithstanding, with the right design philosophy and approach, token ring switches will go a long way to extending the life of existing token ring sites.

Section 2. Historical Perspective

The best way to understand why token ring LANs are currently in go-slow mode is by looking at the history of the medium. If ever the much-overused term *legacy* is appropriate, it's when referring to the legacy of campus LANs left behind as a result of IBM's iron grip on the hearts and minds of Fortune 1000 net planners in the late 1980s. The vast majority of Fortune 1000 customers have been left in a technological twilight zone caused by IBM failing to follow through on its token ring strategy. For all intents and purposes, IBM's efforts to improve the scalability of token ring for large-scale enterprise internetworks ended with its initial announcement in 1985. Specifically, IBM has neglected source route bridging (SRB), token ring's mainstay protocol that allows connections between end devices hooked up to physically separate LANs.

SRB functions as follows: Each token ring LAN is given a number. At session initiation, an "explorer" frame is broadcast throughout the network of interconnected token rings. As it passes through each bridge, the bridge adds the "ring-bridge-ring" numbers that uniquely identify it to the actual frame as it passes through. This is known as the routing information field (RIF). Despite its name, this is not layer 3 routing, but still layer 2 bridging. When the session partner receives the frame, it simply "turns the frame around." The frame then traverses the same path it arrived on, only in reverse. Once the session is established, all traffic between the two session partners follows the same physical path through the network.

The problem with SRB is that its architecture was never extended to deal with complex LAN/WAN internetworks. Rather, SRB was architected primarily for the local area. The RIF did not indicate to the session partners when the session was traversing a WAN link (rather than a high-speed LAN). Thus, the sessions could not adjust timers to deal with the increased latency. Additionally, SRB sessions could not adjust dynamically to reroute when a WAN link either congested or failed. Thus, meshed/redundant networks cannot be taken advantage of. Data link switching (DLSw) was only recently introduced to effectively "overlay" SRB and allow SR bridged sessions to be routed over a TCP/IP backbone. SRB RIF information and LLC2 sessions are terminated by the router. Then, the data is literally routed—using TCP/IP now and advanced peer-to-peer networking (APPN) in the future—over a simple or complex WAN.

Bandwidth growth screeched to a halt after the 1988 introduction of 16-Mbit/s token ring. Rumors of 64-Mbit/s token ring floated around for years—especially after IBM's 1993 introduction of the high-performance LANStreamer chip set—but an announcement was never forthcoming. It was only in 1995, when it shipped its 25-Mbit/s ATM products, that IBM identified a growth path for token ring users.

Section 3.   Source Routing Problems

Token rings don't *have* to use source routing, but in reality they all do. This is a result of the battle between IBM and the-rest-of-the-world. Early innovators like CrossComm, Microcom, and the now-defunct Vitalink applied the proven transparent bridging approach to token ring in the late 1980s. Transparent bridging (TB) has the same end goals as SRB: allowing stations connected to physically separate LANs to communicate. Whereas SRB requires that the end stations be "internetwork aware," transparent bridging hides the internetwork from the end stations. Stations communicate exactly as if connected to the same physical LAN segment. The bridge decides which frames (of which sessions) to forward between LAN segments.

As a result, TB was able to work with very old network hardware and software. In contrast, SRB could work only with products whose drivers had been updated to function with SRB's RIF. This took Novell, for instance, several years to do. Technically, transparent bridging worked just fine. But IBM pushed its own alternative (and nonstandard) source routing (SR) approach, and its campaign won out. Smart vendors began shipping SR bridges. Vendors that held their ground, like Vitalink, went out of existence.

With the ascendancy of SRB, and under the guidance of IBM-sanctioned network designs published in IBM's Red Books, Fortune 1000 campus networks began to fall into a particular pattern. A hierarchical, double-backbone approach was adopted by almost every large customer. Source routing itself was the biggest determinant of network design. The source routing spec (originated by IBM and, years later, adopted by the IEEE 802.5 token ring committee) allowed a maximum of seven bridges, or hops, between any two communicating end stations. What that meant was this: While more than seven bridges could be present in a network, any end stations separated by more than seven bridge crossings simply could not communicate. The seven-bridge limit was a global one. The entire source routing bridged network was considered one logical network and thus the seven-hop limit applied, not just campuswide, but nationwide and worldwide.

This effectively required net managers to build strictly hierarchical structures. At the campus level, all ring-to-ring traffic, which included all LAN-to-mainframe traffic and much LAN-to-server traffic, needed to traverse at least one backbone to reach its destination. And, ultimately, a single backbone would provide the unifying link across the entire campus, aggregating all traffic to and from the lower-level LANs. All this was fine if the aggregating LAN was of a higher speed than the feeder LANs. But this is no longer the case. IBM itself, until recently, effectively rejected FDDI's 100-Mbit/s solution. Thus, most customers were left with a multitude of 16-Mbit/s LANs feeding into several building backbones that would, in turn, feed into a single 16-Mbit/s campuswide backbone.

Virtual rings—extra "hops" added by routers configured to be multiport bridges (such as those by Cisco and Bay Networks)—reduced further net managers' options in planning the physical network topology. These multiport boxes always consumed at least one extra hop because the box would "appear" to have a ring inside it. Thus, as far as SRB was concerned, it "cost" two hops, rather than just one, to cross a single physical Cisco, say, bridge. Help arrived only in 1993–94 when the data link switching (DLSw) architecture allowed routers to terminate SRB hop counts as the sessions entered a TCP/IP backbone across a WAN. Thus, an SR bridged environment could be built with seven hops *into* the cloud, no hop restrictions across the cloud, and seven hops back *out* of the cloud. This update, however, did little to help net managers' massive token ring installations at local campuses.

Furthermore, IBM did recently "update" its SR bridging scheme to allow for double the number of hops—to 14. Making use of this change, however, requires end-station communications programs and adapter NOS drivers as well as bridges that support the extension of the routing information field (RIF), where "hop" info is stored. Unfortunately, few, if any, of the token ring bridge or adapter vendors have upgraded their software in this manner.

Section 4.   Replacing the Physical Backbone

Because of IBM's massive influence in the token ring market, many net managers adopted IBM's PC-based bridges as the basic building block of their campus networks. These bridges were always two-port devices—one port in, one port out. Campus networks built with these bridges required a physical backbone LAN to provide the "switching" point between any pair of LANs. Each departmental LAN would connect to the backbone LAN. From there, the frames could be bridged across to the receiving departmental LAN.

From the beginning, network managers saw the advantage of collapsing their token ring backbones into a single wire center in the basement or in the data center. Instead of token ring bridges located on each floor of a building, segments would be strung vertically to span each floor. Then individual bridges would all be located in a wiring center on one floor.

In these cases, a backbone LAN that would, say, "logically" extend across multiple buildings or floors within the same building would "physically" exist in a single wiring closet at a central point. A lobe (node) from each of the connected LANs would be wired into this collapsed backbone. Either copper repeaters or fiber-optic token ring connections could be employed to accomplish the wiring. This "collapsed backbone" could then be easily isolated from problems occurring on or caused by attached networks. Because the entire backbone existed in one physical location, management and debugging were significantly easier.

Frequently, expensive gear like an FEP (front-end processor) would be directly connected to the backbone LAN. (The FEP-to-LAN connection alone at one time cost approximately $20,000 for an IBM 3745. For that, the customer received two connections. It was not possible to buy just one.) Furthermore, depending on when the customer purchased the FEP connection, that link might be at 4 Mbit/s. The presence of even a single 4-Mbit/s station forces the customer to either run the entire ring at 4 Mbit/s or create a separate ring for the 4-Mbit/s traffic and bridge it to the 16-Mbit/s backbone.

File-and-print servers, along with any AS/400 minis, might be connected either directly to the backbone or to a bridge-connected "server farm." Number is usually the determining factor. Since stability is a very high priority with physical backbones, it is always desirable to limit the number of devices directly connected to the backbone. But as soon as devices are removed from this backbone, the tradeoff is immediate: Session traffic that previously needed to run on only two rings and traverse a single bridge must now span three rings and traverse two bridges. Not only are there additional points of failure—the extra ring and extra bridge—but each frame is subject to additional latency.

As each frame is processed by a bridge, a small but measurable delay is incurred. Since many simple tasks involves hundreds, or even thousands, of frame exchanges, adding bridge hops between clients and servers often has a noticeable negative impact on performance.

Section 5.   The Switching Solution

The token ring switch offers, first and foremost, an easy upgrade for the overburdened backbone. Given a collapsed backbone, the token ring switch can completely replace both the physical backbone LAN and, sometimes, all the bridges that connect to it. The lobe connections previously linking the bridges to the physical backbone are simply plugged into the switch. The switch solution, if planned properly, can easily be implemented over a weekend. The old, two-port bridges can be pulled out (see Fig. 27.3).

For the many customers who built networks based on stacking two-port bridges, the switch alternative is an attractive one. The switch provides a high-speed backplane allowing 16-Mbit/s connections between any two LANs at any time—arbitrarily. The packets are, typically, directed dynamically between the appropriate LANs on the basis of standard SR information fields found in the frame headers.

This multiple 16-Mbit/s channel of bandwidth is a huge improvement over the physical backbone it replaced. That LAN offered a maximum aggregate capacity of 16 Mbit/s to or from any of the connected departmental LANs. A pair of high-performance applications

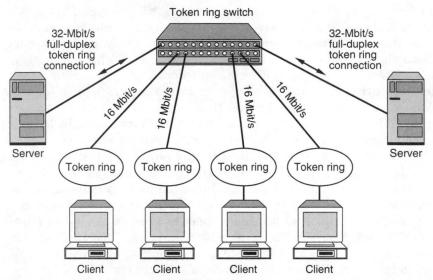

Figure 27.3 The token ring switch solution. Token ring switches use source routing information to establish point-to-point connections between attached token ring LANs, devoting a full 16 Mbit/s to each connection. Some switches include a full-duplex feature that boosts available throughput to 32 Mbit/s.

communicating across the backbone could easily consume the entire backbone. Ironically, advances in token ring bridge performance have exacerbated the problem. Newer high-throughput, low-latency devices allow LAN data to flood the backbone at much higher rates than was possible just a few years ago. The token ring switch, by eliminating the LAN and the bridges, completely eradicates the campuswide (or buildingwide) bottleneck created by backbone rings in hierarchical networks.

Section 6.   Hop Reduction and Latency

With almost all the token ring switches shipping today, the switch approach eliminates the backbone ring both literally and figuratively. The old physical ring disappears completely into the backplane of the switch. The backbone ring even disappears from the view of source routing. Previously, a session across a backbone LAN would show as going from source ring via a bridge to the backbone ring and continuing across a second bridge to the target LAN. With switching in place, the traffic (from source routing's point of view) appears to originate on one LAN, cross a single bridge, and terminate on a second LAN. The backbone ring has now transformed into a backbone bridge. All attached segments see the switch as the same, single bridge number.

Thus, the newly implemented switch reduces hop count consumption by giving network managers additional flexibility in network design. Because source routing is a dynamic protocol, end stations dynamically adjust to this logical reconfiguration. At most, the end stations would need to be rebooted.

Implementing a token ring switch eliminates not only the pair of bridges but the latency (delay) introduced by frames crossing them. Thus, performance even in low-utilization situations can improve dramatically. It should be understood that the effect of latency is directly related to the characteristics of specific applications. While bridge latency itself is easily measured, there is no simple, direct correlation between latency and application performance. Simply put, in cases where the latency of the application (i.e., the speed at which it can process network data) is slower than the latency of the bridge, improvements in latency have little effect on performance. Conversely, when bridge latency can be shown to be the bottleneck, immediate performance improvements can be expected.

Many backbone LANs built in the late 1980s still run at 4 Mbit/s. Since many backbones support then state-of-the-art 3725 and 3745 FEPs at 4 Mbit/s, these LANs have not been upgraded to run at 16 Mbit/s. Replacing the physical backbone with a switch offers a clean workaround for these speed mismatch problems. Since the ports can run at either 4 or 16 Mbit/s, older devices can be deployed on one or more 4-Mbit/s segments and not force 16-Mbit/s-capable devices to run at the slower speed.

Section 7.   Front-Ending the Router

As explained above, many network managers have long since encountered and resolved the physical backbone LAN bottleneck by replacing first-generation two-port bridges with high-density, multiport bridge/routers. These multiport bridge/routers virtualize the backbone LAN and link up to some 20 or more token ring LANs via a high-speed backplane. In most cases, the backplane appears as a virtual ring. Each LAN segment communicates onto the backplane via a virtual bridge instance.

At first glance, it might look like these networks are not candidates for token ring switch solutions. This is hardly the case. High-end, high-density bridge/routers are notoriously expensive. These boxes are put in place primarily because of their prowess in handling complex WANs and an array of routing protocols. Such talents are of little use for "on campus" communications. Raw bridging and LAN-only connectivity work quite well for campus LANs. This allows token ring switches to be used effectively in conjunction with high-end routers. The switch can be placed between the hierarchy of campus LANs and the router. The switch can process all local traffic without involving the router. Only traffic that needs to traverse the WAN would leave the switch and enter the router. Thus, the switch solution can significantly reduce the number of router ports required. And it can save money, since switch ports are usually cheaper than router ports.

Furthermore, the LAN-WAN megarouter stands as a single point of failure in the network. By dividing up responsibilities between a LAN switch and a WAN router, an additional level of isolation and reliability can be achieved. The costs of today's megarouters increase dramatically when redundancy is built in. Most significant is the increase in vendor choice for WAN routers that is gained when port density requirements are lowered by the deployment of LAN switches. Most third-party vendors have already chosen not to fight Cisco Systems Inc. (Menlo Park, CA) and Bay Networks Inc. (Santa Clara, CA) in the high-end router arena. Thus if upward of 10 LAN ports are required, the choices are fairly limited. With switches, a three- or four-port router could now connect to a fairly complex campus network. Advances in WAN port concentration, which allow multiple, independent WAN links (i.e., branch offices) to be handled via a single WAN interface (frame relay), make low-density routers viable options once again. In fact, we may have seen the peak of the megarouter era.

Section 8.   Turbocharged Servers

Up until now, the focus has been on using switches to improve backbone bandwidth. Equally important is the positive impact a properly deployed switch can have on server performance. Because the demand placed on a server is so much greater than that placed on a client, bandwidth draw must be dealt with in a totally different way. Stated simply, many servers are complex, high-cost devices that must service tens or even hundreds of users to become cost-effective. Yet traditional shared-media server deployment places communications constraints on servers that often forces the raw number of servers to go up.

When servers are deployed on LANs with end stations, high server utilization deprives standard clients of bandwidth and can be problematic. The logical solution, then, might be to cluster servers together on a server farm. This would certainly reduce the contention between server and client. Unfortunately, server farms built using traditional shared-media LANs cause more problems than they solve. With total, aggregate bandwidth still locked in at 16 Mbit/s and multiple high-demand servers using it, backbone bottlenecks are not far off. Isolating servers on dedicated LANs is a possible solution. But it is an expensive and not entirely satisfactory solution.

Token ring switches can be employed to build high-powered, flexible, dedicated-bandwidth environments. Server NICs can be directly connected to switch ports, allowing full 16-Mbit/s bandwidth to be allocated dynamically between the server and any end station on any target LAN. Further, for NOSs like Netware that can dynamically load-balance client stations across multiple NICs, a server's bandwidth can be expanded simply by adding an NIC and connecting it to its own port (shared or dedicated) on the switch.

Section 9.   Full-Duplex Token Ring

By definition, traditional shared-media token ring is half-duplex. Information flows in one direction only and the media can be used (at any given time) only by a single transmitting station. When a server is hooked directly to a switch, its shared-media protocol ceases to be relevant. A "nailed up," dedicated, point-to-point circuit exists between the station and the switch. Thus, it becomes feasible to run token ring in a full-duplex fashion. Such operation allows data to run in both directions simultaneously. The server can receive and transmit at the same time.

Using traditional token ring, a server may need to transmit and receive at the same time but cannot. Data on the transmit queue must wait until receive data is processed before it can be shipped out across the network. Thus, even when high-performance CPUs and expensive disk caches are utilized effective end-user performance can suffer simply because the transmit queue is not serviced often enough by the network.

Assuming adapter and NOS support, a switch-connected server can be reconfigured to run in full-duplex mode. (IBM's LANStreamer adapter is one example of an NIC that supports this facility.) In this configuration, a single server NIC can theoretically deliver a combined 32 Mbit/s of transmit/receive traffic. Such a configuration can have an instant impact on end-user response times (actual mileage may vary). Further, only the server need run in full-duplex mode. Clients themselves rarely (if ever) need to transmit and receive at the same time. Thus, providing dedicated full-duplex ports for clients is both expensive and pointless.

In the area of full duplex, switches outshine routers. Even the most sophisticated router still treats each of its LAN ports as a standard, half-duplex, shared-media environment. Thus, a server farm, or even dedicated server ports, hung directly off of a router can never provide the effective throughput of a full-duplex switch.

Section 10.   Comparing Ethernet and Token Ring Switches

Ironically, the most important differences between Ethernet and token ring switches are not technical, though technical differences can still affect the way in which each is implemented. Here's a summary.

Timing.   The Ethernet switch market, in terms of product delivery, was 2 to 3 years ahead of the token ring switch market. Ethernet gear has been available since 1992. Most token ring switch vendors didn't ship product until sometime in 1995. That time frame is important when taking into account competing technologies. Ethernet switching was able to get firmly planted before 100-Mbit/s technologies like 100Base-T and 100VG0-AnyLAN were available. The long delay in shipping token ring switches gives other technologies, especially ATM, the chance to get into the corporate network first.

Cost.   Historically, token ring technology has been more costly than Ethernet. Today, it is still not uncommon to see token ring components (particularly NICs) costing twice as much as their Ethernet counterparts. Switching is no exception. While pricing structures will undoubtedly change over time, token ring switches will remain considerably more expensive than Ethernet switches for the foreseeable future. This will have a significant impact on net managers' deployment of the technology. Given the price per port of most token ring switches, deploying so-called personal token ring (with each user given a dedicated LAN segment) will usually be out of the question. Thus, where many Ethernet switches are naturally positioned as work group products, pricing alone will keep most token ring switches in the backbone.

28

Designing an
FDDI Backbone

Section 1. Overview

Now that network managers have seen for themselves that Ethernet
and token ring don't have the bandwidth to make it on the backbone,
they face a simple choice: Field complaints from angry users on
maxed-out LANs or find a technology that can really deliver.
Industry gurus may sing the praises of ATM and 100Base-T, among
others, but they seem to be oblivious to one high-speed scheme that
boasts a full range of readily available networking products. That
technology is FDDI.

FDDI, which has been around since 1988, has quietly matured into
a stable transport method that's more than capable of handling LAN
backbones. FDDI's biggest claim to fame is its 100-Mbit/s throughput
(a real, rather than a theoretical, limit). But bandwidth on the backbone doesn't mean much if departmental LANs can't exploit it. In
order to design a functional network, net managers need to know
exactly how the equipment that connects the LANs to the backbone
behaves, and what it is truly capable of.

Asking equipment vendors themselves those questions is one of the
more pointless exercises life has to offer. If vendors are to be believed,
all their products are capable of offering stratospheric levels of performance, all the time. Fortunately, there is a far more accurate source

---

This chapter first appeared as an article in *Data Communications* magazine, and
was written by Kevin Tolly of The Tolly Group (Manasquan, NJ) and David Newman of
Data Communications.

of information—independent testing. To date, the only evaluation of the bridges and routers that tie local networks into an FDDI ring has been conducted by *Data Communications* magazine. This chapter describes the *Data Comm* test lab's findings, and how network designers can learn from them.

Section 2.   The Test Rationale

In essence, *Data Comm* was looking to answer one critical question: How many LANs can a bridge or router link to an FDDI backbone? To find out, it put seven FDDI bridges and routers from six vendors through their paces. (The lab invited the industry's top 10 market leaders to participate.) Each product was tested in "Gatling gun" fashion, using a variety of protocols and packets.

The lab found that the FDDI bridges and routers evaluated, while not perfect, generally have enough horsepower to move traffic from the backbone to as many LAN segments as vendors claim they can handle. In some cases, the products even pass traffic at close to the wire speed of each attached LAN. Of the boxes evaluated, two did particularly well. The Backbone Concentrator Node (BCN) from Bay Networks Inc. (Santa Clara, CA) was the overall leader in this round of tests, demonstrating high routing throughput, support for large numbers of LAN segments, and excellent bridging numbers. The Linkbuilder 3GH from 3Com Corp. (Santa Clara, CA) also earned special praise. The Linkbuilder, a bridging hub, sent traffic at near wire speed for all attached segments.

In addition to the Bay BCN and 3Com Linkbuilder, the lab checked out the 3Com Netbuilder II router, the DECnis 600 bridge/router from Digital Equipment Corp. (DEC, Maynard, MA), a hybrid PC-based router supplied by Madge Networks Inc. (San Jose, CA), and the CNX 500 bridge/router from Proteon Inc. (Westborough, MA) (see Table 28.1). The Madge and Proteon devices were configured to link FDDI networks to token ring LANs; all other vendors supplied Ethernet and FDDI interfaces. (Bay and 3Com also offer token ring; Proteon has an Ethernet interface. The lab tested the products that best represent each vendor's chief area of expertise.)

Section 3.   Performance, Configuration, Cost, and Management

To understand why the winners performed as well as they did—and what areas still could use improvement—it's helpful to understand some of the criteria used in these evaluations. The most important of these are performance, configuration, and cost.

TABLE 28.1 Selected Vendors of FDDI Bridges and Routers

Vendor	Product	Software release	Topologies supported	Number of slots; maximum interfaces per slot	Routing protocols	Bridging methods	Price
Digital Equipment Corp. Maynard, MA 508-493-5111	DECnis 600	2.2	Ethernet, FDDI	7; 2 Ethernet, 1 FDDI (2 slots), 8 sub-T1 WAN, 2 T1/E1, 1 T3	IP, IPX, DECnet Phase IV, OSI, Appletalk, Integrated IS-IS	802.1D spanning tree, transparent bridging	Chassis, $11,600; DAS FDDI interface, $14,000; two-port Ethernet interface, $4,800
Madge Networks Inc. San Jose, CA 408-955-0700	Madge adapter cards and Novell Multiprotocol Router software in Compaq Systempro	Adapter drivers: 1.04a; Novell MPR: 2.0	FDDI, token ring	7; 1 FDDI, 1 token ring	IP, IPX	None	Compaq Systempro, $5,000; Madge FDDI adapter, $1,395; Madge token ring adapter, $1,195; Novell MPR, $995
Proteon Inc. Westborough, MA 508-898-2800	CNX 500	13.0A	Ethernet, FDDI, token ring	3; 2 Ethernet, 1 DAS FDDI, 2 token ring	IP, IPX, XNS, OSI, DECnet, Vines, Appletalk	Transparent spanning tree, source route	Chassis, $10,895; FDDI adapter, $10,495, 2-port token ring adapter, $4,295; 2-port Ethernet adapter, $2,495; optional management software for Sun Sparcstation, $8,995
3Com Corp. Santa Clara, CA 408-764-5000	Linkbuilder 3GH	2	Ethernet, FDDI	11; 8 Ethernet, 4 FDDI	Not applicable	Transparent spanning tree	Chassis with single power supply, $12,150; with dual power supplies, $14,950; management module, $10,350; management software, $750; FDDI backbone module, $9,000; 8-port Ethernet module, $12,500

TABLE 28.1 Selected Vendors of FDDI Bridges and Routers (Continued)

Vendor	Product	Software release	Topologies supported	Number of slots; maximum interfaces per slot	Routing protocols	Bridging methods	Price
	Netbuilder II	6.1	Ethernet, FDDI, token ring	4; 1 Ethernet, 1 FDDI, 1 sub-T1 to T1/E1, 1 E1	IP, IPX, XNS, OSI, DECnet, Vines, Appletalk	Not applicable	Chassis, $2,995; 8-slot chassis, $5,495; management module, $5,000; management software, $1,500; FDDI module, $7,500; 1-port Ethernet module, $1,125; 1-port token ring module, $2,995
Wellfleet Communications Inc. Bedford, MA 508-670-8888	Backbone Concentrator Node (BCN)	1.55	Ethernet, FDDI, token ring	13; 4 Ethernet, 1 FDDI, 4 token ring, 1 sub-T1 to T1/E1, 1 T1, 1 E1	IP, IPX, XNS, OSI, DECnet, Vines, Appletalk	Transparent spanning tree, source route	Chassis, $24,000; 1-port FDDI interface, $19,000; 4-port Ethernet interface, $13,000; management software, $200

DAS = Dual-attached station

Performance was the key criterion in the tests. FDDI networks can carry traffic at nearly 100 percent of their 100-Mbit/s capacity. Thus, an FDDI ring can flood 10 Ethernets running at 10 Mbit/s or seven token ring LANs running at 16 Mbit/s—provided the intermediate bridge or router can handle such a load. Obviously, the faster a device is, and the more attachments it can handle, the better it's suited to backbone applications.

But there's more to performance than just traffic. The type of traffic involved and product scalability also must be factored in. Because bridging is less complex than routing, bridged traffic should theoretically pass through a device faster than routed traffic, but that isn't always the case. DEC's device routed 64-byte IP packets faster than it bridged 64-byte frames—an indication that net managers shouldn't take anything for granted when trying to pick the best tool for the job.

Scalability—the ability to add interfaces—also affects performance, particularly in high-capacity bridges and routers. When a device has to service 5 or 10 LANs, throughput can fall off and stability can be compromised. In an attempt to eliminate these problems, some vendors add processors along with interfaces to make sure the load is shared equally. To assess the effect that added interfaces have on throughput, the lab evaluated the DEC and Bay routers with 6 Ethernet interfaces, and then again with 10 interfaces. (These were the only two routers tested that could handle the higher number of interfaces.)

Configuration was judged to be almost as important as raw throughput. Mixing FDDI with Ethernet or token ring can make internetworking even more difficult than it already is. Several vendors made repeat visits to the lab to tweak their devices, and more than one muttered "It's not supposed to do this" in response to unexpected conditions.

Routers, as in past tests, required extensive configuration and tuning to operate properly. IP and IPX had to be enabled and other protocols had to be disabled for each LAN segment. In the case of Bay's BCN, the changes had to be made on a port-by-port basis. The lab also had to choose a common routing method—in this case, RIP (routing information protocol) rather than OSPF (open shortest path first). Further, IP routing required support for SNAP (subnetwork area protocol), which defines how packets and ARP (address resolution protocol) messages are handled when traveling across an internetwork. Even with all these parameters, the test bed represented a relatively simple internetwork. Complexity grows as more protocols must be accommodated.

The one device supplied with a graphical interface—Bay's BCN— was actually the most difficult to configure. 3Com, which uses command-line interfaces, had remarkably straightforward configuration routines, despite the many options available. Obviously, graphical doesn't always mean great.

FDDI itself adds further complexity for token ring users. The technology accepts transparently bridged traffic—the most common type on Ethernet LANs—without the need for any conversion. But the FDDI spec doesn't spell out how to handle source route bridging (SRB) traffic—the most common type on token rings. Some vendors have simply adopted the source routing transparent (SRT) spec spelled out in IEEE 802.1d; others have come up with proprietary schemes. Some approaches add overhead; many are incompatible. Proteon, for instance, encapsulates SRB traffic in frames that are transparently bridged across an FDDI backbone.

Cost also is an important consideration. FDDI interfaces are still significantly more expensive than their Ethernet or token ring counterparts. And backbone bridges and routers are often among a vendor's most expensive boxes. Most of the bridge/routers evaluated ran $25,000 to $50,000 in their basic configurations.

Madge Networks has a novel low-cost alternative—a high-end PC configured with FDDI and token ring adapters from Madge and routing software from Novell Inc. (Provo, UT). By using off-the-shelf components, Madge can deliver a multiprotocol router for around $14,000—nearly half the price of 3Com's Netbuilder II, the next least expensive product tested. But at this point, the Madge box doesn't offer bridging. When it comes to throughput, the Madge box delivers lower per-port data rates than Proteon's CNX 500 (the only other token ring router tested), especially for IP traffic. Still, Madge's solution may be attractive when cost is a big concern.

Section 4.   The Test Bed

Essentially, the performance part of the test sought to send as much FDDI traffic as possible onto as many attached LAN segments as possible. The test bed comprised three main components: an FDDI ring, the router or bridge under test, and the attached LANs (see Fig. 28.1). Test traffic was sent from a frame generator on the FDDI network to a PC on each of the LAN segments. The lab initially offered 100 percent of FDDI capacity to the bridge or router. Since it didn't expect all the products to be able to work at 100 percent of offered load, the lab also measured throughput at 50 percent, 10 percent, and 5 percent of full capacity.

The lab used a DA-30 analyzer from Wandel & Goltermann Inc. (WG, Research Triangle Park, NC) that ran Version 3.3.4 of WG's FlexmitF software to generate traffic. By generating void frames, FlexmitF makes it possible to throttle back on the number of valid data frames sent to the bridge or router. The test traffic was sent using a "Gatling gun" approach: The first packet was destined for segment 1, the next for segment 2, and so on.

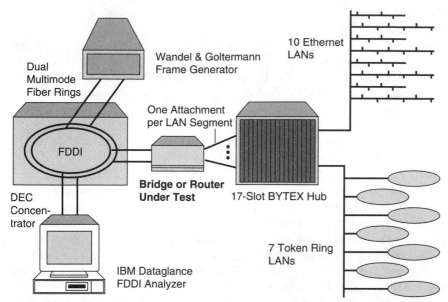

Figure 28.1 The test bed. In order to stress test bridges and routers, the lab linked an FDDI network to multiple Ethernets and token rings. A frame generator on the FDDI network sent traffic at 100 Mbit/s, and a LAN analyzer measured throughput on individual LAN segments.

To decode traffic, the lab used an IBM Dataglance, an FDDI-only analyzer that consists of cards and software that can be added to a high-end PS/2. The Dataglance was employed to verify the contents of test frames, check ring status, monitor FDDI utilization, count packet rates, and measure overall throughput. A concentrator linked the frame generator, FDDI analyzer, and device under test to the FDDI ring. The lab used a DECconcentrator 500 from Digital Equipment Corp. for this purpose.

Because FDDI can carry close to 100 Mbit/s, seven token rings running at 16 Mbit/s and ten Ethernets operating at 10 Mbit/s were attached to the backbone. The theoretical aggregate limits of these segments are 96 Mbit/s and 100 Mbit/s, respectively. One PC was attached to each LAN segment. The token ring PCs used 16-Mbit/s adapter cards from IBM, Madge Networks, and Olicom USA (Plano, TX), while the Ethernet PCs used Etherlink III adapters from 3Com. The lab used a Series 7760 switching hub from Bytex Corp. (Westborough, MA) to link the 17 LAN segments that had been established to the backbone.

Each LAN segment had three attachments: the router or bridge, a PC, and a frame counter that the lab moved from segment to segment. To measure throughput on the Ethernet/token ring side of the test bed, the lab used a Network Advisor from Hewlett-Packard Co.

(HP, Palo Alto, CA), and double-checked its results with a Sniffer analyzer from Network General Corp. (Menlo Park, CA). To simulate three of the most common real-world traffic patterns, throughput tests were conducted using IP and IPX routing and transparent bridging. Support for both IP and IPX was enabled in all the routers tested; bridging was disabled during routing tests to isolate routing performance, and vice versa.

To measure IP throughput from FDDI to Ethernet, the lab attempted to send custom-crafted test packets of 64, 1024, and 1518 bytes from the FDDI network through the router to each LAN segment. For token ring, the lab increased the largest packet size to 4096 bytes—close to FDDI's theoretical maximum of around 4500 bytes. (The lab built these packets from scratch rather than using application traffic. Data consisted of a string of zeros; destination and source address and interframe delay were varied for each test. For the record, the terms *frame* and *packet* refer to the same thing: a discrete amount of data. Bridged traffic is generally referred to in frames, while packets are more common in routing parlance.)

To measure IPX throughput on Ethernet, the lab sent packets of 64 and 512 bytes through each router. For token ring traffic, the maximum packet size was increased to 4096 bytes. Transparent bridging tests used minimum and maximum frame sizes: Ethernet segments received 64- and 1518-byte frames, and token ring segments received 64- and 4096-byte frames.

As indicated, the lab started all throughput tests with 100-Mbit/s offered load on the FDDI side. In some cases, products could not pass traffic under these conditions. Madge's product, for example, would route 4096-byte IP packets only when the FDDI load was throttled back to 10 percent. (In all cases, when an FDDI load of less than 100 percent was used, that has been indicated.) What's more, some products actually worked faster with 50 Mbit/s coming in than with 100 Mbit/s. This isn't surprising, since input overload often degrades performance. For example, Proteon's CNX 500 bridged 64-byte frames 50 percent faster when the FDDI load was throttled back to 50 percent.

Section 5.   Test Results

It's simple to assess the results for IP and IPX routing over Ethernet: Bay and 3Com turned in very similar numbers for IP (see Fig. 28.2). Bay's BCN was always the winner for IPX (see Fig. 28.3). DEC, the only other vendor in the Ethernet IP and IPX routing tests, finished third with all three packet sizes. To ensure a fair comparison, IP routing tests for DEC, 3Com, and Bay were measured with one FDDI and six Ethernet interfaces (six is the maximum number supported by 3Com's Netbuilder II). Because Bay and DEC support 10 Ethernet

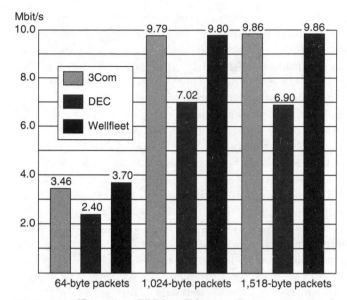

Figure 28.2 IP routing, FDDI to Ethernet. Six segments total, measured on single segment.

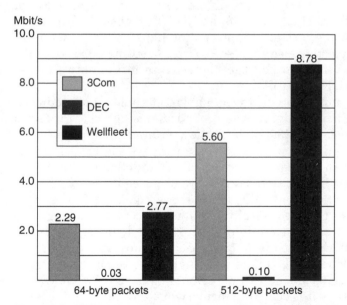

Figure 28.3 IPX routing, FDDI to Ethernet. Six segments total, measured on single segment.

interfaces, the lab also ran the throughput tests with both products equipped with that number of adapters. Bay's throughput was lower with 10 Ethernets attached. IP routing with 64-byte packets fell to 2.18 Mbit/s on each attached LAN—a decline of nearly 60 percent from 3.46 Mbit/s with six Ethernets. Degradation at larger packet sizes was less pronounced with 10 segments: The BCN routed 1024-byte packets at 8.42 Mbit/s on each segment, compared with 9.80 Mbit/s per segment with six segments attached. For 1518-byte packets, performance with 10 segments dropped to 8.96 Mbit/s per segment, compared with 9.86 Mbit/s per segment with six Ethernets.

With 10 Ethernets attached, the DECnis 600 routed 64-byte IP packets at 2.40 Mbit/s (per segment)—the same rate it posted with six segments. Similarly, results for 1024- and 1518-byte packets varied by less than 10 kbit/s. As noted, DEC's software is not optimized for IPX traffic, a shortcoming the vendor plans to remedy. It's easy to see why performance was better with fewer interfaces. With 10 interfaces in place, each port on the bridge/router was offered 10-Mbit/s. When six interfaces were slotted in, each port was offered 15 Mbit/s. In almost every case, performance with six adapters was better: The bridge/routers dropped more frames but they also pushed more frames through.

Ethernet bridging was an easy call: 3Com's Linkbuilder 3GH took the top slot (see Fig. 28.4). With 64-byte frames, the Linkbuilder beat Bay's BCN by more than 1 Mbit/s and the DECnis 600 by more than 2 Mbit/s. With 1518-byte frames, the difference was less extreme: 3Com surpassed Bay by about 100 kbit/s and DEC by about 2 Mbit/s. In token ring IP routing, Proteon topped out at 12.512 Mbit/s when handling 4096-byte packets (see Fig. 28.5). And in routing 4096-byte IPX packets, the CNX 500 clocked the highest rate in the entire test—12.768 Mbit/s (see Fig. 28.6).

As mentioned, not all products were able to handle all offered traffic loads. Token ring bridging was a particular sore spot. Proteon's CNX 500 could not pass 4096-byte frames. Even at the largest frame size the CNX 500 did support—1460-byte frames—the Proteon product was not able to bridge 100 percent of FDDI's offered load. When the lab throttled back FDDI traffic by 50 percent, the CNX 500 bridged 1460-byte frames at 12.240 Mbit/s (see Fig. 28.7). That's more than 75 percent of the theoretical limit of a 16-Mbit/s token ring. The Proteon box had a lot of trouble with 64-byte frames, posting a throughput of 80 kbit/s at full offered load and only 120 kbit/s at 50 percent offered load. Still, this low throughput may not be much to worry about, since such small frames would be used for acknowledgments. Proteon says it is readying memory modules for its token ring interfaces that will remedy its bridging problems.

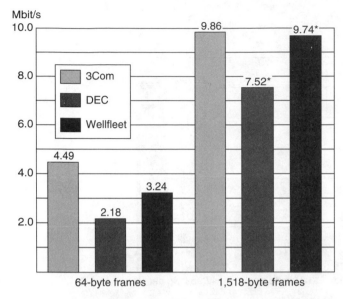

*Tested with 1,517-byte frames, the maximum size supported

Figure 28.4 Transparent bridging, FDDI to Ethernet. Six segments total, measured on single segment.

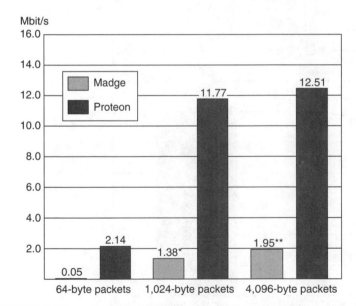

*Offered 48.15 percent of FDDI capacity **Offered 9.85 percent of FDDI capacity

Figure 28.5 IP routing, FDDI to token ring. Five segments maximum, measured on single segment.

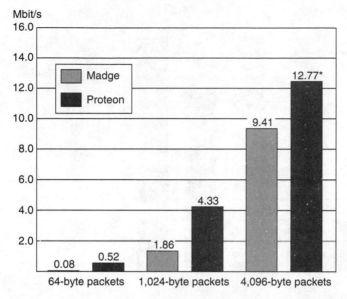

*Offered 47.42 percent of FDDI capacity

Figure 28.6   IPX routing, FDDI to token ring. Five segments maximum, measured on single segment.

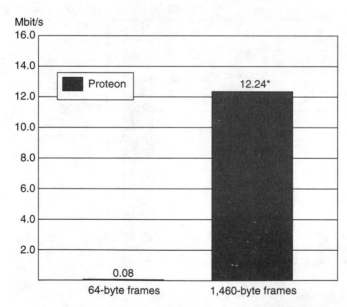

*Offered 50.21 percent of FDDI capacity;
1,460-byte frames were the largest supported

Figure 28.7   Bridging, FDDI to token ring. Five segments maximum, measured on single segment.

29

Analyzing Traffic on Switched LANs

Section 1.   Overview

Ethernet and token ring LAN switches deliver many benefits, but easy traffic measurement isn't one of them. Network managers may be attracted by the switches' high throughput, low latency, and virtual LAN capabilities—but an unfortunate side effect of switches is that they cause net managers to literally lose sight of the traffic flowing through their networks.

The need to analyze switched traffic flow is important on shared-media LANs, but critical on switched networks. Ironically, one of switching's main benefits—fast point-to-point connections—is a major hindrance when it comes to analyzing traffic. The problem is this. In LANs today, a segment consists of multiple end stations and a bridge or router, all attached to a hub. On any one segment, all devices share access to the cabling, so an external analyzer or RMON probe attached to the hub will see all traffic on that segment. Switches, on the other hand, send traffic from one port directly to another. If only one end station is attached to a switch port, there's no place to plug in an external analyzer.

Faced with this problem, many LAN switch vendors have come up with a simple solution—omit traffic analysis facilities from their products altogether. As a result, many corporations are deploying LAN switches now, but leaving figuring out how to add traffic analy-

---

This chapter first appeared as an article in *Data Communications* magazine, and was written by David Newman, director of the *Data Communications* test program.

sis until later. That could turn into a big mistake. Easy access to traffic analysis data is critical to net managers with switched networks, who need a clear picture of traffic flow in order to optimize network performance. For instance, managers can use traffic analysis information to reallocate nodes on several different switch segments that need to communicate to the same switch port—thus reducing the possibility that the switch itself will become a bandwidth bottleneck.

Section 2.   Analysis Trailblazers

Not all switch vendors are ignoring the need for analysis. Some have now developed solutions. The most common of these is putting a special "monitor port" on the switch, capable of copying or redirecting switch traffic to an external analyzer or RMON probe. Another scenario involves embedding traffic measurement capabilities directly into the switch. Vendors of token ring and FDDI switches also can gather some statistics from the management capabilities built into those topologies. Yet another approach is to use statistics garnered from SNMP agents embedded on each port.

All these workarounds have significant drawbacks. The approach that holds by far the most promise for net managers is the plan by some vendors to embed SNMP's RMON agents into their switches. The RMON MIB was first developed back in 1992 for use on shared media LANs. RMON is specifically designed to deliver in-depth traffic analysis. Some switch vendors are also participating in the development of RMON 2; a new version of the standard that will provide greater scalability than existing models.

Section 3.   The Problems

The switched model poses three challenges for today's standalone RMON agents. First, additional RMON agents will be needed as work group switches deliver one of their main benefits—adding segments to relieve congested networks. In other words, one RMON agent will be needed for each segment that's added. With standalone RMON products running roughly $2500 to $5000 per managed segment, the increased cost can be staggering. Further, each new RMON agent collects more data to be sent to a central RMON management application, adding to the network traffic load.

Second, increasing the number of network segments means increasing the number of RMON agents reporting to a management station. Thus, network management systems will need a way to synthesize data from large numbers of agents. The RMON working group of the Internet Engineering Task Force (IETF) is studying ways of reducing the amount of data to be correlated in its forthcoming RMON 2 specification, but has no plans to impose a specific design on vendors of network management systems.

Finally, some switches allow the creation of virtual LANs—logical segments that span multiple physical segments and even multiple physical switches. In virtual LAN environments, the number of segments not only increases but also becomes more fluid. As physical nodes are moved, added to, or deleted from a logical segment, the RMON system tracking traffic patterns must also change.

Section 4. The Missing RMON

To date, few switch vendors have risen to the challenge of building RMON into their switches. Further, the sophistication and usefulness of the RMON implementations from switch vendors that have gone the extra mile in adding RMON to their products vary widely.

The RMON standard defines 10 groups. They include:

- Analysis of network utilization, including data and error statistics
- Historical information for network trend and statistical analysis
- Matrix information describing communications between nodes and the quantity of data exchanged
- Packet traps to provide network alarms
- Packet capture for network traffic decoding and analysis
- Source data to support network accounting/billing applications

All the RMON groups can be useful in designing and tuning a switched network. So it's unfortunate that net managers who buy a switch because its vendor claims to support RMON often end up without some—or even most—of the RMON groups.

The issue is that RMON is extremely power-hungry. In order to conserve CPU processor cycles, many switch vendors are implementing "hobbled" or restricted implementations of RMON standard. The power problem is most acute in uniprocessor LAN switches (which use a single CPU both to switch traffic and to perform management duties). With these products, the simple act of switching on the management facilities can drop packet per second (pps) processing rates through the floor.

Performance problems are bad enough with simple SNMP MIB II agents. Retix (Santa Monica, CA) says that the speed of its eight-port Ethernet switch, which is equipped with a single Intel i960 CPU, may drop by 25 percent when SNMP is activated. However, the demands of running SNMP are as a light buffet to those of running RMON, which quite simply devours CPU cycles. Cabletron Systems Inc. (Rochester, NH) says that accessing basic SNMP stats has no appreciable effect on the performance of the monoprocessor switch modules which it sells for its MMAC hub, because it has built an elementary level of SNMP support into the Ethernet controller on each port. But trying to use all nine Ethernet RMON groups to monitor the traffic on each switch port reduces pps performance by over 50 percent—a fact that Cabletron has been understandably reticent in advertising.

Most vendors with RMON in their switches take either one or two approaches to conserving power. The first is to omit support for some of the RMON groups. (Ironically, the matrix group—which is particularly handy because it delivers an "at a glance" summary of traffic flow between all switch ports—is often the first to go.) The second approach to conserving performance is to limit the number of ports which can be monitored simultaneously, typically to only one. This leaves the onus on the net manager to collate traffic statistics from multiple ports and make sense of it—a time-consuming and inefficient task. Some vendors offer the net manager a choice between the two tradeoffs. With the Catalyst switch from Cisco Systems Inc. (San Jose, CA), the net manager can elect to listen to all ports simultaneously with either one or two RMON groups; or the manager can choose to hone in on one port and apply all nine groups at once.

UB Networks Inc. (Santa Clara, CA) worked with Epilogue Technology Corp. (Albuquerque, NM), a developer of RMON and SNMP source code, to create a distributed management architecture called Access/Empower. The new architecture streamlines management of many UB products, essentially by lightening the load of agents at each port and handing up some tasks for processing by a management application. UB says customers can use Access/Empower to manage its AccessOne and Georim switches. Epilogue also is working with switch maker Optical Data Systems Inc. (ODS, Richardson, TX), which was one of the first vendors to embed RMON agents in its switching hubs.

The bottom line for net managers thinking about investing in a switch with RMON inside is to first check if the RMON agent shares a CPU with the switch itself. If so, it's best to road-test first to see what sort of performance hit is involved. Also, find out which RMON groups are available, and check that they can be applied to more than one port simultaneously.

In an effort to improve their RMON implementations, several switch makers have forged partnerships with analyzer and RMON vendors to address these problems. For example, Bay Networks Inc. (Santa Clara, CA) is working with Network General Corp. (Menlo Park, CA), the leading vendor of LAN analyzers, to embed analysis capabilities into its forthcoming 28000 Ethernet/fast Ethernet switch.

Section 5.   What RMON Does

A major difference between RMON and monitor ports is that RMON selectively captures only a limited amount of the most important information from all ports—a process referred to by RMON vendors as *light monitoring*. The key statistics gathered are port status, segment utilization, protocol distribution, number of broadcasts, and, in Ethernet environments, collisions.

RMON covers these stats both on a per-port basis and on a per-conversation basis, allowing managers to see whether bandwidth is being efficiently allocated. For example, per-port statistics might indicate that a server attached to one switch port sends 1 million packets to that port; but per-conversation reporting might reveal that 900,000 of those packets are destined for a client located across a WAN link. In this case, per-conversation reporting provides strong evidence that the server should be relocated to lessen network traffic. The original RMON standard handled the per-conversation requirement, and RMON 2 added two other statistics—segment utilization and protocol distribution—to the mix.

Section 6.   The Right Stuff

Switch makers and RMON vendors are in broad agreement over what RMON should accomplish in a switched network, but they are still split over how best to implement it. The move to switched environments raises a new challenge: building affordable, scalable RMON agents. Some vendors reckon that embedding full-blown RMON agents on every port is expensive and CPU-intensive. They suggest that rather than putting a "monolithic" RMON agent on every port, it makes more sense to embed a limited-function subagent at each port and then have processing occur at a central entity. This is the approach taken in UB's Access Empower distributed management product.

But some observers say another switching trend—the move away from CPUs and toward ASICs (application-specific integrated circuits)— will increasingly lead to faster, cheaper RMON agents on every port, without consuming additional CPU cycles or rearchitecting the RMON framework. Applied Network Technology Inc. (ANT, Westford, MA) uses ASICs to support nine groups of RMON on every port of its switch, which costs only $320 per port (see Fig. 29.1).

Section 7.   A Port with a View

As an alternative to RMON, some switch vendors give users a detailed view of their traffic by adding a special port for protocol analyzers. This port goes by several names. Alantec says its Powerhub

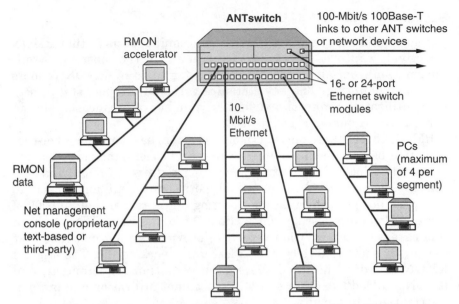

Figure 29.1 Switching views. ANT's LAN switch can be fitted with an RMON accelerator that gives net managers in-depth information on traffic flow to and from each switch port.

was the first switching hub with a "port monitoring" capability. Analyzer maker Wandel & Goltermann Technologies Inc. (WG, Research Triangle Park, NC) has proposed that all switch vendors equip their devices with a universal test access port (UTAP). And Cisco Systems Inc. (San Jose, CA) offers switched port analyzer (SPAN) capability as an option for its Catalyst switch.

Whatever the name, the basic idea is the same—the special port observes traffic as it flows through the switch. Other vendors of work group switches with monitor ports include 3Com Corp. (Santa Clara, CA) and Grand Junction Networks Inc. (Fremont, CA). In total, however, only about a dozen vendors now offer monitor ports, while the total number of switch makers is over 100.

Not all monitor ports are created equal, however. One distinguishing feature is the number of segments that a monitor port can measure. A view of one segment's traffic is imperative in troubleshooting, but it doesn't answer the larger question of how much traffic the switch can handle on all ports before it becomes saturated. For that, a view of all segments is needed—and only a very few vendors' monitor ports can handle that.

Essentially, looking at one segment at a time is fundamentally flawed, since it doesn't measure the total amount of traffic flowing through the switch. Alantec's Powerhub switch uses a shared-memory architecture that can forward traffic from all segments (or a user-defined subset of all segments) to the monitor port. While a view of all segments' statistics is important, not everyone agrees that the monitor port is the right way to gather them. Shunting many segments' traffic to a single monitor port can cause the monitor port itself to become an I/O bottleneck. The problem is that sending many ports' traffic to one port will eventually cause that port to drop packets. The problem is especially severe in larger switches.

Even on a more limited scale, monitor ports will run out of gas when capturing traffic from all ports. For example, in the case of the Etherswitch EPS2015 RS from Kalpana Inc. (Sunnyvale, CA), monitoring all 15 ports under congested conditions would cause traffic to flow to a monitor port at nearly 100 Mbit/s—or almost 10 times the port's rated capacity. For this reason, Kalpana recommends against using the monitor port for full-time capture from all ports.

Section 8.   Built-In Help

Some vendors say their switches can gather global statistics without relying on monitoring ports. These vendors' switches get their traffic measurement data from one of two sources: from the management capabilities built in to the token ring and FDDI topologies, or from embedded SNMP agents on each switch port.

As noted, token ring and FDDI both keep basic traffic statistics, such as the number of stations, frames, and errors on the ring. These statistics can be handed to a switch management application that keep tabs on traffic on all ports. That's exactly the approach taken by token ring switch maker Centillion Networks Inc. (Mountain View, CA). Centillion's Speed Switch 100 uses token ring's built-in reporting capabilities to track active stations, ring errors, and configuration parameters.

The Speed Switch 100's management application reports more data than IBM's LAN network manager (LNM), the application commonly used to manage bridged token ring networks. LNM reports only very basic statistics—such as the number of broadcast and nonbroadcast frames on a ring—even though the IEEE's 802.5 specification allows for considerably more detailed reporting. Centillion says its customers will need more comprehensive reporting in the future, and expects customer demand for RMON to increase over time.

Another low-key traffic reporting approach is to use the SNMP agents built into most switches. An SNMP agent or MIB (management information base) does report very basic information, such as number of packets coming in or out of a device. It does not, however, supply more detailed information about broadcasts, multicasts, errors, and so forth. For that, SNMP's RMON application is needed.

Cabling and High-Speed LANs

Looked at simplistically, there are three basic ingredients to a high-speed LAN: hardware (hubs, switches, adapters); software (network operating systems, drivers, applications); and the cabling scheme (comprising cabling as well as connecting equipment). Whichever way you look at it, cabling tends to get less attention from network press and consultants than the other two network components. That's unfortunate, given that choosing the right cabling scheme is just as critical a part of making the transition to high-speed networking as picking which type of high-speed network to support, or which company's hardware to support it with.

Choosing cabling (and associated connecting equipment such as faceplates, connectors, and patch panels) is getting harder— for two reasons. First, network managers have more types of cabling to choose from, available from more manufacturers, than ever before. Second, and more important, as networks migrate to faster speeds, the demands which are placed on the cabling scheme are becoming greater—as are the chances that problems will occur. Specifically, data's susceptibility to electromagnetic interference (EMI) and near-end crosstalk (Next) increases in proportion to its bit rate. Consequently, cabling which worked just fine at 10 Mbit/s or 16 Mbit/s can be completely unsuitable for service at speeds of 100 Mbit/s or more.

As more and more companies move their LANs to higher speeds, horror stories about cabling catastrophes are emerging. For instance, cabling problems were responsible for a high-speed LAN at a manufacturing plant in Texas being closed down by the Federal Communications Commission (FCC) in 1994. The reason? The plant was situated underneath the flight path into

Dallas International Airport, and the levels of electromagnetic radiation from its cabling scheme were so high that they were interfering with control tower instructions to incoming aircraft.

For most network managers, the penalty for picking the wrong type of cabling will not be so drastic. Nevertheless, a poor choice now will mean a costly refit later down the road. Fortunately, the last couple of years have also seen several significant advances in cabling technology, designed to enable the construction of affordable high-performance cabling schemes.

One example is the development of a new breed of high-performance unshielded twisted-pair (UTP) cabling called Category 5 UTP (also known as data-grade UTP). With Category 5, the copper pairs are twisted tighter to enhance their ability to carry data. Another example is the development of labor-saving techniques that dramatically cut the cost of installing fiber to the desktop, making it an economical alternative to copper cable for the first time. Still another breakthrough has been the creation of a standard—called EIA/TIA-568—defining how high-performance cabling should be installed, and the performance parameters it should meet. EIA/TIA-568 (and its successor, TIA/EIA-568A) provides net managers with a blueprint which they can use to design a high-speed cabling scheme. It enables cable installers to guarantee their work. And it allows cable and connector manufacturers to warranty their products.

The following chapters deal with four different aspects of high-speed cabling:

- Chap. 30 provides an introduction to the technology, including the types of cabling and connectors available, cable management packages, and training.

- Chap. 31 details how to avoid problems when installing Category 5 UTP.

- Chap. 32 discusses the falling price of fiber cabling.

- Chap. 33 deals with standards relating to high-speed cabling.

30

High-Speed Cabling: The Basics

Section 1. Overview

Selecting a LAN cabling type to run to the desktop used to be a confusing business. Network managers had to decide among a variety of different designs, each with its own advantages and disadvantages. These days, however, there's an almost automatic first choice when it's time to recable—a breed of high-performance unshielded twisted-pair (UTP) cabling that's commonly called Category 5 UTP. About 40 percent of U.S. users have switched to Category 5 UTP since its debut, according to recent surveys.

Category 5 UTP comprises four copper pairs twisted together and protected by a thin polyvinyl chloride (PVC) jacket. Its popularity is largely attributable to its status as the lowest-cost, easiest-to-install cable designed to carry high-speed data. (User acceptance of Category 5 UTP also has been encouraged in the last couple of years by endorsement from IBM, which traditionally has been by far the biggest vendor of shielded twisted-pair (STP) wiring. Big Blue launched its first wiring scheme incorporating a Category 5 UTP in 1993.)

Exactly how fast Category 5 can carry data is a matter that is being hotly debated. The challenge for manufacturers is that cables must support data without exceeding the U.S. recommendations on electromagnetic radiation defined by the Federal Communications Commission (FCC). Category 5 was first developed with an eye to carrying 100-Mbit/s FDDI data in about 1991 (when it was known as data-grade UTP). Since then, there have been huge advancements in the data signaling and encoding schemes which adapters, hubs, and switches use to drive data over the line. The first ATM adapters which use Category 5 cable to carry data at 155 Mbit/s are already shipping. Some vendors foresee a time when speeds in excess of 300 Mbit/s may be possible.

Advances in signaling are also causing some observers to question the need to upgrade to Category 5 UTP in order to support high-speed LANs at all. In 1994, the first ATM adapters and switches started shipping, pushing the envelope on Category 3 cable throughput to a mighty 155 Mbit/s. The products incorporate a specialized cable transceiver from Tut Systems (Pleasant Hill, CA).

Section 2. Alternative Cable Types

There are five main alternatives to Category 5 cabling (see Table 30.1).

- *Category 3 UTP.* Like Category 5 UTP, this cable comprises four copper pairs protected by a thin PVC jacket. However, the pairs are not twisted together as tightly as with Category 5 UTP. Traditionally, this factor has limited the data rates supported over Category 3 UTP to 10 Mbit/s. Now some vendors are pressing it into service at far higher speeds.

TABLE 30.1   Cable Basics

Cable type	Description	Maximum speed currently supported
Category 3 unshielded twisted pair (UTP)	100-ohm cable comprising four copper pairs twisted together and protected by a thin polyvinyl chloride (PVC) jacket	155 Mbit/s
Category 4 UTP	100-ohm cable comprising four copper pairs twisted together and protected by a thin PVC jacket	155 Mbit/s
Category 5 UTP	100-ohm cable comprising four copper pairs twisted together and protected by a thin PVC jacket	155 Mbit/s
Shielded twisted pair (STP)	150-ohm cable comprising two copper pairs individually wrapped in metal shielding then sheathed in an additional braided metal shield and a PVC outer jacket	155 Mbit/s
Coaxial	50-ohm cable comprising a single copper core wrapped in polyurethane insulation and sheathed by braided copper wire and a PVC jacket	155 Mbit/s
Fiber	Single strand of 62.5- or 125-micron optical fiber protected by a PVC jacket	All foreseeable LAN speeds

- *Category 4 UTP.* This cable has the same basic construction as Category 3 but—as with Category 5—the copper pairs are twisted somewhat tighter to enhance its ability to carry data. Category 4 UTP was originally intended for use on 16-Mbit/s token ring LANs. Again, some vendors are now claiming that far higher speeds are possible over Category 4 UTP.

- *Shielded twisted pair (STP.)* This cable comprises two copper pairs, individually wrapped in metal shielding and then sheathed together in a braided metal shield covered by a PVC outer jacket. STP's proponents boast that it has the same—or better—data-carrying properties as Category 5 UTP.

- *Coaxial cable.* Coaxial cable comprises a single copper core, insulated in polyurethane, and then sheathed by braided copper wire and a PVC jacket.

- *62.5- or 125-micron optical fiber cable.* This cable comprises a single fiber strand in a PVC jacket; multimode fiber is capable for all foreseeable LAN speeds.

Recently, two other cable types have started to make small inroads into the U.S. market. The first is screened twisted pair (ScTP), or foil twisted pair (FTP); this cable is a hybrid of STP and UTP, comprising unshielded twisted pairs protected by an aluminum ribbon that is wound around the inside of the cable. Supporters reckon that ScTP can carry data as fast as or faster than Category 5, and claim that the additional shield adds only about 20 percent to the cable's cost. Endorsement by France Télécom and Groupe Bull S.A. (Paris) has already given screened cable a large share of the French cabling market, but until recently it has remained relatively unknown in North America.

The second new cabling scheme is a high-performance plastic fiber cable that costs about the same as Category 5 UTP. This plastic fiber, called GIPOF (graded-index plastic optical fiber), is now being sold by Boston Optical Fiber Inc. (Marlborough, MA). GIPOF cabling reduces the signal loss that characterized earlier plastic fiber offerings, Boston Optical says. The vendor claims that its GIPOF cable can transmit 100-Mbit/s FDDI data for 150 meters. That's 100 meters more than earlier plastic fiber and 50 meters more than Category 5 UTP, although far less than the 2-kilometer distance supported by multimode glass optical fiber. As well as being cheaper than glass, plastic fiber is easier to install because it's more flexible. It also shares glass fiber's immunity to EMI.

Although the cost of plastic and glass fiber cabling schemes is now low enough to compete against copper, prices for the adapters, hubs, and other network hardware needed for fiber cabling remain steep. For instance, the 4322-1 10Base-FL fiber PC adapter from Lancast Inc. (Amherst, NH) costs $250. 10Base-T adapters for copper cable can now be had for around $60.

Section 3.   Ease of Installation

Of course, maximum data capacity is not the only criterion to consider when choosing a high-speed cable. Net managers also need to consider how easily the cable can be installed. For example, Category 3, 4, and 5 UTP (and ScTP) cables are terminated using a simple RJ-45 connector, which can be fitted in about a minute. In contrast, STP usually is fitted with IBM's proprietary connector, which takes five times longer to hook up, according to Thomas & Betts Corp. (Bridgewater, NJ), a premises wiring vendor. Installing fiber is a whole different ball game. (The subject is dealt with in Chap. 32, "The Fiber Alternative.")

UTP also is much thinner than STP—about 5 millimeters thick versus 11 millimeters. As a result, it is easier to install and takes up less room in ducts. (ScTP is slightly thicker.) But there's a flip side to UTP's advantages in installation: The cabling is also more susceptible to electromagnetic interference than STP. Consequently, UTP must be installed away from equipment such as photocopiers, elevators, generators, and even fluorescent lighting. ScTP vendors reckon that its foil screen makes it less susceptible to interference—a claim that Category 5's supporters say is specious. All these cables are designed primarily to run horizontally over each floor of a site. For connecting different floors within the same building, or different buildings at the same site, fiber is still the most popular cabling medium.

Regardless of who does the installing, most of today's networks are fitted in star or multistar topologies, in which cables run between PCs and a wiring hub or hubs. This approach allows cable management to be centralized. Another benefit is that hubs add redundancy by isolating failures on individual PC connections, thus minimizing the threat of network crashes.

Section 4.   Choosing an Installer

The four most common wiring schemes in North America are the Systimax Premises Distribution System (PDS) from AT&T (New York), Open DECconnect from Digital Equipment Corp. (DEC, Maynard, MA), the IBM Cabling System from IBM Corp. (Armonk, NY), and the Insulated Building Distribution Network (IBDN) from Northern Telecom Ltd. (Mississauga, Ontario).

But net managers who choose not to use one of the major cable companies to install their scheme should gauge the expertise of smaller companies carefully—for example, by checking out references. A second approach is to ask for certificates showing that the installer's technicians have been independently trained and tested. Several cabling vendors, including Mod-Tap, have recently started running certified installer programs. Another certificate to ask for is the Registered Communication Distribution Designer (RCDD), which is awarded by the Building Industry Consulting Service International Inc. (BICSI, Tampa, FL), an industry association for cable installers. Cable technicians must prove that they have a minimum of 2 years' experience before they can even take the RCDD exam, and it has a 65 percent failure rate.

Avoiding Category 5 Cable Catastrophes

Section 1.   Overview

Over the past year or so, some network managers who've dutifully followed the advice of experts and installed Category 5 unshielded twisted pair (UTP) as part of the transition to high-speed networking have come in for a rude surprise: Many of those Category 5 cabling runs have turned out not to be up to the job of handling speeds of 100 Mbit/s or more.

As companies start to deploy high-speed LANs—such as 100-Mbit/s FDDI and 100Base-T—over Category 5 wiring, they are running into problems caused mainly by excessive levels of electromagnetic interference (EMI) and near-end crosstalk (Next). Such performance problems usually aren't evident at lower LAN speeds, such as 10-Mbit/s Ethernet and 16-Mbit/s token ring, because data is less susceptible to EMI and Next at lower rates.

Cabling consultants estimate that 20 percent of all Category 5 cabling runs now installed may be unsuitable for carrying high-speed traffic—news that's especially troubling for network planners who've spent millions of dollars over the past couple of years on new installations. That's a pretty big group: Category 5 UTP now accounts for about 40 percent of all cable installed in the United States. To add to the angst, the networking rumor mill has been busy cranking out a host of reasons—many of them unfounded—for Category 5's problems. Meanwhile, some vendors of Category 5 UTP have flatly denied the existence of any performance glitches—a kind of stonewalling that isn't helping to ease the fear, uncertainty, and doubt in users' minds.

If all this wasn't bad enough, the stocks of Category 5 cabling themselves have started to run dry—a result of a shortage of the fluoropolymer resin used to insulate the copper pairs within Category 5 cabling. The shortage is delaying deliveries and driving prices through the roof. Net managers are now paying anything from $300 to $400 per 1000 feet of Category 5 UTP—as much as double what they were paying in 1994.

Section 2.   A Reality Check

On closer examination it turns out that, although the Category 5 performance problem is potentially widespread, in most cases it probably is correctable. The good news is that there's nothing inherently wrong with Category 5 cabling. In fact, some early reports of Category 5 performance woes have proved to be groundless. In some cases, early handheld testers built to diagnose faults in Category 5 cabling turned out to be buggy themselves. Poorly developed software drivers running on first-generation 100-Mbit/s FDDI-over-copper adapters also caused mediocre performance—a snafu that has since been corrected.

Most of the trouble found so far can be traced to the way cabling has been installed and connected. A substantial number of companies are experiencing problems caused by contractors that pulled Category 5 cable using improper installation techniques. In other cases, poorly designed cable connectors are at fault. Both instances lead to unacceptably high levels of EMI and Next.

The good news is that net managers who have installed their Category 5 cabling properly, and terminated it using independently certified connectors, can rest assured that their schemes will carry data at 100 Mbit/s just fine. And even those who have been the victim of poorly made connectors or bogus workmanship can take some comfort from the fact that they aren't faced with the prospect of having to tear out entire cabling schemes and start again from scratch. With some additional work—either in reterminating cabling or in retrofitting new connector components—high-speed networking is still within reach.

Justified or not, concerns about Category 5 cabling are already forcing a redefinition of the premises wiring market. The twin scares about Category 5's reliability and its availability have weakened its standing as a low-cost option for high-speed networking, motivating users to consider more expensive but supposedly less problematic alternatives—such as screened twisted pair (ScTP), shielded twisted pair (STP), and fiber. However, it's important to keep the shift to new cables in proportion. Despite setbacks, Category 5 remains by far the most popular cabling medium with net managers, most of whom say they are still confidant in its capabilities (see Fig. 31.1).

Question: Do you think your current cable can meet the demands of high-speed networking in terms of . . . .

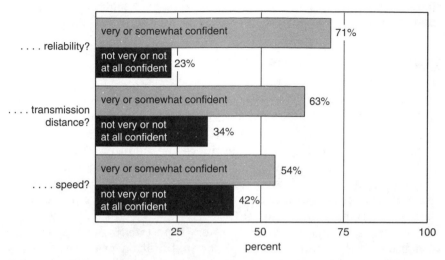

Figure 31.1 Still number 1 with net managers. Despite the negative publicity surrounding Category 5 UTP of late, a survey of 50 *Fortune* 1000 companies (32 in New York and 18 in London) shows that the majority are confident that their current copper cabling system will meet the demands of high-speed networking. 48 percent of respondents run Category 5 UTP; 13 percent use Category 3. One company is using Category 4. The other 16 percent run either shielded or screen twisted pair. (*Source: ITT Datacomm, Santa Ana, CA.*)

Category 5 schemes that have fallen victim to second-rate installation techniques often will not exhibit noticeably degraded performance when used at lower speeds. However, data's susceptibility to EMI and Next increases in proportion to its bit rate. That's why trouble with Category 5 started to surface only recently, as companies began to use their schemes for 100-Mbit/s FDDI-over-copper and IEEE 802.3 100Base-T fast Ethernet networks. As more and more net managers make the move to higher-speed networking, Category 5 performance will become an even greater issue. And problems are likely to intensify once cable and equipment vendors increasingly start to push the envelope on copper performance by using it for even higher speeds, such as 155-Mbit/s ATM.

Category 5 UTP owes much of its popularity to a reputation for being the cheapest way to ready buildings for high-speed data. As well as being less costly than optical fiber, it's cheaper than STP and ScTP. (ScTP, already popular in parts of Europe, recently has started to make inroads into North America, although right now only a handful of vendors offer it.) Put simply, Category 5 UTP costs less because there's less to it. UTP comprises four copper pairs, twisted together and protected by a thin polyvinyl chloride (PVC) jacket. In contrast, ScTP uses four copper pairs wrapped in a foil shield covered in PVC. STP is even more complex: two copper pairs individually wrapped in metal shielding and then sheathed in a braided metal shield covered by a PVC jacket.

Section 3.   Installation Procedures

While less means more when it comes to keeping cable costs down, it also means that greater care must be taken when cabling is installed. ScTP and STP use the additional protection of metal shielding to prevent electromagnetic radiation (from equipment such as elevator motors, air-conditioning units, and fluorescent lighting) from interfering with the electrical signal on the cable. The same shield also serves to keep the intensity of the electromagnetic emissions generated by the cabling to within the guidelines defined by the Federal Communications Commission (FCC).

In contrast, Category 5 UTP uses very tight twisting of copper pairs to achieve the same objectives. Poor installation practices quickly reduce its immunity to electromagnetic radiation from outside sources, while increasing the level of radiation it gives off. Category 5 cabling also is more dependent on the components built into high-speed network adapters to reduce emissions by filtering and balancing the data signal. Ensuring that Category 5 cabling works according to spec and meets FCC regulations means adhering precisely to the installation procedures set out in the Electronics Industries Association/Telecommunications Industries Association (EIA/TIA) 568A premises wiring standard.

For many Category 5 installations, here's where the trouble starts: It turns out that the work undertaken by installers at many sites around the country falls way short of the mark. Users and consultants with firsthand knowledge of Category 5 cabling problems cite three mistakes most commonly made by cable installers: (1) excessive untwisting of copper pairs prior to insertion into punchdown blocks (the maximum amount of untwisting permitted with Category 5 cabling is 13 millimeters, or about half an inch); (2) failure to adhere to the maximum bend radiuses defined for Category 5 cables (bend radiuses should not be less than four times the diameter of the cable); and (3) overcinching of cable bundles with cable ties. Any one of these slipups can result in excess EMI and increased levels of Next—both of which spell trouble for high-speed transmissions. The net result is reduced signal strength and increased noise, manifested as more errored packets on the network. Depending on how many cable runs are affected, these traits will cause one of two symptoms: poor performance or complete network failure.

Cabling consultants estimate that 20 percent of the Category 5 cable runs now in place have problems. One way to spot them is through a visual inspection. Consultants recommend that net managers make sure to test a sample of the work done by every member of the installation team, since each person's work has a very distinct signature. If you get a bad installer, all that person's work will be bad.

For some companies, a 20 percent failure rate would be welcomed. Equippable Real Estate Investment Management Inc. (New York) estimates that none of the Category 5 it wired in an 18-month period between 1993 and 1994 will work when it moves to high-speed networking. Equippable's problem is that its Category 5 cables have been stripped back and unraveled beyond the regulation 13 millimeters. Other users also cite such installation difficulties. Equippable's solution to the problem has been to switch to ScTP cabling.

Section 4. Repairing Problems

The job of correcting installation snafus can range from an inconvenient chore to an expensive reclamation project, depending on how badly the installation has been botched. The average labor charge for copper cable installation is $45 per hour for each worker (although that figure can skyrocket depending on such factors as location and union rates). Reterminating each cable for insertion in a punchdown block takes about 3 minutes ($2.25 labor charge). Mounting a new patch panel in a wiring closet takes about 1.5 hours ($67.50 labor charge). Adjusting cables to meet maximum bend radius restrictions can be even pricier, particularly if the cables are lying in an inaccessible part of the cabling plant. If required, the cost of new connecting hardware pushes the repair bill even higher. Category 5 patch panels cost an average of $8 per port, according to Anixter Inc. (Skokie, IL), a manufacturer of cable and connectors. Category 5 wall outlets cost $11 each, Anixter says. Further, companies must factor in the expense of network downtime caused by outages while problems are located and rectified.

Avoiding problems with EMI and Next means making certain that cable installers have retrained their work force with the skill set required to handle Category 5 cable and connectors. This is especially important, given that many of the practices forbidden on Category 5 schemes—including excessive untwisting, bending, and cinching— come as second nature to technicians used to installing cabling for voice traffic or for Ethernet or token ring data. Experts suggest that one approach to weeding out slipshod cabling installers is to quiz the installer's work force on its knowledge of Category 5 installation techniques. The State of Texas Mental Health and Mental Retardation

Board (Austin) tests every worker with a handout sheet, and reports that about four out of five fail the test and have to be retrained.

Section 5.   Correct Components

Getting the right installer is only part of ensuring that a Category 5 scheme works at triple-digit LAN speeds. Users also need to make sure that their cabling and connectors are designed and manufactured to meet the performance specifications defined in EIA/TIA 568 and TIA/EIA 568A.

Finding good cabling is the easy part. Nearly 50 vendors now offer cabling verified as Category 5-compliant by either ETL Testing Laboratories Inc. (Cortland, NY) or Underwriters Laboratories Inc. (UL, Northbrook, IL). Additionally, nearly a dozen companies now sell "enhanced" Category 5 UTP cables that can handle frequencies higher than 100 MHz. They include Belden Wire & Cable (Richmond, IN), Berk-Tek Inc. (New Holland, PA), Comm/Scope Inc. (Hickory, NC), Helix/Hitemp (Franklin, MA), and Hitachi Cable (Manchester, NH). The premium cables typically are proofed to 350 MHz and cost from 20 to 30 percent more than 100-MHz Category 5 offerings.

These enhanced products are designed to ensure premium performance for high-speed data. Vendors use a variety of different manufacturing techniques to improve the enhanced cable's attenuation, impedance, and crosstalk characteristics. For instance, the wires forming each copper pair within Belden's Datatwist 350 cable are actually bonded together, rather than just being intertwined. As well as improving impedance characteristics, this technique prevents installers from excessively untwisting the copper pairs prior to insertion into punchdown blocks. Manufacturing Category 5 cable, and even enhanced Cat 5, isn't all that difficult. Conversely, manufacturing Category 5 connecting equipment—such as jacks, punchdown blocks, and wall plates—is a much greater challenge. With cabling it is possible to use the twisting of the copper pairs to cancel out crosstalk, but connectors actually aggravate the problem. The crosstalk problem stems from the way UTP pairs are untwisted and assigned to the eight pins in RJ-45 cable connectors. The first and eighth pairs run alongside each other for about three-quarters of an inch within the connector. That's enough to cause significant "bleeding" of data signals (crosstalk) between the two.

Connector vendors use one of two techniques to compensate for this problem. The first is to add capacitors to compensate for signal imbalances. The second is to add a printed circuit board to ensure that data travels over the first and eighth pairs in opposite directions.

The difficulty of producing Category 5-compliant connectors is reflected in the fact that only 15 vendors have succeeded in having their products independently verified. According to Microtest Inc. (Phoenix), a manufacturer of cable testers, the performance of any Category 5 cable will still exceed that of the best, most expensive Category 5 connector. Tests conducted by Microtest of 10 name-brand connectors being sold as Category 5-compliant showed that four failed to meet EIA/TIA 568 performance specs, and some of the others were borderline, it says. Plainly, net managers who choose not to buy an independently certified connector must shop carefully.

Cable consultants suggest a few rules. First, avoid economizing on connector costs. Second, check what the connector is made of (consultants recommend buying connectors with fewer than 50 microns of gold content). Third, insist on a warranty.

Section 6. Cable Warranties

Warranties are one of the strong points of the cabling schemes sold by the four foremost suppliers of turnkey cabling systems—AT&T, Digital Equipment Corp., IBM, and Northern Telecom Ltd. (Mississauga, Ontario). Because these companies not only supply the cable and connectors but also install them—using either their own staff or approved outfits—they can guarantee their schemes end to end. Net managers who buy cabling from one company and connectors from a second, and then install them using a third-party contractor may have a much harder time getting satisfaction if something goes wrong. First, they have to establish which supplier is at fault; then they must prove their case to that supplier. Finger-pointing and quibbling can be expected.

Category 5's problems have not gone unnoticed by the big four. The EIA/TIA 568A standard was intended to open the cabling market to competition by allowing small companies to guarantee the performance of their products. Now that some users are having difficulties working with or finding Category 5, the four major suppliers are again pitching the notion that the only way to guarantee that a cabling scheme works right the first time is to let one vendor handle the entire process.

Section 7. Handheld Testers

While the warranties available from big companies may be tempting, blindly buying from a major supplier is not in itself a guarantee of getting the best price, cable, connectors, or installation work available. Regardless of how well net managers pick their wiring, connectors, and installers, the best-laid cable schemes can still go awry.

When problems do occur, tracking them down is not always easy, since a visual check is sometimes not enough to locate a cabling glitch.

To aid net managers in troubleshooting high-speed networks, several vendors now sell handheld testers for evaluating Category 5 installations. Testers from Microtest Inc. (Phoenix, AZ), Scope Communications Inc. (Northborough, MA), and Wavetek Corp. (San Diego) evaluate the entire link, including cables and connectors. Handheld testers offer several improvements over the only other alternative to testing Category 5 cabling, which is to use a full-blown network analyzer. First, handheld devices are light enough to be toted easily around installation sites. Second, they deliver easy-to-understand test results. Third, at less than $4000 a pop, they cost roughly one-tenth of the price of a full-blown analyzer.

On the downside, handheld testers cannot match the ability of network analyzers to measure network conditions in extremely fine increments. More important, handheld testers have a wider margin of error. In some instances, this has led to network managers and installers failing cable links which were actually Category 5-compliant. To prevent further confusion, the Telecommunications Industries Association (TIA) came out with a document, called TSB 67, which defines not only which tests handheld testers for Category 5 should perform, but also the degree of accuracy with which they should perform them.

TSB 67 defines two levels of accuracy for Category 5 testers: Level I (less accurate) and Level II (the most accurate). All the Category 5 cable testers released prior to the document conform to Level I of the specification, according to TIA observers. The main reason they fall into the inferior group is that they connect to the cable under test via an RJ-45 connector. On its own, an RJ-45 jack can introduce up to 3 decibels of error to a test, according to Wavetek.

Several vendors have already announced testers which they say conform to the spec. Fluke Corp. (Everett, WA) says its DSP-100 LAN CableMeter ($3795) is the first tester to use digital signal processing (DSP)—as opposed to analog signals—to test Category 5 cable. DSP delivers three benefits, it says: high accuracy (in conformance with Level II of the TSB 67), faster test speeds (under 20 seconds), and the ability to detect the location of crosstalk faults on a given length of cable. Wavetek says its Lantek Pro XL (from $4495) is able to conform to the Level II spec because it incorporates new circuitry and uses a DB-15 connector rather than an RJ-45 jack to connect to the cable under test.

In the absence of a standard for certifying installed cabling, cable tester vendors had previously been selling so-called Category 5 tester equipment that implemented a set of draft test parameters featured in Annex E of the EIA/TIA-568A cable standard. Annex E was intended only as an advisory document for use in laboratories. It was never intended for use in testing installed cable.

Unfortunately, TSB 67 may not spell the end of the tester problem. In 1995 it emerged that a flaw in the design of some cable connectors causes handheld Category 5 cable testers to incorrectly fail short cable runs. The problem lies in the way some manufacturers handle capacitance imbalances in their connectors. When these products are hooked up to short cable runs (20 meters or less), they fool testers into thinking that the link exceeds maximum Category 5 levels for near-end crosstalk—even though the link is serviceable, and should actually pass the test. Currently, there's no way to tell which connectors will cause the problem and which won't. As often happens in the cable industry, manufacturers are bonding in a code of silence about which connectors are afflicted with the problem.

The PN2948 task group of the TR41.8.1 subcommittee (which is responsible for the EIA/TIA-568A cabling standard) is now considering developing new design and performance standards for connectors which would eliminate the problem. An alternative solution would be to relax the crosstalk requirements for handheld cable testers when testing short links. No final decision has been taken on when (or even if) either of these approaches will be adopted.

Section 8.   Category 5 Shortage

Poor installation techniques, faulty testers, and connector glitches aren't the only things that net managers have to worry about. A critical shortage in the cable itself is creating a major problem for corporations looking to upgrade their premises wiring schemes. Net managers face two choices: either delay their cabling projects (and then pay massively inflated prices when new stocks of Category 5 UTP finally arrive) or consider cabling alternatives—particularly fiber. Ironically, a run on fiber cabling could have further repercussions for the networking industry, sparking a shortage of fiber-optic transceivers and leading to increased prices for fiber-capable hubs, switches, and network interface cards.

The Category 5 UTP shortfall is being caused by a lack of the fluoropolymer resin used to insulate the copper pairs within Category 5 cabling—called FEP (fluorinated ethylene propylene). Big name, big problem. FEP's fire-resistant and electrical insulation properties make it an essential component in fire-rated Category 5 cabling, which is also known as plenum cable. Building codes require that fire-resistant cabling be installed in all parts of a building where air flows—such as under floors or in ceilings above ceilings.

Unfortunately, FEP manufacturers have grossly underestimated demand for their product. New production facilities won't be up and running until 1996. To date, industrywide efforts to find an affordable alternative to FEP have proved fruitless. In the meantime, the shortage of FEP has caused a Category 5 UTP drought. Cable prices have skyrocketed to previously unheard-of levels—in some cases, to almost double what they were at the end of 1994. Some cable installers are having to wait for upward of 6 months for cable, when they can get it all.

The Category 5 calamity is prompting net managers to reconsider their cabling options. Alternatives to Category 5 UTP include installing the aforementioned fiber, putting in nonplenum Category 5 cable in fireproof conduits, buying into less well-made cable and reducing the length of cable runs by a third, switching to chunkier shielded twisted-pair (STP) or screened twisted-pair (ScTP) cable, or migrating to LAN technologies that can run over Category 3 UTP.

What to Do When Category 5 UTP Runs Out

Supplies of plenum-rated Category 5 UTP are running short. That leaves network managers looking to upgrade their premises wiring to support high-speed data between a rock and a hard place. Here are six alternatives to Category 5 UTP that net managers can turn to today.

The Fiber Diet

As the cost of Category 5 UTP has gone up, the price of fiber has come down. Today fiber can be bought and installed for only around 30 percent more than the cost of copper cable. Fiber can handle all foreseeable LAN speeds, across distances measured in *kilo*meters rather than meters.

Consider Conduits

Plenum-rated Category 5 UTP (the firefighter's friend) may be harder to find than an honest politician, but there's still plenty of nonplenum Category 5 UTP to be had. By using nonplenum UTP in metal conduits or pipes, installers can get the electrical insulation they need—and meet

building codes to boot. But net managers thinking about going with conduits best budget an extra 40 percent on top of their original wiring estimate.

Category 4-and-a-Bit

Mohawk's LAN 75 UTP cable can get net managers out of the Category 5 UTP scrape—provided their LAN is on the small side. The so-called Category 4-and-a-half UTP replaces FEP with a less efficient insulator, limiting it to cable runs up to 67 meters in length. To get around the shortfall, net managers may have to install extra telecom closets, hubs, and repeaters.

Bulk Up

Category 5 UTP relies on FEP to be able to carry high-speed data. Shielded twisted pair (STP) takes a brute-force approach—using metal armor instead. Unfortunately, that makes STP bigger and badder to install. It's also a lot more expensive.

Behind the Screen

Net managers have known about screened twisted pair (ScTP) for some time, but it's never really taken off in the United States. Consequently, there's still a lot of it available.

Look at the LAN

By segueing to a high-speed LAN that can run over lower-quality Category 3 UTP, net managers can circumvent the issue of cabling altogether. There are three choices: 100Base-T and 100VG-AnyLAN (both of which run at 100 Mbit/s) and ATM (available in 25-Mbit/s and 155-Mbit/s flavors). Alternatively, Ethernet and token ring LAN switches (which work over installed cabling) also circumvent the need to rewire.

Section 9.   FEP Suppliers

All these cable alternatives have drawbacks, however. Given the choice, most network managers would rather stick with Category 5

UTP. Unfortunately, there are only two companies in the world that make FEP: DuPont (Wilmington, DE) has the lion's share of the market. A small amount of FEP also comes from Daiken (Osaka, Japan). Neither company anticipated the phenomenal growth in demand for Category 5 UTP, which has been increasing at a rate of roughly 50 percent per year since 1992.

Both DuPont and Daiken are now gearing up to bring new FEP plants on line. But DuPont says it will be 1997 before its $150 million expansion program is complete. Even when the new plants are up and running, it will take months (perhaps more than a year) before DuPont can catch up with the backlog of orders.

Converting other chemical plants to FEP production isn't even an option, DuPont says. FEP possesses two properties which together make it unique—and uniquely difficult to imitate. First, it's fire-resistant. Second, it's an extremely efficient electrical insulator, ensuring that electromagnetic radiation from Category 5 UTP stays within limits defined by the Federal Communications Commission (FCC), even when carrying data at speeds of 100 Mbit/s or more. Other so-called low-smoke fluoropolymer insulators—such as Halar, Kynar, and Tefzel—can match FEP in terms of fire safety. But when it comes to electrical insulation, none of them are in the same league.

Efforts to find an alternative to FEP have so far proved fruitless, despite around-the-clock work in the R&D departments of cable manufacturers across the United States—including those at AT&T, the inventor of Category 5 UTP. It's important to note that the cable shortage does not apply to all Category 5 cables. Nonplenum Category 5 UTP (which is not fire-resistant and can be made using materials other than FEP) is readily available. However, the law prohibits use of non-fire-resistant cable in many parts of modern office buildings (bad luck for the people who build corporate offices, good news for the people who work in them).

Building codes vary from state to state, but plenum-rated (fire-resistant) cable is typically mandated in any area where the cable is in contact with the flow from air-conditioning systems. The official term for this space is the *air-handling environment*. Depending on the design of the building, it's either above the ceiling or below the floor. Though installing nonplenum cable throughout a building is not usually an option, the shortage of plenum cable has prompted some installers to start using nonplenum where before they would have used the fire-resistant UTP.

It's worth noting that corporations in Europe aren't affected by the Category 5 UTP price hike. That's because building standards in Europe call for use of so-called halogen-free UTP cables rather than the fluoropolymer resin set down in TIA specs for North America.

Halogen-free UTP presents a compromise between the flame-resistant characteristics of fluoropolymer resin and the gas emanation limits set down by European environmental laws. According to IBM Europe, halogen-free cables account for about 40 percent of the total cable production in Europe. The remaining 60 percent of cables are insulated using polyvinyl chloride, IBM Europe says.

Section 10.   Category 5 Alternatives

In the meantime, back in the United States, the shortage of Category 5 UTP is getting worse by the day. Depending on whom they ask, some users are finding that Category 5 cannot be had, even for ready money. And the advice for net managers who *do* succeed in finding a source of Category 5 is that they better have plenty of money ready. FEP manufacturers, cable manufacturers, distributors, and installers are all hiking prices. In 1995 the cost of a foot of Category 5 UTP almost doubled—from 12 cents a foot to up to 20 cents a foot.

As it happens, 20 cents is a significant figure in the world of cabling. That's because it's also the cost per foot of fiber cable. Copper's biggest advantage over fiber has traditionally been price. Fiber prices had already plummeted prior to the FEP shortage, primarily because of advances in installation techniques and the availability of cheaper connectorization components like patch panels and wall plates. As the cost of the fiber and copper cables themselves converge, the price rationale for installing copper is fast disappearing.

Fiber also has several major advantages over copper: It can carry data faster (at multigigabit speeds) and further (for distances of several kilometers), and it is completely immune to electromagnetic interference. Nevertheless, while the cost of the cabling, connectors, and installation may not be significantly higher than using Category 5 UTP, the cost of LAN equipment for fiber networks is still way higher than for copper kit. For instance, a 10Base-T Ethernet network interface card (which works over UTP copper cable) can now be had for as little as $60, but the least expensive 10Base-FL Ethernet cards (which work with fiber) still cost more than $250. Even more pricey is 100-Mbit/s FDDI equipment—between $1000 and $1500 for a fiber port on a concentrator or hub, and an average of $1150 for the FDDI NIC which sits in the user's workstation.

While the dearth of Category 5 UTP could do wonders for fiber's fortunes, its unlikely to spark a comeback in use of shielded twisted-pair (STP) cable. STP doesn't rely on FEP, which means there's plenty of it around. But while fiber has gotten cheaper, STP has remained at about the same price—making it actually more expensive than fiber. Also, while STP's meaty construction endows it with the same performance properties as Category 5 UTP, it makes it a bind to install, and means it takes up a lot of room.

Net managers who don't want chunky cable have several other alternatives to consider. One option is ScTP cable—though only while stocks last. ScTP is already a hit in France and Germany, but it has never gripped the imagination of net managers in the United States. Consequently, there are still substantial stocks available. ScTP's reliance on FEP means that if it ever does take off, the same shortages will occur.

Another option is to install nonplenum Category 5 UTP within fireproof conduits, or pipes. Again, the snag here is cost. With conduits, net managers pay two times: for the conduits themselves, and for the labor required to install them. Conduits add 35 to 40 percent to the overall installation cost, and also add to the hassle of making cabling moves, adds, and changes.

The FEP deficit has prompted Mohawk to produce a nonstandard Limited Distance LAN 75 UTP cable—commonly alluded to in the cable industry as Category 4-and-a-half UTP. Mohawk's UTP features the same essential design as plenum-rated Category 5 UTP, but uses a non-FEP insulator, which Mohawk declines to name.

Mohawk specs the cable to provide the same fire-resistant capabilities and the same electrical properties as true Category 5 UTP, provided that it is installed only for cable runs up to a maximum of 67 meters (or 67 percent of the standard 100 meters maximum length defined in the EIA/TIA-568A premises wiring standard). On the face of it, Limited Distance UTP costs the same as Category 5 UTP, but the fact that it covers less ground means that some net managers will end up spending more in another way—when they have to buy additional wiring closets, repeaters, and hubs to go the extra distance in their horizontal wiring plant.

There is another way for net managers to get around the Category 5 problem—one that doesn't involve making changes to the cabling at all. That's to move to a higher-speed LAN technology that can run over the Category 3 UTP cable that most companies already have in their offices. When standards bodies first started working on highspeed LAN technologies, it was thought that electromagnetic radiation would prevent Category 3 UTP from being used to support highspeed LAN traffic. But recent advances in signal encoding and transceiver technology mean that some vendors now believe it will be possible to transmit data at speeds of 100 Mbit/s or more on Category 3 UTP.

Net managers have three choices. The 100VG-AnyLAN standard from the IEEE already specifies an encoding scheme that transmits data at 100 Mbit/s over four copper pairs in a Category 3 UTP cable.

The companies working on the 100Base-T fast Ethernet standard (also from the IEEE) are still hammering out a similar specification. Recently, UB Networks (Santa Clara, CA)—in collaboration with Tut Systems Inc. (Pleasant Hill, CA)—claimed to have developed switches and adapters which can transmit 155-Mbit/s ATM traffic over Category 3. None of these products have yet been independently tested for compliance with FCC regulations. Yet another option open to network managers is to add an Ethernet or a token ring LAN switch. These devices boost performance by dedicating up to the full bandwidth of the network over individual nodes—and they operate over the cabling that net managers already have installed.

32

The Fiber Alternative

Section 1. Overview

Fiber on the backbone, copper to the desktop. For years, that's been the book on premises wiring. Now, that book is being rewritten. Several manufacturers of fiber-optic products have come up with labor-saving techniques that dramatically cut the cost of installing fiber to the desktop. These techniques—combined with continued price reductions for fiber cabling and components—are bringing the overall cost of fiber installation close to that for Category 5 unshielded twisted-pair (UTP) copper wiring.

In such instances, the rationale for installing Category 5 UTP vanishes. Today, Category 5 UTP is widely championed as an interim wiring solution that handles speeds of 100 Mbit/s and faster at a significantly lower cost than fiber or shielded twisted-pair (STP) wiring schemes. Once faster technologies like 622-Mbit/s ATM emerge, users probably will have to rip out Category 5 wiring and replace it with multimode fiber, which not only handles higher speeds (1 Gbit/s or more) but also has a much greater operating range (2 kilometers, as opposed to Category 5's 100-meter operating limit).

The strategy of using Category 5 UTP as an interim solution has been predicated on the wide disparity between the costs of installing Category 5 wiring and fiber cabling. That gap is shrinking considerably. While the material, labor costs, and skills required to install and maintain copper cable supporting 100-Mbit/s transmissions have increased, the costs for fiber cable installation and maintenance are declining. According to figures from IBM Corp. (Armonk, NY), the result is that a fiber plant capable of supporting up to 1-Gbit/s transmissions can be designed and installed for prices within 30 percent of 100-Mbit/s copper systems.

Given that price difference, the decision to install wiring with a fairly limited shelf life doesn't make much sense. The projected drop in fiber cabling costs looks like it will catch most network managers by surprise. In a recent survey of the cabling plans of 100 companies, JLP Associates (San Jose, CA) found that only 3 percent of respondents were planning to run fiber to the desktop. As fiber costs fall, wiring plant managers are going to have to rethink their long-term strategies—or risk investing in technology with rapidly diminishing short-term gains.

Section 2.   Fiber Advantages

The two most obvious advantages to installing fiber are speed and operating range. For the distances involved inside a building, either monomode or multimode fiber will support gigabit speeds. Other than for very short cable runs, copper wiring always will be limited to megabit speeds. Because of signal attenuation, copper becomes unreliable beyond 100 meters, while monomode fiber runs can easily stretch to 2 kilometers before the signal must be repeated.

Beyond speed and range, fiber offers two more key advantages over copper. First, unlike copper cable, fiber is immune to electromagnetic interference, which means that it can be installed adjacent to equipment like photocopiers and fluorescent lights—or in environments like factory floors—without affecting the data signal. Second, fiber cable is an intrinsically secure medium because it can't be tapped: Any break in the cable disrupts the light signal and instantly results in an outage.

Section 3.   Double-Barrel Savings

Vendors say falling fiber installation costs are attributable to two factors. One is a drop in the cost of the fiber cables and components (such as connectors and patch panels). The other, and probably more significant, factor is the development of new techniques that cut the amount of time needed to terminate fiber connections. Cost cuts for cabling and components are being driven by improved production techniques, as well as by the use of less expensive connector materials. In the past, for example, the part of the fiber connector that holds the fiber line in place (called a ferrule) was made of ceramic. Now, less expensive plastic and stainless steel ferrules are being used.

Cost reductions also are reflected in the falling prices of fiber-based network adapter cards. Prices for FDDI equipment, for example, fell by about 50 percent in 1994. Today, the cheapest FDDI implementations cost around $1500 per node (including the cost of adapter and concentrator port), although the average price is still about $2500 per node. Prices are expected to drop further, as vendors start cutting profit margins to compete with copper-based high-speed LAN products, and as cards arrive that implement lower-cost 850-nanometer transceivers, rather than the 1300-nanometer transceivers specified in the FDDI standard. Raylan Corp. (Palo Alto, CA), a maker of fiber concentrators and adapters, says that using 850-nanometer components will allow it to offer FDDI cards for the same price as today's FDDI-over-copper products.

Opinions differ about exactly how far the price of fiber cable and connectors has fallen. 3M Corp. (Minneapolis), which makes both fiber and copper cabling and connectors, reckons that the costs of the fiber cable and connectors are now comparable to copper. But Anixter Inc. (Skokie, IL), an independent distributor of third-party copper and fiber cabling and connector components, says the cost of fiber cabling and components still is more than double that of Category 5 UTP equivalents. Even with the price disparity cited by the vendor, fiber works out to be less expensive than Category 5 UTP on a per-Mbit/s basis when maximum speeds are considered. Table 32.1 shows average cable costs garnered from a variety of manufacturers and cable installers. Net managers can expect to cut themselves better deals by shopping around.

To spread out the cost of migrating to fiber, organizations can opt to use 10-Mbit/s Ethernet or 4- or 16-Mbit/s token ring adapters and concentrators that can run over fiber cable. For example, the 1100 Series Ethernet-over-fiber concentrator from Optical Data Systems Inc. (ODS, Richardson, TX) costs from $180 per port. ODS' 677 Ethernet-over-fiber PC adapter card costs $495. Both products conform to the IEEE 10BaseFL standard for running 10-Mbit/s Ethernet signals over fiber. Another alternative is to convert older Ethernet and token ring adapters to fiber duty using a transceiver like the TRC8223-PC from Andrew Corp. (Orland Park, IL), which costs $395.

Section 4.   Labor Savers

As expensive as fiber components have been, labor costs have contributed the most to fiber's reputation for exorbitance. The basic problem is the amount of time and effort needed to terminate a fiber-optic connection. Early fiber installations were particularly labor-intensive. A specialist had to use a fusion splicer, a bulky and expensive (about $20,000) piece of equipment, to melt fiber strands and fuse them to connectors. The development of epoxy bonding helped cut installation cost to an extent. Epoxy bonding, a four-stage process, is much easier than fusion splicing, but it still takes a lot of time. First, the epoxy

TABLE 32.1 Weighing Wiring Costs

	Category 5 UTP	ScTP (screened twisted pair)	STP	Fiber
Description	Four copper pairs twisted together and jacketed in PVC	Four copper pairs wrapped in an aluminum foil screen and jacketed in PVC	Four copper pairs, with two pairs each wrapped in separate metal shielding before being sheathed in an additional braided metal shield and jacketed in PVC	62.5- or 125-micron optical fiber jacketed in PVC
Materials cost per 100-meter cable run (including cable and connectors)	$91	$107	$174	$193
Labor cost per cable run*	$72	$75	$80	$81
Total cost per cable run	$163	$182	$254	$274
Predicted maximum data rate	300 Mbit/s	500 Mbit/s	500 Mbit/s	All foreseeable LAN speeds
Cost per Mbit/s at predicted maximum rate	$0.54	$0.36	$0.51	$0.27 (at 1 Gbit/s)

*Based on labor charges of $45 per hour.

resin must be prepared and applied to the fiber connectors. Second, the connector and cable must be mechanically spliced, or crimped, with a crimping gun. The third, and most time-consuming, step is to cure, or dry, the epoxy using ultraviolet light or a conventional heat source, such as a portable oven. The final step is to polish the connection by hand. The curing process can take anywhere from 10 minutes to several hours. By doing several connections simultaneously, installers can cut the average termination time down to about 10 to 15 minutes—faster than, but still not nearly as fast as, copper terminations.

The third generation of fiber termination technology is bringing installation time down to 5 minutes or less—making labor costs almost a nonissue (see Fig. 32.1). A couple of fast installation options are available. One approach, taken by Amp with its Lightcrimp product and Siecor (Hickory, NC) with its CamLite offering, involves the use of preterminated fiber cable that simply has to be crimped onto a connector using a crimping gun. Eliminating the epoxy curing process reduces installation time to an average of 2 minutes, according to Amp. The downside to crimping is that it provides somewhat higher signal loss than fusion-spliced or epoxy-bonded connections.

Savings in labor costs that accrue from reduced installation time can be substantial—particularly in large installations where thousands of connections must be made. Amp estimates that the average

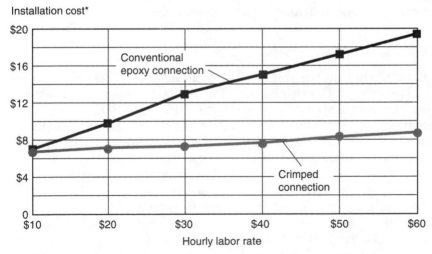

*Includes the cost of connection components

Figure 32.1 Time is money. With preterminated fiber cabling, technicians can use a crimping gun to install a fiber connection in about 2 minutes, compared with the 15 minutes needed for conventional epoxy connections. At a typical labor charge of $40 per hour, that translates to roughly a one-third savings.

hourly rate charged in the United States for fiber installations is $40. At that rate, a 15-minute epoxy bonding installation carries a $10 labor cost. A 2-minute installation with Lightcrimp costs only about $1.30 in labor, Amp says—almost eight times less than the labor costs of epoxy bonding. In areas where labor costs are higher than the average, cost savings are even greater.

As well as being faster, crimping tools are relatively inexpensive (Lightcrimp costs about $650) and easy to use. This means that, depending on their inclination and the strength of the local trade unions, organizations could buy their own fiber installation equipment and do the work themselves, rather than rely on outside experts. In an alternative approach, some vendors are refining the epoxy bonding process to speed installation. 3M's Hotmelt Fiber Connector comes loaded with a fast-drying epoxy glue. To make a connection, the installer heats up the Hotmelt connector to soften the epoxy, inserts a preterminated fiber cable, and then leaves the connection to dry. No equipment is needed to cure the bond. The entire process can be completed in as little as 5 minutes, 3M claims. 3M also says its epoxy is easier to work with than conventional epoxy adhesive. Once ordinary epoxy has been cured, it hardens and becomes unmalleable. But with 3M's epoxy, if a problem occurs during the connection process, the adhesive can be resoftened by reheating the connector.

AT&T has developed an epoxy glue that uses an anaerobic curing process to dry in less than 5 minutes, the vendor claims—faster than some people take to install a coaxial connector.

Section 5.   The User View

Users confirm that the cost of installing fiber cabling is coming down fast. The Federal Reserve Bank (Dallas) says it paid only a 10 percent premium to wire its building with fiber instead of STP copper cable. As part of its move into a new building last year, the bank installed fiber to connect 1000 token ring nodes. It's worth noting that conventional epoxy bonding was used to install the cabling; the bank had tested Siecor's crimp-on connectors but chose the conventional epoxy solution because it provides lower signal loss.

The Richardson (Texas) Independent School District is another organization that was pleasantly surprised by the cost of fiber. It reports that the cost of installing fiber is compatible with that of Category 5 copper. The district has completed eight fiber installations, totaling some 400 LAN nodes. The sites were all installed using 3M's Hotmelt connectors. The first installation tackled by the district, a 30-node site, had an average cost per node of $665 (including adapters); Category 5 UTP would have cost only about $42 per node (about 6 percent) less.

Net managers at both the Federal Reserve Bank and Richardson Independent School District agree that the best thing about installing fiber is that it negates the need to recable further down the road. Similarly, both sites refute the commonly held notion that fiber cabling damages easily and consequently is more expensive to maintain. In fact, the net manager at Richardson Independent School District says that installing fiber has enabled him to reduce the number of staffers allocated to cabling maintenance.

Section 6.   Bad Publicity

Fiber vendors blame the perception of fiber as a delicate cabling medium on misinformation from manufacturers of copper cable and connectors. In fact, fiber's pull strength (the maximum pressure that can be exerted on the cable before damage occurs) is 200 pounds, eight times that of Category 5 UTP.

Fiber vendors also point out that while independently tested and approved fiber cables and connectors are now commonly available, testing labs such as Underwriters Laboratories Inc. (Northbrook, IL) have only just started work on verifying the capabilities of the connectors that vendors are touting as Category 5 products. ITT Datacomm (Santa Ana, CA), a cable installer, estimates the cost of going back and replacing connecting components that are not up to snuff at 10 to 20 percent of the initial installation price of a UTP scheme.

33

High-Speed LAN
Cabling Standards

Section 1. Overview

Prior to 1992, there was no standard for premises wiring. This meant that net managers looking to put in a reliable cabling scheme for high-speed data had to rely on one of a handful of dominant cabling suppliers. Fortunately, all that has changed. The EIA/TIA-568 standard from the Electronics Industries Association/Telecommunications Industries Association defines how to design and install premises wiring, and is now firmly established in North America. In 1995, the standard was revamped and renamed TIA/EIA-568A. Crucially, the new version includes performance specifications for *installed* cabling. Previously, test specs had been provided only for individual components. Progress also has been made on an international equivalent to the standard.

TIA/EIA-568A should be compulsory reading for any net manager about to embark on a migration to higher-speed networking. It presents users and vendors with precise guidelines governing premises wiring installations. In essence, TIA/EIA-568A is a building code for premises wiring. The standard dictates the topology of cabling installations, the cabling types to be used for a given network speed, and the connector types to be used with a given cabling type. It also defines performance specifications that the cables and connectors must meet. This information is invaluable in designing a high-speed LAN. By sticking to the standard, net managers can avoid a plethora of potential problems caused by mistakes such as using the incorrect cable or connectors, or running cable for excessive distances.

Section 2.   History of the Standard

The EIA/TIA began work on its wiring standard in 1985, when the breakup of the Bell System opened the premises wiring market to competition. It took the organization 6 years to ratify the first parts of the standard (known in its first iteration as EIA/TIA-568). The organization subsequently continued to work on performance specifications for cable and connectors, which were published as separate technical specification bulletin (TSB) documents as they became available. Those TSBs have now been rolled into the new version of the standard—TIA/EIA-568A. They include TSB 67, which defines performance testing for installed cable links—including the cable and the connecting components at either end.

Prior to the standard, premises wiring was characterized by proprietary and largely incompatible schemes that locked users into not only a single vendor but also, in some cases, a single product line (see Fig. 33.1). For example, IBM users found that 3270 mainframe and terminal networks required RG-62 coaxial cable in point-to-point configurations, but System/3X networks called for twin coaxial cable in a daisy-chain topology.

There are two parts to TIA/EIA-568A. The first defines the topology, cable types, and connector types to be used in compliant wiring schemes. The second sets down minimum performance specifications for cables and connecting components, using such parameters as signal attenuation, crosstalk, and return loss. Because it addresses only the physical wiring scheme, TIA/EIA-568A complements rather than conflicts with standards such as ATM, 100Base-T, and FDDI, which define methods for transmitting data across specific wiring types.

TIA/EIA-568A does not cover equipment that is attached to the wiring scheme, such as PC cards, hubs, or switches. A complementary standard, 569, specifies the amount of space required by wiring ducts and closets. Yet another standard is available that defines premises wiring administration issues such as how to keep cabling records and how to color-code and number components.

Section 3.   Topology

The beauty of the topology specified in TIA/EIA-568A lies in its simplicity. The standard defines a structured wiring scheme in which all users are connected in a star topology to a central distribution point, a telecommunications closet containing equipment such as patch panels and intelligent hubs. Telecommunications closets also are connected in a star configuration. The maximum cable length from the telecommunications outlet under each user's desk to the wiring closet

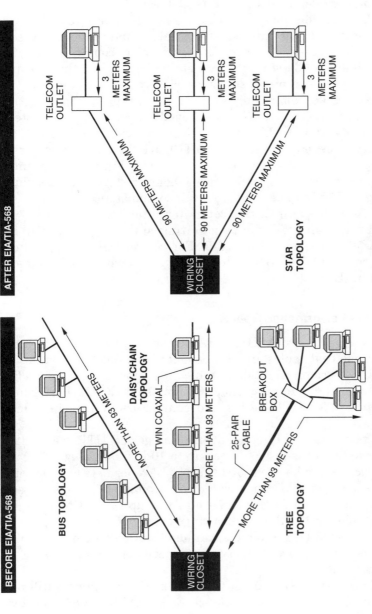

Figure 33.1 A simpler path for premises wiring. Before the arrival of the EIA/TIA-568 standard, wiring vendors used a variety of topologies to link premises computers and equipment (left). The standard calls for each node to be connected to a wiring closet in uniform fashion, no matter what type of cabling is used (right).

is 90 meters (295 feet), regardless of the type of cable used. The maximum length for the cable connecting the telecom outlet to the user's workstation or telephone is 3 meters (9.8 feet).

TIA/EIA-568A specifies five cable types. These are 100-ohm cable, comprising four copper pairs twisted together and protected by a thin polyvinyl chloride (PVC) jacket; 150-ohm cable, comprising two copper pairs individually wrapped in metal shielding and then sheathed together in a braided metal shield covered by a PVC outer jacket; 50-ohm coaxial cable, comprising a copper core wrapped in polyurethene insulation, screened by a layer of braided copper wire, and protected by a PVC jacket; and 62.5- or 125-micron optical fiber. The standard also covers screened twisted pair (ScTP), a 100-ohm cable comprising four copper pairs wrapped in a metal shield. Finally, the standard allows other cable types, including 100-ohm STP, 75-ohm coaxial, or other types of fiber, to be used in certain circumstances.

TIA/EIA-568A specifies two connector interfaces for UTP: a jack, and a punchdown block for terminating multiple cables. For STP, TIA/EIA-568A specifies the DB-9. For coaxial cable, the standard calls for the use of the BNC connector, or bayonet locking connector, specified in IEEE 802.3.

Section 4.   Performance Specs

The second part of TIA/EIA-568A defines minimum performance specifications that cables and components must meet without exceeding the U.S. recommendations on electromagnetic radiation defined by the Federal Communications Commission (FCC). Performance specifications for UTP cables and connectors define three levels (Categories 3, 4, and 5) of performance.

Products that meet TIA/EIA-568A's Category 3 UTP specifications can be used for transmission rates up to 10 Mbit/s. Category 3 cables and connectors can be used for Ethernet LANs or networks operating at lower speeds, such as voice traffic or 4-Mbit/s token rings. Category 4 UTP products handle transmission rates up to 16 Mbit/s, making them suitable for 16-Mbit/s token rings or any other lower-speed network. Category 5 UTP products can handle transmission rates up to 100 Mbit/s. The standard also covers specifications addressing STP cable and connectors.

As with any standard, the possibility exists that vendors will make misleading claims about compliance with TIA/EIA-568A. Not every installer that claims compliance will implement the whole standard. One way for users to spot such discrepancies is by becoming thoroughly familiar with the standard and by carefully combing through each vendor's specs. That task is made easier by TIA/EIA-568A's performance specifications, which enable independent testing labs to verify compliance of cables and components. A certified product is stamped by its manufacturer with its performance level and with the name of the testing facility that approved the product.

Section 5.   A Worldwide Cabling Standard

When TIA/EIA-568A was first ratified, it opened up the U.S. cabling market to competition by enabling smaller vendors to guarantee that their wares would perform as well as those of larger outfits. The net result? Users ended up getting cheaper premises wiring schemes, plus a guarantee that cabling and components from different suppliers could work together.

In 1994, an international cabling standard brought some of the same benefits to users outside North America. Called ISO 11801, the standard was ratified in Geneva and is the work of the International Organization for Standardization. The international standard is very largely based on TIA/EIA-568A. However, the global standard differs from the U.S. standard in one crucial area. TIA/EIA-568A defines the topology of the cabling scheme, the types of cabling and connectors which can be used in the scheme, and the performance criteria which those components must meet. ISO 11801 contains the same information, but includes a get-out clause stating that installers can use different topology, cables, and connectors—provided that they still meet the performance criteria.

This is a crucial loophole. TIA/EIA-568A specifies use of fire-resistant plenum-rated UTP cables. Plenum cables use a fluorocarbon raw material which gives them fire-resistant properties, but once they start to burn they produce highly toxic and corrosive gases. Because of this, European cabling standards typically call for use of so-called halogen-free UTP cables. These represent a good compromise between flame and fire characteristics of plenum cabling and the gas emanation limits required by European directives.

Halogen-free cabling has become a de facto standard for European cable installers, and their use is now mandatory in many European countries in public buildings, hospitals, and anyplace where a high concentration of people is foreseen. Today, halogen-free cables account for about 40 percent of the total cable production in Europe. The remaining 60 percent are PVC-based cables—not plenum-rated cables. Other examples of international regional wiring idiosyncracies include the habit in some European countries of installing two-pair UTP cable, or using cable runs greater than 90 meters in length.

Vendor Index

Knowing who the key players in the high-speed LAN market are is one thing; finding them can be another. Here's an index to more than 800 of the key movers and shakers in the networking industry. In addition to telephone and fax numbers, this index also provides the location of vendor's home pages, where supported.

Able Communications Inc.
 Irvine, CA
 800-654-1223 or
 714-553-8825
 (fax) 714-553-1320

Accton Technology Corp.
 Hsinchu, Taiwan
 886-35-770270 (fax) 886-35-770267
 http://www.accton.com

Accugraph Corp.
 El Paso, TX
 915-581-1171 (fax) 915-581-3437

Ace/North Hills
 See NBase Communications

Acsys Inc.
 Burlington, MA
 800-GO-ACSYS or 617-270-5566
 (fax) 617-270-5575

Actiontec
 Sunnyvale, CA
 408-739-7000 (fax) 408-739-7001

ACT Networks Inc.
 Camarillo, CA
 800-367-2281 or 805-388-2474
 (fax) 805-388-3504
 http://www.acti.com

Adaptec
 Milpitas, CA
 800-959-7274 or 408-945-8600
 (fax) 408-262-2533

Adax Inc.
 Berkeley, CA
 510-548-7047 (fax) 510-548-5526
 http://www.adax.com

ADC Fibermux Corp.
 Chatsworth, CA
 800-709-4624 or 818-709-6000
 (fax) 818-709-1556

ADC Kentrox
 Portland, OR
 800-ADC-KTRX or 503-643-1681
 (fax) 503-641-3341
 http://www.kentrox.com

ADC Telecommunications Inc.
Minneapolis, MN
800-366-3891 or 612-938-8080
(fax) 612-946-3292
http://www.adc.com

Adtech Inc.
Honolulu, HI
800-348-0080 or 808-734-3300
(fax) 808-734-7100

Adtran Inc.
Huntsville, AL
800-326-3700 or 205-971-8000
(fax) 205-971-8116
http://www.adtran.com

Advanced Computer
Communications (ACC)
Cupertino, CA
800-666-7308 or 408-366-9600
(fax) 408-446-5234
http://www.acc.com

Advanced Relay Corp.
Eugene, OR
503-345-9178 (fax) 503-484-0216

Advanced Telecommunications
Modules Inc.
Sunnyvale, CA
408-523-1400 or (fax) 408-523-1410

Advantage Memory Corp.
Irvine, CA
800-245-5299 or 714-453-8111
(fax) 714-453-8158

Advantis
Schaumberg, IL
800-888-4103 or 708-240-3000
(fax) 708-240-3857

Aerocomm Inc.
Lenexa, KS
800-492-2320 or 913-492-2320
(fax) 913-492-1243

Age Logic Inc.
San Diego, CA
800-PICK-AGE or 619-755-1000
(fax) 619-755-3998
http://www.age.com

The AG Group Inc.
Walnut Creek, CA
800-466-AGGP or 510-937-7900
(fax) 510-937-2479
http://www.aggroup.com/

Agile Networks Inc.
Boxborough, MA
800-ATM-XLAN or 508-263-3600
(fax) 508-263-5111
http://www.agile.com

Airaccess Ltd.
Raanana, Israel
972-9-982606 (fax) 972-9-983218

Air Communications
Santa Clara, CA
408-567-8000 (fax) 408-567-9090

Aironet Wireless
Communications,Inc.
Needham, MA
800-449-8038 or 617-449-2111
(fax) 617-449-7937

Airsoft
Cupertino, CA
408-777-7500 (fax) 408-777-7527

Alantec Corp.
San Jose, CA
800-ALANTEC or 408-955-9000
(fax) 408-955-9500

Alcatel Data Networks
Velizy, France
33-1-30-67-34-00 (fax) 33-1-30-67-91-01

Alfa Inc.
Hsinchu, Taiwan
886-35-789625 (fax) 886-35-788983

Alisa Systems Inc.
Pasadena, CA
800-992-5472 or 818-792-9474
(fax) 818-792-4068
http://www.alisa.com/

Allied Telesyn Inc.
Mountain View, CA
800-424-4282 or 415-964-2771
415-964-0944

Alphatronix
Research Triangle Park, NC
800-849-2611 or 919-544-0001
(fax) 919-544-4079

Amber Wave Systems Inc.
Acton, MA
508-266-2900 (fax) 508-266-1159

American Hytech Corp.
Pittsburgh, PA
412-826-3333 (fax) 412-826-3335
http://www.lm.com/netguru

American Power Conversion Corp.
West Kingston, RI
800-788-2208 or 401-789-5735
(fax) 401-789-3710

American Technology Labs Inc.
Ijamsville, MD
800-223-9758 or 301-695-1547
(fax) 301-874-3465

Ameritec Corp.
Covina, CA
818-915-5441 (fax) 818-915-7181

AMP Inc.
Harrisburg, PA
800-522-6752 or 717-564-0100
(fax) 717-986-7575

Ancor Communications Inc.
Minnetonka, MN
800-342-7379 or 612-932-4000
(fax) 612-932-4037
http://www.ancor.com

Ando Corp.
Rockville, MD
800-367-ANDO or 301-294-3365
(fax) 301-294-3359

Andrew Corp.
Orland Park, IL
800-328-2696 or 708-349-5440
(fax) 708-349-5673

Angia Communications Inc.
Provo, UT
800-877-9159 or 801-371-0488
(fax) 801-373-9847

Annexus Data Systems
San Diego, CA
800-505-0019 or 619-530-0019
(fax) 619-530-0096

ANS Co + re Systems Inc.
Elmsford, NY
800-456-8267 or 914-789-5300
(fax) 914-789-5310
http://www.ans.net

Answersoft Inc.
Plano, TX
800-896-2677 or 214-612-5100
(fax) 214-612-5198

ANT Nachrichtentechnik GmbH
Backnang, Germany
49-71-91-13-2384

Apertus Technologies Inc.
Eden Prairie, MN
800-328-3998 or 612-828-0300
(fax) 612-828-0454

Apex Data Inc.
Pleasanton, CA
800-841-APEX or 510-416-5656
(fax) 510-416-0909

Apex PC Solutions Inc.
Redmond, WA
800-861-5858 or 206-861-5858
(fax) 206-861-5757

Apple Computer Inc.
Cupertino, CA
408-996-1010

Applied Expert Systems
Redwood City, CA
415-364-1222 (fax) 415-364-3620

Applied Network Technology Inc.
Westford, MA
508-392-0690 (fax) 508-392-0535

Applied Voice Technology Inc.
Kirkland, WA
800-443-0806 or 206-820-6000
(fax) 206-820-4040

Apsylog Inc.
Palo Alto, CA
800-APSYLOG or 415-812-7700
(fax) 415-812-7707

APT Communications Inc.
Ijamsville, MD
800-842-0626 or 301-874-3305
(fax) 301-874-5255

Archtek America Corp.
City of Industry, CA
800-368-5465 or 818-912-9800
(fax) 818-912-9700

Ardis
Lincolnshire, IL
708-913-1215 (fax) 708-913-1453

Armon Networking Ltd.
Tel Aviv, Israel
972-3-647-9586 (fax) 972-3-490-701

Arnet Corp.
Nashville, TN
800-366-8844 or 615-834-8000
(fax) 615-834-5399

Artisoft Inc.
Tucson, AZ
800-233-5564 or 602-670-7100
(fax) 602-670-7101

Asante Technologies Inc.
San Jose, CA
408-435-8388 (fax) 408-432-1117
http://www.asante.com

Ascend Communications Inc.
Alameda, CA
800-621-9578 or 510-769-6001
(fax) 510-814-2300
http://www@ascend.com

Ascom Timeplex Inc.
Woodcliff Lake, NJ
800-669-2298 or 201-391-1111
(fax) 201-391-0852

Aspect Telecommunications
San Jose, CA
408-441-2200 (fax) 408-441-2260

Astarte Fiber Networks Inc.
Boulder, CO
800-872-8777 or 303-443-8778
(fax) 303-449-2975

AST Computer
Irvine, CA
800-876-4278 or 714-727-4141
(fax) 714-727-8592

Astrocom Corp.
Minneapolis, MN
800-669-6242 or 612-378-7800
(fax) 612-378-1070

Attachmate Corp.
Bellevue, WA
800-426-6283 or 206-644-4010
(fax) 206-747-9920
http://www.atm.com

AT&T Business Multimedia Services
Bedminster, NJ
800-248-3632

AT&T Easylink Services
Bridgeton, MI
800-325-1898

AT&T Global Business
Communications Systems
Basking Ridge, NJ
800-843-3646 or 908-953-7514
http://www.att.com

AT&T Global Information Solutions
Dayton, OH
800-447-1124 or 513-445-5000
(fax) 513-445-4184
http://www.att.com

AT&T Network Systems
Morristown, NJ
201-606-2466
http://www.att.com

AT&T Paradyne
Largo, FL
800-482-3333 or 813-530-2000
(fax) 813-530-2103
http://www.paradyne.att.com/

AT&T Tridom
Marietta, GA
800-346-1174 or 404-426-4261
(fax) 404-514-1737

Aurora Technologies Inc.
Waltham, MA
617-290-4800 (fax) 617-290-4844

Auto-trol Technology Corp.
Denver, CO
303-452-4919 (fax) 303-252-2249

Avail Systems
Boulder, CO
800-444-4018 or 303-444-4018
(fax) 303-546-4219

Avalan Technology Inc.
Holliston, MA
800-441-2281 or 508-429-6482
(fax) 508-429-3179
http://ultranet.com/dtemple

Avdata Systems Inc.
Atlanta, GA
800-876-8001 or 404-523-2848
(fax) 404-420-3072

Avistar Systems
Palo Alto, CA
415-617-1350 (fax) 415-617-1351

AVM Computersysteme GmbH
Berlin, Germany
011-49-30-467070 (fax) 011-49-30-
4670-7299

Axis Communications Inc.
Woburn, MA
800-444-AXIS or 617-938-1188
(fax) 617-938-6161
http://www.axis.se

Axonet Inc.
Harvard, MA
508-772-3590 (fax) 508-772-3196
http:///www.tiac.net/users/axonet/
home.html

Axon Networks Inc.
Newton, MA
617-630-9600 (fax) 617-630-9604

Azure Technologies Inc.
Hopkinton, MA
800-233-3800 or 508-435-3800
(fax) 508-435-0448

Banknet KFT
Budapest, Hungary
36-1-202-7083 (fax) + 36-1-758-364

Banyan Systems Inc.
Westborough, MA
800-222-6926 or 508-898-1000
(fax) 508-898-1755
http://www.banyan.com

Barr Systems Inc.
Gainesville, FL
800-BARR-SYS or 904-371-3050
(fax) 904-491-3141

Barry Test Sets and Independent
Technologies
Omaha, NE
402-498-8400 (fax) 402-493-5100

Batetech Software Inc.
Denver, CO
303-763-8333 (fax) 303-985-0624

B.A.T.M Advanced Technologies
Patach-Tikva, Israel
972-3-9264555 (fax) 972-3-9228899

Bay Networks Inc.
Santa Clara, CA
800-776-6895 or 408-988-2400
(fax) 408-988-5525
http://www.baynetworks.com

Bay Technical Associates Inc.
Bay St. Louis, MS
800-523-2702 or 601-467-8231
(fax) 601-467-4551

BBN Planet
Cambridge, MA
508-369-2100 (fax) 508-369-2106
http://www.bbnplanet.com

Beame & Whiteside Software Inc.
Raleigh, NC
919-831-8989 (fax) 919-831-8990
http://www.bws.com

Belden Wire & Cable
Richmond, IN
317-983-5200 (fax) 317-983-5846

Belgacom
Brussels, Belgium
32-2-202-9972 (fax) 32-2-203-1742

Bell Atlantic Mobile
Bedminster, NJ
800-255-BELL or 908-306-7000

Bell South Telecommunications
Birmingham, AL
800-635-8171 (fax) 205-977-1989

Bendata Inc.
Colorado Springs, CO
800-776-7889 or 719-531-5007
(fax) 719-536-9623

Berk-Tek Inc.
New Holland, PA
800-BERK-TEK or 717-354-6200
(fax) 717-354-7944

Best Data Products Inc.
Chatsworth, CA
800-632-BEST or 818-773-9600
(fax) 818-773-9619

Blast Inc.
Pittsboro, NC
800-24-BLAST or 919-542-3007
(fax) 919-542-0161

BMC Software Inc.
Houston, TX
800-841-2031 or 713-918-8800
(fax) 713-918-8000

Boffin Ltd.
Burnsville, MN
612-894-0595 (fax) 612-894-6175
http://www.boffin.com

Boole & Babbage Inc.
San Jose, CA
800-22-BOOLE or 408-526-3000
(fax) 408-526-3053

Boole & Babbage Storage Division
Conyers, GA
770-483-8852 (fax) 770-388-9453

Border Network Technologies Inc.
Toronto, Ontario
800-334-8195 or 416-368-7157
(fax) 416-368-7789
http://www.border.com

Braintree Technology Inc.
Norwell, MA
617-982-0200 (fax) 617-982-8076

Bridgeway Corp.
Redmond, WA
800-275-6849 or 206-881-4270
(fax) 206-861-1774

Brooktrout Technology Inc.
Needham, MA
617-449-4100 (fax) 617-449-9009

BT Managed Network
London, UK
44-1442-233-961 (fax) 44-1442-239-587

Bull HN Worldwide Information
Systems Inc.
Billerica, MA
800-884-4864 or 508-294-6000
(fax) 508-294-6109
http://www.bull.com/prod/ism

Business Partners Solutions
Westmont, IL
708-323-9292 (fax) 708-323-9330

Bus-Tech Inc.
Burlington, MA
800-284-3172 or 617-272-8200
(fax) 617-272-0342

Bytex Corp.
Westborough, MA
800-232-9839 or 508-366-8000
(fax) 508-366-0244

Cable & Wireless Inc.
Vienna, VA
800-CWS-SOLVES or 703-790-5300
(fax) 703-905-4161
http://www.cwi.net

Cabletron Systems Inc.
Rochester, NH
800-332-9401 or 603-332-9400
(fax) 603-337-2211

CACI Products Company
Arlington, VA
703-841-7800 (fax) 703-841-7882

California Software Products Inc.
Corona del Mar, CA
800-830-3311 or 714-729-2270
(fax) 714-729-2272
http://www.calsoft.com

Callware Technologies Inc.
Salt Lake City, UT
800-888-4226 or 801-486-9922
(fax) 801-486-8294

Cameo Communications
Nashua, NH
603-888-8869 (fax) 603-888-8906

Cami Research Inc.
Lexington, MA
800-776-0414 or 617-860-9137
(fax) 617-860-9139

Campbell Services Inc.
Southfield, MI
800-559-5955 or 810-559-5955
(fax) 810-559-1034

Canary Communications
San Jose, CA
800-883-9201 or 408-453-9201
(fax) 408-453-0940

Canoga-Perkins Corp.
Chatsworth, CA
818-718-6300 (fax) 818-718-6312

Caravelle Networks Corp.
Nepean, Ontario
800-363-5292 or 613-225-1172
(fax) 613-255-4777
http://www.caravelle.com

Cascade Communications Corp.
Westford, MA
800-DIAL-WAN or 508-692-2600
(fax) 508-692-9214

Castelle Inc.
Santa Clara, CA
800-289-7555 or 408-496-0474
(fax) 408-492-1964

Castle Rock Computing Inc.
Cupertino, CA
408-366-6540 (fax) 408-252-2379
http://castlerock.com

Cellware Breitband Technologie
GmbH
Berlin, Germany
49-30-46-70-82-0 (fax) 49-30-46-307-658

Centillion Networks Inc.
Mountain View, CA
800-ATM-LANS or 415-969-6700
(fax) 415-969-6710

Central Design Systems Inc.
San Jose, CA
800-366-2374 or 408-383-9399
(fax) 408-383-9395

Century Software
Salt Lake City, UT
800-877-3088—801-268-3088
(fax) 801-268-2772
http://www.censoft.com

Cerfnet Inc.
San Diego, CA
800-876-CERF or 619-455-3900
(fax) 619-455-3990
http://www.cer.net/

cfSoftware
Des Plaines, IL
800-366-8756 or 708-824-7180
(fax) 708-824-0930

Chase Research Inc.
Nashville, TN
800-872-0770 or 615-872-0770
(fax) 615-872-0771

Checkpoint Software Technologies
Ltd.
Ramat-Gan, Israel
972-3-6131833 (fax) 972-3-5759256
http://www.checkpoint.com

Cheyenne Communications Inc.
Roslyn Heights, NY
800-243-9462 or 516-484-5110
(fax) 516-627-2999
http://www.chey.com/

Chipcom Corp.
Southborough, MA
800-228-9930 or 508-460-8900
(fax) 508-460-8950

Cisco Systems Inc.
San Jose, CA
800-859-2726 or 408-526-4000
(fax) 408-526-4100
http://www.cisco.com

Citrix Systems Inc.
Coral Springs, FL
800-437-7503 or 305-340-2246
(fax) 305-341-6880
http://www.citrix.com

Claflin & Clayton Inc.
Northboro, MA
508-393-7979 (fax) 508-393-8788
http://www.c-c.com/

Clark Development Company
Murray, UT
801-261-1686 (fax) 801-261-8987

Cnet Technology Inc.
Hsinchu, Taiwan
886-35-782-211 (fax) 886-35-782-458

Coastcom
Alameda, CA
800-433-3433 or 510-523-6006
(fax) 510-523-6150

Colcom Inc.
Austin, TX
800-888-1978 or 512-244-6689
(fax) 512-244-6694

Collabra Software Inc.
Mountain View, CA
800-474-7427 or 415-940-6400
(fax) 415-940-6440

Combinet Inc.
Sunnyvale, CA
800-967-6651 or 408-522-9020
(fax) 408-732-5479
http://www.combinet.com

COM & DIA
Raleigh, NC
919-848-0001 (fax) 919-848-7779

Command Software Systems
Jupiter, FL
407-575-3200 (fax) 407-575-3026

Communication Devices Inc.
Clifton, NJ
800-359-8561 or 201-772-6997
(fax) 201-772-0747

Commvision Corp.
Mountain View, CA
800-832-6526 or 415-254-5720
(fax) 415-254-9320

Companhia Portugesa Radio Marconi
S.A.
Lisbon, Portugal
351-1-790-7521 (fax) 351-1-790-7539

Compaq Computer Corp.
Houston, TX
800-345-1518 or 713-370-0670
(fax) 713-378-1442

Compatible Systems Corp.
Boulder, CO
800-356-0283 or 303-444-9532
(fax) 303-444-9595
http://www.compatible.com

Compex
Anaheim, CA
714-630-7302 (fax) 714-630-6521

Complex Architecture
Wakefield, MA
617-224-3344 (fax) 617-224-3380

Compression Labs Inc.
San Jose, CA
408-435-3000 (fax) 408-922-5429

CompuServe Inc.
Columbus, OH
800-433-0389 or 614-798-3356
(fax) 614-791-9298
http://www.compuserve.com

Computer Associates International
Inc.
Islandia, NY
800-225-5224 or 516-342-5224
(fax) 516-342-5734
http://www.cai.com

Computer Knacks Inc.
Shrewsbury, NJ
800-551-1433 or 908-530-0262
(fax) 908-741-0972

Computerm
Pittsburgh, PA
412-391-7804 (fax) 412-391-4964

Computer Network Technology
Cambridge, MA
800-BRIXTON or 617-661-6262
(fax) 617-547-9820

Computer Peripheral Systems Inc.
Atlanta, GA
800-888-0051 or 404-908-1107
(fax) 404-908-1208

Computer Systems Products Inc.
Minneapolis, MN
800-422-2537 or 612-476-6866
(fax) 612-475-8457
http://www.csp.com

Computer Vectors Inc.
Kailua-Kona, HI
808-329-6645 (fax) 808-329-6523

Computone Corp.
Roswell, GA
800-241-3946 or 404-475-2725
(fax) 404-664-1510
http://www.computone.com

Compuware Corp.
Farmington Hills, MI
800-368-4ECO or 810-737-7300
(fax) 810-737-7108

Comstream
San Diego, CA
619-458-1800 (fax) 619-657-5404

Comtest International
London, UK
44-0-171-938-4591 (fax) 44-0-171-938-1649

Comtrol Corp.
St. Paul, MN
800-926-6876 or 612-631-7654
(fax) 612-631-8117
http://www.comtrol.com

Concert Communications
Reston, VA
703-707-4000 (fax) 703-707-4072

Concord Communications Inc.
Marlboro, MA
800-851-8725 or 508-460-4646
(fax) 508-481-9772

Confertech International Inc.
Westminster, CO
800-525-8244 or 303-633-3000
(fax) 303-633-3001

Connectware Inc.
Richardson, TX
214-907-1093 (fax) 214-907-1594

Control Data Systems Inc.
Arden Hills, MN
800-257-OPEN or 612-482-2100
(fax) 612-482-2791

Coronet Systems
Los Altos, CA
415-960-3255 (fax) 415-960-3288

Covia Technologies
Rosemont, IL
708-518-4721 (fax) 708-518-4850

CR Systems A/S
Copenhagen, Denmark
45-44-66-11-44 (fax) 45-44-65-13-88

Cray Communications Inc.
Annapolis Junction, MD
800-FOR-CRAY or 301-317-7710
(fax) 301-317-7535

Crosscomm Corp.
Marlborough, MA
800-388-1200 or 508-481-4060
(fax) 508-229-5535

Crosswise
Santa Cruz, CA
408-459-9060 (fax) 408-426-3859

Cryptocard Inc.
Buffalo Grove, IL
800-307-7042 or 708-459-6500
(fax) 708-459-6599

CSS Laboratories Inc.
Irvine, CA
714-852-8161 (fax) 714-852-0410

Cubix Corp.
Carson City, NV
800-829-0550 or 702-888-1000
(fax) 702-888-1001

Cyberaccess Inc.
Valley View, OH
800-524-5003 or 216-524-5005
(fax) 216-524-5001

Cybersafe Corp.
Redmond, WA
206-883-8721 (fax) 206-883-6951

Cylink Corp.
Sunnyvale, CA
800-533-3958 or 408-735-5800
(fax) 408-735-6643

Cyranex
Ottowa, Ontario
613-738-3864 or (fax) 613-738-3871
http://www.cyranex.com

Danware Data A/S
Copenhagen, Denmark
45-44-53-25-25 (fax) 45-44-53-15-51

Databeam Corp.
Lexington, KY
800-877-2325 or 606-245-3500
(fax) 606-245-3528

Datacom Technologies Inc.
Everett, WA
800-468-5557 or 206-355-0590
(fax) 206-290-1600

Datacraft Asia
Hong Kong
852-2513-3168 (fax) 852-2567-4268

Data Interface Systems Corp.
Austin, TX
800-351-4244 or 512-346-5641
(fax) 512-346-4035

Data Management
Malabar, FL
407-725-8081 (fax) 407-724-4267

Data Race Inc.
San Antonio, TX
210-558-1900 (fax) 210-558-1939

Data Switch Corp.
Shelton, CT
203-926-1801 (fax) 203-924-6400

Data Viz Inc.
Trumbull, CT
800-733-0030 or 203-268-0030
(fax) 203-268-4345

Datacom Technologies, Inc.
Everett, WA
800-468-5557 or 206-355-0590
(fax) 206-290-1600

Datawatch Corp.
Wilmington, MA
800-445-3311 or 508-988-9700
(fax) 508-988-2040

Datax
Berchem, Belgium
32-0-230-28-87 (fax) 32-0-3-230-27-
39

Dayna
Salt Lake City, UT
415-960-3255 (fax) 415-960-3288

Delphi Internet Services Corp.
New York, NY
800-695-4005 or 212-462-5000
(fax) 212-462-6000
http://bosa00.delphi.com/http_home.
html

Deltec Electronics Corp.
San Diego, CA
800-DELTEC-1 or 619-291-4211
(fax) 619-291-2973

Denmac Systems Inc.
Northbrook, IL
708-291-7760 (fax) 708-291-7763

Desknet Systems Inc.
Armonk, NY
800-DESKNET or 914-273-6232
(fax) 914-273-6209

Desktalk Systems Inc.
Torrance, CA
800-DESKTALK or 310-323-5998
(fax) 310-323-6197

Deutsche Telekom
Bonn, Germany
49-130-80-11-80 (fax) 49-228-936-1609

Devcom Mid-America Inc.
Oak Brook, IL
708-574-3600 (fax) 708-572-0508

Develcon
Saskatoon, Saskatchewan
800-667-9333 or 306-933-3300
(fax) 306-931-1370
http://www.develcon.com

Dialogic Corp.
Parsippany, NJ
800-755-4444 or 201-993-3000
(fax) 201-993-3093

Digi International
Eden Prairie, MN
800-344-4273 or 612-943-9020
(fax) 612-943-5398
http://www.digibd.com

Digilog
Willow Grove, PA
800-344-4564 or 215-830-9400
(fax) 215-830-9444

Digital Equipment Corp. (DEC)
Maynard, MA
800-332-4636 or 508-493-5111
(fax) 508-841-5681
http://www.digital.com/info/spd

Digital Instrumentation
Los Alamos, NM
505-662-1459

Digital Link Corp.
Sunnyvale, CA
408-745-6200 (fax) 408-745-6250

Digital Pathways Inc.
Mountain View, CA
800-344-7284 or 415-964-0707
(fax) 415-961-7487

Digitech Industries Inc.
Danbury, CT
203-797-2676 (fax) 203-797-2682

Distinct Corp.
Saratoga, CA
408-366-8933 (fax) 408-366-0153

D-Link Systems Inc.
Irvine, CA
800-326-1688 or 714-455-1688
(fax) 714-455-2521

Dual-Tek Corp.
Kingston, NY
800-835-3017 or 914-331-0142
(fax) 914-331-0195

Duke Communications
Van Nuys, CA
818-781-7600 (fax) 818-782-1412

Dynatech Communications Inc.
Woodbridge, VA
703-494-1400 (fax) 703-494-1920
http://www@dynatech.com

Early, Cloud & Company
Middletown, RI
800-322-3042 or 401-849-0500
(fax) 401-849-1190

Eastern Research Inc.
Moorestown, NJ
800-337-4374 or 609-273-6622
(fax) 609-273-1847

E-Comms, Inc.
Gig Harbor, WA
800-247-1431 or 206-857-3399
(fax) 206-857-3444

E.G. Software
Portland, OR
503-294-7025 (fax) 503-294-7130

Eicon Technology
Lachine, Quebec
800-676-9267 or 514-631-2592
(fax) 514-631-3092

Eiger Labs Inc.
Sunnyvale, CA
800-653-4437 or 408-774-3456
(fax) 408-774-3444

Elan Computer Group,Inc.
Mountain View, CA
800-536-3526 or 415-964-2200
(fax) 415-964-8588
http://www.elan.com/

Elan Software Corp.
Pacific Palisades, CA
800-654-3526 or 310-454-6800
(fax) 310-454-4848

Electronic Specialists Inc.
Natick, MA
800-225-4876 or 508-655-1532
(fax) 508-653-0268

Eliashim Microcomputers Inc.
Pembroke Pines, FL
800-477-5177 or 305-450-9611
(fax) 305-450-9612

Elsner Technologies Company
Fort Worth, TX
800-243-2228 or 817-626-4110
(fax) 817-626-5330

EMASS Inc.
Englewood, CO
303-792-9700 (fax) 303-792-2465

EMC Corp.
Hopkinton, MA
800-258-5528 (fax) 508-497-6904

Emulex Corp.
Costa Mesa, CA
800-EMULEX3 or 714-662-5600
(fax) 714-513-8266

Enabling Technologies Group Inc.
Atlanta, GA
404-642-1500 (fax) 404-993-4667

Engage Communications, Inc.
Aptos, CA
408-688-1021 (fax) 408-688-1421
http://www.engage.com

Ensamble Software
Dallas, TX
214-341-6789 (fax) 214-404-2033

Epilogue Technology Corp.
Albuquerque, NM
505-271-9933 (fax) 505-271-9798
http://www.epilogue.com

Epson America Inc.
Torrance, CA
800-338-2349 or 310-782-0770
(fax) 310-782-5161

Ericsson Inc.
Research Triangle Park, NC
800-227-3663 or 919-990-7000
(fax) 919-990-7451

E-Tech Research Inc.
Santa Clara, CA
408-988-8108 (fax) 408-988-8109
http://www.e-tech.com

Eunetcom
Frankfurt, Germany
49-69-92-90-10 (fax) 49-69-92-08-20-90

Eunet
Amsterdam, Holland
31-20-623-3803 (fax) 31-20-622-4657

EUnet GB Ltd.
Whitstable Kent, UK
44-1227-266466 (fax) 44-1227-266477
http://www.britain.EU.net

Executive Software
Glendale, CA
800-829-4357 or 818-547-2050
(fax) 818-545-9241
http://www.earthlink.net/execsoft

Exfo E.O. Engineering
Vanier, Quebec
800-663-EXFO or 418-683-0211
(fax) 418-683-2170

Extended Systems Inc.
Boise, ID
800-235-7576 or 208-322-7800
(fax) 208-377-1906
http://www.extendedsys.com

Faircom Corp.
Columbia, MO
800-234-8180 or 314-445-6833
(fax) 314-445-9698

Farabi Technology Corp.
North Providence, RI
800-565-3455 or 514-332-3455
(fax) 514-332-3915

Farallon Computing Inc.
Alameda, CA
510-814-5000 (fax) 510-814-5023
http://www.farallon.com

Fastcomm Communications Corp.
Sterling, VA
800-521-2496 or 703-318-7750
(fax) 703-787-4625
http://www.fastcomm.com

Fasttrack Inc.
Germantown, MD
301-990-1500 (fax) 301-977-5491

Faxquest
Sunnyvale, CA
415-380-2560 (fax) 415-380-2570

Fiber Optic Technologies Inc.
Englewood, CO
303-792-0770 (fax) 303-792-0778

Fibronics Ltd.
Haifa, Israel
972-4-313313 (fax) 972-4-550550
http://www.fibronics.co.il

Finisar Corp.
Mountain View, CA
415-691-4000 (fax) 415-691-4010

Firefox
San Jose, CA
800-230-6090 or 408-467-1100
(fax) 408-467-1105
http://www.firefox.com

First Virtual Corp.
Santa Clara, CA
800-351-8539 or 408-988-7070
(fax) 408-988-7077

Fischer International Systems Corp.
Naples, FL
800-237-4510 or 941-643-1500
(fax) 941-436-2586

Fluke Corp.
Everett, WA
800-44-FLUKE or 206-347-6100
(fax) 206-356-5116

The Forefront Group
Houston, TX
800-867-1101 or 713-961-1101
(fax) 713-961-1149
http://www.ffg.com

Fore Systems Inc.
Warrendale, PA
800-884-0040 or 412-772-6600
(fax) 412-772-6500
http://www.fore.com

Fotec Inc.
Boston, MA
800-537-8254 or 617-241-7810
(fax) 617-241-8616

4-Sight
West Des Moines, IA
515-221-2100 (fax) 515-224-0802

France Telecom
Paris, France
44-75-27-28 (fax) 44-76-85-00

Frederick Engineering Inc.
Columbia, MD
410-290-9000 (fax) 410-381-7180

Frontier Software Development Inc.
Chelmsford, MA
800-357-7666 or 508-244-4000
(fax) 508-244-4004

Frontier Technologies Corp.
Mequon, WI
800-929-3054 or 414-241-4555
(fax) 414-241-7084
http://www@frontiertech.com

Frye Computer Systems Inc.
Boston, MA
800-234-3793 or 617-451-5400
(fax) 617-451-6711

FTP Software Inc.
Andover, MA
508-685-3300 (fax) 508-794-4488
http://www.ftp.com

Fujitsu Business Communication
Systems
Anaheim, CA
714-630-7721 (fax) 714-764-2527

Fujitsu Open Systems Solutions Inc.
San Jose, CA
408-432-1300 (fax) 408-432-1318
http://www.ossi.com

Funk Software Inc.
Cambridge, MA
800-828-4146 or 617-497-6339
(fax) 617-547-1031
http://www.funk.com

Futuresoft Engineering Inc.
Houston, TX
800-989-8908 or 713-496-9400
(fax) 713-496-1090
http://www.fse.com

Futurus Corp.
Norcross, GA
404-242-7797 (fax) 404-242-7221

Galacticomm Inc.
Fort Lauderdale, FL
800-328-1128 or 305-583-5990
(fax) 305-583-7846

Gambit Computer Communications
Ltd.
Yokneam, Israel
972-4-989-0140 (fax) 972-4-989-0189

Gandalf Systems Corp.
Deltran, NJ
609-461-8100 (fax) 609-461-4074

GDT Softworks Inc.
Burnaby, British Columbia
800-663-6222 or 604-291-9121
(fax) 604-291-9689

GE Capital Spacenet Services Inc.
McLean, VA
703-848-1000 (fax) 703-848-1010

GEC Plessey Semiconductors
Scotts Valley, CA
408-438-2900 (fax) 408-438-5576

General Datacomm Inc.
Middlebury, CT
203-574-1118 (fax) 203-758-8507

Gentner Communications Corp.
Salt Lake City, UT
800-945-7730 or 801-975-7200
(fax) 801-974-3676

Geotek
Salzgitter, Germany
53-41-21-8301 (fax) 53-41-21-8325

Geotel Communications Corp.
Littleton, MA
800-486-1199 or 508-486-1100
(fax) 508-486-1200

Gilat Satellite Networks
Tel Aviv, Israel
972-3-499068 (fax) 972-3-6487429

Gilltro-Electronics Inc.
Santa Clara, CA
800-445-8769 or 408-727-6422
(fax) 408-727-5508

GL Communications Inc.
Gaithersburg, MD
301-670-4784 (fax) 301-926-8234

Global Village Communication
Sunnyvale, CA
408-523-1000 (fax) 408-523-2408
http://www.globalvillag.com

Globetrotter Software Inc.
Campbell, CA
408-370-2800 (fax) 408-370-2884

GMA Communications
Bala Cynwyd, PA
610-668-2266 (fax) 610-668-4111

GMM Research Corp.
Irvine, CA
800-531-6145 or 714-752-9447
(fax) 714-752-7335

GN Nettest Inc.
Markham, Ontario
800-262-8835 or 905-479-8090
(fax) 905-475-6524

Grand Junction Networks Inc.
Fremont, CA
800-747-FAST or 510-252-0726
(fax) 510-252-0915

Graphnet Inc.
Teaneck, NJ
800-327-1800 or 201-837-5100
(fax) 201-833-3888

Groupquest
Phoenix, AZ
800-864-5061 or 602-234-6949
(fax) 602-234-6950

Gsoft Systems Inc.
Frederick, MD
301-898-7973 (fax) 301-898-0310

GTE Government Systems
Needham Heights, MA
617-455-4381 (fax) 617-455-5222

Hadax Electronics Inc.
South Hackensack, NJ
201-807-1155 (fax) 201-807-1782

Harris Computer Systems Corp.
Ft. Lauderdale, FL
800-666-4544 or 305-974-1700
(fax) 305-977-5580
http://www.hcsc.com

Haventree Software Ltd.
Kingston, Ontario
800-267-0668 or 613-544-6035
(fax) 613-544-9632

Hawknet Inc.
Carlsbad, CA
800-HAWKNET or 619-929-9966
(fax) 619-929-9969
http://www.hwknet.com\netinfo

Helios Software
Cupertino, CA
408-864-0690 (fax) 408-864-0694

Hewlett-Packard Co.
Palo Alto, CA
800-231-9300 or 415-857-1501
(fax) 415-857-5518

Hewlett-Packard Idacom
Alberta, Canada
403-439-4866 (fax) 403-430-2640

Hewlett-Packard Co. Roseville
Networks Division
Roseville, CA
800-533-1333 or 916-786-8000
(fax) 916-785-2683

Hitachi Ltd.
Tokyo, Japan
81-3-3763-2411 (fax) 81-3-5471-2565
http://www.hitachi.co.jp/

Horizons Technology Inc.
San Diego, CA
800-828-3808 or 619-277-7100
(fax) 619-565-1175
http://www.horizons.com

HT Communications Inc.
Simi Valley, CA
805-579-1700 (fax) 805-522-5295

Hughes Network Systems
Germantown, MD
301-428-5500 (fax) 301-428-1868

Hummingbird Communications Ltd.
North York, Ontario
416-496-2200 (fax) 416-496-2207
http://www.hummingbird.com

Hypercom Network Systems
Phoenix, AZ
602-866-5399 (fax) 602-866-5380

Hyperdesk Corp.
Westborough, MA
800-TEAMWRK or 508-366-5050
(fax) 508-366-9140

Hyperlink Technologies Inc.
Boca Raton, FL
407-995-2256 (fax) 407-995-2432

Ibex Technologies
Placerville, CA
916-621-4342 (fax) 916-939-8899

IBM
Armonk, NY
800-IBM-CALL or 914-332-3900
(fax) 800-IBM-4FAX
http://www.ibm.com

IBM Personal Software Products
Division
Austin, TX
512-823-0000 (fax) 800-IBM-4FAX
http://www.ibm.com

IBM Printing Systems Co.
Southbury, CT
203-262-2000

IBM Storage Systems Division
San Jose, CA
800-426-7299 or 408-256-1600
(fax) 408-256-5082

IBM Systems Management
Somers, NY
914-766-1900 (fax) 914-766-9417

ICG Wireless Services
Thornton, CO
800-799-2411 or 303-705-6900
(fax) 303-705-6999

ICL Enterprises North America
Reston, VA
703-648-3300 (fax) 703-648-3326
http://www.icl.co.uk

Imatek Corp.
Sunnyvale, CA
408-244-8864 (fax) 408-244-8864
http://www.imatek.com/

IMC Networks Corp.
Irvine, CA
714-724-1070 (fax) 714-724-1020

Incite
Dallas, TX
800-9-INCITE or 214-447-8200
(fax) 214-446-8205
http://www.incite.com

Incognito Software
Vancouver, British Columbia
604-688-4332 (fax) 604-688-4339

Independent Technologies
Omaha, NE
402-496-4700 (fax) 402-493-5100

Infinite Technologies
Owings Mills, MD
800-678-1097 or 410-363-1097
(fax) 410-363-0846
http://www.ihub.com

Infonet Services Corp.
El Segundo, CA
310-335-2600 (fax) 310-335-2876

Information Builders
New York, NY
212-736-4433

Information Resource Engineering
Inc.
Baltimore, MD
410-931-7500 (fax) 410-931-7524

Informix Software Inc.
Menlo Park, CA
415-926-6300 (fax) 415-926-6593

Infoseek Corp.
Santa Clara, CA
408-982-4450 (fax) 408-986-1889

InfraLAN Wireless Communications
Acton, MA
508-266-1500 (fax) 508-635-0806

Innosoft International Inc.
West Covina, CA
800-552-5444 or 818-919-3600
(fax) 818-919-3614
http://www.innosoft.com/

Insitu Inc.
Boston, MA
617-720-0821

Insoft Inc.
Mechanicsburg, PA
717-730-9501 (fax) 717-730-9504
http://www.insoft.com

Intecom Inc.
Dallas, TX
800-468-3945 or 214-447-9000
(fax) 214-447-8533

Integrated Network Corp.
Bridgewater, NJ
800-345-1365 or 908-218-1600
(fax) 908-218-0804

Integratrak Inc.
Seattle, WA
206-547-3390 (fax) 206-547-2502

Intel Corp. Network Products
Division
Hillsboro, OR
800-538-3373 or 503-264-7354
(fax) 503-629-7580
http://www.intel.com

Intellicom Inc.
Chatsworth, CA
800-922-2882 or 818-407-3900
(fax) 818-882-2404

Interactive Inc.
Humboldt, SD
605-363-5117 (fax) 605-363-5102

Intercon Systems Corp.
Herndon, VA
703-709-5500

Interface Systems Inc.
Ann Arbor, MI
800-544-4072 or 313-769-5900
(fax) 313-769-1047

Intergraph Corp.
Huntsville, AL
800-345-4856 or 205-730-2000
(fax) 205-730-2461

Interlink Computer Sciences Inc.
Fremont, CA
800-422-3711 or 510-657-9800
(fax) 510-659-6381
http://www.interlink.com/

International Data Sciences Inc.
Warwick, RI
800-437-3282 or 401-737-9900
(fax) 401-737-9911

International Network Services
Mountain View, CA
800-3773-INS or 415-254-0800
(fax) 415-254-4288
http://www.ins.com

Intrak Inc.
San Diego, CA
800-233-7494 or 619-695-1900
(fax) 619-271-4989

Intrusion Detection
New York, NY
800-408-6104 or 212-348-8900
(fax) 212-427-9185

Ipswitch
Wakefield, MA
617-246-1150 (fax) 617-245-2975

ISDN Systems Corp.
Vienna, VA
800-KNOW-ISC or 703-883-0933
(fax) 703-883-8043
http://www.infoanalytic.com/isc

ISDN*tek
San Gregorio, CA
415-712-3000 (fax) 415-712-3003

IsiCAD Inc.
Anaheim, CA
714-533-8910 (fax) 714-533-8642

Isolation Systems
Toronto, Canada
416-231-1248 (fax) 416-231-8561

ITK Telecommunications AG
Dortmund, Germany
49-231-9747-0 (fax) 49-231-9747-111

ITT Cannon Network Systems &
Services
Santa Ana, CA
714-754-2259 (fax) 714-754-2098

J&L Information Systems
Chatsworth, CA
818-772-3825 (fax) 818-882-9134

JOLT
Jerusalem, Israel
972-2-710445 (fax) 972-2-710448

Jones Futurex Inc.
Rocklin, CA
916-632-3456 (fax) 916-632-3445

Jupiter Technology Inc.
Waltham, MA
617-894-9300 (fax) 617-894-9700

Kalpana Inc.
Sunnyvale, CA
408-749-1600 (fax) 408-749-1690
http://www.kalpana.com/kalpana

Kasten Chase
Mississauga, Ontario
905-238-6900 (fax) 905-238-6806

Kingston Technology Corp.
Fountain Valley, CA
714-435-2615 (fax) 714-438-2720

Klos Technologies Inc.
Merrimack, NH
603-424-8300 (fax) 603-424-9300

K-NET Ltd.
Camberley, UK
44-(0)-1252-877443 (fax) 44-(0)-
1252-872890

Kokusai Denshin Denwa Co. Ltd.
Tokyo, Japan
81-3-3324-39180

Krone Inc.
Englewood, CO
800-775-KRONE or 303-790-2619
(fax) 303-790-2117

Lagercrantz Communication AB
Stockholm, Sweden
46-8-6260650 (fax) 46-8-7547759

LAN Access Corp.
Torrance, CA
310-328-9700 (fax) 310-328-9696

LANart Corp.
Needham, MA
800-292-1994 or 617-444-1994
(fax) 617-444-3692

LANcast Inc.
Amherst, NH
800-9-LANCAST or 603-880-1833
(fax) 603-881-9888

LANcity Corp.
Andover, MA
508-475-4050 (fax) 508-475-0550

LANnair Ltd.
Tel Aviv, Israel
972-3-645-8423 (fax) 972-3-648-7146

Lannet Data Communications Ltd.
Irvine, CA
800-5LANNET or 714-752-6638
(fax) 714-752-6641

Lanoptics
Migdal Ha-Emek, Israel
972-6-546-222 (fax) 972-6-540-124

LANsource Technologies Inc.
Toronto, Ontario
800-677-2727 or 416-535-3555
(fax) 416-535-6225

The LAN Support Group Inc.
Houston, TX
800-749-8439 or 713-789-0882
(fax) 713-977-9111
http://www.lsg.com

LANtelligence
Las Vegas, NV
909-949-4486 (fax) 909-982-0929

Lantronix
Irvine, CA
714-453-3990 (fax) 714-453-3995
http://www.lantronix.com/

LANworks Technologies Inc.
Mississauga, Ontario
905-238-5528 (fax) 905-238-9407

Larscom Inc.
Santa Clara, CA
408-988-6600 (fax) 408-986-8690

Larus Corp.
San Jose, CA
408-494-1500 (fax) 408-494-0735

Laser Communications Inc.
Lancaster, PA
800-527-3740 or 717-394-8634
(fax) 717-396-9831

LCI International Inc.
McLean, VA
800-296-0220 or 703-442-0220
(fax) 703-821-3368

L-Com
North Andover, MA
800-343-1455 or 508-682-6936
(fax) 508-689-9484

LDDS Worldcom
Jackson, MS
800-364-5113 or 601-360-8600
(fax) 601-360-8533
www:http://www.wiltel.com

Leemah Datacom Security Corp.
Hayward, CA
800-331-2734 or 510-786-0790
(fax) 510-786-1123

Legato Systems Inc.
Palo Alto, CA
415-812-6000 (fax) 415-812-6032

Legent Corp.
Herndon, VA
800-949-5468 or 703-708-3000
(fax) 703-708-3471
http://www.legent.com

Leviton Telecom
Bothell, WA
800-722-2082 or 206-486-2222
(fax) 800-767-5270 or 206-483-5270

Liebert Corp.
Columbus, OH
800-877-9222 or 614-888-0246
(fax) 614-841-6022

Lightspeed Software
Bakersfield, CA
805-324-4291 (fax) 805-324-1437

Linksys
Irvine, CA
800-546-5797 or 714-261-1288
(fax) 714-261-8868

Link-VTC Inc.
Boulder, CO
800-LINK-VTC or 303-473-0200
(fax) 303-473-0220

Litton-Fibercom
Roanoke, VA
800-423-1183 or 703-342-6700
(fax) 703-342-5961

Livingston Enterprises Inc.
Pleasanton, CA
800-458-9966 or 510-426-0770
(fax) 510-426-8951
http://www.livingston.com

Locus Computing Corp.
Inglewood, CA
800-95LOCUS or 310-670-6500
(fax) 310-670-2980

Logicode Technology, Inc.
Camarillo, CA
805-388-9000 (fax) 805-735-6442

Logtel Systems
Petah-Tikva, Israel
972-3-9247780 (fax) 972-3-9247783

Loral Federal Systems
Manassas, VA
703-369-4307

Loral Test & Information Systems
San Diego, CA
800-644-3334 or 619-674-5100
(fax) 619-674-5145

Los Altos Technologies Inc.
Los Altos, CA
415-988-4848 (fax) 415-988-4860

Lotus Development Corp.
Cambridge, MA
800-343-5414 or 617-577-8500
http://www.lotus.com

Madge Networks Inc.
San Jose, CA
408-955-0700 (fax) 408-955-0970

Make Systems Inc.
Mountain View, CA
415-941-9800 (fax) 415-941-5856
http://www.makesys.com/makesys

Markham Computer
Boca Raton, FL
800-262-7542 or 407-394-3994
(fax) 407-394-3844

Mastersoft Inc.
Scottsdale, AZ
800-624-6107 or 602-948-4888
(fax) 602-948-8261
http://www.chaco.com./mastersoft/

Maxat Ltd
London, UK
44-171-430-4400 (fax) 44-171-430-4321

Maximum Computer Technologies
Inc.
Kennesaw, GA
800-582-9337 or 404-428-5000
(fax) 404-428-5009

Maximum Strategy Inc.
Milpitas, CA
800-352-1600 or 408-383-1600
(fax) 408-383-1616
http://www.maxstrat.com

Maxim Systems Corp.
McLean, VA
703-561-0400 (fax) 703-761-0414

Maxoptix Corp. Networks Division
Fremont, CA
800-546-6695 or 510-353-9700
(fax) 510-353-1845

Maxtech Corp.
Rockaway, NJ
800-289-4821 or 201-586-3008
(fax) 201-586-3308

McAfee & Associates Inc.
Santa Clara, CA
408-988-3832 (fax) 408-970-9727

McData Corp.
Broomfield, CO
303-460-9200 (fax) 303-465-4996

MCI Communications Corp.
Washington, DC
800-933-9029 or 202-872-1600

MCI International
Rye Brook, NY
914-934-6110 (fax) 914-934-6863
http://www.internetMCI.com

Medialogic ADL Inc.
Boulder, CO
303-939-9780 (fax) 303-939-9745

Megahertz Corp.
Salt Lake City, UT
800-527-8677 or 801-320-7701
(fax) 801-320-6022
http://www.xmission.com/mhz

Memco Software
New York, NY
800-862-2602 or 212-286-8820
(fax) 212-286-9150

Memorex Telex Corp.
Irving, TX
800-980-6767 or 214-444-3500
(fax) 214-444-3501
http://www.mtc.com.

Memory International
Irvine, CA
800-266-0488 or 714-453-8008
(fax) 714-453-8103

Memotec Communications Inc.
North Andover, MA
508-681-0600 (fax) 508-681-0660

Mercury Communications
London, UK
44-171-528-2000

Mergent International Inc.
Rocky Hill, CT
800-688-1199 or 203-257-4223
(fax) 203-257-1975
http://www.mergent.com

Meridian
Chesterfield, MO
314-532-7708 (fax) 314-532-3242

Meridian Data Inc.
Scotts Valley, CA
800-767-2537 or 408-461-3100
(fax) 408-438-6816

Metacomp Inc.
San Diego, CA
619-674-5000 (fax) 619-674-5005

Metrodata
Egham, UK
44-1784-477421 (fax) 44-1784-
477423

MFS Communications Ltd.
London, UK
44-171-570-5700 (fax) 44-171-571-
5711

MFS Datanet Inc.
San Jose, CA
800-MFS-4USA or 408-975-2200
(fax) 408-975-2210
http://www.mfsdatanet.com

Micom Communications Corp.
Simi Valley, CA
805-583-8600 (fax) 805-583-1997

Microbeam Corp.
Largo, FL
800-879-2727 or 813-546-2727
(fax) 813-541-3278

Microcom Inc.
Norwood, MA
800-822-8224 or 617-551-1000
(fax) 617-551-1021

Micro Computer Systems Inc.
Irving, TX
214-659-1514 (fax) 214-659-1624
http://www.mcsdallas.com

Microdyne Corp.
Alexandria, VA
800-255-3967 or 703-329-3700
(fax) 703-329-3716

Microframe Inc.
Edison, NJ
908-494-4440 (fax) 908-494-4570

Micro-Integration Corp.
Frostburg, MD
800-832-4526 or 301-689-0800
(fax) 301-689-0808

Micromuse PLC
London, UK
44-081-875-9500 (fax) 44-081-875-9995

Micronet Technology Inc.
Irvine, CA
714-453-6000 (fax) 714-453-6001

Microplex Systems Ltd.
Burnaby, British Columbia
800-665-7798 or 604-444-4232
(fax) 604-444-4239
http://microplex.com/

Microsoft Corp.
Redmond, WA
206-882-8080 (fax) 206-936-7329

Microsystems Engineering Co.
Lombard, IL
800-359-3695 or 708-261-0111
(fax) 708-261-9520
http://www.microsystems.com/
products

Microsystems Software Inc.
Framingham, MA
800-489-2001 or 508-879-9000
(fax) 508-626-8515

Micro Tempus Inc.
Montreal, Quebec
800-361-4983 or 514-848-0803
(fax) 514-848-0713

Microtest
Phoenix, AZ
602-952-6400 (fax) 602-952-6490

Microwave Networks Inc.
Houston, TX
800-495-7123 or 713-495-7123
(fax) 713-495-9759

Midnight Networks Inc.
Waltham, MA
617-890-1001 (fax) 617-890-0028

Milan Technology Corp.
Sunnyvale, CA
800-GO-MILAN or 408-752-2770
(fax) 408-744-2793
http://www.milan.com

Millennet
Fremont, CA
510-770-9390 (fax) 510-770-9213

Mil 3 Inc.
Washington, DC
202-364-8390 (fax) 202-364-6182

Miralink Corp.
Orem, UT
801-785-6400 (fax) 801-224-8087

Mitek Systems Inc.
San Diego, CA
800-350-0661 or 619-635-5900
(fax) 619-635-5908

Mitel Corp.
Kanata, Ontario
800-648-3587 or 613-592-2122
(fax) 613-592-4784

Mitron Computer Inc.
Campbell, CA
800-713-6888 or 408-371-8166
(fax) 408-371-8167

MKS Inc.
Waterloo, Ontario
519-884-2251 (fax) 519-884-8861
http://www.mks.com

Mobilware Inc.
Richardson, TX
214-690-6181 (fax) 214-690-6185

Mobius Encryption
Mississauga, Ontario
800-561-6100 or 905-507-4220
(fax) 905-507-4230

Moda Systems Inc.
Cambridge, MA
617-494-0402 (fax) 617-494-1744

Mod-Tap
Harvard, MA
508-772-5630 (fax) 508-772-2011

Morgan Hill Supply Co.
Kingston, NY
800-874-4848 or 914-331-4848
(fax) 914-331-4894

Morning Star Technologies Inc.
Columbus, OH
800-558-7827 or 614-451-1883
(fax) 614-459-5054

Motorola Inc. Wireless Data Group
Schaumburg, IL
800-MOTOROL or 708-576-5000
(fax) 708-576-9595
http://www.mot.com

Motorola Information Systems Group
Network Systems Division
Mansfield, MA
800-446-6336 or 508-261-4000
(fax) 508-337-8004
http://www.cdx.mot.com

Motorola Information Systems Group
Transmission Products Division
Huntsville, AL
800-451-2369 or 205-430-8000
(fax) 205-430-5657
http://www.cdx.mot.com

Mountain Network Solutions
Scotts Valley, CA
800-458-0300 or 408-438-6650
(fax) 408-461-3047

MTI
Anaheim, CA
800-999-MTI or 714-970-0300
(fax) 714-693-2256

Multiaccess Computing Corp.
Santa Barbara, CA
805-964-2332 (fax) 805-681-7469

Multipoint Networks
Belmont, CA
800-872-8958 or 415-595-3300
(fax) 415-595-2417

Multi-Tech Systems Inc.
Mounds View, MN
800-328-9717 or 612-785-3500
(fax) 612-785-9874

Mustang Software Inc.
Bakersfield, CA
800-999-9619 or 805-873-2500
(fax) 805-873-2599

Nashoba Networks Inc.
Littleton, MA
508-486-3200 (fax) 508-486-0990
http://www.harpell.com/nashoba

National Semiconductor Corp.
Santa Clara, CA
800-272-9959 or 408-721-5000
(fax) 408-739-9803

NBase Communications
Lenexa, KS
800-998-4223 or 913-888-4999
(fax) 913-888-4103

NBS Systems Inc.
Enfield, CT
203-741-2244 (fax) 203-745-5030

NEC America Inc. Corporate
Networks Group
Irving, TX
214-751-7000 (fax) 214-751-7002

Neon Software
Lafayette, CA
800-334-6366 or 510-283-9771
(fax) 510-283-6507

Nestor Inc.
Providence, RI
401-331-9640 (fax) 401-331-7319

Netcorp
Montreal, Quebec
800-NETCORP or 514-923-4040
(fax) 514-923-4882

Netedge Systems Inc.
Research Triangle Park, NC
800-638-3343 or 919-991-9000
(fax) 919-991-9060

Netframe Systems Inc.
Milpitas, CA
408-944-0600 (fax) 408-434-4190

Netinc
Humble, TX
800-365-6384 or 713-446-2154
(fax) 713-540-3045

Netlink Inc.
Framingham, MA
800-NET-LINK or 508-879-6306
(fax) 508-872-8136

Netmanage Inc.
Cupertino, CA
408-973-7171 (fax) 408-257-6405
http://www.netmanage.com

Netops Corp.
New Fairfield, CT
203-746-3086 (fax) 203-746-3086

Netrix Corp.
Herndon, VA
800-776-1477 or 703-742-6000
(fax) 703-742-4048

Netscape Communications Corp.
Mountain View, CA
415-254-1900

Netsoft
Laguna Hills, CA
800-776-1477 or 714-753-0800
(fax) 714-753-0810

Netsys Technologies Inc.
Palo Alto, CA
800-638-5065 or 415-833-7500
(fax) 415-833-7597
http://www.netsystech.com

Nettech Inc.
Raleigh, NC
919-781-7887

Netvantage
Santa Monica, CA
800-796-8401 or 310-828-9898
(fax) 310-828-2553

Netware Users International
Orem, UT
800-228-4684 or 801-429-7177
(fax) 801-228-4577

Netwise Inc.
Boulder, CO
800-733-7722 or 303-442-8280
(fax) 303-442-3798

Netwiz Ltd.
Haifa, Israel
972-4-376-656 (fax) 972-4-384-474
Netwiz@actcom.co.il

Network Application Technology Inc.
Campbell, CA
800-474-7888 or 408-370-4300
(fax) 408-370-4222

Network Computing Inc.
Santa Clara, CA
408-296-8080 (fax) 408-296-8329

Network Design and Analysis
Markham, Ontario
800-387-4234 or 905-477-9534
(fax) 905-477-9572

Network Dimensions Inc.
San Jose, CA
408-366-8444 (fax) 408-255-4576

Network Dynamics Pty. Ltd.
Brisbane, Australia
61-7-231-1979 (fax) 61-7-231-1932
http://www.nd.co.nz/

Network Equipment
Technologies Inc.
Redwood City, CA
800-234-4638 or 415-366-4400
(fax) 415-366-5605
http://www.net.com

Network Express Inc.
Ann Arbor, MI
800-553-4333 or 313-761-5005
(fax) 313-995-1114
http://branch.com/netexpress/netex-
press.html

Network General Corp.
Menlo Park, CA
415-473-2000 (fax) 415-321-0855

Network Integrity Inc.
Marlborough, MA
800-638-5518 or 508-460-6670
(fax) 508-460-6771

Network Managers Inc.
North Chelmsford, MA
800-821-5466 or 508-251-4111
(fax) 508-251-8562

Network Performance Institute
Miami, FL
305-864-2744 (fax) 305-868-0530

Network Peripherals Inc.
Milpitas, CA
800-674-8855 or 408-321-7300
(fax) 408-321-9218

Network Resources Corp.
San Jose, CA
800-544-5255 or 408-383-9300
(fax) 408-383-0136

Network Specialists Inc.
Lynhurst, NJ
800-775-4674 or 201-804-8400
(fax) 201-804-2799

Network Systems Corp.
Minneapolis, MN
800-338-0122 or 612-424-4888
(fax) 612-424-4888
http://www.network.com

Network Translation Inc.
Palo Alto, CA
415-494-6387 (fax) 415-424-9110
http://www.translation.com

Networth Inc.
Irving, TX
800-544-5255 or 214-929-1700
(fax) 214-929-1720
http://www.networth.com

New Media Corp.
Irvine, CA
800-453-0550 or 714-453-0100
(fax) 714-453-0114

Newbridge Microsystems
Kanata, Ontario
800-267-7231 or 613-592-0714
(fax) 613-592-1320
http://www.newbridge.com

Newbridge Networks Corp.
Kanata, Ontario
800-267-7231 or 613-591-3600
(fax) 613-591-3680
http://www.newbridge.com

New Era Systems Inc.
Gold River, CA
916-638-8556 (fax) 916-638-8557

Nextest International
Richmond Hill, Ontario
905-882-9455 (fax) 905-882-9454

NHC Communications
Mount Royal, Quebec
800-361-1965 or 514-735-2741
(fax) 514-735-8057

Openvision
Pleasanton, CA
800-223-OPEN or 510-426-6400
(fax) 510-426-6486
http://www.ov.com/

Opis Corp.
Des Moines, IA
800-395-0209 or 515-284-0209
(fax) 515-284-5147

Optibase Ltd.
Herzliya, Israel
972-9-599-288 (fax) 972-9-586-099
http://www.optibase.com

Optical Data Systems Inc.
Richardson, TX
214-234-6400 (fax) 214-234-1467
http://www.ods.com

Optimal Networks Corp.
Mountain View, CA
415-254-5955 (fax) 415-254-5954
http://www.optimal.com

Optimum Electronics Inc.
North Haven, CT
203-239-6098 (fax) 203-234-9324

Optus Software Inc.
Somerset, NJ
908-271-9568 (fax) 908-271-9572

Oracle Corp.
Redwood Shores, CA
415-506-7000
http://www.oracle.com

Ositech Communications Inc.
Guelph, Ontario
800-563-2386 or 519-836-8063
(fax) 519-836-6156

OST
Cesson-Sauvigny, France
33-99-32-50-50 (fax) 33-99-41-71-75

Pacific Bell
San Francisco, CA
415-542-9000

Pacific Century Corporate Access
Singapore
65-296-7877 (fax) 65-393-2892

Pacific Communication Sciences Inc.
San Diego, CA
800-933-7274 or 619-535-9500
(fax) 619-535-0106
http://www.pcsi.com

Pacific Data Products Inc.
San Diego, CA
800-737-7110 or 619-552-0880
(fax) 619-552-0889

Pacific Internet
Culver City, CA
800-572-2638 or 310-410-9700
(fax) 310-410-9727
http://www.pacnet.com

Palindrome Corp.
Naperville, IL
800-288-4912 or 708-505-3300
(fax) 708-505-7917

Patton Electronics Co.
Gaithersburg, MD
301-975-1000 (fax) 301-869-9293
http://www.patton.com/

PC Guardian
San Rafael, CA
415-459-0190 (fax) 415-459-1162

PCX
Solana Beach, CA
619-259-6300 (fax) 619-481-6474

Peerlogic Inc.
San Francisco, CA
800-PEER-601 or 415-626-4545
(fax) 415-626-4710

Penril Datability Networks
Gaithersburg, MD
800-473-6745 or 301-921-8600
(fax) 301-921-8376

Percussion Software
Stoneham, MA
800-438-9900 or 617-438-9900
(fax) 617-438-9955

Peregrine Systems Inc.
Carlsbad, CA
800-638-5231 or 619-431-2400
(fax) 619-431-0696
http//:www.peregrine.com

Performance Systems
International Inc.
Herndon, VA
703-904-4100 (fax) 703-904-4200

Performance Technology Inc.
San Antonio, TX
210-979-2000 (fax) 210-979-2002

Persoft Inc.
Madison, WI
608-273-6000 (fax) 608-273-8227

Petree Technologies Inc.
Roswell, GA
404-667-5663 (fax) 404-667-5652

Phasecom
Jerusalem, Israel
972-2-889888 (fax) 972-2-889889

Philips
Les Plessis-Robinson, France
33-1-41-28-70-00 (fax) 33-1-46-30-
62-24

Picturetel Corp.
Danvers, MA
508-762-5000 (fax) 508-762-5245

Pipex Ltd
Cambridge, UK
44-1223-250120 (fax) 44-1223-
250121

Plasmon Data Inc.
Milpitas, CA
800-445-9400 or 408-956-9400
(fax) 408-956-9444

Plexcom
Simi Valley, CA
805-522-3333 (fax) 805-583-4764

Portfolio Technology Inc.
Newark, CA
510-226-5600 (fax) 510-226-8182

Positron Fiber Systems Inc.
Mount Laurel, NJ
609-222-1288 (fax) 609-222-1744

Practical Peripherals Inc.
Thousand Oaks, CA
800-442-4774 or 805-497-4774
(fax) 805-374-7200

Preferred Systems Inc.
West Haven, CT
800-222-7638 or 203-937-3000
(fax) 203-937-3015

Premisys Communications Inc.
Fremont, CA
510-353-7600 (fax) 510-353-7601

Presticom Inc.
Saint-Hubert, Quebec
514-443-2908 (fax) 514-443-2878

Primary Access Corp.
San Diego, CA
619-675-4100 (fax) 619-674-8800

Primary Rate Inc.
Salem, NH
800-950-ISDN or 603-898-1800
(fax) 603-898-1199

Prism Networks
Waltham, MA
617-890-0002 (fax) 617-890-0111

Process Software Corp.
Framingham, MA
800-722-7770 or 508-879-6994
(fax) 508-879-0042
http://www.process.com

Procom Technology
Irvine, CA
800-852-8600 or 714-852-1000
(fax) 714-852-1221
http://www.procom.com

Proginet Corp.
Uniondale, NY
516-228-6600 (fax) 516-228-6605

Prometheus
Tualatin, OR
800-477-3473 or 503-692-9600
(fax) 503-691-1101

Protec Microsystems Inc.
Pointe Claire, Quebec
514-630-5832 (fax) 514-694-6973

Proteon Inc.
  Westborough, MA
  800-830-1300 or 508-898-2800
  (fax) 508-366-8901
  http://www.proteon.com

Proxim Inc.
  Mountain View, CA
  415-960-1630 (fax) 415-960-1984

Psiber Data Systems Inc.
  La Mesa, CA
  619-670-7456 (fax) 619-670-5427

Pulizzi Engineering Inc.
  Santa Ana, CA
  714-540-4229 (fax) 714-641-9062

QPSX Communications
  West Perth, Australia
  61-9-262-2000 (fax) 61-9-3241642

Quabbin Wire & Cable
  Ware, MA
  413-967-6281 (fax) 413-967-7564

Qualcomm Inc.
  San Diego, CA
  619-587-1121 (fax) 619-452-9096

Qualix Group Inc.
  San Mateo, CA
  800-245-8649 or 415-572-0200
  (fax) 415-572-1300
  http://www.qualix.com

Questronics Inc.
  Salt Lake City, UT
  801-262-9923 (fax) 801-262-9858

Quintessential Solutions Inc.
  San Diego, CA
  800-925-3183 or 619-280-7535
  (fax) 619-280-1628

Quyen Systems Inc.
  Rockville, MD
  301-258-5087 (fax) 301-258-5088

Racal-Datacom Ltd.
  Sunrise, FL
  800-RACAL-55 or 305-846-1601
  (fax) 305-846-4249

Racal-Guardata
  Herndon, VA
  800-521-6261 or 703-471-0892
  (fax) 703-437-9333

Racal Interlan
  Boxborough, MA
  800-LAN-TALK or 508-263-8655
  (fax) 508-263-8655

Racore Computer Products Inc.
  Los Gatos, CA
  800-635-1274 or 408-374-8290
  (fax) 408-374-6653

Racotek Inc.
  Minneapolis, MN
  612-832-9800 (fax) 612-832-9383

Radcom Equipment Inc.
  Mahwah, NJ
  201-529-2020 (fax) 201-529-0808

Radcom Ltd.
  Tel Aviv, Israel
  972-3-645-5055 (fax) 972-3-647-4681

RAD Data Communications Ltd.
  Tel Aviv, Israel
  972-3-645-8181 (fax) 972-3-498250

Radio LAN
  San Jose, CA
  408-526-9170 (fax) 408-526-9174

Radlinx Ltd.
  Tel Aviv, Israel
  972-3-647-5188 (fax) 972-3-647-5057
  http://ady.radlinx.rad.co.il/

Rad Network Devices Ltd.
  Tel Aviv, Israel
  972-3-645-8555 (fax) 972-3-648-7368

RADvision Ltd.
  Tel Aviv, Israel
  972-3-647-6661 (fax) 972-3-647-6669

RAM Mobil Data
  Woodbridge, NJ
  908-602-5500 (fax) 908-602-5736

Raptor Systems Inc.
  Waltham, MA
  617-487-7700 (fax) 617-487-6755
  http://www.raptor.com

Rdc Communications Ltd.
Jerusalem, Israel
972-2-519311 (fax) 972-2-519314

Relational Technology Systems Inc.
Waltham, MA
800-661-7096 or 617-890-2888
(fax) 617-890-2953

Relay Technology Inc.
Vienna, VA
703-506-0500 (fax) 703-506-0510

Remedy Corp.
Mountain View, CA
415-903-5200 (fax) 415-903-9001
http://www.remedy.com/

Renex Corp.
Woodbridge, VA
703-878-2400 (fax) 703-878-4625

Retix
Santa Monica, CA
800-255-2333 or 310-828-3400
(fax) 310-828-1109
http://www.retix.com

Rightfax
Tucson, AZ
520-327-1357 (fax) 520-321-7459

RIT Technologies Ltd.
Tel Aviv, Israel
972-3-496504 (fax) 972-3-496505

Rockwell Network Systems
Santa Barbara, CA
800-262-8023 or 805-968-4262
(fax) 805-968-6478
http://www.rns.rockwell.com

Saber Software Corp.
Dallas, TX
800-338-8754 or 214-361-8086
(fax) 214-361-1882

Sanrex Corp.
New Hyde Park, NY
516-352-3800 (fax) 516-352-3956

The Santa Cruz Operation Inc.
Santa Cruz, CA
408-425-7222 (fax) 408-458-4227
http://www.sco.com

SAS Institute Inc.
Cary, NC
919-677-8000 (fax) 919-677-8123
http://www.sas.com

Satelcom (UK) Ltd.
Ascot, UK
44-1344-872677 (fax) 44-1344-872206

Satellitenkommunikation GmbH
Bonn, Germany
49-22-89-10400 (fax) 49-22-89-10-4015

SBE Inc.
San Ramon, CA
800-925-2666 or 510-355-2000
(fax) 510-355-2020

Scitech
Chicago, IL
312-486-9191 (fax) 312-486-9234

Scope Communications Inc.
Northborough, MA
800-418-7111 or 508-393-1236
(fax) 508-393-2213

Scopus Technology Inc.
Emeryville, CA
800-9-SCOPUS or 510-597-5800
(fax) 510-428-1027

Scorpion Logic
Watford, UK
44-923-245-672

SDL Communications Inc.
Easton, MA
508-238-6338 (fax) 508-238-1053

Seagate
Scotts Valley, AZ
408-439-2276

Securicor 3net
Basingstoke, UK
44-1256-843311 (fax) 44-1256-840429

Security Call Inc.
Los Gatos, CA
408-356-6509 (fax) 408-356-0758

Security Dynamics
Cambridge, MA
617-547-7820 (fax) 617-354-8836

Security Integration Inc.
Lexington, MA
617-861-8800 (fax) 617-861-6576

Server Technology Inc.
Sunnyvale, CA
800-835-1515 or 408-745-0300
(fax) 408-745-0392

Service Systems International
Overland Park, KS
913-661-0190 (fax) 913-661-0220

SFA Datacomm Inc.
Frederick, MD
800-270-CONX or 301-662-5926
(fax) 301-694-6279

SFMT Montana Telecom KFT
Budapest, Hungary
36-1-270-4050 (fax) 36-1-270-4045

Sharp Electronics Corp.
Mahwah, NJ
800-BE-SHARP or 201-529-8200
(fax) 201-529-8919

Shiva Corp.
Burlington, MA
800-977-4482 or 508-788-3061
(fax) 508-788-1301

Shore Microsystems Inc.
Oceanport, NJ
908-229-3009 (fax) 908-229-2324

S.I. Tech
Geneva, IL
708-232-8640 (fax) 708-232-8677

Siecor Corp.
Hickory, NC
704-327-5000 (fax) 704-327-5973

Siemens Rolm Communications Inc.
Santa Clara, CA
408-492-2000 (fax) 408-492-4137
http://www.siemensrolm.com/info/

The Siemon Company
Watertown, CT
203-274-2523 (fax) 203-945-4225

Silicom Connectivity Solutions Ltd.
Kfar-Sava, Israel
972-9-978989 (fax) 972-9-951977

Silcom Technology Inc.
Union City, GA
800-388-3807 or 404-964-9293
(fax) 404-964-9282

Simpact Associates Inc.
San Diego, CA
800-746-7228 or 619-565-1865
(fax) 619-292-8015

Simple Technology Inc.
Santa Ana, CA
714-476-1180 (fax) 714-476-1209

Simware Inc.
Ottawa, Canada
800-267-9991 or 613-727-1779
(fax) 613-727-3533

Singapore Telecom
Singapore
65-838-3388 (fax) 65-732-8428

Sita Group
London, UK
44-1628-773577 (fax) 44-1628-
778097

SNMP Research Inc.
Knoxville, TN
615-573-1434 (fax) 615-573-9197

Societé Anonyme de
Télécommunication (SAT)
Paris, France
33-1-40-77-12-12

Softarc Inc.
Markham, Ontario
800-364-1923 or 905-415-7000
(fax) 905-415-7151

Software AG
Reston, VA
703-860-5050 (fax) 703-391-6975

Software Builders Inc.
Atlanta, GA
404-717-8003 (fax) 404-717-9054

Software Cafe Inc.
Laguna Niguel, CA
714-495-5280 (fax) 714-495-0790

Software Corp. of America
Stamford, CT
203-359-2773 (fax) 203-359-3198

Software Licensing Corp.
Incline Village, NV
800-831-0882 or 702-832-0881
(fax) 702-832-0883

Software Partners/32 Inc.
Topsfield, MA
508-887-6409 (fax) 508-887-3680

Solid State Electronics Corp.
Northridge, CA
818-993-8257 (fax) 818-993-8259

Spaceline Communication Services
GmbH
Dusseldorf, Germany
49-211-967-7580 (fax) 49-211-967-
7576

Spectra Logic
Boulder, CO
800-833-1132 or 303-449-7759
(fax) 303-939-8844

Spectracom Corp.
East Rochester, NY
716-381-4827 (fax) 716-381-4998

Spider Island Software
Irvine, CA
714-669-9260 (fax) 714-669-1383

Spider Systems Ltd.
Edinburgh, UK
0131-554-9424 (fax) 0131-554-0649

Sprint Data Products Management
Reston, VA
800-736-1130 or 703-689-6000
(fax) 703-689-5176

Sprint International Inc.
Reston, VA
703-689-6000

Spry Compuserve Internet Division
Seattle, WA
800-777-9638 or 206-447-0300
(fax) 206-447-9008
http://www.spry.com

Spyglass Inc.
Naperville, IL
708-505-1010 (fax) 708-505-4944
http://www.spyglass.com

Square D
Costa Mesa, CA
714-557-1636 (fax) 714-434-7652

St. Bernard Software
San Diego, CA
800-782-3762 or 619-676-2277
(fax) 619-676-2299

Stalker Software
Larkspur, CA
800-262-4722 or 415-383-7164
(fax) 415-383-7461

Stampede Technologies Inc.
Dayton, OH
800-763-3423 or 513-291-5035
(fax) 513-291-5040

Standard Microsystems Corp.
Hauppauge, NY
800-SMC-4-YOU or 516-273-3100
(fax) 516-273-1803
http://www.smc.com

Starcomm Communications Products
Anaheim, CA
714-375-1241 (fax) 714-375-1244

Starlight Networks Inc.
Mountain View, CA
415-967-2774 (fax) 415-967-0686
http://www.starlight.com

Starware Inc.
Berkeley, CA
800-763-0050 or 510-704-2000
(fax) 510-704-2001

Sterling Software Communications
Software Division
Irving, TX
800-700-5599 or 214-868-5000
(fax) 214-868-5311

Stonybrook Software Inc.
Bohemia, NY
516-567-6060 (fax) 516-567-6648

Storage Dimensions Inc.
Milpitas, CA
408-894-1331 (fax) 408-9444-1200

Stratacom Inc.
San Jose, CA
800-767-4479 or 408-294-7600
(fax) 408-999-0115

Sunsoft Inc.
Mountain View, CA
800-SUNSOFT or 415-960-1300
(fax) 415-961-6070
http://www.sun.com

SVEC Computer Corp.
Irvine, CA
800-756-SVEC or 714-756-2233
(fax) 714-756-1340
http://www.svec.com

Swiss Telecom PTT
Geneva, Switzerland
41-31-338-1111 (fax) 41-31-338-2549

Sybase Inc.
Emeryville, CA
510-922-3500 (fax) 510-658-9441

Symbionics Networks Ltd.
Cambridge, UK
441-223-421025 (fax) 441-223-421031

Symmetrical Technologies Wildsoft
Mobile Computing Division
Amherst, NH
603-598-4477 (fax) 603-598-3505

Symplex Communications Corp.
Ann Arbor, MI
313-995-1555 (fax) 313-995-1564
http://www.iea.com/symplex

Synaptel
Velizy, France
33-1-30-67-17-00 (fax) 33-1-34-65-39-13

Sync Research Inc.
Irvine, CA
800-275-7692 or 714-588-2070
(fax) 714-588-2080

Synergy Solutions Inc.
Mesa, AZ
602-545-9797 (fax) 602-545-9827

Syntax
Federal Way, WA
206-838-2626 (fax) 206-838-9836
http://www.syntax.com

Syskonnect Inc.
San Jose, CA
800-SK2-FDDI or 408-437-3800
(fax) 408-437-3866

Systems & Networks
Foster City, CA
415-378-2900 (fax) 415-378-3601

Systems and Synchronous Inc.
Naperville, IL
708-505-3900 (fax) 708-505-5701

Systems Enhancement Corp.
Chesterfield, MO
314-532-2855 (fax) 314-532-2037

Syzygy Communications Inc.
Scotts Valley, CA
408-438-5111 (fax) 408-438-5115

Tally Systems Corp.
Hanover, NH
800-262-3877 or 603-643-1300
(fax) 603-643-9366

Target Technologies Inc.
Wilmington, NC
800-666-2496 or 910-395-6100
(fax) 910-395-6108

TC Communications
Irvine, CA
714-852-1972 (fax) 714-852-1948

TCG Lanlink
Staten Island, NY
718-983-2000 (fax) 718-983-2147

TCL Inc.
Fremont, CA
510-657-3800 (fax) 510-490-5814

Technical Communications Corp.
Concord, MA
508-287-5100 (fax) 508-371-1280

Technologic Inc.
Atlanta, GA
404-843-9111 (fax) 404-843-9700

Techsmith Corp.
East Lansing, MI
800-517-3001 or 517-333-2100
(fax) 517-333-1888

Tekelec Inc.
Calabasas, CA
800-835-3532 or 818-880-5656
(fax) 818-880-6993

Teknekron Software Systems Inc.
Palo Alto, CA
415-325-1025 (fax) 415-321-3176

Teknique Inc.
Schaumburg, IL
708-706-9700 (fax) 708-706-9735

Tektronix Inc.
Wilsonville, OR
800-547-8949 or 503-682-7300
(fax) 503-685-7454
http://www.tek.com

Telco Systems Inc. Fiber Optics
Division
Norwood, MA
800-221-2849 or 617-551-0300
(fax) 617-551-0539

Telco Systems Inc. Magnalink
Communications Division
Norwood, MA
800-474-8025 or 617-255-9400
(fax) 617-551-0539

Telco Systems Inc. Network Access
Division
Fremont, CA
800-776-8832 or 510-490-3111
(fax) 510-656-3031

Telebit Corp.
Chelmsford, MA
800-989-8888 or 508-441-2181
(fax) 508-441-9060
http://www.telebit.com

Telecom Analysis Systems Inc.
Eatontown, NJ
908-544-8700 (fax) 908-544-8347

Telecom Finland Ltd.
Helsinki, Finland
358-1040-2719

Telecommunications Management
Associates Inc.
Manassas, VA
703-331-2030 (fax) 703-331-2050

Telecommunications
Techniques Corp.
Germantown, MA
800-638-2049 or 301-353-1550
(fax) 301-353-1536

Telefonica Sistemas De Satelites
Madrid, Spain
34-1-337-3009 (fax) 34-1-337-5672

Telehouse International Ltd
London, UK
44-171-512-0550 (fax) 44-171-512-
0033

Telematics International Inc.
Fort Lauderdale, FL
800-833-4580 or 305-772-3070
(fax) 305-351-4405

Telemax Corp.
Lisle, IL
708-241-0909 (fax) 708-241-0943

Tele Media International Ltd.
London, UK
44-171-333-8800 (fax) 44-171-333-
2999

Telenetworks
Petaluma, CA
707-778-8737 (fax) 707-778-7476

Telenex Corp.
Mount Laurel, NJ
800-222-0187 or 609-234-7900
(fax) 609-778-8700

Teleos Communications Inc.
Eatontown, NJ
908-389-5700 (fax) 908-544-6490
http://www.teleoscom.com

Teleport Europe GmbH
Hannover, Germany
49-511-879560 (fax) 49-511-879-5690

Teleprocessing Products Inc.
Simi Valley, CA
800-522-8155 or 805-522-8147
(fax) 805-581-6019

Telequip Corp.
Nashua, NH
800-598-0120 or 603-598-1300
(fax) 603-598-6724
http://www.telequip.com

Telespazio SpA
Rome, Italy
39-6-40791 (fax) 39-6-4079-3639

Telesync Inc.
Norcross, GA
404-246-9662 (fax) 404-246-9733

Telink Systems Inc.
Gaithersburg, MD
301-670-0811 (fax) 301-590-9284

Tellabs Inc.
Lisle, IL
800-445-6501 or 708-969-8800
(fax) 708-852-7346

Teloquent Communications Corp.
Billerica, MA
508-663-7570 (fax) 508-663-7543

Telstra Inc.
Sydney, Australia
61-3-634-6441 (fax) 61-3-364-4556

Teltrend Inc.
St. Charles, IL
800-TELTREN or 708-377-1700
(fax) 708-377-0891

T4 Systems Inc.
Little Rock, AR
800-233-1526 or 501-227-6637
(fax) 501-227-6245

TGI Technologies Ltd.
Vancouver, British Columbia
604-872-6676 (fax) 604-872-6601

TGV Inc.
Santa Cruz, CA
800-848-3440 or 408-457-5200
(fax) 408-457-5205

Thomas & Betts Corp.
Memphis, TN
800-247-9378 or 901-682-7766
(fax) 901-680-5200

Thomas-Conrad Corp.
Austin, TX
800-332-8683 or 512-836-1935
(fax) 512-836-2840

3Com Corp.
Santa Clara, CA
800-638-3266 or 408-764-5000
(fax) 408-764-5001
http://www.3Com.com/home.html

3Com-Sonix Ltd
Cirencester, UK
44-1285-641651 (fax) 44-1285-642098

3M Telecom Systems Division
Austin, TX
800-426-8626 or 512-984-3400
(fax) 512-984-3408

Tivoli Systems Inc.
Austin, TX
512-794-9070 (fax) 512-794-0623

Tobit Software
Santa Clara, CA
800-GO-TOBIT or 408-982-2562
(fax) 408-982-2517

Tom Sawyer Software
Berkeley, CA
510-848-0853 (fax) 510-848-0854

Tone Software Corp.
Anaheim, CA
800-833-8663 or 714-991-9460
(fax) 714-991-1831

Toshiba America Information
Systems Telecommunications
Systems Division
Irvine, CA
714-583-3700 (fax) 714-583-3886
http://www.tais.com

TPS Teleprocessing Systeme GmbH
Cadolzburg, Germany
49-0-91-03-50-60 (fax) 49-0-91-03-
50-62-02

Tracker Software Inc.
St. Paul, MN
800-925-9950 or 612-525-9802
(fax) 612-525-9825

Traffic USA Corp.
Boca Raton, FL
407-995-5282 (fax) 407-995-5272

Transarc Corp.
Pittsburgh, PA
412-338-4400 (fax) 412-338-4404

Traveling Software Inc.
Bothell, WA
206-483-8088 (fax) 206-487-1284

Trax Softworks Inc.
Culver City, CA
800-367-8729 or 310-649-5800
(fax) 310-649-6200

Trellis Network Services Inc.
Princeton, NJ
800-793-3390 or 609-987-0660
(fax) 609-987-9028

Trend Communications
Torrance, CA
310-782-8190 (fax) 310-328-5892

Trendware International Inc.
Torrance, CA
310-328-7795 (fax) 310-328-7798

Tribe Computer Works
Alameda, CA
800-77-TRIBE or 510-814-3900
(fax) 510-814-3980
http://www.tribe.com

Tricord Systems
Plymouth, MN
800-TRICORD or 612-557-9005
(fax) 612-557-8403
http://www.tricord.com

Trioniq Inc.
Chicoutimi, Quebec
418-693-5858 (fax) 418-696-4816

Tripp Lite Manufacturing
Chicago, IL
312-755-5401 (fax) 312-644-6505

Triticom
Eden Prairie, MN
612-937-0772 (fax) 612-937-1998
http://www.Triticom.com

Triton Technologies Inc.
Iselin, NJ
800-322-9440 or 908-855-9440
(fax) 908-855-9608

T3plus
Santa Clara, CA
800-477-7585 or 408-727-4545
(fax) 408-727-5151

Txport
Madison, AL
800-926-0085 or 205-772-3770
(fax) 205-772-3388

Tylink Corp.
Norton, MA
800-828-2785 or 508-285-0033
(fax) 508-285-2738

UB Networks Inc.
Santa Clara, CA
800-496-0111 or 408-496-0111
(fax) 408-970-7337

Uconx Corp.
San Diego, CA
619-627-1700 (fax) 619-627-1710

Unicom Electric Inc.
Santa Fe Springs, CA
800-346-6668 or 310-946-9650
(fax) 310-946-9167

Unified Communications Inc.
Minneapolis, MN
800-272-1710 or 612-851-1710
(fax) 612-851-1716
http://www.uci.com

Unikix Technologies
Billerica, MA
800-765-2826 or 508-663-4170
(fax) 508-663-4194

Unipress Software Inc.
Edison, NJ
800-222-0550 or 908-287-2100
(fax) 908-287-4929
http://www.unipress.com

Unison Software Inc.
Santa Clara, CA
408-988-2800 (fax) 408-988-2236
http://www.unison.com

Unisource Satellite Services BV
Hoofddorp, Netherlands
31-25-03-86002 (fax) 31-25-03-86065

Unisync Inc.
Upland, CA
909-985-5088 (fax) 909-982-0929

Unisys Corp.
Blue Bell, PA
800-874-8647, ext. 576 or
610-993-3081
(fax) 610-993-6152
http://www.unisys.com

U.S. Robotics
Skokie, IL
800-USR-CORP or 708-982-5010
(fax) 708-933-5800
http://www.usr.com

Uunet Technologies Inc.
Fairfax, VA
800-488-6383 or 703-206-5600
(fax) 703-206-5601
http://www.uu.net

Ven-Tel Inc.
San Jose, CA
800-538-5121 or 408-436-7400
(fax) 408-436-7451

Verilink Corp.
San Jose, CA
800-VERILINK or 408-945-1199
(fax) 408-262-6260

Verisign Inc.
Redwood City, CA
415-508-1151 (fax) 415-508-1121
http://www.verisign.com

Viacrypt
Phoenix, AZ
602-944-0773 (fax) 602-943-2601

Videoserver Inc.
Lexington, MA
617-863-2300 (fax) 617-862-2833

Vinca Corp.
Orem, UT
801-223-3100 (fax) 801-223-3107

VIR Inc.
Southampton, PA
800-344-3934 or 215-364-8866
(fax) 215-364-0920

Virtual Reality Laboratories Inc.
San Luis Obispo, CA
800-829-8754 or 805-545-8515
(fax) 805-781-2259

Vivo Software Inc.
Waltham, MA
617-899-8900 (fax) 617-899-1400

Vocaltec Inc.
Northvale, NJ
800-843-2289 or 201-768-9400
(fax) 201-768-8893
http://www.vocaltec.com

Vtel Corp.
Austin, TX
512-314-2700 (fax) 512-314-2792

Vycor Corp.
College Park, MD
800-888-9267 or 301-220-4450
(fax) 301-220-0727

Walker Richer & Quinn Inc.
Seattle, WA
800-872-2829 or 206-217-7500
(fax) 206-217-0211

Wall Data
Kirkland, WA
206-814-9255 (fax) 206-814-4309

Wandel & Goltermann
Research Triangle Park, NC
800-277-7404 or 919-460-3300
(fax) 919-481-4372
http://www.wg.com/wg

Web Technologies Inc.
Souderton, PA
800-724-9300 or 215-723-6400
(fax) 215-723-0333

Webster Computer Corp.
San Jose, CA
800-457-0903 or 408-954-8054
(fax) 408-954-1832

Western Datacom Co. Inc.
Westlake, OH
800-262-2311 or 216-835-1510
(fax) 216-835-9146

Western Telematic Inc.
Irvine, CA
800-854-7226 or 714-586-9950
(fax) 714-583-9514

Whitetree Network Technologies Inc.
Palo Alto, CA
415-855-0855 (fax) 415-855-0864
http://www.whitetree.com

Whittaker Communications
Santa Clara, CA
800-4HUGHES or 408-565-6000
(fax) 408-565-6001

Winchester Systems Inc.
Woburn, MA
800-325-3700 or 617-933-8500
(fax) 617-933-6174

Winfinet Software Inc.
Somerset, NJ
908-805-1931 (fax) 908-805-0030

Wingra Technologies Inc.
Madison, WI
800-544-5465 or 608-238-4454
(fax) 608-238-8986
http://www.wingra.com

The Wiremold Company
West Hartford, CT
203-233-6251 (fax) 203-232-2062

Wollongong Group
Palo Alto, CA
800-872-8649 or 415-962-7204
(fax) 415-962-0286
http://www.twg.com

Workflow Designs Inc.
Dallas, TX
214-991-3569 (fax) 214-661-1147

Workgroup Productivity Corp.
Oak Brook, IL
708-953-8688 (fax) 708-953-1130

Workgroup Solutions
Aurora, CO
303-699-7470 (fax) 303-699-2793

World Software Corp.
Ridgewood, NJ
201-444-3228 (fax) 201-444-9065

Worldcom
Houston, TX
800-744-2220 or 713-650-6522
(fax) 713-650-3331
http:\www.worldcom.com

Worldtalk Corp.
Los Gatos, CA
408-399-4000 (fax) 408-399-4013
http://www.worldtalk.com

Xactdata Corp.
Seattle, WA
206-654-5300 (fax) 206-382-6615

Xcellenet
Atlanta, GA
404-804-8100 (fax) 404-804-8102

Xedia Corp.
Wilmington, MA
800-98-XEDIA or 508-658-7200
(fax) 508-658-7204

Xircom Inc.
Thousand Oaks, CA
800-438-4526 or 805-376-9300
(fax) 805-376-9311
http://www.xircom.com.world wide
web

Xnet Technology Inc.
Milpitas, CA
800-788-0148 or 408-263-6888
(fax) 408-263-8898

Xylan Corp.
Calabasas, CA
818-880-3500 (fax) 818-880-3505

Xylogics
  Burlington, MA
  617-272-8140 (fax) 617-273-5392
  http://www.xylogics.com

Xyplex Inc.
  Littleton, MA
  800-338-5316 or 508-952-4700
  (fax) 508-952-4702
  http://www.xyplex.com

Zeitnet Inc.
  Santa Clara, CA
  408-562-1880 (fax) 408-562-1889

Index

Index notes: The *f.* after a page number refers to a figure; the *n.* to a note; and the *t.* to a table.

ABOUT THE AUTHOR

Stephen Saunders is News Editor at *Data Communications* magazine and a well-known specialist in LAN-related topics. He has won several awards. Most recently, in 1995 he won a Jesse H. Neal Editorial Achievement Award from the American Business Press for an article on LAN switches.